Captain
BEEFHEART

Mike Barnes

OMNIBUS PRESS

LONDON / NEW YORK / PARIS / SYDNEY / COPENHAGEN / BERLIN / MADRID / TOKYO

ISBN: 1.84449.412.8
Order Number: OP 50160

Exclusive Distributors
Music Sales Limited,
8/9 Frith Street,
London W1D 3JB, UK.

Music Sales Corporation,
257 Park Avenue South,
New York, NY 10010, USA.

Macmillan Distribution Services,
53 Park West Drive,
Derrimut, Vic 3030,
Australia.

To the Music Trade only:
Music Sales Limited,
8/9 Frith Street,
London W1D 3JB, UK.

Typeset by Phoenix Photosetting, Chatham, Kent
Printed by Creative Print & Design, Ebbw Vale, Wales

A catalogue record for this book is available from the British Library.

Visit Omnibus Press on the web at www.omnibuspress.com

ACKNOWLEDGEMENTS

This book is dedicated to the memory of Gerry Pratt, 1950–1995. His passion for the music of Captain Beefheart & The Magic Band, which he broadcast via his meticulously researched fanzine, *Steal Softly Thru Snow*, has been an inspiration. Without his inadvertent assistance, the writing of this book would have been even more difficult. R.I.P.

A big thank you …

To all the interviewees, and to those who gave help way above and beyond the call of duty: David Breuer, Michael Eivaz, John French, Gary Lucas, Gary Marker, Elaine Shepherd.

To everyone who provided material for the book. Special thanks to: Don Aldridge, Dean Blackwood, Alastair Dickson, Greg Davidson, Steve Froy, Tim Hill, Henry Kaiser, Billy James, Graham Johnston, Ivor Kallin, Dave Maleed, Michael Werner Gallery, Mark Paytress, Edwin Pouncey, John Platt, Ian Sturgess, Colin Webb, Robert Williams.

To all those who gave their encouragement and support, particularly Len and Peggy Barnes, and Howard and Sarah Farr.

To anyone who had to endure endless updates on the book's progress and excited reports of new minutiae unearthed first time around, only to get more during its revision.

To Chris Charlesworth and Andy Neill, at Omnibus Press.

To the computer salvage crew: Jeremy Cole, Giles Perring and Hilary Cole.

For Dictaphonics: David Stubbs.

Please visit: www.mikebarnes88.co.uk

CONTENTS

1

A HELL OF A WAY TO WAKE UP

"Without being kicked in the butt he would never have started singing, he was too shy."
Frank Zappa, *International Times*, March 1977

Don Glen Vliet was born at 4.25 p.m. on January 15, 1941 at the Glendale Research Hospital, Los Angeles, to Willie Sue Vliet and Glen Alonzo Vliet. It was an event that, thirty-four years later, he still remembered well: "I remember every bit of it. I remember when the jerk slapped me on the fanny and I saw the yellow tile and I thought what a hell of a way to wake somebody up."[1] Don's entry into the world was not without resistance on his part, as he later recollected: "I was born with my eyes open – I didn't WANT to be born – I can remember deep down in my head that I fought against my mother bringing me into the world."[2]

Don's infancy was also far from orthodox: "I whistled when I was two. I refused to talk till I was about three and a half. I told my supposed mother, Sue, when I was three that Mother was a cold word and that I would address her by her surname [*sic*] and that's the way it's been all along ... we are very good friends."[3] In 1980 he looked back on his relationship with his parents: "When I was three I said to my mother: you be Sue, I'll be Don and he [my father] will be Glen. Don't step over the line and we'll be friends. I said that when I was three. I sent my mother home my navel! What else could I do? She appreciated it, she went along."[4]

Don was a precocious and gifted only child who showed skill in sculpting from an early age. One of his earliest memories of childhood creation was bath-time sculpture at the age of three: "... Like everyone does; my genitals first, then a bar of soap and out from there."[5] A mixture of

1

wilfulness, rebelliousness and an obsession with sculpting animals gave rise to a habit, between the ages of three and six, of intermittently locking himself in his room so he could create undisturbed. He claims that he once did this for three weeks – with his parents pushing food "under the door" – during which time he produced "things that I would have tried to move kinetically, try to move these things around. These were my friends, these little animals that I would make, like dinosaurs and… I wasn't very much in reality, actually."[6]

Don would also vacuum the floor and collect hairs from his Persian cat to use as raw material for his sculptures. With a single-mindedness rare in a child, he set about moulding a likeness, of, "every animal on the Northern Continent". He turned his attention next to African mammals, a task he completed by the time he was thirteen: "Aye-ayes, dik-diks and all these obscure lemurs. I love them all. After that I did all the fish of the ocean which is quite a feat. My folks thought I was insane of course…"[7]

This tactile creativity was paralleled in his adulthood by his playing with and sculpting language. Most people have a tendency to alter the events of their life to make them more interesting, often subconsciously. But, as his friends and acquaintances later realised, few had Don Vliet's determination and imaginative facility to make his remarkable life even more so in the telling.

The Vliets lived close to the Griffith Park Zoo, Los Angeles. Now substantially redeveloped as the Los Angeles Zoo, at the time it was principally a home for former circus animals. Don's parents took him there regularly to sketch. The Portuguese sculptor Agostinho Rodrigues noticed young Vliet at work and was struck by the child's talent. Subsequently, Rodrigues invited him to appear on an educational TV show. Every week the precocious youngster would come in to sculpt and draw in the studio. Vliet was, in his own words, 'apprenticed' to Rodrigues between the ages of five and eight, and looked back on the experience with mixed feelings. Speaking on the subject in 1972, he said: "I didn't like the system. Television patting me on the head and pinching my bottom and calling me a prodigy."[8] But he stayed with Rodrigues for a number of years in the Fifties. In a bizarre spin-off, he claims to have lectured at the Barnsdale Art Institute in Los Angeles at the age of eleven.

Seventeen years later, the promising young sculptor – now established as a musician, writer and painter, and going under the pseudonym Captain Beefheart – is being interviewed for a promotional LP that will be sent to radio stations to try and generate interest in his most recent album, *Trout Mask Replica*. He tells the interviewer, a young journalist named Meatball Fulton, about his early years. "I was a sculptor till the age of 13," he says, "I studied under Agostinho Rodrigues from Portugal," chewing over each syllable of his tutor's name in a deep, hip drawl. This information was delivered in the context of an amusing, baffling and intimidating interview full of elliptical wordplays and verbal conundrums, which was suitably far-out for 1969. The interviewer was having problems keeping up, let alone challenging his interviewee, or pinning him down long enough to get more details. That this musician was also a trained sculptor gave good copy and, over time, this information gradually metamorphosed, with Augustinio Rodrigues – as his name was usually mis-spelt – promoted to 'renowned Portuguese sculptor', and his former student gradually embroidering their relationship in future exchanges with the music press.

The Rodrigues story was beguiling and entertaining, like something that would happen in a movie rather than in everyday suburban Los Angeles. One could imagine a scene where this pre-eminent Iberian sculptor, new to America, is spending a pleasant Sunday afternoon at Griffith Park Zoo. While walking past the lions' enclosure, he passes a young boy and his parents. He notices the adults are both watching the boy, who is leaning a sketch pad on the outer rails and drawing with intense concentration. Curious, he catches a glance at what the lad is doing and stops dead in his tracks, struck by the brilliance of the work. He is so moved by what he has seen he feels obliged to come over and introduce himself. "Good afternoon, sir," he says to Glen Vliet doffing his hat and bowing his head slightly with respect. "My name is Agostinho Rodrigues. I am a renowned Portuguese sculptor," he continues in heavily accented English that suggests his authenticity. "I couldn't help but notice your son's work. It is very impressive. I guarantee you that if your son studies with me, he will become a genius." Young Don turns around and smiles. He turns back and is once again immersed in his drawing.

Back to reality, those curious to find out the real story of this enigmatic Portuguese sculptor have had their searches thwarted. Here was a sculptor whom no art historian seems to have heard of, not even art enthusiasts who lived in the Los Angeles area and were contemporaries of Don Vliet. So, for both reader and journalist, the easiest thing to do was just to give in and believe what he said. Many have shrugged their shoulders and thought, well, it *could* be true, even though the whole yarn – not least Vliet's claim of being 'apprenticed' at five years of age – was far more likely to be a total fabrication.

The increased accessibility of the internet over the last decade or so should have clarified the Rodrigues story, but instead has made it even more complicated. There was still no verifiable information on the artist and his only presence on the net is in articles written by Captain Beefheart fans. But recently, some press cuttings – presumably Vliet's own – came to light and finally explained the genesis of the story: Rodrigues was indeed a sculptor, and the spelling of his name indicates that he was of Portuguese descent. An unidentified Los Angeles newspaper article from 1950 carries an article on a children's sculpting competition, and is accompanied by a photograph of young Don Vliet and Peter Conway, both 9 years old. "They Like Elephants," says the caption of the photograph showing the boys holding up clay figurines. Peter Conway won the Achievement Award, but Donald [*sic*] Vliet won first prize.

"Two hundred young sculptors, students of the Griffith Park clay modeling classes, climaxed this year's instruction with an exhibit of their work at Griffith Park Zoo yesterday.

"On display were hundreds of figurines provided by children from 4 to 16 years of age. The modelling class, conducted by Agostinho Rodrigues, Los Angeles sculptor, is reported to be the first of its kind in the United States to use live animals and birds of the zoo as models.

"Award for the finest work of art was made to Donald Vliet of 3467 Waverly Drive with the Achievement Award going to 9–year old Peter William Conway of 5303 11th Avenue. Both exhibited elephants.

"Winner's ribbons were presented by William Frederickson, superintendent of recreation in The Recreation and Parks Department, sponsor of the children's art project."

Another unidentified newspaper cutting from the following year shows a photograph of "Agostinho Rodrigues, center instructor of City Recreation and Park Department clay modeling classes," looking at models with Don Vliet who again won first prize and Ronald Hill, 10, who won second prize.

The *Los Angeles Examiner* (5/2/51) ran the story with a picture of Vliet sitting next to the head keeper, Charles Allen, who was holding a lion cub. "With his clay model of a polar bear, Don Vliet, 10, of 3467 Waverly Drive, won the first place blue ribbon in the monthly modeling contest at Griffith Park Zoo yesterday.

"It was the second straight blue ribbon for the Ivanhoe Elementary School fifth grader, who has attended sculptor Agostinho Rodrigues' free Sunday art class at the zoo for five months."

Rodrigues was no Picasso, then, but Vliet's accounts were more or less true, if somewhat disingenuous. There's little doubt, however, that he realised these stories would assume a life of their own once let loose. But as with so many tales in which he figures, some of the more unlikely details turn out to be true. At the end of the *Los Angeles Examiner* article comes this piece of information: "Second Place went to Ronald Hill, 10, of 2689 Waverly Drive, Don's fellow fifth form grader who moulded his spotted leopard under Don's exclusive direction. Ronald never attended the art class."

If, years later, Vliet had claimed that not only was he the outstanding student in the class, but he even directed another child, who didn't even attend classes, to a second prize, the reaction might well have been an upward rolling of eyes. Alarmingly, one wonders if the young boy might even have come up with that himself for the benefit of the reporter in an early – and successful – attempt at self-aggrandisement. But assuming it was true, and bearing in mind the autocratic, bullying way in which he later treated the musicians in his groups, one's first reaction is of sympathy for Ronald Hill.

Sue Vliet has always confirmed to interested parties amongst her son's friends and associates that he did indeed appear on television as a child, although whether or not this was with Rodrigues is unclear. As he had won a prize in a competition run by the City Departments, it is quite possible this would be the case. Again, even inveterate TV watchers of the same age and in the same area do not recall an educational wildlife show with a child sculpting, so perhaps it was a one-off after the modeling contest. That much still remains shrouded in mystery.

Although the details we have of Vliet's childhood are sketchy and their veracity often open to question, he has often spoken fondly of that time. He is wont to say that in a sense he had never grown up and that to him, playing and creating are still inextricably linked. As a child, he was encouraged to play, by which process he produced what others considered to be art, and continued to do so throughout his adult life. But the adult world's capacity for mindless cruelty introduced a dark shadow even into these halcyon days, as he explained to Connor McKnight in 1972: "You know the MGM lion, Leo, their emblem lion? I used to go into cages with

5

him when I was five down at Griffith Park Zoo in Los Angeles to sculpt him with a good friend of mine. He was very old, the lion, and some idiot threw a cigar on him and it burnt through his skin while he was asleep and killed him. Made me sick. It was one of the most traumatic things I remember out of my childhood. Isn't that awful? That sonofabitch."[9]

Aged thirteen, Vliet won a three-year scholarship from Knudsen's Creamery, to study sculpture in Europe, which was set to commence when he reached the age of sixteen. One of the reasons he didn't take it up was because "they wanted me to look at all those church paintings or something".[10] Another reason he gave was that his parents were convinced that all artists were 'queers', and therefore they declined the offer on his behalf. Although he disliked being treated as a child prodigy, he was also deeply disappointed at being denied this chance to fulfil his artistic potential: "I got out, right out, although at the time I thought my folks were mean pulling me out."[11] Vliet showed the other side of this defiant attitude when he admitted that because he had been prevented from taking up the scholarship, he tried to run away, but 'couldn't do it'. Instead he claimed that, because the experience had embittered him so much, he effectively cut himself off from the products of others' creativity in that he 'never' listened to music and gave up art until he was twenty-three. "Look, if I was that dependent on it they probably did the right thing. I probably would have burned out," he said.[12]

Vliet looked back on his place of birth in 1972: "They call it Glendale but there wasn't much of a dale or a glen left when I was born there."[13] The family subsequently moved from Glendale out beyond the furthest reaches of the sprawling suburbs of Los Angeles to Lancaster, a small town situated in the Antelope Valley, at the edge of the Mojave Desert, and close to the Edwards Air Force Base. Lancaster was spread out geographically and the population of the entire valley at the time only amounted to about twenty-five thousand. Physically dwarfed by the vastness of the Mojave, for Vliet Lancaster was a cultural desert too. But his parents were not in the least interested in art – they had not even heard of Picasso, as he later remarked. His reading of the situation was that they had moved there for the express purpose of putting him off artistic pursuits.

Once in Lancaster, Vliet attended Antelope Valley High School, an experience that he was thereafter keen to forget. An extremely intelligent youth, he also possessed a short attention span and didn't take well to the academic regime. Subsequently, he pursued a revisionist strategy to erase the era from his past, at least publicly. "I *never* read books and I never went to lessons at school – I couldn't take that," he said, also offering the view that "school makes you focus so sharp that if somebody came up and threw something your eyes would shatter".[14]

When interviewed on *The David Letterman Show* in July 1983, he did admit to half a day at kindergarten: "Somebody told me that I stayed too long," he quipped, before continuing, "I was a sculptor. It's good for some people but it wasn't good for me." "So what did you do?" asked Letterman. "Outsmarted the truant officer," he replied. With very few exceptions, he has utterly refused to admit that he attended school, often justifying his side of the story with the comment, "If you want to be a different fish, you gotta jump out of the school." The recent discovery of his school graduation photograph would tend to suggest otherwise.

Vliet's tendency, as an adult, to get other people to read, write or type for him may have been attributable to a form of dyslexia. He has hinted at this himself: "I get people to read things to me sometimes. I have enough trouble getting out what's in me already without having to consider what other people are saying. Besides, I can't concentrate on print. I need one of those kids' books with huge letters."[15]

In 1974 Bill Gubbins asked Vliet to confirm if he'd been to school and got this reply: "No, I never went to school. That's why I have trouble spelling. Probably one of the main reasons why I'm a poet – because I couldn't accept the English language as it was, and I changed it."[16]

Vliet's artistic aspirations may have been thwarted and his schooling wasn't much of a consolation, but his home life was comfortable. Ken Smith lived next door to the Vliets in Lancaster in the mid-fifties. He looked back on this era in 1997: "Don's parents – Glen and Sue as they were called by everybody, including Don – were well liked by everybody. Glen and Sue were never condescending and treated everybody with genuine friendship, and would even talk to a pimple-faced geek (me) as if he were an adult. Once you got used to the crustiness (Glen and various uncles) and noise (everybody), it was a very warm and loving household. Sue had a habit of always locking the doors, regardless of the time of day or how many people were with her inside the house or just outside the door, then Don would immediately think of something he needed inside the house.

"Banging on the door, bellowing in an amazing basso profundo for a fifteen-year-old, Don would say, 'God damn it, Sue, open up this back door jam.' This scene might repeat several times a day, and was funny every time. I recall one day when Sue was gone somewhere and Chuck Sherwood [older brother of Vliet's friend and contemporary Jim] locked the door when Don went outside. Looking at Sherwood through the window and knowing his mother was gone, Don still yelled, 'God damn it, Sue, open up this back door jam.'"[17]

Living across the street was Sue Vliet's mother, Anne Warfield, now known to all as Grannie Annie. She was second cousin to Wallis Warfield, better known as Wallis Simpson whose relationship with the Prince of Wales, later King Edward VIII, resulted in him abdicating from the throne. She was also related to cowboy star Slim Pickens and the explorer Richard Halliburton. Her husband, Amos Warfield, had owned a plantation in the South and she had stories of seeing blues legend Howlin' Wolf playing there. She always called him 'The Howling Wolf', which Vliet thought was really hip.

In 1956 a Sicilian/Greek kid, Frank Zappa, just a few weeks older than Vliet, moved to Lancaster from San Diego. He was less than impressed with the stifling heat and the sprawling layout of the place. The Zappa family had already moved a number of times in Frank's lifetime, but he reckoned Lancaster was one of the worst places he had lived. The Zappas ended up living "on a tract of little stucco houses. Okies with cars dying in their yards. You know how you always have to pull up a Chevrolet and let it croak on your lawn."[18]

Zappa was musically precocious. He had already been active in San Diego, drumming from the age of fourteen in The Ramblers, an R&B group who specialised in early Little Richard material. As a parallel activity, he had begun writing avant-garde orchestral pieces inspired by Edgard Varèse. He felt nothing if not stranded in Lancaster, as he later explained to Michael Gray: "For me, living in places like Lancaster – it was good but it was very frustrating. Because things were really happening in Los Angeles, which was 80 miles away. Can you imagine how that felt – knowing that there it all was, but 80 miles away! I mean, so near and yet so far."[19]

Zappa and Vliet met at high school and found out that they shared a similar taste in music. They'd meet up at Zappa's house and then cruise around the streets in Vliet's powder-blue Oldsmobile, which sported a terracotta werewolf's head he had modelled himself on the steering wheel. They had a fruitless quest, in Zappa's words, "looking for pussy – in Lancaster!"[20]

Vliet would ask Zappa round to his place to play records in sessions that often extended into the early hours, the pair having to bunk off school the next day. The two friends were obsessive in their love of (almost exclusively black) music. Favourite listening ranged from doo-wop groups like The Spaniels and The Orchids to Lightnin' Slim and Slim Harpo, Clarence 'Gatemouth' Brown, Johnny 'Guitar' Watson, and the Chicago blues of Muddy Waters and Howlin' Wolf – which refutes Vliet's claim to have never listened to music until he was twenty-three. Vliet's father, Glen, had a job running a delivery truck for Helm's Bakery, which they raided for leftover pineapple buns during these elongated listening sessions.

Zappa had assessed Vliet as being rather narcissistic and described him in his teens as dressing in the latest Pachuco fashion, "a certain style of clothes that you had to wear to look like that type of teenager – khakis and French-toed shoes".[21] Many years later, Vliet remembered he had gone to a party full of "cholos, heavy Mexicans, bad cats, women in angora sweaters, the bunny shoes and stacked hair". He had brought some unorthodox music with him. It was "a record for teaching a parakeet to talk, you know, 'say hello, Tweetie'. I thought it was pretty hip. I got it when I was about five. I took that record and slipped it into a stack of 45s and they just couldn't take it!"[22]

Being an only child inevitably made Don the centre of attention within his family. He admitted that he used his unique position to help him get his own way. Another school friend and musician who lived close to the Vliets was Jim Sherwood, who would later play saxophone with Zappa in The Mothers Of Invention. He remembers one of Vliet's extraordinary abilities: "Don was kind of strange because he would get embarrassed when there were things to do and he didn't really want to do them. I remember [when we were] in high school when his mother would make him clean up his room and he'd get mad and yell at her, 'I'm not gonna clean up my room, I'm sick.' He could actually physically break out in a rash so he didn't have to do things."

From childhood, Vliet had been asthmatic and prone to allergies. This inspired Sherwood and Zappa to play some teenage practical jokes on him. Sherwood: "What happened originally was, he was allergic to some kind of cologne and he got a rash when he put that cologne on. What we'd do is tease him and say we'd dumped the cologne all over the front seat of his car and he wouldn't get into it for weeks. We never did it, we'd just tease him."

Less allergenic cologne came in as a useful deodorant when the two friends went off on weekend jaunts to the metropolis. "Don and I would take off to LA and hang out in the clubs and listen to groups. We'd go to drug stores and splash on cologne as we had to sleep in the car – we went through a lot of cologne. I played harmonica and Don played a little harmonica and we'd sing a lot of these old blues things we'd pick up on the radio, driving down in his car. But Don wasn't really interested in [performing] music until much later. He was more into art and things like that."

Towards the end of Vliet's spell at high school, his father suffered a heart attack and so Don was obliged to contribute to the family income. Zappa told Nigel Leigh: "He had dropped out of school by that time and spent most of his time staying at home. Part of the time Don was helping out by taking over the bread truck route and driving up to Mojave, and the rest of the time he would just stay at home and listen to rhythm and blues records and scream at his mother to get him a Pepsi."[23] Vliet was a reluctant surrogate bread delivery man, but Sherwood remembers one of his quips about his new duties: "He told me he used to be embarrassed because he had to open his drawers for all these women."

Vliet loved music but was very reluctant to participate in any organised music-making. He would sing for his own amusement and obviously possessed talent, but he had to be cajoled or tricked into having his voice recorded. When called upon to perform he became self-conscious and embarrassed and his timing would go awry and, likely as not, he would try and cover his embarrassment by becoming angry.

Having graduated from high school, Zappa went on to study harmony at Antelope Valley Junior College, where Vliet also enrolled as an art major before dropping out after a single semester. It was here that Zappa coerced him into making his first recording, in an empty classroom in 1958 or 1959. The song, 'Lost In A Whirlpool', was recorded on a Webcor reel-to-reel tape recorder which, Zappa recalled to Rip Rense in 1993, "just happened to be sitting there waiting to be plundered – maroon, with the green blinking eye".[24] Zappa played lead guitar, even though he had only just learned to play a few months before under the tutelage of his brother Bobby, who played rhythm on this song. "Frank and I had a good time. We were just fooling around," was how Vliet remembered it.[25]

Ostensibly a primeval twelve-bar blues parody, the song also showcases the teenage Vliet's spectacularly repulsive toilet humour. Like some never-to-be-screened episode of *The Twilight Zone*, it chronicles the fate of a spurned lover floating around the U-bend, opening with the lines 'Since my baby flushed me ...' Gripped by scatological terror, Vliet sings of encountering a big brown eyeless fish. There are few areas of basic human activity that have not been dealt with in rock'n'roll, but a song about being pursued by a giant stool stands in a field of one. The hapless victim ultimately calls for a plunger.

'Lost In A Whirlpool' is an example of teenage guys messing around and being as viscerally disgusting as only teenage boys can. But at the start of the song, a combination of Vliet's astonishing falsetto and the primitive recording technology makes him sound uncannily like a bona fide female blues singer. As the song progresses, the roots of Vliet's inimitable singing style are revealed, both in his improvisational ability and in the impact of his voice – he gets a hard-edged sound by constricting the vocal cords while forcing the air through with considerable power. He sounds at least twice as old as his seventeen or eighteen years.

Dropping out of the education system cut down Vliet's immediate employment prospects, but he has since made claims that he undertook a number of jobs from his late teens into his early twenties: in the aviation industry, as a graphic designer, as the manager of a shoe store and as a vacuum salesman. Ken Smith has confirmed that Vliet was something of a hotshot in retail sales, quickly becoming top salesperson at Kinney Shoes in Lancaster. He then moved into vacuum cleaner sales, although whether, as he claims, he sold one to the author Aldous Huxley is open to debate. This could well have happened, as Huxley lived in Pearblossom, a small town in the then sparsely populated Antelope Valley. The story goes that Vliet knocked on his door while holding a vacuum cleaner and, when Huxley appeared, introduced himself, then said, "Sir, this thing sucks."

Lancaster was a satellite of LA, but as often happens in towns geographically removed from the centres of innovation, the environment threw up some of its own interesting hybrids. By the late fifties there was considerable musical activity in the area. While still at high school, Zappa played drums in a multiracial R&B group called The Blackouts, which got its name after some of its members passed out during a peppermint schnapps binge. The group's uniform consisted of white peggers with brown plaid or blue lamé shirts, and metal belts, which, Zappa explained, could be used as chains in case of post-gig disturbances. One of the group's haunts was Sun Village, a black enclave just outside town, where they played what Zappa has described as 'huge Negro dances'. These kinds of goings-on upset the citizens of

Lancaster and it was no doubt more than coincidence that Zappa once got arrested for vagrancy before one of their shows.

In 1959, Zappa's peripatetic family moved once again, this time to Claremont. The time was right for Frank to leave both his family and Lancaster. He moved to LA with the intention of establishing himself as a writer of film soundtracks. His first piece of work was the soundtrack for the low-budget Western *Run Home Slow*. Due to production difficulties which held up the film, the score remained unrecorded. He also worked on the music for a film called *The World's Greatest Sinner*. With Zappa gone, The Blackouts disbanded. Alex Snouffer, who had played trumpet alongside Zappa's drums in the high-school band, formed an R&B group, The Omens, from the remnants of The Blackouts. Jim Sherwood was one of the horn players.

Zappa's next step was particularly significant. In 1961 he moved to Ontario on the outskirts of LA. After hiring a session at Pal studio in nearby Cucamonga for one of his own projects, he ended up spending more and more time there. Pal was owned by Paul Buff, an electronics expert, and the two of them collaborated in an attempt to make the studio into a hit factory. They wrote, produced and played on a number of recordings under different 'group' names and would then go up to Hollywood with acetates to try and hustle a record deal. 'Tijuana Surf' by The Hollywood Persuaders became a hit in Mexico, although it was actually Buff playing all the instruments. Other concoctions were 'Hey, Nelda' by Ned and Nelda, a parody of the Paul and Paula hit 'Hey, Paula', and 'How's Your Bird' by Baby Ray and The Ferns, which featured singer Ray Collins.

Zappa and Collins began writing songs together. One of their successes was 'Memories Of El Monte', recorded by doo-wop group The Penguins (who had topped the R&B charts in 1954 with their single 'Earth Angel') on Art Laboe's Original Sound label. In early 1963, Buff moved out to build the new mixing desk at Art Laboe's Original Sound Studio, leaving Zappa more or less in control. He had an ambivalence towards writing doo-wop and pop music, ultimately because he found it impossible to take seriously, as 'Hey, Nelda' shows. His satirical view on pop culture, which stayed with him throughout his career, was exemplified by 'Fountain Of Love', from 1963. Written with and featuring Collins, the song is a magnificent yet utterly hollow doo-wop parody, the lyrics to which Zappa later described as 'submongoloid'.[26]

Concurrent with his desire to get a hit record, Zappa was also keen to move away from pop pastiches and play his own music. Drummer Vic Mortensen, who had known Zappa years before at high school, arrived back on the scene. They started playing together and formed the core of a new group, The Soots. A more confident and enthusiastic Vliet was drafted in on vocals, recording material at Pal, which Zappa was now referring to as Studio Z.

"This album is not available to the public. Even if it were, you wouldn't want to listen to it," announces Vliet at the start of 'Tiger Roach', recorded in 1963. As the tune begins, Vliet delivers a few seconds of slurping, farting and gargling noises, and then an amazing porcine squeal. Zappa was on guitar, Janschi on bass and Mortensen on drums. While they were playing in the studio, Vliet was standing out in the hallway, which doubled as the vocal booth, listening to the sound that leaked through the door to the live room. His vocal performance is a primitive incantation, with ideas for lyrics generated by looking through an X-Men comic book, which was pinned to the notice board, and by observing his surroundings, coming up with such profundities as 'Light switch'. 'Tiger Roach' is an R&B tune flecked with a few spots of surf guitar spray. Surf music was big in Lancaster at the time, with blond floppy hair and white Levi's *de rigueur*, even though the surfing options in the Mojave Desert were limited.

Other Soots songs recorded around this time included an instrumental, 'I'm Your Nasty Shadow', 'Metal Man Has Won His Wings' and 'Slippin' and Slidin' '. 'Metal Man' is slower than 'Tiger Roach', but shares a basic twelve-bar format over which Vliet improvises a similar vocal line. Zappa had formed a publishing company, Aleatory Music, which he ran from his home in Ontario. Through it he tried to interest Dot Records in some of his new material, including a Vliet-led 'Slippin' and Slidin'', but they were not impressed. Dot A&R man Milt Rogers returned a politely negative letter, dated September 19, 1963: "The material has been carefully reviewed and while it does have merit, we do not feel strongly enough about its commercial potential to give you any assurance of a recording." Zappa called Rogers to try some first-hand persuasion, but he would not relent, justifying his rejection by saying 'the guitar was distorted'.

Jim Sherwood moved in with Zappa for about six months in 1963, and they set to work on a "lot of recording and just a lot of bizarre stuff" to be added to the burgeoning reservoir of sonic oddments he had amassed, with Vliet or Ray Collins coming in to add some vocals. The main project was to be the first-ever rock opera, *I Was A Teenage Maltshop*. The opening theme is a ramshackle oddity with Mortensen on drums, Sherwood on acoustic guitar and Zappa on piano. Vliet was to play a character in the opera called Captain Beefheart.

The opera, which unsurprisingly was never performed, was based on the characters Ned and Nelda from the single 'Hey, Nelda'. Songs written for the project included 'Ned The Mumbler', 'Ned Has A Brainstorm' and two later recorded by Zappa's group The Mothers Of Invention, 'My Guitar Wants To Kill Your Mama' and 'Status Back Baby'. Sherwood explains: "It was supposedly about a kid, Ned the Mumbler, who came into one of these small closed-up towns where they didn't allow rock'n'roll and so he wrote these songs. He was going to get the whole town singing and enjoying music." The project, later described by Zappa as a 'stupid piece of trash', was eventually rejected by Joseph Landis of KNXT, a CBS-TV station, in December 1964 on the basis of an outline. "We remain unconvinced that the outline submitted can insure a quality show," he wrote.

Run Home Slow, starring Mercedes McCambridge, was finally shot in 1963. With the $2,000 soundtrack royalties, Zappa was able to buy Pal outright in the summer of 1964, officially renaming it Studio Z. The studio had already been filled up with props, such as giant cardboard rockets, and with the money left over, Zappa bought some old movie sets, which he began adapting for his next project, a sci-fi film entitled *Captain Beefheart vs. The Grunt People*, the 'grunt people' being Zappa's name for the 'straights' of the time. At least that's one interpretation.

Sherwood explains that the movie was to be set on Mars, and that Zappa wrote the movie so Vliet could play the 'magic man'. There is a snatch of monologue by Vliet, entitled 'The Birth Of Captain Beefheart', on Frank Zappa's *Mystery Disc* released in 1998. "Hi, it's your old friend Captain Beefheart," says Vliet, who then explains that the character travels through time and space and is "invisible and all that jazz". The story steers well clear of a linear narrative. Sherwood describes his own role in the film: "I was supposed to play Billy Sweeney, a kind of retarded kid whose father was rich and owned this huge ranch. I wanted to ride the ponies so I ran away from home and took over an old pony ride in a little town."

Zappa was fascinated by the Vliet household and Don's relationship with his mother. Some of the script for the movie has surfaced over the years and despite it being set on a different planet, there are some domestic scenes involving Captain Beefheart that bore a close resemblance to goings-on in the Vliet household back in Lancaster, Planet Earth.

Sherwood recalls how they found their way into the script: "Frank wrote some funny lines in the movie. Don was supposedly talking to all the little kids in his room and his mother comes in and says, 'Don, clean this place up, it smells like a camel's been eating peanut butter in here,' and he says, 'Shut up, Sue, and get me a Pepsi' – that's what he used to say to his mother all the time."

Cal Schenkel, a young artist and designer friend of Zappa, contributed some storyboard-like sketches for the film, one depicting Vliet with wings and another of him asleep on the floor with the TV on in the background. But there was no specific brief and his recollections of the project suggest that although ideas were being bounced around, it was very much a work in progress.

Although Zappa had moved away years beforehand, he kept up his connections with Lancaster and Studio Z became a focal point of activity for musicians from the town. Vliet would go there with guitarist Doug Moon and Jerry Handley, who'd had a spell as a guitarist in The Omens. Zappa and Vliet had been playing around with a rock'n'roll version of the 'Death March' to which Handley contributed some guitar. This helps explain where Vliet got the basis for one of his more cryptic, fantastic tales. He claimed that while listening to the radio he heard a place where he could fit in and decided he was going to 'fix' the formality of music.

In 1973 he described to Elliot Wald how he popped out of the 'egg' and into music, aged twenty-four, which would have been 1965: "I took this sax and went into the studio, where they were playing this thing called 'Logan Incident', a song written about this incident in… oh, San Diego. Something really corny like the 'Death March', only hyped up, like the Fifties. So I grabbed the sax and started blowing how I felt about this thing. I was saying, 'Hey, this is me playing.' They said 'Hey, look, it's too weird.' 'How can you say that to me in this day and age?' I asked, and they replied, 'Well, we're saying it to you. As a matter of fact you're fired.'"[27]

Studio Z, with its invitation to 'Record Your Band' painted in giant letters on the outside, was an intrusion into the day-to-day life of Cucamonga, whose population of seven thousand made it an archetypal small town. A news article in the *Ontario Daily Report* on *Captain Beefheart vs. The Grunt People* had hoped – a little misguidedly as it turned out – that Zappa might bring some of Hollywood's glamour to Cucamonga. Other parties in the town were less enthusiastic about his presence, and in a police set-up Zappa was arrested for making a pornographic tape. He had been commissioned to produce this item to accompany some stag night blue movie and he and his girlfriend Lorraine Belcher set about making some ersatz sexual noises, in between laughing at the absurdity of it all. It was no laughing matter for the police, who paid him a visit and took the by now edited tape. Zappa ended up with ten days in jail. "From what I understand, the guy who busted him used to hang out in the [public] bathroom and bust gay guys going in. The guy was really sick," says Sherwood. "But the thing that was really bad was they confiscated all Frank's tapes, everything. And it took Frank years and years and years to get them back." Studio Z effectively ceased functioning after this fiasco and *Captain Beefheart vs. The Grunt People* was abandoned. Zappa moved off to LA with the fledgeling Mothers Of Invention, to be joined later by Sherwood. The Cucamonga-Lancaster scene was over.

2

ETHEL HIGGENBAUM AND HER MAGIC BAND

"Strange, hit-record-like noises have been emerging from a group with the highly unlikely name of Captain Beefheart & His Magic Band. Captain Beefheart is a rather ominous-looking huge fellow by the name of Don Van Vliet."
Derek Taylor, *The Great Gnome Biography*, press release, 1966

Alex Snouffer arrived back in Lancaster in the winter of 1964–5, after a spell working in a casino at Lake Tahoe. He wanted to get a group together and start playing guitar again, so he called up Jerry Handley, Don Vliet and Doug Moon. Handley moved from lead guitar to bass and Doug Moon was invited to play guitar alongside Snouffer. Although Moon was relatively inexperienced and Vliet was still largely an unknown quantity, the nascent group were unified in their love of the blues. They had also become used to each other's playing on an *ad hoc* basis during the jams at Studio Z.

The musicians were competent, if no virtuosi, but original drummer PG Blakely was found to have a timekeeping problem and soon departed. Vic Mortensen was the obvious choice as replacement, and the group, who took the name Captain Beefheart & His Magic Band, began in earnest in early 1965. In Zappa's film, the Captain Beefheart character was conceived as the 'magic man', and so this would be his magic band. Vliet took his mooted film character and placed him in a new musical dimension. But although he was the front man, Snouffer had formed the group and was to all intents and purposes the leader. At least to begin with. He decided to

17

ditch his surname, replacing it with his middle name, Clair, which he changed to St Clair. Vliet followed suit, adding the Van to his surname. The following year, in a slice of typical Sixties zaniness, St Clair/Snouffer claimed the two of them had to change their names as they were wanted by the police for "smuggling sponges into Nevada".[1]

There have been numerous explanations of both the genesis of the name 'Captain Beefheart', and how it became appropriated as the name of the group. Zappa has claimed that he named the film character with reference to one of Van Vliet's uncles, known as the Colonel. One of his habits was to use the toilet with the door open, especially if Van Vliet's girlfriend was likely to walk by, offering the information that his 'whizzer', as Zappa put it, was built on such generous lines that the end looked like a beef heart. Other explanations and theories were that it was something to do with a tomato, or that the group's name was dreamed up by Van Vliet and/or Zappa, and/or some of the other guys in the band, on a stoned/drunk excursion to the desert. Van Vliet later steered the meaning away from such phallic grotesquerie, saying that it had nothing to do with anything in particular. Late on in his career, he explained that it derived from the beef that he had in his heart against the world and its attendant evils.

The first live performance by Captain Beefheart & His Magic Band is cited in a 1966 press release as being a 'Battle of the Bands' show at Claremont and Pomona Colleges in early 1965. St Clair is quoted as saying, "I don't think we really knew how to play together but we knew that we had sufficient music in us to beat the other group (who will remain nameless) in the contest. Our motivation for the Battle of the Bands was determination to destroy the opposition."[2] Van Vliet's version of their first concert is astonishingly different. He has confirmed that St Clair called him up to ask him to join the group, saying that they would be playing that evening. This prompted Van Vliet to admit that he knew nothing about music, and that his voice would sound like a 'burro'. Supposedly, St Clair insisted anyway, and the group played that night in Lancaster. During the intermission Van Vliet claims that, 'out of paranoia', he plugged a vacuum cleaner into an amplifier and did some tricks with Mexican jumping beans. "I was doing an artistic show, and the people dug it," he concluded. "That's what got me on the wrong track..."[3]

In common with just about every upcoming group at the time, Captain Beefheart & His Magic Band needed to get some Rolling Stones covers together for their live set. An upfront harmonica-totin' singer who could jump around like Jagger was more or less obligatory during the British 'invasion' of the mid-Sixties. So successfully did they assimilate this style that some people were convinced they actually were an English group. They started out rehearsing at Handley's house and then later at the Van Vliets' place, on Carolside Avenue. From these archetypal garage beginnings they soon moved inside the house due to noise complaints. Van Vliet justified their playing of Stones covers as being a necessity, more or less, as the rapid escalation in the group's popularity meant that they hadn't had time to sort out their own new material. Don Aldridge was a Lancaster-based singer-guitarist and a friend of Van Vliet. He was also a regular at the group's early rehearsals. On the subject of Rolling Stones covers, he recalls that Van Vliet's incumbent Jagger-esque role was beginning to rankle with him. "They did enough of them that on one occasion Don sent a copy of 'Get Off Of My Cloud' sailing past my head," he says. "He thoroughly hated Jagger by then."

At first the Magic Band was an all-for-one collective, with St Clair a dominant organisational force at rehearsals. More often than not the early material was completely collaborative. The group would start playing a riff or blues figure and Van Vliet would rummage around in his ubiquitous brown paper sack of lyrics to try to find something suitable.

The group soon became a melting pot of ideas and some typical antagonism began to emerge. Van Vliet was coming up with new ideas; but although he was rapidly developing into an impressive blues harmonica player, he had difficulty in getting his ideas across to the other musicians. He had to describe what he wanted verbally, or get the group to start playing something and then try to shape it from there. Frustration and arguments inevitably arose and the musicians' way of getting at Vliet was to remind him that, in the way that chords worked with each other and songs were structured, he didn't really know what he was talking about.

He was nevertheless beginning to assume greater control of the group. Aldridge – the fly-on-the-wall, so to speak – gives this perspective: "Don was so kind to me that I may have failed to recognise what a driving force he was from the very beginning. He was a heck of a guy to know during those early years. Don was always in charge, I thought at the time, by Al's default. Today I'm not so certain. I think Al appeared more dominant than he truly was.

"One night, as was the custom before practice, we smoked a couple of joints. As the band was firing up the first song, Don said something – a song title or something – and Doug made a wisecrack that broke me up. Immediately, Don lashed out, 'If you guys can't handle the stuff [referring to the dope], then we won't have it any more!' Everything instantly fell into line. He wasn't in control in the sense that he was later, but nevertheless they all looked to him for leadership. From the beginning, Don knew what he was about. The more it's discussed, the more certain I am."

Interviewed for the 1997 BBC documentary *The Artist Formerly Known As Captain Beefheart*, Doug Moon told Elaine Shepherd the reasons for the group's local popularity: "Don was a master at capturing the nuances of blues artists, their vocal. He could catch the sound of Howlin' Wolf and Muddy Waters – he didn't copy exactly, but he could re-create that sound. He had a tremendous blues voice and basically we played a lot of those [blues] tunes in the early days. And even in spite of the fact that we were different, I think the name the Magic Band really stuck, because no matter what we played, we played with conviction. We became local heroes amongst the community."[4]

Lew Stults was a member of a local car club, The Cordials, who regularly booked the Magic Band for their concerts and dances. They sold out every time they played, and the club made a profit even when paying the group the hefty sum of $250. "They were different, innovative, arrogant and spectacular," he recalls.[5]

Captain Beefheart & His Magic Band's big break came at the Teenage Fair at the Hollywood Palladium, which was held over a few days in April 1965. Legend has it that as a result of their appearance, the group spawned a number of fan clubs ahead of their first record deal. It also heralded the first major ruction within the group. The event was a big promotional deal for makers of teen-oriented products, like guitars, amps, surfboards and clothing. Groups were hired to demonstrate instruments in booths and then play a show or two on the main stage. Van Vliet was keen to keep on top of what was going on in the local scene. He was impressed by a sixteen-year-old drummer, John French, playing in a booth with his surf group The Maltesemen. The group were 'trading' alternate songs with a group in the next booth who were making their live début: The Rising Sons. They were fronted by a black blues singer, Taj Mahal, but the band member Van Vliet became fixated on was their seventeen-year-old guitarist, Ry Cooder. Gary Marker, the group's bass guitarist, remembers the event well: "Beefheart didn't demonstrate instruments, as I recall. They were getting local action and somehow just got booked on the big stage. It was the first real gig for The Rising Sons; we were hired by McCabe's Guitar Shop in Santa Monica – a big folkie hangout where Ryland cut his teeth – in combination with Martin Guitars.

"The Rising Sons were really just winging it, playing lots of Jimmy Reed, Muddy Waters and Howlin' Wolf, all off the tops of our heads. But we were a stark contrast to the bleached-blond surf bands, so we snagged some attention. Especially with a black dude singing really nasty blues and the added novelty of Cooder's bottleneck guitar. So one night I'm digging Cooder just wailing on some Howlin' Wolf tune – 'Down In The Bottom', I think.

"I looked up at the crowd and right up front was this really weird-looking guy with baby-blue eyes set in a kind of very pale moon-face. It gets pretty toasty in Hollywood in April, even outdoors at night-time, but this dude with an unruly shock of hair was wearing a leather coat that hit him about mid-thigh. He had an absolutely stunned and perplexed look on his face, as if he'd just discovered his best friend's corpse in his living room. He was flanked by a couple of guys who weren't quite as scary-looking, and I pegged them all as being musicians right away. The song wound down, and this weird dude turned to one of the guys with him and grabbed him by the arm – and I mean grabbed him really hard. He pointed at Cooder, then snarled at his prisoner through clenched teeth, 'There, *that's* the shit I mean. That's what I've been fucking talking about. Get it? Now do you know what the fuck I'm talking about?'

"One thing led to another and we quickly got acquainted. It was Don in the leather coat, of course, and the focus of his rage was his long-term whipping boy, Doug Moon."

Marker and Van Vliet ended up becoming good friends, but that night he had a definite agenda. Marker: "Ryland got more chummy than I did with them right off – because Don started making moves on him right away. Don told us he had a record deal cooking, but I was sceptical." Subsequently, The Rising Sons were invited up to Lancaster to jam with the Magic Band, with Van Vliet trying to conceal his ulterior motive.

The Teenage Fair appearances led to the group's first management deal. Dorothy Heard, who apparently already knew about the group, saw them play and, after a subsequent meeting, she passed them on to Leonard Grant, who offered to manage them, his first foray into that area. Once signed with Leonard Grant & Associates, the group began to get a lot more live work on and around the West Coast. By the end of 1965, on the strength of some early acetate demos, including a recently unearthed version of 'Call On Me', Leonard Grant landed the group a two-single deal with A&M Records, a company recently set up by Herb Alpert and Jerry Moss.

John French, who saw this early version of the group a number of times in Lancaster, in 1996 recalled Van Vliet's vocal transition into a full-blown lycanthropic bellow: "[Initially] his voice was totally different and they never changed the key of anything. So when he started singing, his voice was actually quite high. As he sang [more] his voice would get hoarse, get lower and deeper."[6]

Jim Sherwood also noticed the way it had changed from the early days: 'He would wash his hair and keep it wet and do things to get a cold. He used to stay sick with a cold so that he'd get that voice and sing like Howlin' Wolf. Then when I saw Don a few years later, his voice was really torn. I don't know what he did, whether he tore his vocal cords, but he had a real gruff voice and it pretty much stayed that way. That's what he wanted and he got it.'

Shortly before recording commenced, The Magic Band were rocked by the news that Mortensen had received the dreaded Vietnam draft letter. St Clair came up with a radical solution to this problem – he took Mortensen's place behind the kit, proving himself a competent drummer. Guitarist Richad Hepner, whom the group had seen in Denver playing with The Jags, was brought in to play alongside Moon. The recording sessions for A&M took place at Sunset Sound Recorders, Sunset Boulevard, Hollywood, in early 1966, probably January. There is some conjecture as to whether these were financed by the management to then get a deal, or were recorded after they secured a deal with A&M. As a producer had been drafted in, the latter seems more likely. The producer in question was David Gates, who later fronted the soft-rock giants Bread.

"Their record company asked me to produce four sides with them," he says. "They were very new to recording, and this may have been their first real recording session. They only had two songs and, as Don's voice was so R&B, I suggested we remake my favourite Bo Diddley song, 'Diddy Wah Diddy'. They did not know the song, but loved it right away."

Why Bo Diddley's mid-fifties classic had apparently eluded such R&B obsessives up to that point is a difficult question to answer. More importantly, Gates took control of the sessions, arranging the music and playing keyboards on 'Diddy'. As it turned out, four other tracks were recorded. 'Who Do You Think You're Fooling?', 'Frying Pan' and 'Here I Am, I Always Am', were written by Van Vliet, while Gates also contributed a song: "I wrote an R&B type song for – or with – them called 'Moonchild', on which I played a slide guitar. This gave us the songs that the label wanted. I do recall that the record company was shocked when they heard 'Moonchild' as it was so 'out there' compared to what I guess they had expected from the group.'

As a friend of the group, Aldridge was present at the recording sessions. "I didn't know that David Gates produced those sessions until two years ago," he says. "He was like wallpaper. I remember thinking, 'Moonchild', how silly. Not Beefheart at all.' Don had a terrible time with the vocals on 'Moonchild'. I didn't know David Gates, although Bread was a great studio session band. But Beefheart? A terrible match. Placing 'Moonchild' on the project was an old Hollywood producer's ploy. If it got airplay and mechanicals, even if it was a B-side, the producer just supplemented his take on the project. Phil Spector did this all the time. Everyone did. But to release 'Moonchild' as the A-side, to me was insanity. Still, on the tunes they created, they absolutely cooked. The guys appeared relaxed and jovial. They were trying very hard to make it look like another day at the office. I was seated, not in the control room, but in the studio. We spoke back and forth during breaks. Jerry and Alex joked with me. Don was more subdued: too hip for the room."

The first Van Vliet composition (credited on the label to Don Vliet) ever released was 'Who Do You Think You're Fooling?', the B-side of 'Diddy Wah Diddy'. It was a critical comment on the US government using the Statue of Liberty as a symbol, he later claimed. The stand-out sound on the A-side is Handley's fuzz bass, distorted by Gates into a floor-shaking monster. The bass guitar was still principally used as background colour, but the more adventurous producers of the era would occasionally soup it up into a big, bad, brutal hot-rod of an instrument.

'Diddy Wah Diddy' was released in or around April 1966. After a slow start it succeeded in pricking up some crucial ears. One of the first people to pick up on it was English DJ John Peel, who was then working for the radio station KMEN, based in San Bernardino. "My best pal on the station was the music director Johnny Darren. And I was that rare thing even then, a DJ who was interested in music," he says. "He used to let me trawl through the rejects and I used to go out of there with twelve, fifteen, twenty records a day. A lot of times you knew they would be mildly interesting because they would have a Dylan song on the B-side and sometimes you picked them out because you liked the name.

"So when I saw 'Captain Beefheart & His Magic Band' on a record, I thought, 'Oh, that sounds pretty neat.' Having played it myself, I took it to Johnny and said, 'We really ought to be playing this.' As much a favour to me as anything else, it was play-listed for a week. So it was probably the first time – I like to think – that a Beefheart record was ever play-listed anywhere."

The record became a 'turntable hit', getting radio plays, but without the high sales to match. It was being tipped as a national hit, but in a strange quirk of fate, over on the East Coast, Massachusetts group The Remains released a cover of the same song at the same time. The story was big enough for *Beat Magazine* to devote a page to the two groups, asking readers to decide which version was better. Good publicity, if it had not been in such adverse circumstances. Neither version reached the national charts, but by June the Magic Band's version had become a local hit.

The Crowell–Collier Broadcasting Corporation's magazine, *KFWB Hitline*, proclaimed that, "This delightful group is currently riding the KFWB Fab Forty with 'Diddy Wah Diddy'." The article made use of the ten-page press handout, *The Great Gnome Biography*, written by Derek Taylor for Leonard Grant & Associates. It proved an inspired vehicle by which to purvey information in a quintessentially Sixties, tongue-in-cheek, oddball kind of way. Here are some extracts:

"How did the name 'Captain Beefheart & His Magic Band' come about?"

"The Great Gnome of Rock'N' Roll gave us a choice of two names: Captain Beefheart and The Warts, and Ethel Higgenbaum and Her Magic Band. We just combined them. I can't wait until Ethel Higgenbaum and The Warts cut a record," said Alex.

"We feel very fortunate that we are associated with A&M," said Beefheart. "Our music is down home Chicago type country blues and we work well together."

"What is the trend in popular music as Beefheart sees it?"

"The Supremes may want to change their name to Ethel Higgenbaum and the Warts if Motown goes out of style."

"Thank you, Captain Beefheart."[7]

The group's visual image was quirky, to say the least. Their publicity shots found them photographed on a climbing frame, and posing with brass instruments and an old wind-up gramophone outside an antiques shop. The most absurd photo, and the one used for the *Hitline* article, found Van Vliet and the group looking as mean as they could surrounded by huge cuddly toys. A face from the group's earliest days was seen in the photographs – that of P. G. Blakely. The reason for his reappearance was that Hepner left shortly after the sessions with Gates had been completed. In another game of musical chairs, St Clair returned to his role as guitarist, leaving the drum stool free for the original drummer to return, his timing problem now deemed cured.

In these heady times, the Magic Band cemented their local celebrity status with an appearance on a youth TV show *Where The Action Is*. Miming to 'Diddy Wah Diddy', they were surrounded on set by healthy-looking Californian youth doing the frug and having a good time. As a result of Peel's enthusiasm, an A&M Records representative got in touch, with an invitation to see the group at the Whiskey-A-Go-Go in Hollywood, supporting Van Morrison's first group, Them. Critic Pete Johnson, who reviewed the show for the *Los Angeles Times*, remarked on Van Vliet's 'guttural throaty shout' and described his Howlin' Wolf vocal timbre as his 'tortured pinched-trachea sound'.[8] This could well have been the same show at which Van Vliet later claimed to have seen the popular crooner Andy Williams in the audience. That in itself was not so unusual, as Williams had a reputation for being something of a scenester in those days. But the singer was allegedly fried on LSD, coming down to the front of the stage between numbers and loudly proclaiming: "You're great."

John Peel gives his assessment of his first exposure to the group in concert: "I remember Beefheart and the band being really quite exceptional in a shambolic way and doing something which I'd never heard anyone else doing before. It was blues-based, but they attempted these long rambling interpretations of Howlin' Wolf tunes and stuff like that. I was sold straight away."

A second single, 'Moonchild', emerged a few months later, backed by 'Frying Pan'. The group were not impressed by the A-side – Van Vliet claiming that he sang it like crooner Vaughan Monroe – but it's a much maligned song. Van Vliet plays unison harmonica with the guitar and there are some spidery slide-guitar decorations, played by Gates. Whispered backing vocals and echoed tambourine add to the proto-psychedelic atmosphere.

'Frying Pan' is a propulsive R&B number, about the lesser of two evils, as Van Vliet later commented. The most interesting song from the sessions is 'Here I Am, I Always Am'. The staccato chorus and the restless rhythmical shifts were unusual for the time and presaged the developments that would soon take place within the group. The guitars navigate this bumpy ride with crisp, almost banjo-like picking. And Van Vliet was becoming increasingly confident, the proclamation "Here I's always am" rolled around in his mouth with a sexy arrogance. This track was originally planned as the B-side to 'Moonchild', but only got as far as some white-label test pressings. A&M were essentially a pretty conservative label and they were no doubt happy to see this oddity put in the dumper, and 'Frying Pan' taking its place. The song lay dormant in the vaults until it was released with the other four tracks on a 12-inch EP, *The Legendary A&M Sessions*, in 1984. Gates came up with another song for the group, 'Mississippi Bound', but Van Vliet would have nothing to do with it. 'Moonchild' was, as Gates recognised, perhaps a bit too *outré* for mass taste and the single flopped. Even Peel was unable to get it play-listed.

The group's local status continued to grow. Otis Owens, who later worked on the design side of Zappa's Bizarre and Straight record labels, particularly rated the 1966-era group whom he saw at the Antelope Valley fairgrounds. "There sprang up this whole high-desert blues subculture and each of our bands had these cliques, with Don as the reigning kingpin,"[9] he said.

Don Aldridge offers his views on the band's development: "The early gigs in Lancaster were mundane events, really. For us, though, at the time, I suppose the fact that Beefheart had broken the 'hair barrier' was a novelty. I don't believe the Magic Band was any better than The Omens or any one of several other groups that played the car-club gigs over the years – that is, in the beginning. They were definitely a band in development. By late 1966, though, the last local gig I remember them playing, they were awesome. They just kept getting better."

Photoshoots with cuddly toys and climbing frames gave a wrong impression, as the group were actually cultivating a tough-guy image, with Moon allegedly carrying a small firearm on his person in case there was any trouble. In the mid-Sixties, having long hair and looking mean gave you hip kudos. But in the wrong company, having long hair was just as likely to get you beaten up for being a faggot – even though the rumours, spread in the Seventies, that the group had waist-length hair at this time were completely untrue.

Van Vliet was an automobile enthusiast and had been a member of the car club at school, but was less than enamoured with the associated culture. Aldridge describes the sort of events that took place at car-club dances in the Lancaster area: "These gigs were typically rural gropefests. The 'Gomers' [country boys] in the car clubs were all about their 'lowered Chebies' [Chevrolet lowriders] with 'twice pipes' [twin exhausts], and cases of Olympia beer. The guy with the coolest car and the most beer got to grope the coolest babe. Don and I shared a disdain for those clowns."

On one occasion Captain Beefheart & His Magic Band found themselves double-booked for a car-club dance and a gig in Hollywood. They chose the latter and invited The Rising Sons to play at the car-club bash. Marker found it an instructive experience: "At first the crowd was wary, but with the knowledge that Beefheart had tapped us personally for the gig, they warmed quickly. But it did degenerate into a fiasco, with airborne beer bottles and fist-fights popping up every minute or two – none of it directed at us. We certainly got a taste of the environment Don and the band cut their teeth in."

The group moved on to play some bigger West Coast venues in 1966, including shows at The Avalon Ballroom, San Francisco, where they appeared alongside groups like The Charlatans, The Family Dog and The Chocolate Watch Band. Marker occasionally stood in on bass for Jerry Handley, "when he had problems with the draft board or some rinky-dink marijuana bust which meant he couldn't leave the county". One such show was at The Avalon Ballroom in May 1966, on the same bill as Big Brother & The Holding Company (featuring Janis Joplin) and Love. He remembers that Van Vliet's timing would occasionally waver on stage and St Clair had to cue him in, using his guitar neck like a conductor's baton. As well as the group's own material they played John Lee Hooker's 'Tupelo Mississippi', Howlin' Wolf's 'Evil' and 'Somebody In My Home' and a song that Marker insisted on playing if he appeared with the group, 'Old Folks Boogie' by Slim Green & The Cats From Fresno. He recalls that Love played their familiar trick of pretending they had lost their amps in transit, so they could save money by just turning up with their instruments and borrowing another group's gear. They also managed to blow out a couple of the Magic Band's speakers that night.

Van Vliet and Marker struck up a friendship, sharing an extramusical interest in art and the hot-rod culture of the time. Marker: "There are some parallels in his music and his personality in that no matter what you do with Don, even going out to get something to eat, he always keeps you a little off kilter, you never know what he's going to do. He'd fictionalise his life to make himself more interesting. The music business, it's all showbiz anyway. You combine Truman Capote and Thelonious Monk and put them into rock'n'roll and you get Captain Beefheart."

Marker's musical roots lay in jazz bass – he had played sessions with saxophonist and multi-instrumentalist Roland Kirk and had occasionally depped for Charlie Haden of Ornette Coleman's group. One night he persuaded Van Vliet to go out to LA club Shelly's Manne Hole – run by the legendary jazz drummer Shelley Manne – to see Kirk play. Van Vliet was aware of Kirk's recordings but wasn't prepared for his awesome live performance. Already buoyed up with mind-altering substances, when Kirk began stomping on stage and letting rip on his numerous saxes, then playing the police siren he wore round his neck, he became so excited he started to hyperventilate. Marker introduced him to Kirk after the show and remembers him being 'like an awe-struck kid' at first. But both Kirk and Van Vliet were voluble conversationalists and the two of them hit it off.

The Hepner/Moon/St Clair/Handley line-up had recorded a number of demos in early 1966 at Wally Heider's studio, Hollywood. Leonard Grant had been talking with A&M about an album of original material to follow the singles and these recordings were to show that the group could come up with the goods. The musicians played well and Van Vliet's voice began to loom larger in the frame. The songs were all composed by the singer: 'Just Got Back From The City', 'Here I Am, I Always Am' (which suggests that the 'official' version, was recorded at a later date than the other A&M material), 'I'm Glad' and 'Obeah Man'. There also exists a slightly later recording of another outstanding early song, 'Triple Combination', with Blakely on drums, which was made at the Carolside Avenue house. The songs, which featured in their live set, were tough, original R&B, with an occasional dash of soul. They proved that the 'magic' in the group's name was more indicative of Mojo-man hoodoo than mere party tricks. But as far as A&M were concerned, Captain Beefheart & His Magic Band had failed to register a hit and were now threatening to produce an album of material far less conventional than the controversial 'Moonchild'.

After the two A&M singles, the group were effectively dropped by the label. The well-known story, later propagated by Van Vliet, is that the group brought in a new song, 'Electricity', to Jerry Moss, who thought it 'too negative', and that it wasn't safe for his daughter. Other than being a pun on the title of the song, this is little more than fanciful as it had not even been demoed at that point. Although A&M were no longer interested in releasing their music, the group had to go through the process of legally severing themselves from the company. A brief honeymoon, a barely consummated marriage, then divorce proceedings to follow.

By the autumn of 1966, PG Blakely had left the group for the last time and a month or so later, John French left Blues In A Bottle, with whom he was featuring as a vocalist, and took his place behind the drum kit. The Magic Band had played their last car-club dance and moved *en masse* to a rented house in Laurel Canyon, on the northern outskirts of Los Angeles – geographically, at least, nearer stardom.

3

MAY THE BABY JESUS SHUT YOUR
MOUTH AND OPEN YOUR MIND

"Alex St Clair was generally, and tacitly, acknowledged as leader, though it was clear that Don Van Vliet, as lead singer and, therefore, frontman, would be Captain Beefheart. And who would have it otherwise?"
Derek Taylor, The Great Gnome Biography, press release, 1966

After splitting from A&M, Captain Beefheart & His Magic Band soon found an ally in Bob Krasnow, head of Kama Sutra Records' West Coast office. He had been hugely impressed by 'Diddy Wah Diddy' and was enthusiastic about having Captain Beefheart & His Magic Band record for the label's new subsidiary, Buddah. He had already met Van Vliet and wanted the group's début album to be the first release on the label. He knew that all he had to do was interest Kama Sutra president Artie Ripp and they could get things moving. Meanwhile, The Rising Sons had disbanded and Marker was now working on promoting Taj Mahal, Canned Heat and Spirit. He was also keen on working with the Magic Band, convinced they could become commercially successful.

Van Vliet remained obsessed with getting Cooder to join the group and ousting Moon – in that order. Moon was a capable blues guitarist and was starting to expand his playing within the new material. But Van Vliet reckoned he wasn't up to the more complicated, syncopated music that he was coming up with. At group meetings at the house, he would be reduced to gripping the seat of his chair and bouncing around in frustration, browbeating the other musicians by coming up with more and more reasons why, in his opinion, Moon wasn't up to the job.

At this time Cooder was studying at Reed College in Oregon. He was frustrated by both the academic regime and the local music scene and in a break between semesters came back to LA, unsure of what he wanted to do next. Marker, realising that Moon was on his way out and that the group were on the verge of being signed, made a deal with Van Vliet: if he could get Cooder to join, he would produce the forthcoming recording sessions and manage the group. Cooder liked Van Vliet and had already jammed with the Magic Band, but he was still reluctant to join. Marker was a few years older than Cooder and had known him since he was twelve. This put him in a good position, as he says, to 'work on' Cooder. He told him: "You can virtually control this band. This will be your band and Don will think it's his band, but really it will be your baby. This will work. It'll be good for you, it will look great on your résumé." Two weeks later, Marker was able to tell Krasnow, "OK, he's softened up. You can nail him."

Cooder was still dubious about the whole enterprise, but Krasnow's enthusiasm was persuasive. He called Cooder, telling him that Captain Beefheart & His Magic Band were going to be bigger than The Beatles and The Rolling Stones, that they had a good promotion deal, and that Cooder would be credited for his work.

Cooder gave his side of the story to Elaine Shepherd in 1995: "So Krasnow called me up and said, 'It's going to be the biggest thing since The Beatles, bigger than The Beatles. It's gonna be big. I need your help.' I said, 'Well, what do you want me to do?' He said, 'Well we need you to kind of get them ready for the recording.' I said, 'OK, look, let's just see what you're doing.'"

Interviewed by Alexis Korner on BBC Radio 1 in 1983, Cooder said, "He used to come around, Beefheart, 'cause he was having trouble with his guitar player at the time [Moon], who was suffering from nervous exhaustion brought about by Captain Beefheart." Although Cooder reckoned that Van Vliet was 'an imposing figure and very funny'[2] and liked some of his musical ideas, he likened the experience to stirring up the proverbial hornet's nest.

At this time the intra-group atmosphere was disorganised and fractious. French recalls gathering together and writing out Van Vliet's lyrics, which had now found their home in a box. "They were written on torn-up scraps of paper, napkins, matchbook covers, even toilet paper," he told Marc Minsker in 1998.[3]

Krasnow put the group into Art Laboe's studio upstairs from the Buddah company offices to record some demos, with Marker producing. Gordon Shryock from the label was there, checking to make sure everything went along OK. They recorded three new songs featuring both Moon and Cooder, 'Plastic Factory', 'Yellow Brick Road' and 'Sure 'Nuff 'N Yes I Do', and a version of 'Electricity' without vocals. The main men at Kama Sutra/Buddah were impressed.

Clashes between Van Vliet and the other group members were on the increase and Moon's days were numbered. Cooder described what greeted him when he arrived at rehearsals: "[Van Vliet said,] 'Well, I'll tell you what we're doing and what we're not doing. First goddamn thing is this goddamn guy here' – he points to Doug Moon again. 'Get outta here, Doug, just get outta here. You're no use to us now.' I can't remember what language he used but it was something like 'go away and let us do this'… 'Another damn thing I should tell you, the bass player Jerry, he doesn't remember the parts half the time. I told him, I taught him the music.' And I'm going, 'Whoa, all right. One thing at a time.'"[4]

Moon left soon after. Cooder has claimed that the suddenly disenfranchised guitarist pulled a crossbow on the musicians, shouting, "Don't nobody move", but none of the other witnesses at the scene remembers it as dramatically. There was a crossbow in the house which would occasionally be used in an attempt to clear the garden of an infestation of squirrels, but Moon apparently did no more than put it back in its place. His official departure was far less dramatic. He was formally asked to leave by Krasnow, who had been delegated to do the dirty work. With Cooder drafted in immediately following Moon's departure, tensions in the group were high.

Moon gave his side of the story to Elaine Shepherd: "By the time the album finally came out, those songs had evolved to become a little bit more avant-garde and a little bit more hinting at things to come in Don's later albums. That was the transitional period and that's why I left, because of those influences. I did not have that calling. When it got a little too far out, a little too weird, unsyncopated and bizarre and avant-garde, it just did not work with me."[5]

Another problematic factor was entering the equation – Van Vliet was becoming prone to panic attacks. He would hyperventilate, fear he was having a heart attack and be driven off by whoever was in attendance to the hospital at UCLA. Marker: "His father had died of a heart attack a couple of years before and it was always the same story: 'You know my dad died of a heart attack?' The story was that the paramedics couldn't get to him. His other story was, 'He died in my arms.' So he had this pathological fear of dying of a heart attack."

Van Vliet's voracious consumption of LSD was not helping matters. It had the effect of channelling his fears and anxieties into physical symptoms. Don Aldridge feels the panic attacks were also 'success-related'. He explains: "It seems to me these attacks may have been literally acid reflux. I don't recall Don having them before he started messing with all that LSD. You get enough hits of some of that Windowpane we were licking up, and success – and everything else, for that matter – could appear very large."

On arrival at the hospital he would be advised that it was simply a case of his pulse and respiration being up, and that he had a predisposition towards anxiety attacks. He was offered prescription tranquillisers to calm him down, but inevitably refused to take them, fearing they would somehow blunt his creative drive. Marker: "I'd say, 'You won't take a prescription drug that'll make you feel better and might keep you from having your fake heart attacks, but you'll take any sort of dirt acid that someone will hand you on the street – don't you see a contradiction here?' And he'd go off on some rant, a diversionary tactic to get you off of what was going on." These attacks were dubbed, 'The Don Patrol' by Alex St Clair, a play on words of the old war flick *The Dawn Patrol*, because, in Marker's words, "whenever Don decided to have some kind of freak-out or mental break, it was always around dawn, when most people were trying to get some sleep". He remembers one particular incident which took place at his house and which he inadvertently caused.

"Don came to spend a couple of days with me at my place in Venice, California. As usual, he popped some street acid someone gave him, with absolutely no knowledge about its quality or quantity. He got buzzed and for some odd reason I recall we watched an awful, unintentionally hilarious, late night film on TV called *Legs Diamond* – or something like that – starring the now mostly forgotten actor Ray Danton.

"Anyway, Don started coming down off his peak, but was still hallucinating somewhat and was feeling a tad paranoid. He wanted something to drink. I reminded him he left his orange juice and various alcoholic drinks in the fridge – he seemed to prefer even whiskey well below room temperature. So he wandered into the kitchen, didn't turn on the light because he claimed acid made it possible for him to see in the

33

dark – like a cat. I could hear him opening cupboard doors, looking for a drinking glass. As I was a bit buzzed on weed myself, it was too much of an effort to tell him which cupboard the glasses were in.

"A couple of months earlier I went to a friend's big pot luck Thanksgiving Day bash and my task was to make a big, traditional baked yam/sweet potato casserole dish, and a couple of sweet potato pies. So, for some reason I bought a huge 15 pound bag of yams - but of course couldn't possibly prepare all of them, so when I finished, I put the remaining potatoes, in their net bag, up in the cupboard. I was seldom home then and forgot about the unused potatoes.

"Don found the potatoes when he opened the overhead cupboard they were in, while looking for a drinking glass. Any kind of tuber of the potato family, left in the dark for a couple of months, will grow long tendrils whilst seeking root space and/or sunlight. And that's what almost ten remaining pounds of yams did: grew lots and lots of two to three-foot long tendrils. When Don opened the cupboard door in the dark, hundreds of long, thin white tendrils cascaded down on him. He let out a shriek like James Brown's opening volley in 'I Feel Good', but about an octave higher. Seconds later, he bolted out through the kitchen door, ashen, eyes the size of boiled eggs, still screaming and waving his arms frantically. Bits and pieces of severed yam tendrils were flying everywhere and hanging from his hair. A huge cluster had plastered itself to the front of his shirt, another hung from his pocket. He started flashing that he'd been attacked by aliens hiding in my kitchen cabinet.

"It took me two hours to get him calm enough to understand what had happened. But by then he was in a full blown 'heart attack' mode, one of his frequent panic attacks. Pulse and respiration were way, way up. This precipitated another episode in the 'Don Patrol' chronicles and he had to be transported to the UCLA medical center emergency room at 4:30 AM, where they were becoming well acquainted with him. 'Back in town again, Mr. Vliet?' asked the intern/resident who had already dealt with Don on previous occasions. 'What is it this time? Another heart attack, or were you attacked by space aliens?'

"'How the hell did he know?' Don asked me, absolutely stunned. 'Is he psychic?' I thought I'd gotten him to understand about the potatoes, even showed him a couple, but he was slipping back into some acid-induced haze and fantasy world. Don eventually calmed down - or got as calm as he ever got - and drove himself back home to the desert the next afternoon. Several times after that, when the topic came up, he asked me not to tell anyone that he'd been freaked out by a bag of yams. Because, he explained, 'It's kind of embarrassing. You know what I mean?'"

Once within the hornet's nest, Cooder was given the role of musical director, arranger and translator of Van Vliet's musical ideas. He found these a good deal less specific than he was used to, as he explained a decade later to John Tobler of *Zig Zag*: "In a selection of notes he wanted this and he wanted that. How you did it wasn't important, it's just that he wanted a sound... he'd look at music in this real un-linear way". Cooder took to his new role with authority and began to assemble and organise the music. In 1996 John French assessed his contribution: "Ry was the musical director on *Safe As Milk*. He didn't have the power that Don had as far as controlling people and getting people to do what he wanted, but he had this respectability and yet he was fairly easy to work with. Ry had a lot of technical ability and he knew how to take normal things and piece them slightly differently – just shift it a little bit and then it became unique."[7] Once the material had been knocked into shape, Krasnow brought in Richard Perry to produce the sessions. Van Vliet accepted this decision without question, keeping quiet about his deal with Marker – who had lobbied the label for the sessions to be recorded on the eight-track machine at Sunset Sound Studios. Annoyed at Van Vliet's 'treachery', he abandoned any ideas of management and, after briefly helping with the engineering, took no further part in proceedings. Perry, however, was unfamiliar with the mixing desk and the group soon decamped down the road to RCA Studios to finish off the recording on a four-track machine. He also helped in arranging the music and cueing Van Vliet, who was often in a disorganised state in the studio.

Krasnow really was convinced that the group could be bigger than the Beatles and the Stones, and although this was to prove beyond their capabilities, they were beginning to sound like no one else. And his faith in them was total. In an undated quote reprinted in *Goldmine* in 1996 he said, "Beefheart was like an inspiration to me. His brain, his liberated ideas, his multi-talents. To me it wasn't even about rock'n'roll. It was about where rock'n'roll came from. And about the linear concept of music and how it evolved."[8] After all the preliminary palaver, Captain Beefheart & His Magic Band recorded their début album, *Safe As Milk*, in spring 1967.

"Well, I was born in the desert," Van Vliet sings on the opening song, 'Sure 'Nuff 'N Yes I Do', and takes off on a metaphorical journey from

Lancaster into new territory. Accompanied solely by slide guitar at the outset, he gives a thumbnail sketch of his travels to New Orleans, through tornadoes and into a landscape drenched in sunlight, all observed with the moon sticking in his eye. In these first few bars he again sounds much older than his 26 years, but drunk on life. When the Magic Band kick in, the sound is immediately different from the A&M material: French's drumming is filled with hi-hat snatches and stop/start interjections, Cooder and St Clair's guitars cut out new rhythmic shapes, and Handley's supple bass is given plenty of space in which to roam. These were the crucial differences between the Magic Band and their peers, many of whom would have played this sort of song with a straight-ahead backbeat. But 'Sure 'Nuff 'N Yes I Do' showed that the restless, shifting metres of 'Here I Am, I Always Am' were no quirky aberration and indeed were becoming an integral part of the group's developing style.

In amongst the turbulent nature imagery, the song is also a vehicle for Van Vliet's braggadocio – he is driving around in his brand-new Cadillac, inviting "all the young girls" to come around and check it out. And he introduces the high vocal 'hiccup' which became one of his vocal trademarks. The song structure is based on a perennial blues tune that goes back to Muddy Waters's 'Rollin' And Tumblin' ', Howlin' Wolf's 'Down In The Bottom' and further back in time to Charley Patton.

The gongs and whispered "zig zag" at the start of 'Zig Zag Wanderer' set the psychedelic/garage rock agenda, and the track is thereafter driven by Handley's massive, elastic 'Diddy Wah Diddy'-style bass. The two guitars chop into the rhythm, while an urgent call and response develop between Van Vliet and French, who had been drafted into the group as a vocalist as well as a drummer.

'Call On Me' is a prime example of how the group could cobble together the sounds and styles of the time and then add enough otherness to produce a Captain Beefheart song. Tremolo guitars pick out plangent figures that sound like The Byrds (or even The Searchers), and integrate them the way The Beatles had moulded Byrdsian elements on 'If I Needed Someone' from the previous year's *Rubber Soul*. Handley's playing is particularly mellifluous and Perry's clavichord joins in the fray. Just when it seems fairly straightforward, the flow is momentarily broken by a bizarre interlude of tremolo and pizzicato guitars. Percussionist Milt Holland adds tambourine and under this sonic weight the drums end up as virtually inaudible.

Van Vliet's ability to mimic other singers was legendary. Marker remembers him once breaking into a James Brown impression that was so accurate it almost made him drive off the road in shock. Here he does his best Soul Man routine, sounding uncannily like a cross between Otis Redding and Wilson Pickett. The coda is delicious, based on the four-note refrain that ran through The Crystals' 1963 hit 'Then He Kissed Me', over which Van Vliet whoops, hollers and finally exclaims, "I'm down on my knees!"

Although he was now living in Laurel Canyon, the songs 'Plastic Factory' and 'Dropout Boogie' are grounded back in Van Vliet's home-town environment. Pianist and composer Harold Budd grew up in Victorville, on the southern fringe of the Mojave Desert, and recalls the socio-economic underclass of that environment: "I look back now and see that it's a sub-class or a distinct class of American who are disenfranchised, what people disparagingly call 'White Trash' − hard-working, never successful at anything."

"Factory's no place for me," Van Vliet sings on 'Plastic Factory', then snarls, "Boss man, leave me be", sneering back at a work regime that he had escaped. He blows distorted harmonica against St Clair and Cooder's aggressive, jagged guitars. The standard R&B verse and chorus format is broken up by a waltz-time link that is both elegant and delightfully out of context. Don Aldridge recalls that the song was specifically about a factory job he had taken at Lockheed in Burbank. "'Get out of that lame factory, man!,' Don would shout. 'You're too hip for that!' But he saw all of the car club set as losers, destined to end up working at Sears Roebuck. 'Plastic Factory' was against the Establishment in general, but it was specifically about me. I wanted out of the factory as much as he wanted me out. But Don neglected to consider that it was my salary that was keeping him in tobacco and smoking dope."

'Dropout Boogie' takes counter-cultural spokesman and uncompromising LSD advocate Timothy Leary's 'Tune in, turn on, drop out' dictum, and turns it on its head. The option to 'drop out' and be a part of the emergent hippie milieu was there if you had the means to support yourself, but if you were dirt poor, and trying to set up home with a dependant or two, it simply wasn't a possibility.

Van Vliet addresses these difficulties in his lyrics. Slipping into his 'pinched-trachea' snarl, he reels off a list of instructions like "get a job" and "you gotta support her". The subject of the song has told his girl he loves her, so Van Vliet sarcastically tells him to "bring her to mother". Whether the addressee drops out or makes a decision to ride on the stultifying small-town marriage-kids-work-death conveyor belt is in the balance and Van Vliet's relentless line of questioning always returns to 'And what about after that?'

The song crackles with aggression. The opening two vocal lines sound nasty enough, with the rhythm guitar chopping chunks out of French's syncopated rock 'n' roll patterns. But then a second, ultra-belligerent fuzz-guitar joins in, carrying a mean sneer all of its own. As well as tracking the vocals, it sounds like it's trying to scythe them down. The by now inevitable interlude at odds with the prevailing song structure arrives; this time a lovely motif, again in waltz time, with Van Vliet playing marimba to flesh out the melody and, he later claimed, with an uncredited female harp player doubling up the line.

The awesome 'Electricity', which would remain a live favourite for well over a decade, finds Van Vliet breaking away from tradition and heading off into thrilling new areas that he made all his own. At least that's the commonly held opinion, but the truth is a little more complex. The original song was conceived in a more overtly Eastern/psychedelic modal form and was rearranged, almost rewritten, by St Clair, Marker and Cooder during rehearsals, Cooder's bluegrass-style motif becoming the song's principal guitar line.

The short introduction still retains a psychedelic expansiveness, with Van Vliet singing in unison with Cooder's slide guitar. It runs the gamut of his vocal style within thirty seconds, from a creaky, melancholic tone to an astonishing feral bellow, as, by way of introduction, he sings the title of the song.

St Clair's playing deserves to be singled out for praise. His drummer's sense of timing enabled him to become a rhythm guitarist of rare incisiveness. At his best – as on this track – he was untouchable. So was Van Vliet, whose voice spreads over this rhythmic mesh, from relaxed choruses welling up to verse sections squeezed out with amazing intensity. The group had come a long way from the stiff-limbed creature that had played at The Avalon Ballroom less than a year before. Here they play with a flair that leaves the listener on the edge of their seat. John French was on the edge of his seat too, but for different reasons: "The original drumbeat before I was in the band was sixteenth notes on mallets. The part had hardly any rhythm to it – it was just sort of a glide. As they were getting ready to do the song in the studio – Don is famous for doing this – he came up and said, 'I'd like to do this slightly different drumbeat.' And we've got three producers in there looking at their watches."

What Van Vliet vocalised to French was a completely different drum pattern. French was only eighteen years old and in his first recording session, but he remained unfazed, learned it on the spot, and played it brilliantly. Everyone was pleased with the way it all turned out. "I was quite relieved at the end of that session," he has since admitted.[10]

The tune needed something else and Van Vliet had an idea to overdub the sound of a hand-held circular saw screaming through a sheet of aluminium. In the end the buzzing sound of the theremin was chosen instead, which shoots into the distance at the fade, like an aural approximation of the lighthouse beacon flashing across dark seas described in the lyrics. Sam Hoffman played the instrument and Van Vliet described his contribution to Elliot Wald in 1973: "The guy who played it on the album was a friend of Dr Theremin's, also a doctor – a psychiatrist. This fella was able to relate to me because I wrote out what I wanted like a graph – I don't write music – and snap, first cut, he did exactly what I had been thinking of."[11]

If the song wasn't intense enough, the recording session spawned one of the first and most famous pieces of Captain Beefheart lore. What is apparently audible at the end of the track (but remains impossible to discern even with an unnaturally enthusiastic desire to hear it) is Van Vliet's voice overloading and blowing out the vocal microphone. The 'Apocrypha Alert' warning signs immediately start flashing.

Accounts like this help to feed the legend, but on a radio phone-in show on WBAI in 1984, host Tom Pompasello recalled a similar incident on *The Woody Woodberry Show*, a late-night TV show from the Sixties. Captain Beefheart & His Magic Band made an appearance on the show, dressed, he remembered, 'in the most outrageous garb'. Woody Woodberry had heard of the infamous mike-blowing incident and invited Van Vliet to repeat his feat. "The microphone not only overloaded, but short-circuited the other sound-reinforcement equipment," Pompasello recalled.

The radio show included a phone interview with Van Vliet conducted the previous year. "It was a piece of cake to break up that microphone. I did it," he said. "Yeah, they told me, they said, 'If you can break this thing, like you did at the studio when you did the album, do it.' I said, 'Aah, come on, I don't have that kind of money. Are you going to pay for it?' They said,

'Yeah, go ahead, give it your best shot.' And I did and I broke the damn thing. Did you hear that thing bubble on that show? I thought, 'Now what have I done? Now I won't be able to finish the song.'"

One Herb Bermann was also involved in the realisation of *Safe As Milk*, contributing lyrics to most of the songs. Van Vliet explained his role to Connor McKnight of *Zig Zag* in 1973: "He was a fellow that I met up in the desert, a writer, and we collaborated on a few songs. At the time, the group I was with wouldn't listen to a thing I said... they said my songs were too far out for them. I thought that if I worked with someone they considered to be a professional writer, then they'd at least listen to it, and maybe even play it."[12]

That all seemed straightforward enough, except that Van Vliet was casting him as a shadowy, enigmatic character. "I got introduced to two or three different people who were supposed to be Herb Bermann," recalls Marker. "I would always get a different story." Van Vliet offered a number of explanations: that he was someone with whom he had collaborated on the lyrics; that he was his attorney; that as Van Vliet was in dispute with his former manager, who owned his publishing, he wanted to divert 50 per cent of the royalties to this fictitious name in case there was any problem. Vic Mortensen also claims to have written 'Call On Me' before being drafted, but the only other group member who gets a writing credit on the album is Jerry Handley for 'Plastic Factory'.

Born in New Jersey, Herb Bermann moved to California in the early Sixties. Tracked down by the *Malibu Times* in 2000, he told Susan Bunn, "Captain Beefheart and I hooked up in 1966, I was a poet. I was an actor on the run. I had done [Dr] *Kildare* and *Asphalt Jungle*, the TV series, and I decided I could write. I lived on the Sunset Strip where the best music was happening. As all writers do, I had a trunk of fragments of work and poems and inspirational whatever."[1] Thereafter Bermann moved out to the artistic community of lower Topanga Canyon. He went on to write a screenplay for a mooted film project *After The Goldrush* with Dean Stockwell, who had had a starring role in *Dr Kildare*. Inspired by the idea, Neil Young wrote a soundtrack of sorts. Ironically, while Young's *After The Goldrush* album became a massive critical and commercial success, the film was never made. In 2003 some of Bermann's work appeared in the compendium *Idlers Of The Bamboo Grove: Poetry From Lower Topanga Canyon*.

"Don called him the Poet," recalls Don Aldridge. "We were all gagging out: 'The Poet's *heavy*, man,' or 'Geeeeeze, that's *heavy*, the Poet wrote that.' I was in hysterics watching Snouffer react to all of this. Al and I agreed that Herb's most superlative quality was that he'd managed to con that [significantly younger] woman [Bermann's partner] into taking up with him." The reason for Van Vliet's evasiveness was that he didn't like the idea of having to share the writing credits with anyone – there are even rumours that Bermann wrote all of the lyrics to 'Electricity'. He had also been quite noticeably impressed by Bermann, and wanted to restore his cool after letting his guard down.

Van Vliet's idea that artistic processes should be like child's play is given a literal demonstration on 'Yellow Brick Road'. The rather absurd, twee lyrics, set to a kind of two-step rhythm, depict an idyllic environment, with obvious *Wizard of Oz* connotations. "Smiling children" romp about in the sunshine with "bags of tricks" and "candy sticks". When Van Vliet requests his "sunshine girl" to come to his "abode", he sounds positively goofy. Holland's tuned percussion tinkles away in the background, and just when it all seems to be erring towards the mawkish, the chorus is bellowed out with counterbalancing force.

'I'm Glad', which dated back to 1965, exemplifies the doo-wop style on the cusp of its mutation into the soul ballad. The lovelorn protagonist chronicles the break-up of a relationship, yet keeps asserting that he is glad about the good times. His true feelings are belied by the falsetto backing refrain of "So sad baby" – which bears a strong similarity to the Smokey Robinson & The Miracles song 'Ooo Baby Baby', released on Tamla Motown in 1965. A horn section, which sounds as though it has been spirited from the Stax Studios in Memphis lifts the chorus. Van Vliet's vocals are superb, and if it still smacks a little of pastiche, it's more heartfelt than the similar material Zappa recorded at Studio Z.

While 'Electricity', in all its mike-busting glory, is the most exciting, visceral cut on *Safe As Milk*, 'Abba Zaba' – a song that was featured most frequently in concert performances over the years – is more innovative. A tricky cowbell and tom-tom pattern, which French played as an approximation of an African rhythmic style, forms the backbone of the song. It rolls forward with sparse ornamentation from Holland's percussion, sharp chord-work, guitar filigrees and a delightful duet between the drums and Cooder's bass in the middle section. On a more prosaic note, Abba Zaba was the name of a candy bar, 'taffy' with a peanut butter filling, that Van Vliet had consumed in his childhood. He has claimed that the song was about evolution, but in another facet of meaning the repeated lyric 'Babette Baboon' was his childhood name for the little monkey depicted on the wrapper.

'Where There's Woman' is a relatively perfunctory rock/soul excursion augmented by languid congas. Despite Van Vliet's sensuous, melodic vocals, the song comes across as rather furrowed-browed and earnest – until the group race into the raucous chorus, with French joining in on backing vocals. Van Vliet's high exclamatory wail, which would become another of his vocal trademarks, makes an appearance as the song winds down. In complete contrast, he wears his influences on his sleeve on a version of 'Grown So Ugly' by blues singer/guitarist Robert Pete Williams. The original was released on *Free Again* (1960), Williams's first recordings following his release on parole for murder. He was forty-six at the time and the song reads like a requiem for a wasted life. Williams looks in the mirror and, horrified at his ageing face, exclaims, "I've got so ugly I don't even know myself." The Magic Band's version is radically different and exemplifies Cooder's skills as an arranger. The rhythmic quirks inherent in Delta blues are exaggerated in an agitated, complex arrangement, with spells of nine and seven time. The Magic Band sound confident, tearing into Cooder's arrangement. Van Vliet had some initial problems absorbing the time changes – hardly surprising considering the song's rhythmic complexity – but ended up substituting the existential panic inherent in the original with a droll, wry reading.

The most haunting track on *Safe As Milk* is the episodic closer, "Autumn's Child". Van Vliet is found looking back into a dreamscape of the past, with French featuring on the eerie "Go back ten years ago" choruses. In the verse section, theremin buzzes ominously against plangent guitars and Perry's Baroque clavichord, while Van Vliet's lyrics verge at times on free association. Again, some currently fashionable pop elements are featured, but here they are put together in unfamiliar conjunctions. The sections are joined by delicate guitar links, slightly different each time. In the suite-like nature of this song, a brief straight rock passage sounds strangely intrusive.

Cooder had pushed the blues into new configurations on 'Grown So Ugly', and he was impressed by Van Vliet's more radical ideas, as he told Elaine Shepherd: "'Autumn's Child' was the one that got me, 'cos it had a little 4/4 time… You see, he had a couple of ideas. One thing was if you sustain a groove for too long it's corny and he didn't want to do that, you know, getting a thing happening where you're actually in a tempo like 4.

Just to make those tunes work was a heck of a job of work. It was not easy. Certainly none of it was written out and certainly none of it was too well understood, but that was part of the appeal."[13]

The group were all unhappy with Perry's production and Krasnow remixed the album. Cooder has gone on record as rating *Safe As Milk* as a great record, except for the production. The final choice of studio gave them less tape space to play with and the tracks had to be 'bounced down' from four tracks to two, leaving two tracks for the vocals and overdubs. This process can result in a loss of quality, and is the likely explanation for why the drums all but disappear on 'Call On Me'.

Safe As Milk was an exceptional début and quite an achievement for a group with two teenagers in its ranks. Captain Beefheart & His Magic Band looked on course to take their confident, groundbreaking music to the public at large. After the near miss of 'Diddy Wah Diddy', which was a decade-old R&B tune, they were now touting an individual blues/soul/psychedelia/rock'n'roll amalgam that was tailor-made for the expanded minds and musical tastes of 1967. The group's chance of a big break came when they were booked for the Monterey Pop Festival on 16 June, on a bill that also featured the Jimi Hendrix Experience, Otis Redding and Janis Joplin. To get used to the big arena they had a warm-up of sorts at the Magic Mountain Fantasy Fair, at Mount Tamalpais, north of San Francisco, the week before the festival. It was an outdoor love-in type of event, but without much press attention. It gave them the ideal opportunity to test-drive their new set.

The Magic Band's set was an unmitigated disaster. Van Vliet was still having his anxiety attacks and by all accounts his synapses were being prised apart by some psychedelic substance on the day. The farce began just after the start of the show when he noticed a woman in the crowd looking up at him. Her face suddenly transmuted into a fish's face, with bubbles coming out of her mouth. At which point he freaked out.

French to Elaine Shepherd: "We started 'Electricity' and Don comes out with this 'EE-LEC-TRIC-ARTY' and he's pointing out to the audience and suddenly he just stops and we start playing the song and he's just standing there. And he turned around, very composed, straightening his tie, and walked off the back of a ten-foot stage and landed on the manager."[14]

Cooder: 'We continued on instrumentally. Nobody cared. Everybody's out [of their heads] anyway. The audience is there for a good time, they don't give a shit. Got in the Rent-a-car, drove back to the town, got on a plane and went home. That was it.'[15]

French followed Cooder to the car to try to talk him out of leaving, but he would not be swayed this time. If Van Vliet could do that at Mount Tamalpais, what would happen under the spotlight at Monterey? He wasn't prepared to stay and find out. He had done the job asked of him and after a few months he had already had enough: "The thing with Beefheart was so horrendous, it would kill you to be stuck in a thing like that. I figured if I didn't get out of town, it would kill me."[15]

In 1977, Cooder told John Tobler: "The guy at the time seemed an odd person to me, like a circus figure, a carnival sideshow guy, who's entertaining for a while, and then I decided to be less entertained by this spectacle... I couldn't see we had any future together; and besides, he ran a pretty militaristic routine, and everything was very brownshirt-like with him."[16]

Van Vliet gave his views to Connor McKnight of *Zig Zag* in 1973: "He walked out on me just before the Monterey Festival, which I thought was a terrible thing to do... He should have told me how he felt before it got too far."[17]

The Magic Band had built up a reputation, but one that was largely confined to San Francisco and Los Angeles. Had the Mount Tamalpais débâcle not occurred, one can only speculate how the Magic Band's career might have progressed if they had played a good set at Monterey, and been included in the feature film of the event. It certainly did no harm to the reputations of Hendrix, Joplin and Redding. But although Van Vliet's bathetic performance had prompted Cooder to leave, he soon sorted himself out and Captain Beefheart & His Magic Band supported The Yardbirds at the Santa Monica Civic Auditorium the following month.

After Cooder's abdication, guitarist Jerry McGhee had a brief spell in the group, but left soon after he was exposed to their new material. He was replaced in October 1967 by guitarist Jeff Cotton, who had played alongside French in Blues In A Bottle. Prior to that, Cotton had played in Merrell & The Exiles, which featured vocalist–guitarist Merrell Fankhauser. Cotton was blossoming into an innovative blues player with a willingness to experiment. In *Goldmine* in 1996 Fankhauser remembered that Van Vliet had been interested in Cotton for some time: "Back when Jeff and I were rehearsing in The Exiles, Captain Beefheart would come over to my house, sit outside in his black Jaguar sedan and listen to us and then get people to come in and report on who was playing with me."[18]

Safe As Milk was released on Buddah in September 1967 and was the first record on the label, as Krasnow had intended. The original US sleeve featured a grotesque photomontage of the group (including images of Krasnow and Richard Perry), bearing the cryptic message 'May the baby Jesus shut your mouth and open your mind'. In a bizarre marketing ploy, a free bumper sticker was included with the name of the album set next to an image of a baby's head. *Safe As Milk* is better recognised by a later sleeve which features fish-eye lens photos of the besuited group looking like well-dressed thugs. Guy Webster's photos are framed by a black and yellow chequerboard design based on the Abba Zaba wrapper. It all looked promising now. Although the Magic Band had been evicted from their house in Laurel Canyon, they had found new accommodation in nearby Tarzana (where Edgar Rice Burroughs, creator of Tarzan, owned a large estate) and their new guitarist moved in, adding to the group's stability. Crucially, they had a label with some clout behind them and, in Krasnow, an ambitious manager who loved their music. Unfortunately Kama Sutra Records, who were more adept at plugging groups like Sopwith Camel and The Lovin' Spoonful, were unable to get much airplay for the album, even on the album-oriented FM stations. Without this vital exposure, sales were disappointing.

4

YOUR PSYCHEDELIC SELTZER, SIR

"We're making a new album – it's really far out. I hope we don't get in vogue."
Don Van Vliet to Tony Wilson, *Melody Maker*, 3 February 1968

The next Magic Band project was to be a double album, provisionally titled *It Comes To You In A Plain Brown Wrapper*. The group went into TTG studios in Hollywood to begin recording in November 1967 with Bob Krasnow on production duties. After the concision of *Safe As Milk*, Van Vliet wanted to stretch out and be far out, spurred on, no doubt, by his increasing interest in the free end of the jazz spectrum and his own mind-expanding recreational habits. The first sessions found them all stretching out – lengthways at least – and delivering three massive, psychedelic blues jams. John French's whole-kit patterns took his explorations on parts of *Safe As Milk* one step further and Jerry Handley's bass – which managed to sound both woody and rubbery at the same time – bounced around in this greater space. Meanwhile, Alex St Clair and Jeff Cotton's guitars were beginning to weave a new mesh, the founder member's liberated rhythm work clashing deliciously with the newcomer's melodic inflections and spidery, singing slide guitar.

'Tarotplane' takes its title from 'Terraplane Blues', a song Robert Johnson wrote about the popular Twenties car. A few lines of that song crop up, together with snatches of Blind Willie Johnson's 'You're Gonna Need Somebody On Your Bond', Son House's 'Grinning In Your Face' and Willie Dixon's 'Wang Dang Doodle'. Van Vliet also adlibs some lyrics of his own. The nineteen-minute ride in the Magic Band's mutant new craft stretches their blues attachments to breaking point. But as the song winds to its conclusion, it feels as if the musicians have already said all they can a long way back in time and they finish the song on autopilot. Van Vliet's voice sounds different, too, occasionally filtered through a Fender guitar amplifier, which gives a shuddering tremolo effect and an added edge to his 'pinched-trachea' sound. He blows some gusty harmonica, and a highlight of sorts is his entrance on the shenai (an Indian reed instrument that Ornette Coleman gave to him), on which he lets out a garbled call in an unrelated key. Given its content and format, it comes as some surprise that, like the other tracks, it is credited solely to Van Vliet.

On "25th-Century Quaker", a meeting takes place between a "flower child" and a 25th-century Quaker which leads into an image stream of "blue-cheese faces" and "eyes that flutter like a wide-open shutter", before petering out at around nine minutes. Around this time the group wore black Quaker coats on stage and actually played one or two shows as The 25th-Century Quakers before reverting to their original name. Guy Webster recalls a photo session where all the group posed dressed as Quakers. This brief change of identity came from a concept that Van Vliet had been cooking up with Don Aldridge (who came from a Pentecostal background) the previous year. Aldridge explains: "Although Don and I were serious about it, it never really got beyond the discussion stages. I think Don's twist on the idea was to star me as a Fifties-esque rocker. I looked a lot like the stereotypical Ricky [Nelson]/Elvis type in those days. Don considered Jeff Cotton to play lead in that group, before finally taking him for Beefheart. Merrell Fankhauser and I went to work on a new project* and Quaker fizzled out."

'Mirror Man' originated in rehearsals back in Lancaster in 1966 when, according to French, Doug Moon would use the song as a springboard for exploratory guitar excursions. Here they all ride out on a lengthy, mesmeric groove, but although their playing is more than capable, they remain ultimately shackled to what is in effect a three-chord riff. Its fifteen-minute running time ends up as way too much of a good thing. But if this format sounds like potential commercial suicide, one needs to bear in mind that sprawling blues jams were part of the contemporary musical fabric. On Love's 1966 album, *Da Capo*, the brilliance of side one seduces unwary listeners, only to leave them stranded in the subsequent side-long

---

* Aldridge, Fankhauser and Lotspiech – a precursor to Fankhauser's later group, Fapardokly.

splurge, erroneously titled 'Revelation'. The Grateful Dead take listeners on a mind-boggling trip throughout the first side of their 1968 album, *Anthem Of The Sun*, but the comedown begins when the record is turned over, in the shape of their tedious quarter-hour blues workout 'Alligator'. Yang to side one's Yin, perhaps.

These songs were conceived as the 'live' part of the double set, in the free-roaming style that was beginning to dominate their live shows. But the songs recorded in the subsequent *Brown Wrapper* sessions over the next few weeks saw Captain Beefheart & His Magic Band on an exponential growth curve. The soul pastiches and exploratory blues-rock of *Safe As Milk* had ceded to a startlingly original batch of new material – kaleidoscopic, polyrhythmic songs with psychedelic elements, some cut with free-form passages: 'Trust Us', 'Beatle Bones 'N' Smokin' Stones', 'On Tomorrow', 'Kandy Korn', 'Safe As Milk', 'Moody Liz' (with its serpentine dual guitar coda), the sparse, enigmatic 'Korn Ring Finger', 'Gimme Dat Harp Boy', 'Big Black Baby Shoes', 'Flower Pot' and 'Dirty Blue Gene'. The proposed format of *Wrapper* may well have been prompted by The Mothers Of Invention's double album *Freak Out*, which was released in 1966, and Van Vliet's keenness to be seen competing on equal terms with his friend and rival Frank Zappa.

One can now only hazard a guess at how *Brown Wrapper* might have turned out, as a number of the songs were left at the backing-track stage. This indicates that the work as a whole was abandoned. Why this happened is difficult to explain. Record company and contractual problems were moving onto a new level of complexity and details remain clouded, not because of the fading memories of those concerned, but because no one seemed sure what was going on even at the time. The most plausible explanation is that, echoing the views of A&M before them, Buddah were turned off by this radical new material. They kept Captain Beefheart & His Magic Band on their books for the time being, but their new project was put on hold.

A Buddah 'package show' had been set up, principally to give exposure to the newly launched label at the annual MIDEM (Marché International du Disque et de l'Edition Musicale) music business convention in Cannes, France. Captain Beefheart & His Magic Band were scheduled to make their first visit to the UK, before joining up with their new labelmates in France. Although they had yet to play on the East Coast of America, it made sense for them to stop off in London. The group's reputation was growing fast, with *Record Mirror* referring to them as "one of the best-known American groups in Britain". This was almost entirely due to John Peel, who had regularly played tracks from the then import-only *Safe As Milk* on his *Perfumed Garden* and *Top Gear* radio shows. On the business side, the UK based Pye Records were planning a takeover of Kama Sutra/Buddah. The group arrived on January 18, 1968, booked to play at The Speakeasy, a trendy music industry hangout, and do two shows at Middle Earth, unofficial headquarters of the London's colourful underground scene. A single, 'Yellow Brick Road'/'Abba Zaba', was released on Pye to tie in with these appearances, soon to be followed by the belated UK release of the album.

The tour was co-ordinated by Peter Meaden, a one-time protégé of Rolling Stones manager and music business svengali Andrew Loog Oldham and briefly publicist for The Who when they were known as The High Numbers. Meaden, a dedicated Mod, became a Beefheart convert after buying an import copy of *Safe As Milk*. In *Record Mirror* in 1972, Norman Jopling looked back at the era, claiming that "Peter hustled himself almost out of business"[1] in his work with the Buddah package show, and also in bringing Captain Beefheart & His Magic Band over to London. But trouble started as soon as the group landed at London's Heathrow airport. Meaden had overlooked some paperwork and they arrived without work permits. The full extent of the bizarre situation at immigration was documented in an official report which was found – along with other Immigration Department papers – on a rubbish dump in Hounslow, near London, in 1986.

Dated January 24, 1968, the document, entitled *Refusal of Leave to Land Report (Remarks)*, outlines the reasons for their four-and-a-half-hour detention. The 'remarks' include unnecessarily detailed and, by implication, incriminating descriptions of the group's physical appearance: "Mr VLIET is the leader of an American 'pop group' known as Captain Beefheart's Magic Band, which specialises in so-called psychedelic music and is currently very popular with a certain section of the West Coast of the United States. The group arrived together and presented a very strange appearance, being attired in clothing ranging from 'jeans' to purple trousers with shirts of various hues, and wearing headgear varying from conical witches hats to a brilliant yellow safety helmet of the type worn by construction engineers.

"Officers on the control were given ample opportunity to form an initial assessment of the group, as they took fully ten minutes to complete the relatively simple operation of filling in their landing cards. When they eventually approached the desks, it proved somewhat difficult to interview them, as they appeared to think on a completely different mental plane and found it difficult to grasp the rudiments of a passport control.

"All five members of the group possessed tickets from London to Nice and on to Los Angeles and they said that they merely wished to spend a week in this country on the way to France. None of them appeared very certain what the purpose of the visit to this country was, some saying that it was purely for a rest and others saying that they were to meet representatives of the press. However, all of them denied emphatically that they had any intention of taking any form of employment during their stay. Examination of the funds carried by the group showed that they had very little money, Mr VLIET having £2.10.0; and 20 marks (£2)."

The report describes Meaden as "a gentleman dressed in the American style with long unkempt hair and a cigarette dangling from his lower lip". Meaden said that he was representing New Wave Records, who were co-ordinating the visit with Kama Sutra/Buddah. Meaden's offer to produce the necessary information to establish his authority was undermined when "he was unable to prove his connection with these companies beyond producing a press handout and some blank headed notepaper".

Meaden was viewed with even more suspicion by the Immigration Officers when a Special Branch Officer informed them that, "Mr MEADEN was known to have convictions for illegal possession of a Bren gun, taking and driving away a motor vehicle and selling intoxicating liquor without a licence." In a situation of increasing farce, Meaden also denied that the group were in the UK to work and were simply booked in to meet the press.

The Immigration officials were more clued up than the guileless Meaden and the even more guileless group realised. They looked through the recent edition of *New Musical Express*, saw advertisements for the gigs and confirmed over the telephone that the band were expected to play full shows at the venues. The report continues: "Faced with this Mr MEADEN at first protested his innocence but finally both he and the group admitted that the engagements had been arranged. Mr MEADEN then pleaded for clemency on the grounds of his own stupidity, a plea which was rejected."

The Home Office, the Chief Immigration Officer, the Ministry of Labour, Pye Records, Artie Ripp from Kama Sutra head office and Equity were all involved in a tangled web of negotiations that resulted in the group being temporarily flown to Frankfurt, and Meaden apparently being told by Ripp that his association with Kama Sutra "ceased forthwith". Meaden later tried to vindicate himself, telling *Melody Maker*: "Frankly I don't think Pye realised what they had on their hands, but lack of liaison has been negated by the success of Captain Beefheart."[2]

In his recent article on the incident in the Home Office IND (Immigration and Nationality Department) staff magazine *Focus*, Steve Earl added a postscript: "Other accounts of this incident record that when asked by the IOs [Immigration Officers] who they were, Beefheart replied that they were pilgrims from the 25th Century. When asked about a camera around his neck he said it was a member of the group."[3]

After being sent to Hanover for the night, the Magic Band arrived back in the UK the following day – legitimately this time. John Peel had the honour of introducing them on their UK début. It was an emotional occasion: "I started to introduce them at Middle Earth but was so overcome with emotion that I started crying, so I had to abandon my announcement half-way through. I said, 'I never dreamed that I would have the opportunity to say these words to you… This is Captain Beefheart & His Magic Band.'"

The show was reviewed in *International Times*: "With both guitarists using bottlenecks and a pounding [Mitch] Mitchell-style drummer, the heaviness of the sound provided a solid rhythmical spring-board for Beefheart's amazing voice, which sounds like a young Howling Wolf with a ring modulator in his throat and blends in with the backing like a sixth instrument.

"Some of their use of straight feedback and various other basic electronic noises, like an amplified flour sifter, didn't go down so well among Middle Earth's young groovers but made an interesting addition to the straight rock numbers, giving a John Cage feel to some of the instrumentals."[4]

Even in the psychedelic sixties, the amplified flour sifter failed to break through as a rock'n'roll instrument. One can surmise that any 'young groovers' who went to see Beefheart on the strength of a piece of (admittedly bizarre) pop candyfloss like 'Yellow Brick Road', or other *Safe As Milk* songs, would have been shocked by the sheer length of some of their live excursions. 'Tarotplane' hit the half-hour mark at one of the Middle Earth shows. Others loved it. Writing in 1995, Jean Scrivener recalled Van Vliet being 'a little overwhelmed' by the reception he received there, proclaiming, "This is the most fantastic light show I have ever seen."[5] The Speakeasy crowd were, however, largely unimpressed. "Man, the bad vibrations in that place,"[6] said Van Vliet to *International Times*.

The UK press were keen to get their first face-to-face with the Captain Beefheart phenomenon. *Melody Maker*'s Tony Wilson was welcomed by a convivial Van Vliet in his hotel room after the second Middle Earth show. He was told that the musicians were so excited they hadn't slept since the previous night's performance. They were busying themselves in the background, apparently working out a new song, with John French playing on some cases with his sticks. Wilson described him as 'tall and mysterious'. French is of average height, but in the heady atmosphere of the time, he probably seemed a colossus.

Van Vliet enthused about the forthcoming *Wrapper* double album and explained the origins of the Magic Band. "We recorded a song called 'Diddy Wah Diddy', which was a turntable hit in the US, then the turntable stopped turning and we stopped doing 'Diddy Wah Diddy' – and started realising that everything was nothing. We had a year of isolation in the desert and got ourselves together. We got high in the desert," he concluded enigmatically. Referring to the alleged comment by Jerry Moss of A&M that 'Electricity' was too negative and not safe for his daughter, Van Vliet was enthusiastic about their current liaison with Krasnow. "We found Bob Krasnow, who didn't think our music was negative. He put the record out and it did OK in the US."[7]

Van Vliet's proclamations of the existence and imminent release of new material became a recurrent theme in interviews throughout his career – in this instance, a new song, 'Fifth Dimensional Judy'. The music press has always been full of such assertions, whereby musician X states that they've got some exciting new direction, or hot new side project, or they're going into acting, or whatever. If all that was talked up in this way actually happened, rather than remaining unrealised, most rock groups' output would be doubled and they would have become neo-Renaissance men (or women). The gulf between what Van Vliet casually promised and what was produced was far wider – and far more tantalising – than the boasts of most rock journeymen. The interview with Wilson was concluded by Van Vliet quoting a few lines from one of his new songs, 'Trust Us': "What I would like to say is 'Let the living live and the dying die'. That's from one of our new songs, 'You Gotta Trust Us'. Man, I'd like to have sung that in front of the Immigration Bureau. The customs people were so state-ly. Yeah, it's with a hyphen."[8]

Captain Beefheart & His Magic Band recorded a session for Peel's *Top Gear* show in late January at the BBC studios in Maida Vale, London. To help promote the album's belated release, they chose tracks from *Safe As Milk*. The session was broadcast in February and comprised 'Yellow Brick Road', 'Abba Zaba', 'Electricity' and 'Sure 'Nuff 'N Yes I Do'.

The quaint journalese of the time featured throughout the review of *Safe As Milk* in *Melody Maker*. The writer (name unknown) claimed that it sounded "oddly old-fashioned" and "rocks along with a mighty beat, but why it should appeal to London's 'in' clubs is a major mystery". The "brave Captain" was described as being like "a cross between Tommy Bruce and Lord Sutch".[9] If he was familiar with those artists it's unlikely that he was too flattered by the comparison.

After the Middle Earth and Speakeasy dates, Captain Beefheart & His Magic Band flew off to Cannes to play the MIDEM festival, meeting up with their labelmates Penny Nichols and Anders & Poncia. With hindsight one wonders what they were doing at such a music business junket, especially on a label that was heading in a completely different musical direction. Penny Nichols was a Joni Mitchell-esque singer-songwriter and Anders & Poncia were songwriters and studio musicians who were behind studio-based acts such as soft-rock harmony groups The Tradewinds and The Innocence.

Captain Beefheart & His Magic Band were famously filmed performing on the beach on some boarding, raked by the winter sun, in front of the lapping Mediterranean. Video footage of the group performing 'Electricity' and 'Sure 'Nuff 'N Yes I Do' was shown on the French TV programme, *Bouton Rouge*. The band gave a tight and tough performance with Van Vliet's choice of headgear – a top hat – eclipsed by Jeff Cotton, who wore the yellow hard hat that had aroused such suspicion at Heathrow.

The performance was a publicity coup, but had actually been set up because the group were not invited to the MIDEM gala. Van Vliet ironically dedicated the performance to his friends in the music business. The group did, however, play in the Casino at Cannes on a bill that included The Crazy World Of Arthur Brown, Fairport Convention and Blossom Toes.

At the time The Crazy World Of Arthur Brown were pushing the boundaries of English psychedelia and Brown possessed a remarkable voice that competed with the Captain's ursine baritone. But he was uneasy about Van Vliet's presence. Drummer Drachen Theaker recalled the group's experience at MIDEM to Mark Paytress in 1990: "Back in '67 [*sic*], we spent a week in the South of France with Beefheart at the Cannes MIDEM Festival. I was absolutely spellbound. I thought Arthur was the craziest, most soulful, vocal showman on the scene, but after seeing Beefheart he was put into second place. Arthur was into him, but it was important for him not to be seen as a Beefheart clone. So he tried to put down our Beefheart influence, which was wrong."[10]

Back home, business affairs had reached labyrinthine complexity and Buddah dropped the group soon after they got back from Cannes. Krasnow had convinced them to sign Captain Beefheart at the outset, but now the label was becoming more interested in the production team of Jerry Kasenetz and Jeff Katz, who coined the term 'bubblegum music'. Before the end of the year Buddah had released their single 'Quick Joey Small' by The Kasenetz–Katz Singing Orchestral Circus. The sleeve notes of the 1969 compilation, *Buddah's 360 Degree Dial-A-Hit*, state, "When Buddah records was formed two years ago, most songs were about crime and war and depression. At the time we felt there was a place for a new type of music that would make people happy." Fitting Captain Beefheart & His Magic Band's new material into this wide-eyed, teen-appeal template would have been difficult, to say the least.

Rumours still persist of all manner of shady dealings between Krasnow – who was now getting the wheels in motion to set up his own Blue Thumb label – and one or more record companies, in order to bankroll the recording sessions that would eventually yield the second Captain Beefheart album, *Strictly Personal*. His machinations were alleged to include securing advances from two separate record companies before putting the album out on Blue Thumb. Other commentators have it that the album was recorded for Buddah and that Krasnow stole the tapes and put them out on his own label. Krasnow was totally focused on getting the new Captain Beefheart material released in some shape or form and was actively trying to get someone to sign the group. MGM reputedly did just that, or were at least on the verge of doing so, but the deal went down.

Gary Marker offers this perspective: "I've heard a number of stories. I heard that Buddah heard the follow-up [to *Safe As Milk*], 'Mirror Man', that kind of stuff, and said, 'We don't want that shit on our label. What is this stuff – 'Mirror Man', 'Tarotplane'?' They didn't want it. It would be more like Krasnow not to tell Don 'They hate you', because he'd already been through that with A&M. He probably said, 'Don't worry, I'm going to start my own label', and got him as a severance deal, 'cos that's the way they do things.

"Another one was that Krasnow recorded *Strictly Personal* for Buddah and stole it from them. That's a very unlikely scenario. Krasnow was not the kind of person who was going to take something from Buddah Records or Kama Sutra unless they didn't want it. He's not going to steal tapes, for chrissakes, 'cos he'll find his ass in jail. And when Blue Thumb wasn't doing well, Warners wouldn't have hired him [as a producer and A&R man] for all those years if they knew he had that kind of history. It just wouldn't have happened."

However the task was achieved, Krasnow got Captain Beefheart & His Magic Band into Sunset Sound, Hollywood, where they recorded *Strictly Personal* over eight days in April/May 1968. But at the time, nothing was straightforward. French feels that the material on *Strictly Personal* was not as well played as the earlier *Wrapper* versions, as the group had little or no time to rehearse. This was due to Van Vliet getting arrested and spending some time in police custody. He had been visiting Lancaster and went into a schoolyard with a guy and a girl to smoke a joint around midnight. A local cop, named Grier, came to investigate. He guessed what they were doing, but Van Vliet managed to swallow the evidence, further torturing his vocal cords. He was charged for loitering in a schoolyard and Grier was apparently keen to up the stakes and press for a child molestation charge ("He hated long hairs," says Don Aldridge). As it was midnight and the school wasn't even in session, the case against Van Vliet was next to non-existent. He also received legal assistance organised by a mysterious benefactor whom Aldridge remembers only as being a well-dressed older woman. Van Vliet later told him that she was acquainted with the judge. The case was thrown out of court.

The striking packaging of *Strictly Personal* preserves some of the themes of the *Wrapper* concept. The sleeve is designed like a brown envelope, rubber-stamped FOURTH CLASS MAIL and STRICTLY PERSONAL, with the group's heads superimposed on postage stamps of different nationalities. The sender's address, written in the designer's approximation of Van Vliet's handwriting, is "25th Century Quaker, One Ray Gun Drive, Celestial Plainees". The addressee is "Capt. Beefheart &

His Magic Band, 5000/mgs, Tubular Falls Estates, Glassdom, Glassdom". Open the gatefold sleeve and Guy Webster's gloomy, monochrome group photo is like a portal into an absurd, nightmarish world.

On the far right, a figure in silhouette, sporting a metal headdress like an inverted funnel, looks across to St Clair, who is wearing a wide-brimmed black Spanish-style hat, his deathly pale features squeezed into a stocking, robber-style. Next to him stands Van Vliet in a leather trench coat, wearing a ritual mask, playing the shenai. Then one comes across a shadowy figure wearing a Fifties sci-fi-style spherical space helmet, with a small glass panel and a tube coming out of the side. The creature on the end looks like the lobotomised brother of the Tin Man from *The Wizard of Oz*, with a bell as a head, on which is painted an idiot grin.

Strictly Personal is Captain Beefheart & His Magic Band's acid-rock statement, although anyone deciding to take a trip whilst listening to the album would have been advised to hide the sleeve out of eyesight to prevent psychological trauma. 'Ah Feel Like Ahcid' opens, its country blues blues foot-stomp slyly substituted with a recording Krasnow made of Van Vliet's heart beat, the apparently troublesome organ pumping away in a regular metre. Its owner roars a standard "Got up this morning" intro, then borrows the second line from Son House's anguished 'Death Letter': "How do you reckon it read?" In 'Death Letter', House has just received correspondence informing him his girl is dead, but here Van Vliet immediately veers off into a mischievous part blues pastiche/part blues-as-surrealism ramble, with 'read' transformed into the "Red, blue and green", the colours that are swirling through his head. He quickly comes to the conclusion that the "postman's groovy" and makes a reference to licking a stamp and then seeing a "movie". After all this, the recipient of the mail "ain't got t'blues no more". It's hardly surprising his mood has changed, as 'licking a stamp' was contemporary southern Californian acid-head slang for taking a hit of LSD. Owsley Stanley, The Grateful Dead's notorious 'pharmacist', reputedly started the trend of selling hits of acid on postage stamps.

'I said' is changed in the title to 'Ahcid', a phonetic pun on the way Son House sang, his "I said" emerging as "Ah-ci-yud". Son House's influence is also found in the guitar lines. The song then perambulates off into an adlibbed tale featuring quacking ducks, hard-boiled eggs and chicken legs. The blues are dragged into the psychedelic milieu, which Van Vliet alternately embraces and sends up throughout *Strictly Personal*. 'Ahcid', then, is one of the most obvious drug songs on record, but simultaneously one of the most tongue-in-cheek. Van Vliet was on the defensive when questioned about the song a year later, totally denying any drug reference. He said, unconvincingly, that he couldn't understand why anyone would think like that. By way of explanation he offered, even less convincingly, that someone else (implicating Krasnow) must have made it look that way.

'Safe As Milk' exemplifies the distance between this new material and the older songs. All the more radical elements from the album of the same name had been moulded into a new style, which was far more satisfying than the group's long blues-based workouts. The guitars are not so much underpinned as jostled by French, whose drumming was becoming more individual – incisive accents incorporated into rolling, roaming tom-tom, snare and hi-hat patterns. In 1996, French explained one of the reasons for this stylistic shift: "Bob Krasnow decided to use compression on the drums like The Beatles had done [on songs like 'Tomorrow Never Knows' from *Revolver*] so he told me [to] just use tom-toms because they're easier to compress than cymbals – they stand out too much. So for a long time I would practise for this album using no cymbals at all."[11]

Now solely responsible for the lyrics, Van Vliet's burgeoning imagination found an outlet in tales with no easy literal translation. After the wry lyrics of 'Ah Feel Like Ahcid', Beefheart watchers also put the song 'Safe As Milk' on the acid agenda. But it was, he said, intended as a serious warning about the radioactive isotope strontium-90 being absorbed into the body, and hence into the milk of breast-feeding mothers. As Van Vliet himself sings, he's never heard it "put quite that way" before. He describes the shape he's in, which seems a pretty bad one, judging by these slobbish sketches. He admits his cigarette "died when I washed my face" and the contents of his fridge – cheese with a "mile-long beard", decomposing "blue" bacon and "dog-eared" bread – are pollutants in themselves.

The track ends with a passage of semi-free form, rim-clicking drums and splintered slide guitar, then into tom-tom depth charges, and thunderous rolls, heavy with reverb and fizzing with phasing. This effect, which had been on the recording studio's sonic menu since the late Fifties, involved source signals being run out of phase to give a spacy, whooshing sound. In the psychedelic era it became increasingly popular as a way of approximating the acid head-rush in sound. Well-known examples of this effect include The Small Faces' hit single 'Itchycoo Park' from 1967, and 'Rainbow Chaser', a UK hit for Nirvana in early 1968. Although the effect is still used today, an excessive amount of 'whoosh' sounds corny and dated. Van Vliet himself likened the effect to the effervescent antacid Bromo-Seltzer. Much has been made of the phasing spoiling the album, but although a few tracks on *Strictly Personal* were over-treated in this way, all in all the negative effect has been overstated.

The cornerstone of the album is 'Trust Us', an epic United Nations of Youth rallying cry, a wake-up call to get moving "before you turn to dust". The role of musician as a messianic, healing figure had recently been played by The Beatles on 'All You Need Is Love' and with less sincerity by The Rolling Stones on 'We Love You'. But 'Trust Us' is musically more adventurous than either, continually metamorphosing throughout its seven-minute course.

The lyrics promised love and trust, but ran counter to vacuous everyone-is-everybody-else hippie homilies. Van Vliet presented a list of conditions that had to be met. They are vague, perhaps, but proscriptive nonetheless. Anyone wanting to get in on this trip had to 'touch without taint' and 'feel to reveal'. They also had to be ruthless and 'let the dying die', so they could slough the skins of their past attachments, go forward and live. Just as 'Ahcid' was a funny, idiosyncratic take on acid culture, this massive song took the prevailing positive currents and diverted them into a very personal dictum.

The opening monastic chorales, swathed in phasing, are soon disrupted by the basic swung 4/4 rhythm, which is full of unexpected twists. Van Vliet gives vent to his metaphysical musings via a huge tremolo-enhanced vocal sound, backed up by hoarse exclamations from French. Sustained feedback notes link orchestral-style drum and guitar crescendos and then the song cruises off on a monolithic, multi-tracked refrain of "Let the dying die", with massed, whispered pleas of "Trust Us", before cutting dead into another fragment of 'Ahcid'.

'Son Of Mirror Man – Mere Man' is a phenomenal, condensed version of its parent track. After a few bars of guitars in an on/off polka rhythm the ensemble dive into a similar jumpy Delta blues canter, but now phasing gives the guitars a strange, iridescent sheen. Van Vliet, his voice heavily treated, intones the title a few times, before blasting it out at full force from the murk. After a few minutes a massive, over-mixed, phased bass cuts in, playing a waltz-time pattern. It is soon joined by the drums and then goes into a frenzy of phased everything – including the recorded début of the amplified flour-sifter. Van Vliet comes out again from behind this sonic cascade, calming things down by playing his (phased) harmonica and making an incantation on the title as the group re-emerge before the fade.

'On Tomorrow' differs from the original *Wrapper* version in that the abstract guitar and drums interlude is omitted. It also lacks the bite of the original, but it is still the most innovative song on *Strictly Personal*. French's tom-tom patterns shift in a way that reflects his interest in tabla rhythms, and the guitar lines cut across each other, one instrument playing staccato phrases while the other circles around. The entire group play in a hovering, polyrhythmic way that was scarcely precedented at the time. The details in the guitar lines show new developments as they shift from modal lines into sudden flurries of notes and idiosyncratic arpeggios. Van Vliet's lyrics again embrace the 'One World' ethos, telling us that we are "all brothers on tomorrow" with frantic backing vocals – Cotton, presumably – echoing his proclamations.

'Ah Feel Like Ahcid' is edited into pieces that recur throughout the album, creating a continuity that could, at a push, be a reference to the way The Beatles' *Sergeant Pepper's Lonely Hearts Club Band* is structured, with the reprise of the title track. 'Beatle Bones 'N' Smokin' Stones', however, is an unequivocal and hilarious swipe at The Beatles. Zappa had leered at them from the *Sergeant Pepper* pastiche sleeve of The Mothers Of Invention's 1968 album, *We're Only In It For The Money*, but here Van Vliet specifically takes on 'Strawberry Fields Forever'. Although the tracks are musically very different, he employs some backwards tapes, and even uses John Lennon's lyrics in the nursery rhyme-like "Strawberry Fields Forever" refrain, which is echoed by a mocking, sublimely daft little guitar motif. Sadly the strings that were on the *Wrapper* version are absent here.

Lennon had once been photographed in his Weybridge home with a *Safe As Milk* sticker on the fridge behind, a clear indication of his interest in the Magic Band's music. But he was definitely not amused by this warped paean to one of his best songs. Van Vliet had both mocked him and completely trumped him in terms of surrealism. Van Vliet nods to the themes of Englishness that ran through the original, with *Alice In Wonderland* references to Cheshire cats. He then moves out through a kaleidoscopic rural landscape populated by a "Strawberry moth", a crumbling "Chalk man" and "Winged eels". When Lennon and Yoko Ono were ensconced in their post-wedding bed-in in 1969, Van Vliet sent them a telegram of support. It remained unanswered. In 1994, guitarist Bill

Harkleroad, who joined the Magic Band later in 1968, offered another explanation of the song: "Beefheart's thing was it was about the insects after the [nuclear] holocaust. Like cockroaches and the beetles are going to live through this shit and the stones smoking. I could understand that, but I'm sure he could be very brutal and meant it the other way too."[12]

'Gimme Dat Harp Boy' is a thinly disguised and rather elephantine take on Willie Dixon's 'Spoonful' riff. But the main attraction is a magical tussle between one man and his mouth organ (the blues harp). Throughout the history of blues and rock, there have been instances of vocalists introducing solos: Jimi Hendrix introduces his own guitar solo on 'Fire' from *Are You Experienced* with "Move over, Rover, and let Jimi take over". And on The Pixies' 'Monkey Gone To Heaven' from *Doolittle*, Black Francis prefaces Joey Santiago's solo with the command, "Rock me, Joe." In this instance Van Vliet talks to his instrument throughout the song as if it were a living thing, commanding it to "cry", "smile", "smoke" and "toke". If the backing is somewhat perfunctory, Van Vliet's harmonica playing is a blast. He scat-sings, then plays his harp, sometimes scat-sings into it, reminiscent of the way that Roland Kirk would blow and sing into his flute (a style adapted and heavily used by Jethro Tull's Ian Anderson). The essence of the song is exemplified in a few seconds of abandon about half-way through when Van Vliet blows a blues lick, cuts off, grunts, lets out a high whoop and crams the instrument back into his mouth then continues playing with delirious abandon.

The inspiration for the song came when Van Vliet went off with Gary Marker to the Whiskey-A-Go-Go to see Canned Heat. Van Vliet was interested in checking out the group's slide guitarist, Al Wilson, but was less impressed by their enormous singer, Bob 'The Bear' Hite, not least because he was another blues-based vocalist and harmonica player and therefore a rival. Marker recalls that Van Vliet kept leaning over to him and complaining, "What the fuck is that fat guy doin' up there on stage tryin' to sing all that dead Negro music? What's his problem? Jesus Christ Gawdalmighty! Gimme dat harp boy – ain't no fat man's toy." Van Vliet wrote the bulk of the lyrics that night at one of his favourite late-night LA haunts, Canter's Deli.

'Kandy Korn' is, like 'Abba Zaba', a paean to confectionery, the group sharing it around by throwing bags of the stuff into the audience when playing the song live. The lyrics are Van Vliet's most throwaway, and ironically could have been used for a bubblegum pop tune. But musically the song, again originally recorded during the *Wrapper* sessions, demonstrates a new sophistication. After the vocals have subsided, a circular guitar sequence appears like a dramatic movie theme, echoing Van Vliet's love of the music of Henry Mancini. This is soon cut by a staccato guitar pattern in 6/8, to which a few more bars are added each time around. Then more monastic chorales, and a massive coda of beautiful dual-guitar lattice-work. At one point one of the group members can be heard yelling out in affirmation. But something was up in the production room: the monolithic guitar edifice is battered by what sounds like backward cymbals – maybe phased backwards cymbals? – and the drums all but disappear completely under the onslaught. In its entirety, despite the sometimes heavy-handed effects, *Strictly Personal* was like nothing else around at the time.

The recording completed, the group returned immediately to the UK and Europe for more live dates. While in London, they recorded another session for Peel, featuring new material – 'Safe As Milk', 'Beatle Bones 'N' Smokin' Stones', 'Kandy Korn' and 'Trust Us'. When Peel broadcast the session, he said that there were problems getting the new album released and that the group were very confused about the situation.

The tour was a low-budget affair and Peel ended up driving Van Vliet and French to gigs in a hired Mini, whilst the other group members travelled in the Transit van with the equipment. The group played a number of UK dates, including a particularly inappropriate booking at an end-of-term dance at Southampton University. The bill included Chicken Shack, Cliff Bennett & The Rebel Rousers, a rock'n'roll revival show and Tyrannosaurus Rex playing in an upstairs room, with Peel DJing. Captain Beefheart & His Magic Band came onstage in the main hall at 5.30 a.m. Van Vliet's elongated shenai solo on 'Tarotplane' prompted both cheers and booing. One can only wonder how they went down at the Zodiac Club blues night at the Star Hotel, Croydon. The group were due to go on and play four dates in Holland, including shows at the newly opened Paradiso club in Amsterdam, but these were cancelled due to lack of funds.

One of the most famous concerts on the tour was at the Sunday Club at Frank Freeman's Dancing School in Kidderminster. A relatively unknown provincial venue in the Midlands, it had acted as a platform for a number of up-and-coming groups – Kidderminister's most famous son, Robert Plant, had played there with his pre-Led Zeppelin group, Band Of Joy. Peel had DJed there a number of times previously. He describes what took place: "When I told them [where they were playing], they said, 'Wow, it's a really groovy name.' I said, 'No, it's not a groovy name, it's a dancing school run by a bloke called Frank Freeman.' Frank was a really straight kind of bloke, but wanted to do something for people in Kidderminster and put on these gigs. When you turned up, they were there with pots of tea and cucumber sandwiches. They were really sweet people.

"[At] any gig that they [the Magic Band] did about half the audience would leave during the first number when he [Van Vliet] started playing that strange instrument [shenai] – which in a sense he couldn't play terrifically well. If you'd said to him, 'Play "God Save The Queen"' he'd have been hard put to do it. A lot of the numbers consisted of him bellowing and a lot of honking through this machine, but nevertheless the band were rocking away like mad behind."

Despite Captain Beefheart & His Magic Band having just recorded an album of stunning new material, they gave a performance in their more drawn-out style, which included some blues material and a back-to-the-roots version of 'Sure 'Nuff 'N Yes I Do' played as 'Rollin' And Tumblin''. Peels recalls an incident after the show: "When we were coming back from Frank Freeman's, he [Van Vliet] asked if he could listen to a tree. I've always thought that's a really strange thing to have done, but of course it could have been his way of saying that he wanted a pee – probably was. He might have said 'listen to a tree', because it rhymed with 'having a pee'. His thought processes were not like those of other men – you could well believe that he wanted to listen to a tree.

"If anybody else had said it, I would have said 'stupid bastard' under my breath. But with Beefheart you thought, well, he knows more than I do and if he wants to listen to a tree, and I'm in a position to enable him to do so, then I'm going to give him a chance to do it, because it would be quite wrong not to. So he got out of the car and disappeared. It was one of those things where Pete Frame ought to have arranged for a plaque to be put there. Beefheart probably just went and had a pee, I don't know. Or he may have just listened to a tree. I'd like to say that I can see him silhouetted against a gibbous moon with his ear firmly pressed to a fine old elm, but I just don't know."

5

I WANT MY OWN LAND

"Much has been made about Beefheart's singing voice, but it was his speaking voice that could really draw you in. It was hypnotically supple, and resonant with a fake intimacy that belied an intuitive and predacious grasp of every nuance of manipulation. The unwitting became his pets."
Mike Bugbee, *Captain Beefheart's Wedding* ©2002

Captain Beefheart & His Magic Band returned home from their European dates in June 1968 and immediately lost a member. Prompted by financial and domestic considerations, Alex St Clair ended his tenure with the group after nearly four years. Don Aldridge offers these views on his departure: "At some point, Don made a radical turn, a deliberate decision, I believe, to change direction. I always will believe Frank [Zappa] was the catalyst. Frank was actually becoming wealthy and famous doing what they had experimented with as kids. Don could not accomplish his goal with the *Safe As Milk* band. I saw the look in Don's eyes the day he brought Jeff into the group. The handwriting was on the wall. I had no idea Don would take it as far as he did, but I knew without a doubt that everything had changed.

"I was told that Alex was using substances, and that he walked out one night in San Francisco. Don and I never discussed it. I have discussed it with other band members and I just think Alex wasn't happy with the direction things were going. [To say he was] pushed would be severe, but Alex was a blues man. He was possibly one of the most talented of all the Magic Band personnel, but he wasn't into what Don was doing. I don't think Don pushed him out, I think he willed him out.

St Clair's replacement was nineteen-year-old Bill Harkleroad. Back in the mid-sixties, when the Magic Band were enjoying their reputation as the hippest band in Lancaster, Harkleroad, then aged fifteen, was already a precociously talented guitarist. He played in a local group, BC & The Cavemen, who, like the early Magic Band, included Stones covers in their set to help them get gigs. But he was also beginning to take notice of the spiky guitar playing of Hubert Sumlin from Howlin' Wolf's group and black avant-garde jazz, to the extent of drifting asleep with the far-from-soporific John Coltrane playing over his headphones. Harkleroad saw the Magic Band live and on occasions ended up at the Carolside Avenue house, joining in the mass jam sessions, initially when the group's line-up included Paul Blakely (himself a former Caveman) on drums.

Harkleroad recalled these events in 1988: "We started showing up at parties where Beefheart was playing. One of the members of the group I was in was closer to their age. I'd sneak in bein' sixteen, bein' the kid, and I'd jam with them and they'd notice, 'Hey, the kid can play!'"[1]

Harkleroad already knew French and Cotton, and hoped that he'd made a big enough impact to eventually earn himself an audition with the band. On St Clair's exit, and now aged nineteen, he received his call-up. The audition was held at the group's rented house on Ensenada Drive, Woodland Hills, close to the border of Tarzana. The audition was a loose blues jam of the type the group had been playing live on the 1968 tour. It went well. Harkeroad: "I just let fly – I hadn't played in a while. The response was, 'Oh, you're great – you're cool!' and I officially became a member of the Magic Band late June '68."[2]

Harkleroad was still rather overawed by Van Vliet and after the audition was given a baptism by fire under the guise of a good time out, when his new band leader drove him over to the Laurel Canyon house of another of his heroes, Frank Zappa. Chez Zappa was the focal point of a burgeoning freak scene which included the 'groupie' band GTOs (Girls Together Outrageously). The group's most notorious members were *über*-groupie Pamela Des Barres, and Miss Christine, who acted as governess for Zappa's daughter, Moon Unit. Zappa himself was often *in absentia*, working in his downstairs studio. This night he was putting together some kind of rock'n'roll circus that predated The Rolling Stones' similarly titled film extravaganza. More than coincidentally perhaps, Mick Jagger and a very stoned Marianne Faithfull were in attendance that night, and members of The Who joined in the jam sessions. Harkleroad found himself playing guitar on 'Be-Bop-A-Lu-La' and 'Rollin' And Tumblin''. "I was pretty much too scared to death to even play," he confided to John Ellis in 1994.[3] Jagger was an admirer of Van Vliet's voice, but Van Vliet was often disparaging about him thereafter, complaining that Jagger had given him a bad mike to use that night.

Harkleroad was even more astonished by an incident at Shelly's Mannehole, where he and Van Vliet went to watch jazz and blues groups. On this particular occasion Muddy Waters, who had apparently jammed with Van Vliet prior to Harkleroad's arrival in the group, came over to excuse any vocal blemish in his performance as he had a bad cold. The young guitarist was amazed that Van Vliet was held in such respect by the blues legend. Waters respected Van Vliet's ability and his greater commercial success, but not so much that he couldn't remind him where his roots lay.

Gary Marker remembers an earlier encounter: "Muddy said, 'Hey, Van Vliet, you still rippin' off my stuff?' Don's face went white and he said, 'Why, I, I never ripped anything off in my life!' Don had similar encounters with Muddy Waters over the years. I was also with Don and Muddy one time when what Muddy was pissed about was Don's 'Sure 'Nuff' N Yes I Do' on *Safe As Milk*, which was a direct cop from Muddy's 'Rollin' And Tumblin'' blues classic. What Mr Morgenfield [Waters] apparently didn't care to acknowledge was that the format he used on that song had been around for decades before he retooled it a bit for 'Rollin'…'"

Robert Pete Williams's manager was after some money too. Either Van Vliet was experiencing problems with the Buddah contract or he was being disingenuous. He described the episode to Michael Tearson in 1972: "Waterman, the fellow that takes care of Robert Pete Williams, he came up and asked me why I wouldn't give the money that was owed to Robert Pete Williams for the song I recorded ['Grown So Ugly']. I told him that it was because Buddah didn't give me my money, you see?"[4]

Back from the rock'n'roll circus at Zappa's place, Harkleroad moved into the group's house and into a social situation that turned out to be far less glamorous but far more extreme. An immediate problem arose when Van Vliet aired some of his new material. Jerry Handley decided that it was time to call it a day. In his book *Lunar Notes*, Harkleroad writes: "I'll never forget him turning round and saying, 'Where's the blues tunes?'"[5] Handley was the last of the original Magic Band to depart. Van Vliet looked back on this watershed in the group's history with this rather uncharitable view: "The first group wasn't the most desirable type of people I've ever met, you know. They turned out to drink a hell of a lot and things like that. So I got out of that group."[6]

Aldridge suggests that Handley's departure was largely motivated by financial considerations. "Don used to go on weekly rants about how Snouffer and Handley were 'afraid to make it, man!' Sue Handley was a strong woman and her idea of making it was actually getting paid. In summer or fall of '67, she confided in me that she and Jerry had taken a job with one of the local newspapers, delivering papers door-to-door in their car, to make ends meet. I was shocked. I mean, I was under the illusion that Beefheart was a successful group, making large money. They were headlining gigs with The Doors and others who were on their way to stardom."[7]

After his initial involvement in *Safe As Milk*, Marker had decided to curtail his working relationship with Van Vliet, whom he felt had "left a trail of pissed-off people behind him from the get-go", including himself. But Van Vliet persuaded him to join the group, albeit on a temporary basis. He explains why he came back to help out: "The funny thing is, every one of them, even me, wanted to see him succeed. And eventually, if he asked, they would go back and work with him again. It's the abusive-husband thing. He would jerk them around, then say, 'Gee I'm sorry, I really need help, I didn't mean it, that was a terrible thing to do. It was drugs. I don't do that any more.'

"He's a very complex individual. He's got this arrogance, this tyrannical aspect, and yet there is this patina of him being an overgrown baby, helpless. He'd say, 'Can't you just help me?' And you'd buy it – his big, sad eyes like a blue-eyed beagle that had just got stuck in the mud and said, 'Please pull me out.' Everyone would do that. They fell for it hook, line and sinker. I came back and helped him out, but I never got paid."

Around this time, Van Vliet met up with Ry Cooder – who was applying his talents to more traditional material – and tried to sell him the idea of rejoining the Magic Band. He told him he was hooked up with Zappa and he should hear some of the new material he had written. And anyway, why was he still playing this 'old dead people's music'? "He was teasing him," recalls Marker. "But there was just this thing like 'just maybe...'" Cooder declined.

In 1968, Frank Zappa formed his own record company, Bizarre, principally to release material by The Mothers Of Invention. Bizarre was distributed through Reprise, and its subsidiary label Straight had independent distribution. Zappa decided to give his friend a chance to fulfil his potential with complete artistic freedom. Van Vliet thus unilaterally disassociated himself from Krasnow and Blue Thumb. Zappa's manager Herb Cohen later explained that it took six months before he could extricate him from his legal entanglements.

Van Vliet led Harkleroad to believe he was planning to re-record *Strictly Personal* with some new tunes, but Marker was told he was to be involved in the recording of an album of new material that would include a reworking of 'Kandy Korn'. Whatever its exact shape, Van Vliet was determined to push ahead with the project and wanted Marker to join the group full-time. Happy with the temporary arrangement, Marker declined.

Cotton was in charge of teaching Harkleroad the songs and rehearsals were going well. The temporary line-up went to Sunset Sound, Sunset Boulevard – in the same room where they had begun recording *Safe As Milk* – to record the new material. With Zappa producing, they recorded 'Veteran's Day Poppy' and 'Moonlight On Vermont' – both of which eventually found their way onto *Trout Mask Replica* – and a new version of 'Kandy Korn', which was never fully completed. Marker soon noticed that Zappa and Van Vliet were experiencing problems working together: "The real operative current in the studio that night was the competition between Zappa and Don. If there's any tension in that stuff, it's there. It was very obvious. When Don went out to do his vocal overdub, they were setting up the mikes and Zappa was saying, 'Come on, Donny, do your bird whistles for us. Come on, you can do 'em.' He was just teasing him about it and Don says, 'Come on, Frank, cut it out… OK, just one for you.' He was an artistic whistler. Fabulous, actually."

In *Lunar Notes*, Harkleroad recalls a rehearsal session when Van Vliet's cousin Victor Hayden arrived with a finished copy of *Strictly Personal*, and Van Vliet going into a state of complete shock at seeing the artefact they were supposedly re-recording. The story of *Strictly Personal* has become perhaps the most notorious in Van Vliet's career. He chose to portray himself as the hapless artist exploited by Krasnow, who unilaterally added all the backwards tapes and phasing effects to help the record appeal to the burgeoning psychedelic market, and, unbeknown to the group, sneaked the record out on his Blue Thumb label. The label's name was even his idea, he said. To this day Krasnow is vilified by aficionados for ruining one of Van Vliet's better albums. Van Vliet himself took this line for years, acknowledging that Krasnow had apologised, but criticising him for adding the fizz. He maintained that the music still shone through like a diamond in the mud. Using a less savoury simile, he told Roger Ames in 1974: "I was angry about that for a while because I produced it, arranged it, and while I was away they changed it. It's like someone peeing on the *Mona Lisa.*"[7]

To add to the confusion, Harkleroad qualifies Van Vliet's apparent apoplexy at seeing the album by remarking that the experience couldn't have been so traumatic, as he was soon friends with Krasnow again. And it's difficult to explain why Van Vliet was so 'shocked' that an album recorded and set for release was then released, especially as he had already heard acetates of the finished product. "I think there was the separation of him and Bob Krasnow," says Harkleroad. "They got married and divorced quite a few times."

Van Vliet had initially approved of the 'phasing' mix, and evidence suggests that he realised he'd made a mistake – borne out by reviews of the album in which the heavy use of the effect was criticised – and had to look no further than Krasnow for someone to blame. There is also an alternative version of the earlier, unreleased song 'Moody Liz' – reputedly an acetate – which is doused in phasing. Marker remembers seeing Krasnow spending hours in the studio with the tapes, achieving the phasing effects manually. He was regularly fried on acid at the time, but if this was a unilateral move on Krasnow's part, it was an unprecedented one for a producer who had cut his teeth working with R&B artists like James Brown and Hank Ballard on the Federal and King record labels. Marker gives his views on the subject: "Krasnow was much maligned," he says. "He was the whipping boy for the phasing stuff. Don allegedly got pissed off about the mix of that album. But Don came over to my house and gave me a copy and said, 'I think you're going to like this. This is really good.' I put it on and I'm hearing all this phasing going on. I said, 'Went a little crazy with the phasing and flanging,' and he says, 'Yeah, but it has a feel to it.' So that was his position then. The plain fact is, Bob Krasnow was in such awe of Don that he would never, ever release anything without Don's personal stamp of approval."

Strictly Personal could have been an extremely influential album, but its failure in the United States ended any chance Captain Beefheart had of making a Beatles-esque commercial success without artistic compromise. Van Vliet's ambivalence towards (other people's) commercial success was, it seems, fired by scepticism and jealousy: he hated The Byrds, for example. But although he felt this kind of success was really cheap, a mixture of his burgeoning ambitions and unfolding events got him thinking of how he could be successful by pushing his music out into uncharted territory.

Harkleroad soon realised that something odd was going on within the group. He writes, in *Lunar Notes*, that "the vibe was strange – John and Jeff were not the same guys I used to know. They both had a seriously dire look in their eyes, yet at times would flip into an almost over the top excitement."[8] Initially, the Magic Band was a democratic unit and so Van Vliet had to either canvas hard to get his point across, or try and play the group members off against each other – as when he wanted to oust Doug Moon. This he found both frustrating and difficult. Harkleroad found him easy to get on with when he joined the group, but was beginning to realise where the 'strange vibe' was coming from. Now all the original members had left, Don Van Vliet was becoming Captain Beefheart, and the Captain was inexorably assuming control of his younger charges.

During rehearsals for 'Veteran's Day Poppy', Marker had broached the idea of adding a boogie/shuffle section to the middle of the song. His idea became incorporated, despite the group's initial reaction. "Everybody would get this look like [*hushed*], 'Oh no, you can't do that, I don't think Don will like this.' He heard us rehearsing on this riff and came pounding upstairs. 'What is this, what are you doing?' I said, 'I've just got this little riff here, this classic boogie thing.' Once he'd figured out I'd done it he said, 'Well, maybe that's OK.' I could get away with it, but the other guys couldn't. They were standing there cowering." Van Vliet had often asked for his views on his musical works-in-progress. "He would listen to advice a lot of times and he would take it," says Marker. "It's just that he had this little problem – somewhere along the line he'd think he made it up."

Years before, Van Vliet had risked having some of his more idiosyncratic ideas dismissed out of hand by the musicians. Marker recalls that the 'oddball songs' Van Vliet was coming up with were in danger of being rejected because they were not blues tunes. "He had battles with those guys to play a 3/4, 6/8 rolling thing like 'Here I Am, I Always Am'. They didn't want to do it. It was too complex."

He recalls a pivotal conversation which clearly pointed to the direction in which Van Vliet was heading and what he was trying to leave behind. During his unsuccessful attempt to persuade Marker to commit himself to the group, he cranked the drama up a notch or two. "He said, 'Well, the thing is, this is going to be my last band. I'm going to *teach* them to play it the way I want. I'm not going to have no more Alex St Clair telling me I don't know anything about music'... and he went off on this rant. I realised that he was really intimidated for a long time [about] how every one else in the band knew about music and he didn't.

"Alex would have this attitude like, 'Man, it doesn't work. That's not the way you play things, that's not the terminology you use.' That really pissed him off 'cos he had all these ideas in his head and he had no way of getting them across to people. Then he got these 'goddamn kids' – he called them that. Most of them were ten years younger."

Jeff Cotton, who was already finding the band's communal lifestyle stressful, was twenty, as was John French. Harkleroad's friend Mark Boston soon joined as a replacement bass guitarist for Marker. Another former Caveman, he had also played with French in Blues In A Bottle. Like Harkleroad, Boston had been a fan of the Magic Band for a number of years. Van Vliet claimed he was already aware of this, having spotted him in the audience at Magic Band shows in the past. He was nineteen and in for a bit of a shock.

"I walked into the thick of *Trout Mask Replica* thinking I was going to be playing blues and stuff off of the *Safe As Milk* era," he recalls. "They used to be an excellent hard rock blues band, fairly comparable to The Rolling Stones back then. That's what I thought I would be playing when I joined the band. I was surprised, but at the time it was a challenge and it was a band that I wanted to be in – I didn't want to be in any other band than that one. And I figured if they want me to play weird music, I'll play weird music – I just went in with an open mind."

Van Vliet had, by his own admission, always enjoyed being in control. Fearing the loss of that control, he made sure he held on to it, even if that necessitated manipulation or despotic measures. He was sure in his own mind that if he moulded the group to serve his vision, he could be a star on his own terms. The music would be his now and he would unquestionably have the final say. To portray an artistic, far-out image, someone called Captain Beefheart needed to be surrounded by other eccentrically named characters. So Harkleroad was renamed Zoot Horn Rollo, Boston became Rockette Morton and Cotton was rechristened Antennae Jimmy Semens. Victor Hayden, Van Vliet's cousin and an artist himself, had come into the periphery of the picture playing bass clarinet and, via a flamboyant description of the instrument, became The Mascara

Snake. John French was given the most amusing name. In an inspired and endearingly silly pun on Disney's aeronautical elephant, he became Drumbo.

Harkleroad was unsure how much he liked this nickname becoming his 'official' name as a musician, but concluded: "So, the name was cool but it wasn't like I was having to adopt a completely new identity because of it."[9] But surely that is exactly what Van Vliet had in mind. It would be ludicrous to suggest that Harkleroad suddenly became a different person once he'd been given this name, but Van Vliet was reinforcing the musicians' role as players within his elaborate scheme. When asked by Co De Kloet on Dutch radio in 1993 why he had given them new names, Van Vliet replied: "I didn't care for their names. And they seemed to be related to their mama and papa. And I don't think that I'd get along with their mama and papa. So I gave them the names. The Mascara Snake [*laughs*]. That's a relatively true name. He is a snake and he does wear mascara."[10]

With his newly named acolytes around him, Van Vliet was ready to get them playing the new music that would constitute the bulk of *Trout Mask Replica*. But there was more to his method than mere Machiavellian ego-flexing. When Van Vliet set about composing the music for the album, he began sowing the seeds for one of the few truly unique musical statements of the twentieth century. In an inspired, unprecedented move he composed most of it on the piano he'd had moved into the house. Superficially there was nothing unusual about that, except that Van Vliet couldn't really 'play' piano in the technical sense of the word. To compose a masterpiece on an instrument on which he was a beginner took a huge amount of self-belief, but then he had plenty to spare.

Harkleroad looked back in 1998: "We're dealing with a strange person, coming from a place of being a sculptor/painter, using music as his idiom. He was getting more into that part of who he was as opposed to this blues singer."[11] "It amazed the hell out of me" was Jim Sherwood's reaction to Van Vliet's new method of composing and the music it produced.

His compositions in this vein were, in methodology, more or less the inverse of John Cage's 1951 solo piano piece, *Music Of Changes*, which was based on the *I Ching*, the ancient Chinese Book of Changes (which can be used for divinatory purposes through following chance or, more accurately, synchronous procedures). Cage was a composer who displayed a maverick irreverence towards classical tradition. *Music Of Changes* found him abandoning straightforward scores altogether, instead giving the pianist instructions which added aleatoric or chance elements, ensuring that every performance would be partly indeterminate. It was not meant to be repeatable.

Van Vliet, meanwhile, was coming from the opposite direction, playing an instrument on which he had no training. He approached it in a totally intuitive way, finding his way around the keyboard in an exercise that was more an outpouring of raw material than a controlled improvisation. He was unencumbered by technique as he possessed none. The lines he produced were themselves semi-aleatoric passages, which were recorded and then several were pieced together to form a composition. Gary Lucas, a guitarist in the last incarnation of the Magic Band, learned some of his parts from Van Vliet's piano tapes. He likened the composer's process to throwing a pack of cards in the air, photographing them as they fell and then getting the musician or musicians to reproduce the frozen moment.

The Polish composer Witold Lutoslawski also used aleatoric elements in his work from the Sixties onwards, but they were sporadic and their parameters were tightly controlled. *Music Of Changes* employed far more aleatoric elements, but Cage still saw the composer as being in charge of the overall musical concept – he became concerned that as the music made virtuosic demands, it would focus too much glory on the player. As far as Cage was concerned, the performer's function was analogous to a contractor who constructs a building from an architect's plan. There are overlaps, certainly, between these views and those of Van Vliet's towards his music and the role of the Magic Band.

The way the music of *Trout Mask Replica* was composed was unprecedented and French played a vital role in this process. Indeed, it is difficult to imagine how the album could have been made without his input as facilitator and arranger. Prior to the piano being brought in as the main compositional tool, French had operated the tape recorder used for capturing Van Vliet's whistled or vocalised lines. After once incurring his wrath by erasing something by mistake, French decided to sabotage the machine, putting it out of action. He'd bought some manuscript paper to write down drum patterns and surprised Van Vliet by memorising one of his spontaneous piano lines, writing it in notation and playing it back to him.

French would sit with Van Vliet for hours each day as he played these passages, transcribing them and playing them back to Van Vliet. He recalled the beginning of this "marathon" in 1996: "The first thing he wrote was

'Dali's Car' and because the electricity had gone out on the street, we did that by candlelight. The music has candle wax on it."[12] A good way to gain an insight into this compositional process is to attempt to play the guitar duet 'Dali's Car' on piano. Even with my own, sub-Van Vliet piano ability, it is possible to roughly approximate the piece, or at least to see how it is based around a primeval 'root' chord, with the lines of each guitar assigned to each of Van Vliet's hands. But he wasn't just an *idiot savant*, gleefully bashing away. French confirms that he could replicate some of his lines. "It was difficult for him but he could really do it. [But] I would say that he mostly sat down and experimented."[13]

Van Vliet's improvisatory through-composition was a simple – and expedient – idea, and one with no attendant theory. Rather than borrowing from avant-garde techniques, it became his own unique avant-garde technique. It was too intrinsically personal to be transferable – a 'better' musician could not have got past the self-awareness, the application of learned technique, the "'I' consciousness", as Van Vliet called it. Even his famously erratic timing ended up being a vital part of the music.

Some of the lines were eventually smoothed out, while others preserved the original staccato note clumps that distantly echoed the jagged time signatures of Stravinsky's music. Although it would be inadvisable to draw any more than the most tenuous of comparisons between the two composers, each episode of 'Dali's Car' pivots around a handful, literally, of notes in an unusual time signature. In this respect it does share common ground with some of Stravinsky's chamber pieces.

There is a reason for this. Igor Stravinsky wrote *The Five Fingers* in 1920/21 as five finger piano exercises – revolving around benchmark notes – specifically for beginners and these fragments were later orchestrated and premiered in 1962 as *Eight Instrumental Miniatures*. He used a similar technique in larger scale pieces like *Four Etudes For Orchestra* (1917-1929), about which he said: "They [the woodwinds] play a four-note chant (the *Four Fingers*, you might call it), the same music endlessly repeated but at varying rhythmic distances."[*]

However coincidental it may be, the spiky opening fanfares of his *Symphonies of Wind Instruments* (1920) do share similarities with 'Dali's Car'. Van Vliet's music and rhythmically agitated, homespun technique needs to

---

[*] Stravinsky quote on sleeve notes for Miniature Masterpieces CD. Igor Stravinsky edition. Sony Classical. Compilation released 1991.

be described in some way, and although the overlap with Stravinsky (one of his favourite composers) is small even here, the comparison is as apposite as to anything else in rock 'n' roll at the time.

When the lines for the two guitars and bass, often in different keys and metres, were overlaid, things got far more complicated. French: "I would consider if you were building a foundation, like bricks of unequal lengths, putting them all down, then you're laying the next [part] down, starting to figure that out – that's what I had to do a lot. So I always felt that I should have got some arrangement credits, but it never happened."[14]

French assesses that 75 or 80 per cent of the music was composed and transcribed in this way, and other songs, like 'Pena' and 'My Human Gets Me Blues', were whistled. Harkleroad remembers Van Vliet's skill in that area: "He was an expert whistler. Just awesome. He could sit there and blow smoke rings while he was whistling."[15]

Van Vliet generated a lot of rhythmic ideas himself and French assesses that with practice he could have been a good drummer. He had a particular fondness for a groove he called 'the baby beat', as it reminded him of being rocked back and forth in his bassinet as an infant. French played some of these rhythm parts as taught, modified others and also wrote a number of patterns himself. His drumming was fuelled by a desire to square the rhythmic circle – to become the focal point that linked the disparate guitar and bass parts. This required a rare autonomy of limb movement and yielded some spectacular results. Harkleroad describes how the group meshed rhythmically: "The cool thing about John French's playing is that one foot would be on one part of the beat, the other foot and the hands would be on other parts of the beat, all within the same [musical] part and all at different dynamic volumes. It was so fucking funky it would drive you crazy! His 'moments' were the most explosive creative drumming I've ever heard. Bass, guitar and drums – everything had an equal, divisional place. We all played rhythm and we all played melodically. Even [jazz drummer] Elvin Jones just did a kind of smooth tumbling, a real predictable tumbling that you could build something on. John was not to build upon."

Although this way of composing gave the musicians unprecedented new musical forms to learn, their reaction was positive. It was much easier now to realise what Van Vliet wanted musically than struggle with the verbal descriptions and whistling. But learning to play these formidably complex compositions proved a daunting task. Sometimes the musicians would have

to sort out passages where different-length parts in different metres had to
hit a cue, or where sections were missing. Van Vliet would typically say,
"You guys know what to do", or would just run his hands over the piano
to give the hitherto missing part. Van Vliet controlled proceedings in that
he had the ultimate say over the shape of the compositions, but would
rarely rehearse with the group. He compared his spontaneous method of
through-composition to "going to the bathroom" and after his creative
movement he was averse to looking too closely at what he had produced.
But if he didn't spend a lot of time teaching them himself, they certainly
had to learn. Or as Marker puts it, unconsciously echoing Cage's
metaphor: "He was the architect but he didn't hammer that many nails in."

Rehearsals commenced in the autumn of 1968 and went through to the
following spring. There were twenty-one new compositions to learn. To
rehearse what was in effect a totally new approach to rock music from
scratch in six months or so was quick work, but the workload demanded
an almost monastic dedication. On joining the group, Harkleroad had seen
French as a serious, focused character and the furrows on his brow were
deepening from the task he had brought upon himself.

French: "Everybody would get a part, go off to the room and stand in
the corner playing. And I'd be sitting in the middle of the room writing
stuff out, trying to arrange paperwork. I could hear everyone playing at the
same time. I'd hear someone making a mistake: 'No, that's the wrong note!'
That's how nuts I got from doing this… Didn't have a lot of fun in those
days. Didn't have a car, didn't have a lot of money, so it was tough."[16] In an
obsession bordering on the monomaniacal, French would also practise on
his own out in the small wash-house.

The Magic Band were far from the non-musicians Van Vliet later
claimed they were. They were young, dedicated and exceptionally talented.
Harkleroad and Boston had been under the impression they were joining
a psychedelic blues band, but they were prepared to take the leap of faith
required to play this new music, without the safety net of what they had
previously learned. And once a piece was honed down to Van Vliet's liking,
he refused to allow any deviation. Jim Sherwood came up with these
observations: "It was a necessity. Don had to control what he really wanted
there. The guys [maybe] wanted to play some rock'n'roll or blues licks or
something like that. That didn't fit into Don's music style." He also remarks
that Van Vliet was 'overbearing' in the exercising of this control.

Cotton had already played the challenging material on *Strictly Personal*, but both he and Harkleroad had to radically change their styles to play these new piano-generated compositions. In 1995, Harkleroad explained the technicalities to *Guitar* magazine: "Almost everything changed when I joined Beefheart, even down to the way I played – using fingers as opposed to a plectrum. I was aware of wanting my Telecaster or ES-330 to sound like, uh, shrapnel! Often I was literally torturing the guitar with these metal fingerpicks, and of course it made a difference whether I was playing 'steel appendage' or 'glass finger' – metal slide or glass. But I'm not sure how much the sonics were an issue. It was always more of an issue of, 'How in the hell am I going to play this?' That was the constant thought, so the sound kinda came afterwards."[17]

In his book *Modern Music*, Paul Griffiths highlights the point where tonality wrenched itself out of the Austrian/German classical tradition: "Mahler, in the Adagio, which was the only completed movement of his Tenth Symphony (1909–10), came suddenly to the atonal chasm with a ten-note chord which makes an awesome point of punctuation, and it is impossible to imagine where he might have gone had he lived beyond the following year."[18]

Half a century later, the Magic Band were wrenching tonality out of the rock music tradition. They too came upon an atonal chasm and were obliged to jump in. Van Vliet might, for example, crash both hands on the keyboard, producing a ten-note chord that he demanded be played on guitar. The fact that the instrument only had six strings wasn't always accepted as an adequate excuse. Harkleroad recalls how he adapted his style to these demands: "Some of the seven-, eight-, nine-note stretches I needed to make to get the intervals we were after meant that I had to have my whole hand in front of the fretboard with my thumb pressing down on the face for the bass note."[19]

He also praised Mark Boston for his equally radical bass technique: "Mark was playing chords and stuff on his Danelectro double-neck with his claw-hammer technique. At the time it was quite scary! I think he was doing a whole different thing on the bass, much more so than we were doing on the guitar."[20]

Harkleroad describes how he saw Van Vliet's methods of composition and the way the results were learned: "You could just form a bunch of rubbish up into a corner and move it over there and learn how to do it the same way every time. And then take a picture of it – and that works. I'm not demeaning it by that at all. There is no way the music of that period would have sounded anything like that except by the vision of Don Van Vliet. I'm just saying how haphazardly the individual parts were done, worked on very surgically, stuck together, and then sculpted afterwards. Boy, as a nineteen-year-old kid, what a learning experience on how to express music."

Over the years myriad comments have been made by ex-Magic Band members on the issues of composition and arrangement, for which Van Vliet claimed total credit. Taking into account their claims of misreporting or misrepresentation by a music press that had never come across these methods of composition in rock before, the cuttings, in total, still present an ambivalent view: that Van Vilet was a genius, that it was his music, but also that he didn't really know what he was doing in respect of the mechanics of the music, and how all the parts worked together. One later Magic Band member even said that anyone who'd had to translate Van Vliet's less specific musical ideas should have got credit as the composer. These views seem to harbour a covert suspicion of his intuitive, exploratory methods, as rock musicians, indeed most musicians, need to have an idea of what they are doing – or if they don't, they aren't very good. It all comes across like the early group's comments to Van Vliet that he didn't know anything about music, and that his process was somehow less 'valid' than more conventional methods of composition.

Harkleroad refutes this: "[They were] certainly not less valid. But from my side to be brutalised to adhere to a perfection that didn't exist only shows my lack of ego, and his amazing overabundance of ego." Creative processes are often set in motion to see where they are going to lead the creator, so to not have a specific, fully formed vision, even to use chancy, vague procedures, often produces results. Harkleroad's bone of contention is not on this aspect of the composition – "Who's to say what process creates art?" he asks rhetorically. But as the musicians had worked so hard to make the music playable, Harkleroad feels that Van Vliet's insistence on total credit reflects unfairly on them: "He claimed that he knew what he was doing to every note. In the BBC documentary [*The Artist Formerly Known as Captain Beefheart*, 1997], he said, 'Would Stravinsky allow a note not to be played perfectly?', alluding to the fact that he knew where every note was in place and that he intended it beforehand. Again, it was about fulfilling his ego, when there is no way he had a complete knowledge or intention for a completed work in the head. He wasn't a composer of that type. I'm not saying what he did was an invalid way to do it, it's just he claimed that he did it in a different and a much more knowing way. He took credit for *everything* and he was full of shit on that count – he was not what he claimed to be. But was he super-creative? Absolutely. Did he teach me how to play guitar? No. Did he influence how I played guitar? More than anybody."

Van Vliet wanted to change the very way the group thought about playing music. He employed a 'twisting of ideas' to steer them away from traditional, rock'n'roll modes of expression. Harkleroad: "He would say, 'Play a high note like a low note. Play a low note like a high note. Play something staccato but play it like you're imagining it lasting longer.' Any way to change something to make it less predictable in the musical sense. I see it as the way he wanted to see the world. Music almost seemed secondary to that!"

Van Vliet's shenai playing had been idiosyncratic to say the least, but in another display of self-confidence he announced to Marker that he was going to play saxophone on the album. He felt that if it was good enough for Ornette Coleman it was good enough for him. One night he had got loaded with Marker, who played him Coleman's monumental album *Free Jazz* (1960). Van Vliet was overwhelmed. Marker: "I think it made a big impression on him and maybe it's when he mistakenly got the idea he could play a reed instrument. He didn't really understand that Ornette wasn't just noodling randomly, there was actually some kind of organisation." Mistaken or not, Van Vliet wanted a piece of the free-jazz action and wasn't going to be stopped by lack of technique, or anything else for that matter.

The group's lifestyle was rigorous in ways beyond the superhuman dedication required to learn the music. Their living conditions were grim. The house had two main living rooms; they would rehearse for up to twelve hours – sometimes longer – in the larger room, where they slept, then wake up and do it all over again. There was a rota for sleeping in the spare room, which was the only time anyone had any privacy – except Van Vliet who slept in his own room with his girlfriend, Laurie Stone. At first French had problems with practising, as a neighbour would call the police when he started playing. After several visits, French kept the peace by damping the drums and cymbals with cardboard.

Winding forward to 1970, after *Trout Mask Replica* had been recorded, Lynn Aronspeer took up the lease on the Ensenada Drive house after it had changed hands in a bet in Las Vegas and the Magic Band had been asked to move out. She remembers that the new owner wanted more conventional tenants. "The owner didn't even know what he had," she recalls. "He thought it was bigger than it was and I could tell that when he was showing me around, he was a little aghast at the inside of the house. Beefheart had painted the inside of the house in primary colours. The whole living room and ceiling were a red enamel and the kitchen was a brilliant mustard and the upstairs bedroom was a French blue enamel. The yard was just covered in debris. Apparently there was a little bit of a [noise] problem… I know when I looked at the house there were huge pieces of foam rubber over the front window panes and surf boards, things like that which they decided would cut the noise."

Even as an outsider to the situation, Lynn Aronspeer soon realised Van Vliet's dominant position within the group: "I remember coming round one time and we were all standing round outside and he was lecturing about how great chitlins were. It seemed to me that he tended to lecture to, rather than relate to, people. I saw that almost as a defence mechanism. It struck me as a little bit of a cover. As long as he was talking he didn't have to answer questions, and as long as he was holding forth and putting forth this very strong demeanour, no one would be challenging him."

There was a strange mixture of religions and philosophies in the house. Van Vliet went for a mixture of Transcendental Meditation and the occult in lieu of psychedelic drugs. Jim Sherwood recalls that in their earlier acid phase, "Don thought he was from a different planet. In fact he knew he was from a different planet." Later Van Vliet told him that by the time they were preparing for *Trout Mask*, he had reached the point of acid burn-out and stopped his consumption. He also claimed the house was built on a Native American burial mound and that he had communicated with the spirits. Harkleroad remembers the group "were into the Maharishi",[21] and within this framework there was French, a devout Christian going through his period of doubt, which was an aberration in a lifelong faith, and Cotton, who was a practising Rosicrucian.

Harkleroad had a ferocious appetite for dope and acid when he joined the group, and had initially shared some with Van Vliet. But later, when he produced his nefarious wares, he was viewed by the rest of the group as the 'drug guy' and desisted. Such activity did take place, though, but at Van Vliet's behest. He sent out for some hashish that he had the group smoke along with him each evening, in what French describes as a 'cult-like ritual'. He didn't particularly like these smoking sessions, but felt obliged to participate, not least to avoid attracting Van Vliet's negative attention.

Basic essentials like food and money were in short supply. Zappa had agreed to release a record which would give Van Vliet total artistic freedom, but no contract had been signed and so the group had no income except welfare. Harkleroad's mother was helping out her impecunious son and his colleagues by sending cheques from a savings account that had been set up to see him through college. Van Vliet's mother, Sue, and Grannie Annie also contributed subsistence payments. French remembers surviving for an entire month with a cup of soya beans his entire daily food intake, a diet that made him feel like an 'Eastern mystic'. Even taking this level of deprivation into account, the group's later assertion that Harkleroad nearly died and Boston had been too weak to get out of bed was mischievous.

Having said that, when Don Aldridge and Merrell Fankhauser went round to visit, they found the atmosphere and the appearance of the group disturbing. Aldridge: "That place was plugged in! If they weren't doing acid, all that juice was coming from somewhere. The environment in that house was positively Manson-esque. When I saw Laurie Stone – for the first time in a while – I was completely astonished at her cadaverous appearance. It was the same with everyone but Don. I was told by one of the members that Don was taking vitamins and eating well because Sue was sending him 'care' packages. The rest were on a barely liveable diet. These were not the people I had known in Lancaster. They all looked in poor health, but Jeff, Laurie and Mark were the worst as I recall. Harkleroad, who I didn't know well, hadn't changed – he always looked like a cadaver."

Aldridge looks back on the time as being particularly negative. "It was not the Don I knew, apart from that brief period," he says. "I never took acid with Don, nor did I ever knowingly see him on acid. I believe he tried to keep me away from it. Don treated me like a little brother. He and Laurie used to tell me repeatedly what a bummer acid was, which is why I was so astonished to hear they were using it at the house." He explains that it was later confirmed to him by a group member, that acid had been used as part of the ongoing regime of control. "If Don stopped using acid at this time, he was alone in doing so," says Aldridge. "During one recording session, just before a take, one member found himself 'coming on'. Someone had allegedly been directed to drop acid in his drink."

Some things are stranger, even, than acid. Van Vliet's personality was powerful, overbearing at times and Aldridge has vivid memories of an incident which puzzles him to this day. "I have seen Don control events," he says. "One night on Carolside he, Doug [Moon] and I were in the front yard. It was late and a man in a car passed. He went to the end of the block and turned back our way, the way he came. Going back and forth for more than ten minutes. I counted eleven times he came up and down the street at a snail's pace, looking straight ahead. Finally, Don said, 'I'll let him go now'. The man drove away as if he knew exactly where he was going."

Sharing a house with other people can be fraught with difficulties, even if they are all easygoing, lifelong friends. But put five men together in this sort of environment and it's no wonder the atmosphere often became fractious. Add to this a band leader who exacerbated the tensions by his increasingly tyrannical behaviour – which he exhibited to constantly remind them that they were in his thrall – and the social structure began to buckle. Van Vliet looked back on his methods in 1993, saying: "It's sometimes difficult to go through somebody when they don't want to be gone through. But they will definitely be gone through if I'm doing it. I'm a stubborn man."[22] To 'go through' someone implies using them as a conduit for his music, just as he was a conduit for his own muse; and also 'running through', impaling them on his ego, wielding his power to quash a mutiny that hadn't even happened.

Van Vliet was rarely present at rehearsals, which stirred up resentment within the group. And when he was with the group he generally ruled extracurricular activities by demanding to be the centre of attention, becoming annoyed and suspicious if someone wanted to do something on their own. If he wanted to watch TV, they would all watch it, or sit in attendance as he played an impromptu sax solo, or listen to Cotton reciting his poems.

One of the reasons that Van Vliet had his strangely named coterie around him is that the ideas started pouring out but he couldn't – or didn't want to – do things himself. In a letter to *MOJO*, John French wrote: "Just think what he could have achieved if he could have written down music."[23] But with French at hand, he didn't need to. Cotton found himself the secretary to Van Vliet's verbal flow, the Boswell to his Dr Johnson, noting down or taping Van Vliet's recitations to catch them at the point of flash and then reading them back to him.

Interviewed by Elaine Shepherd in 1993, French found this amusing with hindsight:"Jeff's role was to read the poetry, our role was to be excited by hearing it; hearing it dozens of times sometimes! Don tried to create an atmosphere where we were almost living this album. It was like we didn't have a private life, we were onstage any time he was in the room. We had to be enthusiastic, we had to act as though we were really excited about this. And that's kind of hard to keep up for a year."[24]

Then there were the 'brainwashing sessions', when Van Vliet turned on one of the group and systematically criticised him to break him down. His personal mix of ego and insecurity drove him into further subjugating the 'kids'. "Like a comic book Mansonish Gestalt Therapy kind of thing" was how Harkleroad described it to John Ellis in 1994.[25]

But these sessions could be taken to ludicrous lengths. Harkleroad certainly wouldn't want to go through the experience again, but recognises that whether or not it was right or wrong, he became stronger as a result of this mental battering:"I was a kid. Being exposed to all of that, no matter how negative... having him say, 'You hate your mother', working at you for 30 hours in your face. 30 hours, now. It was intense. It makes me wonder what made the man tick. I don't know where he got the energy. Then he would sleep for 27 hours like a hibernating bear and I could jump up and down on his bed, kick him in the legs, and he would still be asleep. I think things came from emotional distress and his intelligence – the guy was really smart. He was driven from other things than normal, for sure. I learnt a lot, it took me into areas I would never [have gone]. Would I, at 19 years old, have looked internally that deep and looked at shit like that? I was very fortunate to have had those kinds of experiences to make me grow and learn from them. Not in any way do I regret it."

But that still doesn't explain *why* he engaged in this kind of psychological warfare, or what drove him to expend so much of his own mental energy in waging it – and to what ends, if any. Harkleroad remembers Van Vliet saying he was chosen for the group because "he wanted someone young and pliable... who would want to change". Perhaps, then, this is how he was trying to effect these changes. It appeared that being in control was putting him under a new type of stress. French has gone on record as saying that Van Vliet had once confided to him that he had been diagnosed as a paranoid schizophrenic. On another occasion he was told by one of Van Vliet's ex-girlfriends that he was undergoing therapy for being a 'compulsive lair'.[26] Which ultimately doesn't get us very far.

Mark Boston offers these views: "It took determination to stick with it sometimes, I tell you, especially through the band meetings and talks. One day we were talking about the songs, or something, and Don said, 'Who's thinking in "c"? Somebody here is thinking in "c"'. I said, 'No, no it weren't me.' And then you sit there trying not to think in "c". I think he did that half the time just to mess with us. He's a highly intelligent person and he had a funny sense of humour some times. He'd try to act real intimidating, but he's really just poking people to see what they'd do. A lot of times it worked against him; he'd make more trouble for himself than if he was just friendly with somebody – I'm talking about the way he dealt with people in general. He's an intense person. It's like standing next to a nuclear reactor. You don't know what it's going to do next but you can feel the energy there – he's definitely a source."

Where most group fights are usually metaphorical, the Magic Band's became physical. Harkleroad admitted to John Ellis that "there were some ridiculous things that happened and violence was not excluded".[27] But through all this the group kept to their task, aware that what they had was so original – unique, even – that it might be a commercial success. French: "I think we all kind of sensed that there's something going on here that had never been done before and was artistically sound. We knew that there was a market, there were people out there who were listening to things that weren't conventional, and I was excited about the fact that we were doing something that wasn't conventional, even though sometimes I really wanted to be somewhere else. That's really what motivated me to stay."[28]

Harkleroad was still overawed by Van Vliet to the point of 'hero worship'. Even though the initial easygoing friendship had turned into a more adversarial master-pupil relationship, one of the reasons he stuck with the harsh regime was because Van Vliet was "this big shy person that put on some other front... a little kid in a lot of pain. That's why I like him, [otherwise] I wouldn't have put up with near as much stuff."[29]

Come March 1969, the Magic Band were ready to start recording *Trout Mask Replica*. Frank Zappa was again on production duties, but from the outset it was obviously going to be different from the average production job. He went over to the group's house with Dick Kunc, who had engineered most of the releases on Bizarre and Straight, including The Mothers' *Uncle Meat*.

In 1993 Zappa recalled the circumstances: "The original plan for the album was to do it like an ethnic field recording. I wanted to take a portable rig and record the band in the house, and use the different rooms in the house. The vocals get done in the bathroom. The drums are set up in the living room. The horn gets played in the garden, all this stuff. And we went over there and set it up and did the tracks that way."[30]

Some provisional backing tracks were recorded in the house on reel-to-reel. They highlight what an astonishingly tight group the Magic Band had become. Dick Kunc describes the apparatus used to capture this field recording: "We had a little Uher portable two-track stereo recorder. It was a tough little machine and it made spectacular recordings. Sometimes I used just the single stereo microphone that came with it; other times I set up four separate mikes or so and fed them to the Uher through a pair of simple Shure mixers. The whole mess was monitored through headphones. Not exactly ideal conditions."

Ideal or not, these raw, vital 'field recordings' are excellent, superior to those on the album in many respects. "Field recordings of the beasts that live in this house,"[31] as Harkleroad later quipped. Zappa was pleased with the way they turned out, but Van Vliet became suspicious of the whole enterprise and accused Zappa of being a cheapskate. They had already discussed recording the vocals in a studio and so Zappa gave the group some studio time. The album was recorded at Whitney Studios, Glendale. Kunc: "I was the one who 'discovered' Whitney for us [Frank and me]. Whitney had been almost entirely a gospel studio up to then. After we used it, lots of other groups tried it. They had a monstrous pipe organ with rooms full of pipes and remote instruments. The group were certainly well rehearsed. I was already the proud owner and appreciator of *Safe As Milk* and *Strictly Personal* and was ready for anything. But as a neophyte to that galaxy of music at the time, I wondered how to tell the difference between good and not-so-good performances."

In an extraordinary display of intuition, Van Vliet famously put down his vocal tracks without the use of headphones. The coincidence of his voice and the material that he had spent little time rehearsing and now couldn't even hear properly is astonishing. If he was winging it, he was doing so brilliantly. A similar thing had happened during the initial *Trout Mask* sessions, prompting Marker to surreptitiously leave some sets of headphones in the live room, so Van Vliet would hear their tinny sound added to the control room leakage. Zappa had certainly not worked with anyone in this way before – except perhaps Van Vliet himself, when he had recorded his vocals in the hallway at Studio Z. To Nigel Leigh in 1993:

"You couldn't explain, from a technical standpoint, anything to Don. You couldn't tell him why things ought to be such and such a way. And it seemed to me that if he was going to create a unique object, the easiest thing for me to do was keep my mouth shut as much as possible, whatever he wanted to do whether I thought it was wrong or not – like covering the cymbals and the drums with cardboard and overdubbing his vocals with no earphones, hearing only vague leakage through the studio window, rendering him only slightly in sync with the actual track that he's singing on. That's the way he wanted it. I think that if he had been produced by any professional, famous producer, there could have been a number of suicides involved."[32]

Van Vliet mentioned this incident to Steve Peacock in *Sounds* a few years later, explaining that he was "just a plumber who dug to take the fitting off his pipes so the water runs. It's no big thing."[33] He also told *Zig Zag* in late 1969: "I did it without the music. I was playing – just like the whales. I don't think there is such a thing as synchronisation… that's what they do before a commando raid, isn't it?"[34]

Even allowing for these unorthodox examples of studio craft, the speed with which *Trout Mask Replica* was recorded was amazing. "I know we rushed through everything," says Kunc, "and I quickly sensed that Frank didn't want any of my suggestions about possibly getting an overall better take. It was happening too fast for more than one commanding general; no time for comparing combs about anything." Harkleroad told *MOJO* in 1995: "We just went in there, played every tune once, and he [Zappa] recorded it. And then about five or six hours later, we went home. I'd guess there were a couple of days spent on vocals, a day mixing, and in four days the album was done."[35]

Zappa was in his home studio when he spoke to Nigel Leigh: "I remember I finished editing the album, it was on an Easter Sunday, and I called them up. I said, 'The album's done.' And he made all the guys in the band get dressed up. They came over here early in the morning and sat in this room and listened to it and loved it."[36]

6

OUT RECORDING A BUSH

"If there has been anything in the history of popular music which could be described as a work of art in a way that people who are involved in other areas of art would understand, then Trout Mask Replica is probably that work."
John Peel (interview with author 1995)

"Trout Mask Replica shattered my skull, realigned my synapses, made me nervous, made me laugh, made me jump and jag with joy. It wasn't just the fusion I'd been waiting for: it was a whole new universe, a completely realised and previously unimaginable landscape of guitars splintering and spronging and slanging and even actually swinging in every direction, as far as the mind could see... while this beast voice straight out of one of Michael McClure's Ghost Tantras growled out a catarrh spew of images at once careeningly abstract and as basic and bawdy as the last 200 years of American Folklore... I stayed under the headphones and played Trout Mask straight through five times in a row that night. The next step of course was to turn the rest of the world on to this amazing thing I'd found, which perhaps came closer to a living, pulsating, slithering organism than any other record I'd ever heard."
Lester Bangs, *New Musical Express*, 1 April 1978

The fusion Bangs had been waiting for was a new music that used the earthbound drive of primal rock as a platform from which to launch the untrammelled 'atonality and primal shrieks' employed by black free-jazz players like Ornette Coleman, John Coltrane and Albert Ayler. He got so much more than he was expecting when *Trout Mask* dropped into his head – the experience was epiphanic. He was still writing about the search for other examples of this fusion the following year, referring then to The Stooges' *Fun House*, with its clash of ultra-hard-nosed garage-rock cut with Iggy Pop's more sophisticated taste for Coltrane and his ilk. Superb though that album is, the comparisons were far more tenuous, but then fusioneers that could meet Bangs' criteria were thin on the ground – Detroit group MC5's mixing of astral jazz into their malevolent rock'n'roll made them another candidate, but Bangs remained unconvinced by them. It was becoming obvious that the *Trout Mask* 'style' was exclusive to Captain Beefheart & His Magic Band.

On the opening song, 'Frownland', the new universe of *Trout Mask Replica* is glimpsed in a one-and-a-half-minute microcosm. For the listener, at least, the tortuous rehearsals, hardship and deprivation had all been worth it. The standard role of the two guitars, bass and drums rock line-up is subverted to the point where nothing ever settles or is repeated to any extent. Stuttering drums vie for space with an angular bass and atonal guitar motif in a different metre, and soon a keening lead guitar line rips its way out of the tangled undergrowth. Less than fifteen seconds in, it dissolves into a torrent, the instruments thrashing around each other in complex contrapuntal patterns. But the music carries an inexorable forward motion – it rocks, in other words. The last piece in the puzzle is Van Vliet's vocal roar. He bellows out a yearning, soulful blues that further warps the already warped structure, pleading, 'I want my own land', realising that his wish is becoming fulfilled as he sings the words.

Here at last was his free record: 'free' as in 'unconstrained'. And he barged into this new territory with adrenalised power. Some of the musical elements are recognizable from previous albums – French's tom-tom rhythms and cross-hand hi-hat snatches hark back to the syncopations of songs on *Strictly Personal* – but with his radical new approach they now fell over themselves, as if his entire drum kit was being rolled down a bumpy slope.

The interlocking guitars that had sounded radically jagged on 'Kandy Korn' here wrestle with each other, before struggling free to run along separate paths, only to meet again head on. Boston's bass playing is equally astonishing, corresponding with the other instruments in an unprecedented way. The instrument's sound is flat and woody and it is clawed, strummed, its neck wrung. The production sounds different too, exacerbating the music's astringency and giving the sound a flattened, desert dryness. Paradoxically the shifting planes produced hologram-like illusions of three-dimensional shapes. And Van Vliet's voice was liberated, expanding into a gallery of new vocal styles.

Even when one understands the methodology of composition and the mechanics of the music, *Trout Mask Replica* still resists demystification. There is an untouchable magic at its core. In 1991 Van Vliet assessed the album retrospectively. To Lars Movin: "It is trying to break up the mind in many different directions, causing them not to be able to fixate, this is what I was trying to do."[1]

Fred Frith was guitarist of Henry Cow when he offered these perceptive views in *New Musical Express* in 1974: "It is always alarming to hear people playing together and yet not in any recognizable rhythmic pattern. This is not free music; it is completely controlled all the time, which is one of the reasons it's remarkable – forces that usually emerge in improvisation are harnessed and made constant, repeatable."[2]

Trout Mask Replica is, to coin a phrase, pretty far out. On first listening it comes across as an avant-garde statement with few precedents and sharing little or no overlap with other styles or genres. But within its unique structures are found a multiplicity of lyrical and musical ideas that tie in with other strands of American culture and music, especially the blues.

As the Sixties moved towards the Seventies, groups in the rock mainstream saw the blues as a vein of raw material to be plundered with impunity. The genre proved strong enough to withstand the mauling of the blues-rockers on both sides of the Atlantic, from the group in the local pub knocking out a twelve-bar blues to the biggest arena rockers. While Led Zeppelin made no apologies for taking the blues and using them as fuel for their hard-rock juggernaut, Electric Flag and The Butterfield Blues Band took a more reverential tack. Jimi Hendrix was miles ahead of the competition, setting the blues tradition on fire and marvelling at the beauty of the flames. But the treatment that Cream meted out to Willie Dixon's 'Spoonful' substituted the rough-hewn power of Howlin' Wolf's version with insubstantial flash. Such was the cost of progression – the Europeanisation of the blues appeared complete.

WC Handy was a black musician and bandleader active in the early part of the century whose interest in blues was awakened, according to legend, when he saw a guitarist (reputedly Charley Patton) by Tutwiler railway station playing a guitar using a knife as a slide. At this point blues tunes often hinged on a standard change based around one chord (initially derived from the limitations of an earlier one-stringed instrument, the Diddley Bow). Or the pattern could be based on a shifting number of bars, with irregular chord changes. In John Lee Hooker's case, there would sometimes appear to be a chord change in the offing, but instead he would sing a different melodic passage over the same backing.

In his heyday, Handy was more of a populariser and publisher than a blues performer (although his orchestra did play a formalised version), and documented a lot of blues music as sheet music. In doing so he had to pin down its mercurial nature, standardising it with chord changes within a twelve-bar structure. This was accepted by many schooled musicians of the time, thus strengthening the format and making it more 'musical' in a European sense. By the Sixties the one-chord blues style was unusual, although it lived on in the work of northern Mississippi bluesmen like Mississippi Fred McDowell and Mississippi John Hurt.

Van Vliet's own take on the 'Spoonful' riff was 'Gimme Dat Harp Boy' (from *Strictly Personal*). There he eschewed any blues-rock guitar fireworks for a neo-urban blues approach that echoed Howlin' Wolf, when the latter claimed his band played music 'Low down and dirty as we could'. Van Vliet's interest in the blues encompassed all points from country blues to urban R&B, but the blues that informs *Trout Mask* is the older, almost 'songster' style.

On *Trout Mask*, the syncopation of the Delta blues is echoed in the piano lines which yielded the raw musical material, and is still evident in French's drum patterns. That Van Vliet might not have been able to play the same line twice actually sits him comfortably alongside a blues tradition where structures of songs were so flexible that every performance would be different to some extent. Taken individually, the guitar lines played by Harkleroad and Cotton are not so far removed from the way John Lee Hooker's staccato guitar articulations jump around the linear flow of his music, often sounding as if he's trying to race ahead of himself. Likewise some of Hubert Sumlin's guitar work with Howlin' Wolf has a peculiar keening quality that would cut deep into the music before shooting off on a tangent.

Howlin' Wolf said of his mentor, Patton: "It took a good musician to play behind him because it was kind of off-beat or off-time."[3] A 'sliding shifting rhythmic pulse' was how Giles Oakley described Patton's timing in *The Devil's Music*.[4] It would not be stretching the point to draw comparisons with Van Vliet's own sense of timing and the way the instruments react to each other on *Trout Mask*.

Robert Pete Williams (whose 'Grown So Ugly' was covered on *Safe As Milk*) was a prime exponent of the old spontaneous never-played-the-same-twice form of country blues, where the vocal and guitar lines were interwoven as if in a conversation. Van Vliet's music was also a conversation, but with five conversationalists. Although first recorded in the late Fifties, much of Williams's music harked back to the Thirties, when he first learned to play, and was as strange, haunted and death-obsessed as anything by Robert Johnson. Legendary American guitarist John Fahey's memories of Williams make him sound like one of the amphibious, half-human, half-race of Dagon monstrosities from one of HP Lovecraft's Gothic horror tales. "[He was] the strangest person I ever met. He was like some alien from another world who was part alligator or something."[5]

Blues lyrics dug deep back into the collective unconscious of folk tradition and brought with them echoes of a semi-tangible, ancient strangeness. Howlin' Wolf rewrote Tommy Johnson's 'Cool Drink Of Water Blues' as 'I Asked Her For Water (She Gave Me Gasoline)' and came up with disturbing tales like that of the hapless abattoir worker who looks back on his missed chances in 'Killing Floor'. In the Sixties Bob Dylan summed up folk tradition thus: "The main body of it is just based on myth and the Bible and plague and famine and all kinds of things like that which are nothing but mystery and you can see it in all of the songs. Roses growing out of people's hearts and naked cats in bed with spears growing right out of their backs and seven years of this and eight years of that and it's all really something that nobody can really touch."[6]

On *Trout Mask*, Van Vliet's lyrics showed a quantum leap from his previous work, mixing up folk tales with a sort of neo-Beat poetry and his own highly individual, non-linear narratives. This new take on the American cultural mythos was mixed up with the kaleidoscopic imagery of surrealism-through-psychedelia, beautifully etched lines and droll wit – not forgetting the corny puns. According to Van Vliet, a number of the lyrics were originally poems. As such they have a similar sort of musicality to that which Robert Creely attained in the Fifties, when he addressed jazz and blues modulations via poems like 'The Joke' and 'Jack's Blues'.

Sonically and structurally *Trout Mask Replica* was still way outside the prevailing trends in rock music, not least in the brevity of the material. The impetus of psychedelia was petering out, but the lengthy explorations born from that music – in which Van Vliet had dabbled the previous year – were about to be further extended into the even lengthier formalised structures of progressive rock. This path was epitomised by the English group The Nice, who went from the psychedelic freak-outs of 1967–8 to keyboard player Keith Emerson's classical adaptations and twenty-minute suites within a year. The longest track on *Trout Mask* was just over five minutes, the majority clocked in at less than three.

'Moonlight On Vermont', from the initial recording sessions, stands on the threshold of the full-blown *Trout Mask* style, though it still casts a backward glance towards *Strictly Personal*. Harkleroad's guitar lines are razor sharp and it all locks together into a complicated, serpentine activity. Lyrically it refers to the Forties pop song 'Moonlight In Vermont', with the moon exerting a strange pull on the locals' behaviour. As the song closes, Van Vliet sings a tongue-in-cheek version of the old gospel hymn 'Old Time Religion', mixed with the refrain 'Come out to show dem' from Steve Reich's 1966 piece *Come Out* (on which he subjected a 'found' voice to tape loop phasing).

In her book *I'm With The Band*, Pamela Des Barres of the GTOs described an incident when they went round to the Magic Band's house, ostensibly because one of the group had a crush on French. "We smoked a lot of pot and Don put on a record [Reich's *Come Out*]. We lounged around the living room while a guy with a really deep voice repeated the phrase overandoverandover until it turned into many different ideas. When the record was over, the needle skipped and skipped, so we listened to that for a while too. I, personally, could find no meaning in it, but I tried. We went outside and stood around in a circle, in a semblance of meditation. I rolled my eyeballs in one direction and then the other, trying to stop them in midspin. It was almost impossible."[7]

From the same sessions, 'Veteran's Day Poppy' is full of R&B elements, but the guitars lend aggressive syncopation to the lengthy instrumental coda. Conscription to fight in Vietnam was a real threat, and here Van Vliet chronicles a bereaved mother's lament for her son. Vietnam was a messy conflict which didn't yield many heroes, and Van Vliet finds a powerful anti-war metaphor in the defiant mother who refuses to make the empty gesture of buying the poppy, as "It can never grow another son".

A wide time span of American culture is recontextualised on *Trout Mask Replica*, demonstrated by the obvious quote from 'Old Time Religion'. But another stylistic device is one so personal to Van Vliet that few people have noticed. He had demonstrated on earlier recordings that he had a magpie mentality, putting together musical styles and quotations that he particularly liked. Throughout the album the guitars play snippets of melody from the music of his youth and childhood, which he had whistled for them to replicate. In this instance, the main slide guitar refrain on the first part of the song is a direct lift from a song that was popular in California in the Forties entitled 'Ranchero Grande'.

'Sugar 'N Spikes' half-conceals another one of Van Vliet's favourite tunes. It starts off on an agitated Delta blues rhythm, but the mood swiftly changes as the singing guitar lines shadow the vocals in the chorus. This section is constructed around a melody lifted directly from Miles Davis and Gil Evans's version of Joaquín Rodrigo's *Concierto De Aranjuez* from *Sketches Of Spain* (1959), an album he and Zappa used to listen to as teenagers. The lyrics, however, take the listener back to his homeland. A tale is told of a man in a cold-water flat with "No H on my faucet" and "no bed for my mouse". But the lyrics are wry and humorous and the music melodic, with a later instrumental 'Aranjuez' chorus disrupted by French suddenly rushing off in a flurry of free-time playing.

'Ella Guru' is a pop tune that audibly fractures as the guitars begin to pull in different directions. Meanwhile Van Vliet is hanging out, watching the girls go by and one in particular. The name 'Ella Guru' was one he'd had kicking around for a number of years and the subject of the song was a particular female fan who turned up to live shows wearing an eccentric and colourful garb, which incorporated sheepskin, tie-dye and ostrich feathers. He casually, but in this case accurately, informs us in a deep, bestial voice, "Here she comes walkin' lookin' like uh zoo", before going into a series of colourful verbal puns, "Hi/High", "yella/Ella" and "High blue she blew". In fact "Hi yella" derives from "High yellow", a phrase, now thankfully out of commission, to describe a person of a particular racial mix. Meanwhile, Cotton joins in the fun, gurgling and giggling like a hyperventilating cartoon character.

'Sweet Sweet Bulbs' is the album's most touching song. It explores a romantic theme: Van Vliet meeting his true love in her garden, where 'warm sun fingers wave'. Carrying on the 'sun' theme he embraces her but becomes detached just before a kiss, looking up and exclaiming that he can see the sun – 'Phoebe' – in her bonnet "with the sunset written on it". The music is in a languid mid-tempo, with a gorgeous bass refrain, though the song goes through patches of turbulence before the melody reemerges. A few years later, Van Vliet explained the 'bulbs' in question, saying that he and his wife, Jan, "have a garden and we eat a lot of sprouts, all kinds of sprouts".[8]

These songs, although hardly straightforward, are still constructed on recognizable lines. At the opposite end of the spectrum sits 'Dachau Blues', a refractory composition over which Van Vliet virtually drowns out the music with the intensity of his incantations. It sounds as if he's using his bass clarinet to rail against the atrocities of war in some desperate, garbled language, horrified by visions of a death-dance of skeletons "dyin' in the ovens". At the end, three children appear bearing cautionary doves, "Cryin' please old man stop this misery". The music is dark and convoluted, but on the recordings made in the group's house the instrumental backing track sounds surprisingly different without Van Vliet's massive voice. When he sings across the instrumentation with this kind of power, it creates a sort of auditory hallucination that blurs the music, the drum parts in particular.

These more turbulent, multi-metred songs demanded a new style of singing. If an American avant-garde/roots version of *Sprechgesang* – a half-singing, half-speaking, melodic oratory – could be deemed to exist, then this is it. Van Vliet sings, recites and sometimes splashes the lyrics over the instrumental backing like a sonic action painting. This initial flash was an important part of his process and his tactic of staying away from rehearsals, preferring instead to opt for maximum spontaneity, is vindicated here for the simple reason that it worked.

Another song which displays a similar chemical relationship is 'Neon Meate Dream Of A Octafish'. Van Vliet narrates the lyrics over ensemble playing of staggering complexity which evokes the mythical octafish thrashing about in the water. The remarkable lyrics work on a number of levels. To make his point, Van Vliet alludes to the Imagist concept of being very precise in descriptions, and the Surrealist concept of juxtaposing opposites to generate new forms so, as André Breton said, "forgotten meaning becomes primary": "Whale bone farmhouse", for example. The song is a journey through a luxuriant forest of language which Van Vliet recites in pinched, breathless tones, onomatopoetically evoking the slippery wetness of sex. The procession of words like 'incest', 'in feast', 'syrup', 'semen', 'squirming' evokes the Futurist concept of using words purely for the meaning conveyed in their sound, but his alliterative lists are chosen for their semantic meaning also. In contrast comes the darker image-stream of 'tubes', 'tubs', 'bulbs', 'mucous mules', 'dank drum' and 'dung dust'. The delirious, drooling carnival stops en route to inspect the centrepiece of the 'Meate Dream', "Meate rose 'n' hairs", the female pudenda, with the orifice displayed as a succulent, pungent, sap-oozing, hothouse flower. In the background Van Vliet wheezes away on musette and simran horn as if asthmatically gasping with excitement.

'Pena' rolls along on an even keel musically until French races off on a spectacular tangent towards the end, leading the band into sounding as if they're suddenly playing the song inside out. Cotton recites the lyrics hysterically, declaiming the tale of a girl who was out enjoying the sun "whilst sitting on a turned-on waffle iron", with the result that "smoke billowing up from between her legs" made him "vomit beautifully". He confides that he then "band-aided the area" before once more adapting his cartoon chuckle. In the background, Van Vliet howls like an animal. The tension between the vocal lines with their painful lyrical content and the astringent music makes it one of the most unsettling songs on the record. It was also physically painful for Cotton, who would hurt his throat when singing in this way.

The brief, abrasive 'Bill's Corpse' was written about either Bill Harkleroad on a bad day or Van Vliet's goldfish, Bill, who died after his enthusiastic young owner overfed him. Maybe both. Ken Smith recalls that, as a youth, Van Vliet and his family had a funeral service for the deceased pet, who was interred in a matchbox coffin. Bill could well be the goldfish in the bowl that "lay upside down, bloatin'". The lyrics also paint an apocalyptic scene of "plains bleached with white skeletons", a cremation, and finally a plea to a female figure, perhaps symbolic of nature.

Another song where Van Vliet stares death in the eye, to a soundtrack of guitars scratching in the dust, is 'Fallin' Ditch'. It falls somewhere between Robert Pete Williams's 'Almost Dead Blues', which he wrote during serious illness with the grave, or ditch, awaiting and Dylan Thomas's poem 'Do Not Go Gentle Into That Good Night', where the addressee is implored to "rage, rage against the dying of the light". A mellifluous bass line leavens Van Vliet's assertion that in his bleak, "frownin'" moods "things just turn t' stone". But even at this nadir he insists that "Fallin' ditch ain't gonna get my bones".

Van Vliet plays the role of raconteur over a complicated, melodic backing on 'Old Fart At Play'. The narrative comes across as a folk tale, rich in imagery – or maybe a grown-up children's story – chronicling the activities of a character, the Old Fart, who hides behind a knoll and dons a wooden fish head, "a very intricate rainbow trout replica", with breathing apparatus attached. He arrives at a farmhouse kitchen as Momma is cooking, and the excited Old Fart surveys the spread of food: "fat goose legs", "special jellies", rows of jars with "crumpled waxpaper bonnets". Van Vliet claimed on a number of occasions that the song was an extract from a novel of the same name – it certainly flows that way – but it was never published.

Trout Mask Replica was the first album on which Van Vliet's ecological concerns were clearly stated. 'Ant Man Bee' rides along on shuffling, swung 4/4 rhythm that Van Vliet named "P-K-Ro-P" and tells an allegorical tale of man squabbling with fellow man in "God's garden". Humankind experiences another fall from grace from a mythical Eden, which is now relocated into the twentieth century as a teeming anthill, with the denizens squabbling over "that one lump uh sugar". Ants have recently been found to be more intelligent than humans realised, but, unlike humans, they still don't have the ability to temper their behaviour. His singing over, Van Vliet gets out his tenor and soprano saxes, playing them simultaneously like car horns or dog barks over the perambulating coda before loosening up for a primitive, visceral solo.

When asked about his views on the human race's capacity for destruction by Co De Kloet in 1993, Van Vliet replied: "Horrible. Human beings. It goes way back. I can think way back to when I wrote 'Ant Man Bee'. It's scary to find the things you're saying acted out in front of your very eyes. I was right. That's one time I'd like to be mistaken."[9]

A more dramatic first-person tale of disruptions to the natural order is conveyed in the back-to-nature ethos of 'Wild Life'. The protagonist flees from the painful reality of a situation where the oppressors have "run down all my kin". Now the endangered species himself, he confides to the listener, "Folks, I know I'm next", before fleeing to the mountains with his wife, hoping the bears will take them into an ursine utopia. "Wild life is ah man's best friend," he says, already assuming they will be more hospitable than humans. 'Steal Softly Thru Snow', a complicated, propulsive song that shifts through a series of episodes powered on by staccato guitar, touches upon some of the same themes, this time more poignantly. Van Vliet is heartbroken by seeing the geese flying off for the winter. He is left behind to witness highways being built over fields of grain, and with only murderous humanity for company.

Some of the *Trout Mask* songs show more overt R&B influences. 'When Big Joan Sets Up' is based on a boogie whose forward thrust comes from the guitars playing a repetitive push-pull riff. Apart from a lengthy hiatus filled by a scribbled sax solo, momentum is maintained throughout. The lyrics describe a large woman who, Van Vliet observes, can't go out in daylight, the reason being people laugh at her body, "Cause her hands are too small". Hardly sylph-like himself, Van Vliet pledges to be there for her when she emerges. His exclamation, "Hoy hoy, is she uh boy?", is a tongue-in-cheek misquoting of "Hoy hoy, I'm the boy" from Howlin' Wolf's '300 Pounds Of Joy', where he uses his giant frame as a selling point over his rivals in romance.

After numerous diversions, including an opening section with a Boston bass line that Van Vliet deliberately engineered to be out of sync with the other players, 'Pachuco Cadaver' develops into a mutated shuffle beat with tricky accents. In one of his best lyrics, Van Vliet runs through a number of contemporary cultural references, including Kathleen Winsor's best-selling novel *Forever Amber*, the antacid "broma' seltzer" [*sic*] and "brody knob", which was a slang term from the hot-rod and motorcycle culture of the Forties and Fifties for the "turn knob" on a vehicle's handlebars or steering wheel, which allowed it to be turned quickly, to give a 'brody', a 180-degree skid. He obliquely eulogises a Hispanic dame who is cruising around in a Chevrolet, with a bolero jacket, high heels or "high tap horsey shoes". Although ninety-nine years old she is still the centre of attention, with "Yellow jackets 'n' red debbils buzzin' round 'er hair hive ho", like drones around the queen bee's beehive hairstyle. Another example of Van Vliet's music accommodating details from his musical past within its radical structures is found at the end of the song, where the group keep returning to a refrain which is the children's song 'Mammy's Little Baby Loves Shortnin' Bread', a tune he still loved.

Similar rhythmic propulsion is whipped up by the slashing guitar chords of 'My Human Gets Me Blues'. Van Vliet's urgent singing keeps riding the rails throughout the song's rollercoaster path. The home straight is an onward-rushing irregular time signature, with Boston's bass holding on to the drums with a rubbery grip. One of the main guitar motifs breaks out again like a clarion call over the final bars, then a final drum roll and two cymbal crashes punctuate Van Vliet reciting the song's title. As well as being one of his most brilliantly realised songs, 'My Human Gets Me Blues' became a live favourite throughout the rest of his career.

'She's Too Much For My Mirror' is a tale of a mismatch in love. Van Vliet sings about a woman who is so vain that he's loath to look in the same (overused and abused) mirror. He's moved to Chicago, "hungry and cold", and regrets leaving home, longing nostalgically for "that little red fum [farm]". Maternal advice to be 'choosey' (*sic*) was ignored, a bad move as it turns out. "Now I find out she's uh floosey," he sings, before admitting that he still longs for her.

The formidable a cappella song 'Orange Claw Hammer' finds Van Vliet playing the role of an old sailor who has returned to port after thirty years at sea. He ends up on skid row, on the edge of town, by the side of the railway tracks "on the bum where the hoboes [*sic*] run". He's down on his luck, with only a dollar to his name: "An eagle shined through my hole watch pocket" is his description. Although encumbered by a peg leg, he is looking for any odd jobs to increase his resources. After his lengthy sojourn at sea he marvels with heightened senses at nature around him. The end section of the song is as moving as it is bizarre. He sees a young girl and howls, "God, before me if I'm not crazy is my daughter". The fact that the subject of his paternal affection is still a girl after he has been away for thirty years is incongruous. Maybe he just sees her that way. Or maybe he is simply crazy. But after memorably offering to buy the 'child' a "cherry phosphate", he explains to her how he was shanghaied, and describes her messy conception in a "banana bin". In a tearful denouement, he takes her down to the harbour to see the ship from which he has disembarked, resplendent with erotic figurehead, "the wooden tits on the Goddess".

This song exemplifies Van Vliet's ability to take traditional material and mould it into a highly personal language. In his teens, Zappa lent Van Vliet *Blow Boys Blow*, a collection of traditional songs of the sea sung by AL Lloyd and Ewan McColl. By 1980 he claimed that it was still his favourite record. He never gave it back. The idea for 'Orange Claw Hammer' may well have sprung from this root, as although the song is a narrative, the tune is in simple, repetitive cadences reminiscent of a sea shanty. It also evokes the atmosphere of the 'Cutty Sark' section of Hart Crane's epic poem from 1930, *The Bridge*. There, an old mariner back disoriented from a long voyage. "I don't know what time it is – that damned white Arctic killed my time," he says. Crane deliberately constructed this poem around American speech rhythms and it reads from the page like phrases jotted down from a conversation.

Van Vliet's performance on 'Orange Claw Hammer' was, in effect, also jotted down. It is one of the 'field recordings' done at the group's house, with the pause button on the recorder audibly clunking down as he thought of the next line. Van Vliet also referred back to folk idioms of speech. He wrote his lyrics from *Trout Mask Replica* onwards in a sort of personalised phonetic transcription of the vernacular, with, for example, "uh" or "ah" replacing "a"; "t" replacing "to"; "'er" replacing "her"; "m'" and "'n" replacing "my" and "and"; "thata" replacing "that'd".

'Well' is like a field holler, sung in a stentorian baritone, with the refrain "well, well" at the end of each line. In an interview in 1980 – after he had come up with his by then stock phrase, "Everyone's coloured or you wouldn't be able to see them" – he looked back on the song. And took care to cover up his blues roots.

"Yeah, who said an albino can't have soul? What I'm saying is that I think a poem like 'Well' and I have that voice… I have an awfully powerful voice. I haven't heard the likes of it. Although if I could parrot it'd feel so funny… like putting on the sleeve of someone else's coat".[10]

Here causal narrative is eschewed in favour of a juxtaposition of image-rich snapshots within a feeling of impending darkness, a hypnogogic state with the mind filled against its control on the edge of sleep. The light which brings day time is described as sailing on the river of day on a "red raft of blood" – presumably a reference to bustling humanity. Ultimately night "blocks out d'heavens like a big black shiny bug". Van Vliet drops into a dream state that gathers its own momentum, picking up fantastic debris as it goes.

Spanish poet Federico García Lorca was affiliated with the Surrealists in the late twenties (although he found that some of their techniques based on subconscious processes lacked the clarity he sought). In Lorca's view, the juxtapositions that "unlock the potential of meaning" need not necessarily be purely imagination-based or Surrealist. In his terms of reference, if poetry was just from the 'imagination', then it would be largely bound by existing human knowledge and logic. His own processes of juxtaposition were more deliberate and produced poetry born of 'inspiration', which incorporated the idea of the *hecho poético*, or poetic fact. (Robert Graves labelled these two types of poetry 'muse' and 'Apollonian' respectively.)

In *García Lorca: Poeta en Nueva York* Derek Harris explains the *hecho poético* as "an image which seems as inexplicable as a miracle, for it is devoid of any analogical meaning. Based on the *hecho poético* and bound together by *la lógica poética*, the poem becomes a self-sufficient entity without reference to any reality outside itself."[11]

Like Van Vliet, the Andalucian Lorca dealt with deeply-rooted native folk archetypes and wrenched them out into a new, often shocking context. The apogee of this approach is in the collection *The Poet in New York*. The striking illogicality and haunting, self-contained images within these lines from 'Well' can be seen as a Van Vlietian *hecho poético*: "The white ice horse melted like uh spot uh silver well. Its mane went last then disappeared the tail."

'The Dust Blows Forward 'N The Dust Blows Back' is the third of the a cappella songs and another 'field recording' – again the tape pause button is audibly pressed down after each line. It sounds as if it comes from some forgotten oral tradition, with Van Vliet singing in creaky tones, like a septuagenarian farmhand sitting on his porch reminiscing about a fishing trip. Down by the riverside, he casts his rod with a cork float "Bobbin' like uh hot red bulb". He notices a riverboat pass by and a lipstick-smeared Kleenex caught on a twig. He sounds happy, drinking "hot coffee from a krimped-up can" with his girl named 'Bimbo Limbo Spam' – presumably to make the last line scan. Day turns to night under a moon that looks like a giant dandelion.

Van Vliet told Roger Ames in 1974: "'Dust blows forward, dust blows back' [*sic*] was recorded in the house on a cassette. It was just me with the cassette. That was an impromtitudinal [*sic*] poem. I used the clicks from switching the mike on and off to create the space. A lot of the songs on that album were poems."[12]

To many people, *Trout Mask Replica* is best known for the snatches of conversation between songs. In the most famous exchange, Van Vliet engages Victor Hayden (The Mascara Snake) in a call-and-response, the notorious "Fast 'n bulbous" routine. "I love those words," chuckles Van Vliet as Hayden recites his lines, then butts in. "Yeah, but you've gotta wait until I say: 'Also a tin teardrop'," he continues, leaving Hayden both amused and bemused. So what exactly is it that is fast 'n bulbous? "A squid eating dough in a polyethylene bag," he informs us during another spoken link. These links, together with the inclusion of a few spontaneous home recordings, compound the feeling of *Trout Mask Replica* as a sonic scrapbook on to whose pages the contents of Van Vliet's psyche have also been pasted. On 'Hobo Chang Ba', Van Vliet revisits the hobos of 'Orange Claw Hammer'. The song is specifically about Oriental immigrants who came over to America looking for work, but ended up becoming hobos, riding the trains into uncertainty. The subject of the song – 'Chang Ba' is his name – now lives nomadically. He is found waking up in the early morning cold in a railroad boxcar – "'Mornin' time t'thaw", as he says. There is a defiance and dignity in his predicament – an elegiac figure disappearing into the unknown, who, because he is disenfranchised, becomes a frontiersman by default. He covers endless miles in search of a new future and if it isn't found on the horizon, there are always horizons beyond. This constant movement becomes an end in itself. He feels that "Standin' still is losin'" and that each new sunrise at least carries potential. He has become so rootless his mother is now the ocean and "the freight train is m' paw [pa]".

Van Vliet told Kurt Loder in *Rolling Stone* in 1980 of an encounter when he had "split a bottle of wine" in the High Mojave with a black hobo. "He'd hitchhiked down from Oakland. He didn't take a train any more. He said, 'I don't ride the rails because the young people they kill tramps now, you know.' I said, 'That's disgusting.' He said, 'It isn't like it used to be, Don.'"[13]

Van Vliet sings this poignant tale – one of his best lyrics – in a ridiculous voice that was apparently his approximation of an Oriental accent. Typically, his vocal presence is inescapable, but his diction is unorthodox to the point where the meaning of the lyrics is obscured. A good enough reason to sit down and read the lyric sheet of *Trout Mask Replica*, one of the few rock albums that warrants such an exercise.

'China Pig' is an example of Van Vliet at his most spontaneous. Doug Moon visited the house, and after he and Van Vliet had played an impromptu version of 'Candyman' by Mississippi John Hurt, Van Vliet asked him to "play one of those 'chunga, chunga, chunga'…" Moon is captured on cassette playing a neat blues figure to Van Vliet's improvised tale of penury with the subject of the story agonising about whether or not to break open his piggy bank, howling, "I don't wanna kill my china pig". He describes this glazed pottery beast with decorative painted flowers and a curly tail, and recounts how a little girl "used t' put her fingers in its snout". A decade later, Van Vliet gave another shading on the song, saying: "It's about how fragile a human being is. I mean the body as opposed to all the forces."[14] Moon received no credit for the music.

The stand-out oddity of the album is 'The Blimp (mouse trapreplica)', a spontaneous poem, apparently based on the newsreel of the Hindenburg airship crash, read by Cotton with Van Vliet playing sax in the background. "Master master, this is recorded through uh flies [*sic*] ear," he informs, gasping, then describes the huge craft, the "mother ship" with "uh trailin' tail". Zappa explained the unusual circumstances of the recording in 1993: "I was in the studio mixing some other tapes, and the band that's actually playing on 'The Blimp' is actually The Mothers Of Invention. The vocal on 'The Blimp' was recorded by telephone. He had just written these lyrics, and he had one of the guys in the band recite it to me over the phone. I taped it in the studio, and recorded it onto the piece of tape that I had up at the time, which was my track. The piece is called 'Charles Ives'. We used to play it on the '68–'9 tour."[15]

Of the three instrumentals on *Trout Mask*, 'Dali's Car' is the most concise. Two guitars lock together in almost Baroque formality but the tone is unremittingly harsh. The piece derives its title from an installation by Salvador Dali – a car containing a mannequin, painted sea shells and other organic matter – that Van Vliet and Harkleroad had seen at the LA County Museum.

There are two versions of 'Hair Pie' (one of the more grotesque slang terms for cunnilingus): 'Bake 2' is a group-only studio take and 'Bake I' was recorded with the group playing in the house, while Van Vliet and Victor Hayden played sax and bass clarinet out in the garden. Their dialogue sounds like the mating ritual of two gigantic birds. Van Vliet gave this tongue-in-cheek explanation shortly after the album was released: "Vic had only been playing bass clarinet for three days and I had only played the horn 120 times or so, something like that – somebody was keeping tally on me." Nearly thirty years later Harkleroad described the spontaneity of the occasion: "We're practising in the living room, thinking that we're rehearsing, and they're out in the weeds playing the horn, 'Oh, that's a take!'"[16]

When 'Bake I' finishes, there follows a conversation between a couple of kids and Van Vliet, recorded when he and Hayden were still wandering around in the garden. The bemused youths had come over to eavesdrop on the band playing in the house. They are asked by Van Vliet what they think: "Sounds good," they reply unconvincingly. Van Vliet helpfully informs them that, "It's a bush recording. We're out recording a bush."

They had in fact gone there for a specific purpose. Eric Drew Feldman – who joined the Magic Band in 1976 – was a Captain Beefheart fan in his teens, and had gone over to the house himself a couple of times, just to hang around outside and listen to what was going on. The incident captured on tape involved two of his friends. Feldman: "One was a musician trying to put bands together and his friend said, 'Hey, there's this band playing up the street, they're really terrible, but they have a really good drummer. Maybe you can get him for your group.' They were thirteen years old, or whatever, and they go over and happen to come upon them when they were recording that version of 'Hair Pie'. After Don says it's 'Hair Pie', there's that uncomfortable silence, nobody says anything. He [Van Vliet] explains who they are and they realise they're a signed band – that's big time. One says, 'I guess you don't get the drummer' and the other one goes, 'Huh'…"

7

CARP HEAD REPLICA

"A trout in a stream. If you have to say psychedelic, that's psychedelic to me."
Don Van Vliet, *Zig Zag*, 1969

"According to him he invented the planet and always made it fun to listen to him telling you how he did it. So it was easy to buy it. I bought it for a lot of years!"
Bill Harkleroad (interview with the author, 1999)

Q: *"People often say they find you frightening. Why do you think that is?"*

A: *"Dumb people. Dummies. They certainly can't carry on a conversation. 'Cos they're afraid. Afraid of themselves. Of course I tease them. What else can I do?"*
Don Van Vliet to Vivien Goldman, *Sounds*, 22 November 1975

Trout Mask Replica was the most literally mind-expanding album released in the Sixties – even though it was the complete antithesis of virtually all psychedelia. Accordingly, the spectacularly strange gatefold sleeve managed to keep clear of psychedelic clichés, while incorporating some of the most memorable visual images of the era.

The most immediately recognizable image – and the one still most closely associated with Captain Beefheart & His Magic Band, Van Vliet specifically – is the front-cover photo. He is clad in a fur-lapelled green coat and a stove-pipe hat with a cut-down brim, standing in front of a plain magenta background. His right hand waves 'Hi!' and a fish's head placed in front of his face gawps at the viewer. Cal Schenkel, who had first met Van

Vliet in the heyday of Studio Z, had become the art director for the Straight and Bizarre labels and had already designed striking covers for Mothers Of Invention albums like *We're Only In It For The Money* and *Uncle Meat*. He and Van Vliet talked over the concept. It was decided that the wooden "intricate rainbow trout replica" mask, as worn by the character in 'Old Fart At Play', would be replaced by something more natural. Schenkel explains: "It was a carp's head that I got at a big fish store in the Fairfax Avenue section, a big market section of LA, near my studio. I just went over there looking for a fish head, brought it back and had my assistant hollow it out, and then basically we strapped it to Don's head like a mask. In fact it was so heavy that he had to really hold it up there, that's why his hand's in the position that it's in."

In 1973 Van Vliet came up with a rather tenuous explanation for the shot for Connor McKnight: "What I was saying was that the carp seems to be able to thrive in polluted waters, and I'm waving to tell people that no one else thrives in polluted waters."[1]

In Anton Corbijn's short film *Some Yo Yo Stuff* (1993), Van Vliet still remembered the incident with disgust: "It stank so *bad*," he said. Not so bad that he couldn't have a bit of fun with it, though. He ending up playing his soprano sax with the reed stuck through the fish's mouth once the session was completed. A few seconds were captured by Schenkel on 8mm film in the hallway outside the photographic studio.

Schenkel staged the cover shots for Ed Caraeff to photograph. The inside cover features photos of the group which the two of them later solarised and otherwise chemically altered. The images are striking and deliberately so. Schenkel: "Doing Bizarre was to do a little bit more outrageous artwork as well [as the music] and that was certainly my philosophy in general with the work I was doing then. I knew Don's work and that was the kind of work I was doing, so it was just a nice mesh. I just took images and played with them into place – I designed it spontaneously, I guess you could say. I took the shots that we had, printed different colour variations, then chopped them up. The other thing is, I didn't have a great deal of control over the colours as I was experimenting with the chemicals and with filters. I wasn't after that [psychedelic] look," he continues. "I liked a funkier, thrown-together look and experimenting with the image in ways that were less pleasing: colours that were edgier, that didn't quite work together." His only disappointment is with the lettering – which he felt could have been stronger – but in this respect he was overruled by Zappa.

"I really like the way it turned out," he concludes. "It was one-off, but at the time everything was a one off."

The back cover was the visual embodiment of why the Magic Band weren't going to be saddled with any of the beads, bells and incense hokum of the increasingly disparate hippie tribes. Especially as Van Vliet was becoming increasingly antipathetic to contemporary drug culture – if not the drugs themselves. And the band's lifestyle had hardly been an exemplar for the tenets of "peace, love and good vibes".

Standing on a rickety wooden bridge in the sloping grounds of the Ensenada Drive house, the Magic Band look as if they've been teleported in from another planet for the photo session. Sporting a top hat and his green coat, Van Vliet looks sullen, detached, staring blankly through shades. He holds a lamp with the former shade now just a wire skeleton surrounding the bulb and points it into the middle distance. Jeff Cotton appears confused, as well he might be, clad in a baseball cap, big boots and a rather becoming dress. Bill Harkleroad sports lipsticked lips, a skullcap, a medieval cape and trouser bottoms a full four inches adrift of his shoes. Mark Boston, studiously bespectacled under his Afro-style shock of hair, wears a natty bottle-green zoot suit and dog tag. John French lurks beneath the bridge, holding the flex to Van Vliet's light contraption, his features impassive beneath a black cap and wraparound insectoid shades.

The bridge had been built across a gully that turned into a creek during heavy rain. French explains what he was doing down there: "They wanted to take a picture on the bridge and said, 'There's not enough room, you need to bunch up closer together.' I was the only one who had enough nerve to crawl under the bridge because everyone else was afraid of spiders. I had that long hat on, a chimney sweep's hat, with a bill that hung way down your back, so I wasn't too worried about it.

"Don was holding the lamp out and the wire just happened to be hanging in front of my face so I just pulled it over and that's how we got that shot. [The sunglasses were] 'Girl Watchers'. They were really cheap sunglasses that came for free with suntan oil. Don used to wear those onstage a lot as a joke. He said, 'You should try wearing these sometime.' I put them on one day and he said, 'Perfect'."

Harkleroad gave his recollections of the shot in 1995: "Those were my clothes actually. The cape was something some woman had given me, and I thought it looked fine. Black fingernail polish? That's cool. Lipstick?

That's cool too. I'm breaking it all away at that point. Nineteen years old – who had *brains* at nineteen?"[2]

Gary Marker remembers that Van Vliet had been thinking awhile about his new look. A number of months before the sessions he offered to take his picture on an Instamatic, and he put on his coat and posed with the skeletal lampshade and an umbrella. "When I gave him some dupe prints of the pictures, he said, 'Yeah. That's about what I'm looking for. You know what I mean? An image.'"

He certainly had one now. In the neighbouring houses, the residents of Woodland Hills were going about their business as usual. And maybe seconds after the shot, the Magic Band simply wandered off chatting to make some coffee or check to see if there was anything in the larder. But in that instant they looked untouchable, at odds with everything.

Marker remembers Van Vliet talking to him at length about his ideas for the group in the run up to *Trout Mask*. "He seemed to be obsessed with a total vision/concept of what he wanted the band to sound like and how they should appear, on stage and off," he says. "He had a long list of weird names for people and particular notions of how they should be dressed. They were all more-or-less 'characters' in his personal travelling circus.

"There were times, hearing all his grand notions about staging and such, that it almost seemed like the music was incidental to the total presentation. He wanted to put on a show that people wouldn't forget, complete with props, sets and carefully staged performances. So he experimented with attention-getting costumes, such as the silly glasses, moth-eaten coat and 'Mad Hatter' lid he was wearing when I snapped a couple of pics of him.

"I made it clear to him that if I played any live gigs with the band, there wasn't a snowball's chance in hell that he'd get me out in front of an audience wearing an ape mask, mini skirt, chain mail vest and white vinyl go-go boots. 'Well, then YOU can be Captain Beefheart and I'll wear the mini skirt,' Don said. And I think this was a very revealing remark - Don probably would've been perfectly happy to just conceptualise a staged musical presentation, without actually having a burning desire to be an active participant. He just wanted to direct.

"Personally, I think he wanted to one-up his old pal Zappa, with the extravagant, overblown stage production. I also tried pointing out to him that all his grandiose ideas needed a great deal of rehearsal time, especially since he had ideas of incorporating dancers, actors and even trained seals, if he could get away with it. I knew it would never happen, of course - because he was too lazy to even rehearse his vocals with the band. So, the only elements that survived were the costumes - and the occasional dancer, clown or oddball prop. Personally, I thought his ideas would detract from the music - and further, wild, psychedelic road shows were pretty much already 'old hat' by 1969; he was a bit behind the times, other bands had been doing it for years, including Zappa."

Lynn Aronspeer later found out more about the group's activities from her new neighbours. "My understanding was that they would roam the neighbourhood in costumes and were really whooping it up. The neighbourhood still mentions the Captain in a huge witch hat and also I think he had a stove-pipe hat, like The Cat In The Hat. I have a feeling he was a pretty benign presence here except for the noise – we live in a hilly community, so noise bounces around; you can never quite tell where it's coming from and it can be quite loud."

Trout Mask Replica was first released on Straight in the US via Reprise in July and came out a few months later in the UK, so press reactions filtered out gradually. Zappa enthused about the album to Dick Lawson of *Zig Zag* just prior to its US release: "The new album that he's just made is a two-record set and the roots of that music are in Delta blues and also in avant-garde jazz – like Cecil Taylor, Thelonious Monk and John Coltrane and a lot of other things. You can really hear that influence and it's all perfectly blended into a new musical language. It's all his."[3]

Lester Bangs submitted a review for *Rolling Stone* which he later described "as unqualified a rave review as was ever written."[4] For advertisements it was whittled down to the summary: "The most outrageous and adventurous album of the year". Bangs noted that a few other rock critics apparently liked it, but suspected that left to their own devices they would far rather listen to something else.

As the methodology of the composition and arrangement has only relatively recently been clearly described, it's not surprising that most journalists simply couldn't get to grips with what was going on in the music. The processes were radical enough compared with the methods of the avant-garde, but within the rock milieu they were unique. Some writers assumed that the drums led the music; or the guitar harmonies were accidental; or the whole thing was a fluke; or it was as difficult and as scrupulously arranged as the music of Varèse; or Van Vliet was ruling the musicians "superconsciously".

DJ John Peel rates *Trout Mask Replica* as his all-time favourite record, and played it in its entirety when it was released in the UK. But he admits that he had his own problems assimilating the music on first hearing: "My initial response would have been similar to my response to [first] hearing Little Richard or The Ramones: you didn't know what you thought. You suspected that it was crap just because it was unlike anything else you'd ever heard in your life. Whoever you are, your value systems are based on comparative judgements and you can't listen to something in a kind of state of grace, and *Trout Mask Replica* had no reference points. You could approach it from any direction, you could interpret it in any way, because it bore no resemblance to anything else you'd experienced. And I'm sure my initial response was 'he's blown it'."

In 1993 Matt Groening, the creator of *The Simpsons* and *Futurama*, talked to Dave DiMartino in *MOJO* about his experiences: "The first time I heard *Trout Mask*, when I was 15 years old, I thought it was the worst thing I'd ever heard. I said to myself, they're not even *trying*! It was just a sloppy cacophony. Then I listened to it a couple more times, because I couldn't believe that Frank Zappa would do this to me – and because a double album cost a lot of money. About the third time, I realised they were doing it on purpose: they meant it to sound exactly this way. About the sixth or seventh time, it clicked in, and I thought it was the greatest album I'd ever heard."[5]

Dick Lawson got rather carried away when he wrote about Captain Beefheart and his 'magic men' in a later edition of *Zig Zag*: "They tear and slash at the guts of their music, ripping its lungs out, grinding and crushing the bones, then pull it all together in a couple of bars." Lawson praised the "beautiful, stoned, surrealistic lyrics… groups of hallucinatory alliteration and repetition," and assessed Van Vliet as "so freaked out and so positive."[6]

In the late Sixties, more serious notions of music as art brought with them a significant sea change in music journalism. The stilted prose of the early to mid-Sixties seems quaint, almost comical now, especially the group profiles where the line of questioning rarely got past the 'What's your favourite food?'/'What's your favourite colour' stage. Pop and rock artists – most notoriously Bob Dylan – began to give increasingly outrageous answers to subvert the banality of the format. Now the music press was becoming part of the scene rather than simply reflecting it, with writers becoming both more serious and increasingly flamboyant in their prose. The independent UK magazine *Zig Zag* is a case in point. It sprang up in

1969, taking its name from the Captain Beefheart song 'Zig Zag Wanderer' and constantly championed him thereafter.

As *Trout Mask* was stirring up the pond, producing shock waves of ecstasy and/or incomprehension, music magazines suddenly took a far greater interest in what the Magic Band were doing. The time was ripe for Don Van Vliet to publicly road-test his Captain Beefheart persona. An interview can be a difficult experience for the interviewer when the ground appears to be slipping away beneath his or her feet, or if they are already overawed by meeting the interviewee – "pre-intimidated," as John Peel puts it.

Peel noticed that Van Vliet could be intimidating without consciously trying. He explains: "You never really quite knew where you were with him. Even those of us who were really fond of him just found him utterly mystifying. His thought processes were just not the thought processes of anybody else that you were ever likely to meet. He was a classical lateral thinker.

"He'd make these gnomic remarks and two or three days later you'd just realise what he meant. One of the first things he said to me was – almost by way of introduction – 'You have to excuse me, but I'm seven people away from myself at the moment, but I'm getting closer all the time.' And at first you'd think it was hippie bullshit, but then you'd think, 'I know what he means.'

"He didn't set out to be weird, like a lot of people did at the time. He was just different, in the same way that someone like Viv Stanshall was different. I was with him when people would come up and say something in a perfectly friendly way and he, in a perfectly friendly way, would say something rather enigmatic back to them. Of course they would be confused by this, because they didn't know if it was a form of hostility or indeed what it meant at all. It was kind of attractive and he established a distance at the same time. People found it, I think, a little difficult to work out exactly how to take him. But if he was in a good mood, he was a genuinely entertaining chap to spend time with."

Among friends and associates, Van Vliet was known as an entertaining and provocative conversationalist, so all he had to do in the interview situation was turn it all up a notch or two. Having flexed his artistic muscle so spectacularly on *Trout Mask Replica*, his interviews became as extravagant, off the wall and capricious as his music and lyrics. He loved to talk with people anyway, and turned these situations into a good-natured game, playing with language – and with it the interviewer – like a sea-lion playing with a ball. Or, as put more bluntly by one ex-associate, he "fucked with the interviewer's head".

However they are labelled, these traits were committed to posterity on a promotional interview LP for radio stations which was issued by Reprise to coincide with the release of *Trout Mask*. One side was devoted to Captain Beefheart, the other given over to promote Ry Cooder.

Meatball Fulton was the journalist entrusted with the interview. Sometimes he kept up to speed, at other times he was obviously baffled. Van Vliet ran the gamut of his conversational idiosyncrasies for Fulton's benefit. He also started what would become a career-long habit of turning the tables in the interview by becoming the inquisitor, asking his own questions, appearing genuinely interested in the answer. In this extract, Van Vliet pulls the conversation around to the then current moon landing:

MF: Do you ever think of leaving the country?

DVV: Do you mean the earth? You mean the country, the United States? I don't think they even know I'm here now.

MF: (*Laughs*)

DVV: Better not laugh too much if we want to get this on the radio. They're likely to get us for breathing with all our holes open!

MF: (*Bursts out laughing*)

DVV: You know they're about to poke their genitals into our cream cheese moon right now. What do you think about that? That's my eye.

MF: What do you mean 'your eye'?

DVV: The moon, it's part of me.

MF: Mmmm… I don't understand.

DVV: Why don't they poke it in the sun, man? Are they afraid to do that? They might get burnt up, right? They're not very daring are they?

MF: What do you think about that?

DVV: Err, if they'd cut the nose off the rocket, you know, I think it would be a little more natural, do you know what I mean? If they could get up there without having the hole in the front closed up, I think they would enjoy it more or I'd like them more. You know what I mean?

MF: Yeah … No, I don't.[7]

When quizzed by Fulton about *Trout Mask Replica* and his standing in the music business, he became more serious: "I wonder why all of our musicians, like Don Cherry, John Coltrane, Charlie Parker and all those people, had to go to Europe to be able to play in front of people, don't you?

I know that somebody playing free music is not as commercial as a hamburger stand. Is it because you can eat a hamburger and see it and hold it in your hand and you can't do that to music? Is it too free to control, maybe?'

Going off the track completely, he is here fancifully describing his spells of truancy, when he went out walking with the "trangents" of Mojave (either Van Vliet's idiosyncratic pronunciation of "transient", or a pun combining that word with "tangent"): "Well, what's a "trangent", do you know what I mean? Someone who likes to go for a walk farther than somebody who is a resident. So the thing is, what's a resident? What's a residue? What's a reservoir? What's a resolution? What's a rhinoceros? Get the point? And he's even been attacked because his horn's good medicine for sex, right? They grind up his horn, man. Hair horn. We're lucky they haven't found out about our teeth."[8]

In August 1969, the Van Vliet/Zappa alliance continued on 'Alley Cat' a lighthearted R&B tune recorded in Zappa's basement – which lay unreleased for over 20 years - and more significantly on Zappa's first solo album, *Hot Rats*. The album was recorded at a number of studios around Los Angeles. Van Vliet added vocals to the track 'Willie The Pimp' back at TTG studios, in a session again engineered by Dick Kunc. Later interviews with Van Vliet suggest that the relationship was beginning to show signs of strain but Kunc remembers the recordings going well, although there were "stories of harsh words passing between them".

English journalist Barry Miles had been staying at Zappa's house at the time and was present at the sessions at TTG's. While Zappa was downstairs working on 'Willie The Pimp', he and Van Vliet were taking a coffee break at 2 a.m. in the studio's 24-hour snack bar. Van Vliet told Miles that he could break glass with his voice. He tried, but after letting out a yell, the window was still intact. He admitted to feeling "a little tired". But moments later Zappa burst in, asking, "What the hell was that?",[9] having heard the noise downstairs in the soundproof control booth. Although declining to add his vocals to the track that particular night, the song became one of Van Vliet's best-known vocal performances. It stands out among the more arranged pieces on the album, being a loose-limbed R&B workout. Van Vliet announces himself as the "Little pimp with my hair gassed back" and tells his story over Zappa's guitar and Sugarcane Harris's violin, before scat-singing in the background and disappearing after only a couple of minutes. His cameo is a telling one and for the remainder of the nine-minute track, Zappa pulls off one of his longer, more inspired guitar solos.

Van Vliet's growing antipathy towards Zappa has generally been put down to the inevitable problems resulting from a clash of titanic egos and personal rivalry. Miles feels that other factors were also becoming important: "I think it was connected with the business side of things. I know that he, Frank and Herb Cohen [Zappa's manager] were having endless meetings when I was there. Frank was becoming intrigued with the idea of having his own record label and becoming a little record business mogul. And he was. He was taking on all of that LA music business thing, calling records 'product'. And Beefheart couldn't stand that. He really hated 'suits' and he thought Frank was basically being taken in by Cohen – which indeed he was and later on had to have a lawsuit to separate himself out from him. They'd all three be in the house having a big meeting and then Beefheart would come stamping out and march around the garden with me, cursing them and saying how Frank was selling out."

One incident implied that things weren't going too well in the Van Vliet psyche at the time. Zappa was alarmed to hear that he had become depressed and destroyed hundreds of poems and songs. Miles: "He told Frank that and Frank was very, very upset, but I think it later turned out that it wasn't strictly true, that there were copies of them at least. But the thing was the manuscripts were beautiful. They were decorated, according to Frank, and the whole thing was a terrible loss. I think he was going through quite a bad phase."

Miles himself found Van Vliet to be "a very friendly guy. Very egotistical". He had been doing a lot of work with Allen Ginsberg, which prompted Van Vliet to proudly proclaim that not only was he a better poet than Ginsberg, he was also a better painter than abstract expressionist Willem De Kooning and was a better sax player than John Coltrane. "There was no irony there," Miles continues. "I was quite shocked when he laid all that stuff on me."

Captain Beefheart & His Magic Band did little live work immediately after *Trout Mask*. A slot on the bill at Woodstock was even turned down as, according to Harkleroad, "A certain person said, 'No, let's not play there. It's just a bunch of drunken hippies sitting in the mud.'"[10] French and Harkleroad only recall doing one gig with the *Trout Mask* line-up. They appeared as part of a big show in LA, with a number of groups including The Mothers and Jethro Tull. French: "I wish there would have been a film made of it. It was right after we finished *Trout Mask* and it was a benefit for something. It was a big place originally called The Hullabaloo. It had this big revolving stage, so they could set up one act while the other one was playing. And I think Buddy Miles opened, and then we came out and Frank Zappa afterwards. We played all stuff from *Trout Mask* and The Mascara Snake was there.

"It was a pretty amazing concert to watch people's reactions, 'cos they'd just gotten to listen to Buddy Miles then suddenly we'd walk on. And we did a theatrical thing like I'd come out first with a broom and for the first ten minutes of our show I swept the stage. We did a few of the really tough pieces and the band was tight, we'd been rehearsing for nine months with this band. Those poor people didn't know what hit them."[11]

The group's penury, near-starvation and ill-treatment by Van Vliet were not mandatory – the musicians always had the option of quitting, but at that age they understandably didn't have the psychological tools to deal with this unprecedented and intimidating situation. But it couldn't go on indefinitely. Shortly after this show, Cotton left the group in what Harkleroad has referred to as "ugly circumstances".[12] French had already disppeared back to Lancaster on a couple of occasions during the rehearsals for *Trout Mask*, but had always returned. Now he made his departure. The whole experience had been too much and when Van Vliet physically threw him out of the house, it was one fight too many. His input into *Trout Mask* had been crucial, but as he had the temerity to leave, he received some shoddy treatment. Not only was he denied the arrangement credits to which he felt entitled, but his name was also left off the album sleeve. Van Vliet felt snubbed by his defection, but later brushed off the subject, denying that he had requested French's name to be removed. The issue was finally resolved when the album was reissued on CD with French's name – Drumbo, actually – at last included on the insert. French has since strengthened his side of the story via his solo drum album, *O Solo Drumbo*, released in 1998. He plays and expands on drum tracks such as 'Steal Softly Thru Snow' and 'Hair Pie', for which he claims compositional credit.

During Zappa's brief spell as their "road manager", the Magic Band went to Belgium to play at the Amougies Festival in October. Zappa had been invited to be MC at a large outdoor rock festival in France but, due to problems with the authorities, the organisers decamped the whole event at short notice to a cow pasture, complete with turnips, in Amougies,

Belgium. The extensive bill featured some high-calibre groups, including Soft Machine, Pink Floyd and The Art Ensemble of Chicago, but the facilities were grim. Zappa recalled that the fifteen thousand punters "basically froze and slept through the entire festival, which went on 24 hours a day around the clock".[13] Zappa spoke no French and few people spoke English, so his function was rather limited. When he could borrow a guitar, he occupied himself by sitting in with a few of the groups.

With French gone, Jeff Burchell, a roadie with virtually no drum experience, learned five songs and just about got through them. The line-up included another rare appearance by Hayden, with Zappa standing in on guitar in place of the departed Cotton.

The following month Van Vliet and Zappa visited London, staging a press conference at the Whitehouse Hotel to promote their activities on Bizarre and Straight, and hopefully landing a UK distributor for the labels. During the press conference, Van Vliet had this to say on the festival: "I don't know what they were doing... they were throwing what looked like bird's nests at us, and then one fellow out of the audience – between one of the compositions – said my name was Captain Bullshit, and I said, 'Well, that's all right, baby, you're sitting in it'. You know what I mean? But it was awfully cold – 20 degrees – the people in the audience... I don't know how they did it. I think it was probably nice for them to leave their bodies... but the amplifiers were blown out by the time we got to them, and we need clarity for that, and there wasn't any. I hope they enjoyed it. I enjoyed it."[14]

Roger Eagle, a UK concert promoter and DJ, met Van Vliet and Zappa for the first time on their London visit. He told John Crumpton in 1995: "There were all kinds of people from the record company there but Don was sitting on his own, nobody was talking to him. Photographers were asking him to put his top hat on, take his top hat off and stand in front of a display stand with album covers on it. I sat down between Zappa and Beefheart and Zappa was coming on like an adding machine. He was talking about everything in business terms and Beefheart just seemed like a very warm human being who seemed to be thinking, 'Oh, my God, I'm surrounded by all these people, I haven't got a clue what I'm doing here, I suppose I should be here.'"[15]

Among the many strange stories associated with the recording of *Trout Mask Replica*, two of the most notorious are actually true. Van Vliet apparently asked for a tree surgeon to come round to the house to check the trees, as he felt that the music the group were producing in rehearsals might frighten or damage them and the one nearest the kitchen might fall on the house. This incident did actually take place. After being astonished to receive a list of expenses including $800 for a tree surgeon, Herb Cohen talked the matter over with Van Vliet. "I felt it was a bit extraneous as an expense – but I'll be goddamned if I didn't get another bill for $240 which I *paid*," he told Michael Gray.[16] A decade later, Van Vliet checked up on them again. He told Co De Kloet in 1993: "When I went down to see the exhibit I had in Los Angeles [in '89 or '90], I went by and saw those trees. They're still living. A male and a female eucalyptus. They're still getting bigger. I'm glad that I helped out."[17] The trees were planted when the area was first developed in the late twenties. Both have since died.

Then there was the tale of the sleigh bells he ordered for the recording (which are featured on 'Hobo Chang Ba'), twenty sets in total. Cohen noticed a record of the order and questioned why he needed so many as even if he, the group, Zappa and Kunc all played two sets there would be six sets left over. His answer came back that they would overdub them. Cohen: "I got him 20 sets of sleigh bells. I couldn't argue with that logic."[18]

Van Vliet's story-telling harks back to the tradition of the American con man; the tall-tale teller, the snake-oil salesman, the kind of guy who would sell you a remedy at a Medicine Show, then next time he was in town would convince you it had worked. Michael Smotherman played briefly with the Magic Band in 1974, but long enough to see similarities with another famous American: "WC Fields. That's who he reminded me of a whole lot – irascible and putting the whole world on, and having a laugh up his sleeve about it."

This icing on the Captain Beefheart cake was addictive, and as the media were hungry for amazing stories and far-out happenings, he was only too willing to serve up a slice or two. These tales would circulate and often end up even more fantastically embroidered. He enjoyed changing details of a story to make it more interesting, and self-mythologising was something he took to brilliantly. It was provocative, entertaining and had the desired effect of drawing people to his work.

The true story of *Trout Mask* was astonishing enough, but although near-starvation had long been associated with artistic endeavour, first fights, tyranny and "brainwashing" sessions weren't such attractive selling points to the Woodstock generation. All that was kept under wraps and over time Van Vliet has been instead quoted, or paraphrased, as saying that

115

the Magic Band worked by telepathy; or that Boston had only been playing bass for six months, and Harkleroad the guitar for seven months on joining; or that he had written all the music in eight and a half hours at the piano with variously named persons (French or Hayden) frantically transcribing his fevered outpourings; or that they regularly rehearsed for twenty hours a day; or that he had not left the Ensenada Drive house for over three years.

Outside the claustrophobic mental assault course of life at the house, Van Vliet was generous in his praise of the musicians. But he was also unequivocal in taking credit for both writing and arranging all of the music. And the myth was certainly helped by his disingenuous portrayal of the musicians as *idiot savant* types who had never played before and whom he had taught from scratch. But in effect he did teach them from scratch. Certainly none of them would have come up with anything like *Trout Mask Replica* on their own. When he was over in London for press duties with Zappa, Van Vliet was asked by *Zig Zag* if the group were involved in music before the Magic Band. He made the point: "They were always involved, but now they're playing."[19] And later to Elliot Wald from *Oui* he said: "The musicians worked so hard on it. They were born on that album."[20]

Conversely, Van Vliet could never have made it without their commitment. He was almost always the sole interviewee and his typical claims had the dual effect of reiterating his total control via the media and sowing the seeds of resentment within the group.

As years went by Van Vliet coloured the picture more vividly. In 1972, he told *Sounds'* Caroline Boucher: "One guitarist that I had made bird noises. He walked into the bush at full moon and ate bread. I thought that was rather artistic. Sometimes you couldn't understand the bird noises too well but otherwise he was pretty normal."[21]

Quotes like this helped reinforce the notion of Captain Beefheart, the shamanic Leader of the Pack, or the top-hatted ringmaster smiling benignly as he presided over the far-out goings-on in his artistic Shangri-La. But apparently ridiculous reports reproduced in the press, like that of a group member wearing a dress (making Cotton the prime suspect) being spotted wandering off with a dazed expression in search of food, had their basis in reality. One time, driven by hunger, the conspicuously dressed group went on a shoplifting spree, were arrested and had to be bailed out by Zappa.

That the Magic Band had originated in 'the desert' was unremarkable to people in the US, but for European journalists unfamiliar with the geography of California, the word conjured up all manner of romantic notions of strange desert men. Woodland Hills is one of the myriad suburbs of Los Angeles, but that didn't stop Phil McNeill writing this in the *New Musical Express* in 1976: "The only people who could play like he wanted must be primarily *non*-musicians. Musicians were too bound up with what they had learned. Accordingly, he gathered around him a core of artists, poets and freaks, and, like a wolf pack bringing up human babies to live and think like wolves, he took these guys to a house in the desert, virtually imprisoned them there and taught them from scratch."[22]

Rewinding to the supposed freaks' playground at the house, Van Vliet's assertion to Fulton that he wanted to record a blues album because "Blue feeling, blue is the colour of peace"[23] is, with hindsight, steeped in irony. After the album had been recorded, the group's hermetically sealed pressure-cooker lifestyle had taken its toll and the uneasy social structure began to fragment. Van Vliet explained Cotton's departure to *Zig Zag* thus: "Antennae Jimmy Semens went back to the desert... I don't know why, and I can't ask why. He got into a little fight with Rockette Morton and broke his dentures but it all ended up all right. It was just a natural reaction I suppose... if there is a natural reaction... but for some reason or other, he's happier out of the group."[24] This was a shocking revelation, not least to Boston himself, as it was, in fact, Van Vliet who had punched him and then had to pay for him to go to a dentist and have new dentures made.

The 'ugly' circumstances of Cotton's departure were even uglier. One night Cotton got into an altercation with Burchell, who beat him up so brutally that he suffered broken ribs and was taken to hospital. This was a genuinely strange period for all concerned and the rumours to which it gave rise were even weirder. Then, as now, it was difficult for those who were associated with the group to figure out what was going on. Some were saying that Van Vliet was behind this incident but with hindsight, Aldridge cannot believe this: "I must say that I have seen Don angry, but never violent. It's a stretch for me to believe today that he orchestrated a beating. The one time I ever saw anything remotely physical on Don's part was the day he locked Grannie Annie in the closet. He was joking, but it was definitely in poor taste."

Looking back in 1996, Merrell Fankhauser, Cotton's friend and former band mate in The Exiles, gave an account that is darker and more fantastic than any of the press material that circulated in the sixties and seventies. After Fankhauser's group H.M.S. Bounty had disbanded, he moved into the area and was invited to all-night jam sessions at the group's house. He told *Goldmine*: "People in their neighbourhood were scared of Van Vliet and his band because they all looked so strange, with beards and long hair, and were all pale because they hadn't seen the sun in a year. The house would be dimly lit at night with all this weird music coming out of it and there were all these trees with moss hanging on them. It was a spooky scene."[25]

One night Cotton admitted to Fankhauser that the atmosphere at the house was worsening and the intra-group friction was so bad that he'd had enough. He wanted to leave and get back with Fankhauser and play guitar in a more relaxed environment. This was not to be as easy as he thought. Van Vliet was unhappy about losing Cotton and Fankhauser alleges that he was physically restrained from leaving the house, even dosed with LSD. The increasingly troubled Cotton would disappear now and again. Fankhauser was suspected of harbouring the fugitive and so Van Vliet's car would pull up outside his house in the middle of the night, and group members would attempt to search it to try to find the missing guitarist.

After being beaten up, Cotton, according to Fankhauser, "somehow ended up in the Olive View mental hospital". After several weeks under sedation, his parents took him back to Lancaster and visits from the Magic Band met with stern rebuffs. Cotton got back into shape and started gigging with Fankhauser as part of MU, but six months later they were invited back to the house for a social evening.

"Don had this strange look in his eye," Fankhauser recalled, "and they locked all the doors in the place. Don gets Jeff and I to go with him into this large bathroom they called the Magic Bathroom." Once inside, the door was locked and Van Vliet "started to demoralise Jeff, saying all this negative stuff about him. I felt like I was dealing for Jeff's soul, because all of a sudden Jeff turned to putty and was agreeing with Don, saying, 'Yeah, maybe I should go back with Don.' It seemed like Don was trying to hypnotise us both. Jeff started crying and fell into the bathtub and slumped into a fetal position.

"Then Don brings out this little cage that had all these spiders in it, including a black widow. Then he says, 'What would you think if I could make one of these spiders smoke a cigarette?' He pulled his beard and said, 'Wouldn't that be heavy, ha ha ha?' So I kept having this weird conversation with Don and eventually he got tired, opened the door and I grabbed Jeff and we walked out of that house and that was it. They never bothered us again and we went on with our new band."[26]

Some people feel that walls store an impression of events that have taken place within their boundaries. It's a shame they can't be checked to verify the above-mentioned events. But Captain Beefheart & His Magic Band did leave behind a more tangible reminder of their occupation of the Ensenada Drive house. Lynn Aronspeer: "There were paintings all over the woodwork − mainly black grease pencil, little drawings. It was like an artistic whim would strike them and, wherever they were, they would just write on whatever surface was available."

8

COUNTING THE PASSING CARS

Meatball Fulton: *"How do you feel about it?"*
Don Van Vliet: *"What, Trout Mask Replica? Good. I feel real good about it."*
Reprise promotional record, 1969

"I was in love with a female mandrill before I met my wife... very high style with a rainbow across the nose. Beautiful."
Don Van Vliet to Vivien Goldman, *Sounds*, 22 November 1975

"It's convenient to say something's a masterpiece, so that the next thing that comes along isn't."
Don Van Vliet on *Trout Mask Replica*, amateur video, 1983

In early December 1969, *Trout Mask Replica* peaked in the UK album chart at number 21, but failed to chart in the US. It was followed in March 1970 by Zappa's *Hot Rats*, which sneaked into the UK Top 10, although it only reached a lowly 173 in the US. Superficially, things were going well for the Bizarre and Straight labels, but beneath the surface, the tension between Van Vliet and Zappa was becoming acute.

Van Vliet became openly hostile towards Zappa. He was convinced that his *meisterwerk* was not being taken seriously and that he was being promoted as a 'freak'. This was prompted by the release, shortly after *Hot Rats*, of the Bizarre/Straight compilation album *Zappéd*, a sampler of Captain Beefheart & His Magic Band and their labelmates. 'The Blimp' and 'Old Fart At Play' were included from *Trout Mask* and Van Vliet also features on Zappa's 'Willie The Pimp'. These tracks sit alongside cuts by The GTOs (the group even recorded a tribute to him, or more specifically his expensive taste in footwear, on their song 'The Captain's Fat Theresa's

Shoes'), the unhinged a cappella singer Wild Man Fischer, raconteur Lord Buckley and Alice Cooper – to whom Van Vliet was antipathetic to say the least. Cooper's alleged cruelty to animals onstage, although hyped up, annoyed him so much he warned Cooper, via the press, that if they met again he'd spank his ass.

Despite the distinct likelihood that no one but Zappa would have facilitated the recording of *Trout Mask Replica*, Van Vliet felt that he was in danger of being perceived as some sort of weird novelty act and he was the man to blame. He later said that he was promised a release on Straight rather than Bizarre and Zappa had put him on Bizarre on purpose. (In fact the album *was* released on Straight.) And then there was the group's visual image, which was extreme even for the time. He had been its principal designer, and realised how easily Captain Beefheart & His Magic Band could now slip into what he saw as the Bizarre/Straight freak show. Derived from the hip vernacular of the late Sixties, the word 'freak' has now been assimilated to the extent that *Chambers Concise Dictionary* defines it as 'a weirdly unconventional person'. To be called a freak was a compliment of sorts because it showed everyone you were apart from the conformists, the 'straights'. But the epithet bothered Van Vliet greatly.

His resentment continued to grow over time. When asked by Steve Peacock in *Sounds* in 1972, if he liked the way *Trout Mask* had turned out, he replied: "No, because I don't think they had their distribution together, so they kept it away from all those people. And I thought there was a very important message of energy – to people, everywhere. I don't care about their age or their hairdos or whether they've paid their dues, or realise there's no point in it, that was an important message... and it was treated as some kind of freak show by Zappa and Cohen – all that Straight/Bizarre... Bizarre, what the fuck, man?"[1]

In that same year he had built up enough of a head of steam to make these vituperative comments to Nick Kent from *Frendz*: "Zappa is the most disgusting character I have ever encountered. Look what he did with Wild Man Fischer. He tried to exploit a man who was not a freak; the word 'freak' just doesn't exist as far as I'm concerned. I haven't seen any freaks – I've seen people who say they're deformed. I do not know what deformed is because I like art and form – that's all beautiful." Obviously there were exceptions to this positive outlook as, oblivious to any irony, Van Vliet continued: "Herbie Cohen, Zappa's manager, reminds me of a red marble in a can of lard, Zappa reminds me of a cataract."[2]

Barry Miles feels that Van Vliet's disowning of Zappa was designed to punish him for becoming so embroiled in the business side of the music industry that he himself disliked and didn't fully understand. Van Vliet also maintained that he had been taped by Zappa in conversation years before – something Zappa liked to do when visitors to his house or studio were coming up with interesting or bizarre ideas – and had effectively had his ideas (or phrases) stolen. These reappeared as Zappa/Mothers album and song titles. Examples he gave included "Hot Rats", "Uncle Meat", "Burnt Weeny Sandwich", "Lumpy Gravy", "Suzy Creamcheese, What's Got Into You?" and "Brown Shoes Don't Make It".

He was still indignantly reiterating this point some six years later. Zappa's role in the realisation of *Trout Mask* was subsequently played down. Van Vliet claimed that he had just gone to sleep at the mixing desk; that it was all above him; that Zappa liked to work but he liked to play, in a lengthy and relentless disparagement.

On the very rare occasions that Van Vliet was complimentary, it was usually in a backhanded way, like the following to David Reitmann in *Rock*: "I felt he would like to join the group because he's a very good guitar player and could have exuded himself in this group. Everybody does in this group. I thought maybe he would like to be Frank Zappa for a while without all those restrictions of success." Zappa was a friend, the same age, from the same area, and now 'in charge' of his musical outlet – it all reads like a surrogate sibling rivalry that had got out of hand. Don Aldridge offers these views: "I believe Frank's success had a great deal to do with everything Don did. In the end he may be greater than Frank, but I don't believe he ever knew it."

Away from all this animosity, Captain Beefheart & His Magic Band were becoming hot property, and the increasing press interest culminated in Van Vliet landing the coveted front cover of *Rolling Stone* in May 1970. Langdon Winner's cover story, entitled "I'm not even here, I just stick around for my friends", opens dramatically: "'Uh oh, the phone,' Captain Beefheart mumbled as he placed his tarnished soprano saxophone in its case. 'I have to answer the telephone.' It was a very peculiar thing to say. The phone had not rung.

"Beefheart walked quickly from his place by the upright piano across the dimly lit living room to the cushion where the telephone lay. He waited. After ten seconds of stony silence it finally rang. None of the half-dozen or so persons in the room seemed at all astounded by what had just happened."[4] This was the first of many accounts of Van Vliet's special ability: telepathic, psychic or deeply intuitive, depending on your semantic preference. Those within Van Vliet's circle were blasé about such incidents, but they came as a shock to newcomers.

Along with his increasing fame, Van Vliet was becoming acutely wary of everybody. Although this is a useful character trait for anyone fighting their corner within the music business, in Van Vliet's case wariness often developed into hypersensitivity, even paranoia. "A little paranoia is a good propeller," he claimed many years later, obliquely acknowledging that it was inextricably linked with his creative drive. Winner wrote an eloquent and thoughtful appraisal of his work, but at one point during the preparation of the article, he claims that Van Vliet suddenly decided he was "public enemy No. 1". As well as being a good propeller, his paranoia would steer him into needless adversarial relationships with his allies.

With Zappa now officially his *bête noire*, he became suspicious of his deal with Straight. But although the label was experiencing money problems, it was gradually being osmosed into Warners/Reprise, which had by this time taken over distribution. Captain Beefheart & His Magic Band also had a new manager, Grant Gibbs, who had set about trying to resolve the contractual complexities that had already built up.

Despite the rift between the respective bandleaders, there followed the first of a throughput of musicians from The Mothers of Invention to the Magic Band. An unlikely and temporary replacement for Cotton came in the shape of prodigiously talented multi-instrumentalist Ian Underwood, who had played horns and keyboards with Zappa since 1967 and had most recently featured on *Hot Rats*. One instrument he was not known for, however, was the guitar. He managed to learn some of the parts, but the task soon proved too much. A keyboard player, Tom Grasso, rehearsed for a short while with the group, but he was an outspoken character and soon clashed with Van Vliet.

The drum stool was taken over by Art Tripp, whom Harkleroad first met at the jam sessions round at Zappa's house. Tripp had played with Zappa on and off since 1967, and had last featured on The Mothers of Invention's *Weasels Ripped My Flesh*. Tripp specialised in percussion at the Cincinatti Conservatory, where he had studied under John Cage. Looking back on his work with Zappa, Tripp said, "For years Frank had had lots of percussion ideas that no one could play, and obviously from my background it was comparatively simple."[5] But less than a year after joining the Magic Band, he was already dismissing Zappa's music as "formal crap".

He told Nick Kent: "All that stuff with Zappa was hard work. This band is like total liberation. Work doesn't come into it at all. We've been released."[6]

Harkleroad was now the musical director, which necessitated the arduous task of listening through tapes of whistling and piano and arranging the parts. He used his own form of notation. "I did more tablature, physical shapes to remember things," he says. "I knew every note every person was playing and I personally taught everyone every note they were playing other than their solo things." As with *Trout Mask*, some of the more unplayable elements and knuckle-busting guitar chords were modified in rehearsal, but Van Vliet reserved the right to make the final sculpting.

Most of the hard graft was left to the group members, although Van Vliet worked on parts and tried out some vocal arrangements with them. In his view, music was dishonest, in that it was like a training programme, and he refused to train himself. He needed to be spontaneous and enjoyed playing rather than working as he didn't have the powers of concentration, or the inclination, to do the latter.

The group had moved out of the anthropological-experiment environment of the Ensenada Drive house and went their separate ways (with the exception of Boston, who stayed there for a while with Van Vliet's ex, Laurie Stone, with whom he had started a relationship). This dissipated some of the tension and spirits were higher, although the same could not be said of the group's income. Meanwhile, Van Vliet had been involved in an archetypal whirlwind romance with Jan Jenkins, a young student in her first year of college. They married weeks later in November 1969. She had been curious about Captain Beefheart as her former boyfriend was a fan, but when they met at a party in the fall of 1969 it was love at first sight. Two days later she had moved in with Van Vliet. An intelligent, well-read, artistically minded 17-year-old, her father was a principal at a public school and her mother a housewife. Both parents were distraught that their talented and attractive daughter had, apparently on a whim, taken up with someone as unorthodox as Van Vliet, whom they had never even met, and who was 12 years her senior. But Jan had immediately got a handle on Van Vliet's Captain Beefheart persona and, more importantly, fell in love with Don. She professed that he was "cute" and although some friends might have questioned her use of the adjective, it was obvious they were right for one another. The wedding took place at a brief ceremony at the Los Angeles County Courthouse, with Harkleroad as best man. From then on they were inseparable.

Shortly before they started recording the new album, *Lick My Decals Off, Baby*, John French was persuaded to rejoin the Magic Band. Van Vliet was hoping to get the group to make some money, and claimed he wanted to make things up to him and that it would be different this time. Art Tripp had found the drum parts a little too far removed from what he was used to, and lacked French's obsessional focus. French, meanwhile, was simply told to use parts he had played on *Trout Mask*, as Van Vliet thought it was a style people could now relate to. French commented on the dual drums arrangement in 1996: "He [Tripp] was really good at fine buzz rolls and things like that, the intricate needlework. I was good at clubbing the drums to death over these weird rhythms that no one else wanted to take the time to play."[7]

Fortunately, Tripp's considerable skills were deployed in another area. As well as adding drum and percussion ornamentations, he was moved to marimba, hence his new name, Ed Marimba. At the time, marimba in a rock band was unheard of. Van Vliet himself had played bass marimba on 'Dropout Boogie' from *Safe As Milk*, but its presence was nigh on subliminal. Tripp integrated its sweet, chunky textures into the group's sound to stunning effect.

The album was recorded in the summer of 1970 at United Recording Corp., Sunset Boulevard, Hollywood. The job was done quickly, although without the benefit of the superhuman six-month rehearsal regime this time, they needed a number of takes to get the definitive version of each song.

In an apparently trivial semantic shift – but one that would assume greater importance later on – the group was now called Captain Beefheart & *The* Magic Band. The design of the album cover was inspired by the place where the group had been rehearsing. Underneath the florid title lettering, the group are photographed dressed in tuxedos. A be-monocled Art Tripp descends the staircase; Boston leans jauntily on a cane, his features distorted by make-up; Harkleroad stands arms folded; and French and Van Vliet are holding glasses as if in a post-prandial brandy and cigars session. The set looks like the staircase of a stately home, with balustrades, a candelabra and an Italianate vase full of flowers. The figures within this tableau have the air of an internationally renowned string quartet rather than a penniless avant-rock group.

Harkleroad revealed what was going on to Connor McKnight of *Zig Zag* in 1973: "That's the Warner Bros sound stage… a set from a movie called *Hotel* – that's where we rehearsed. We sometimes went and played on the set of [TV show] *Bonanza* too, and Mark would run around wearing huge teeth… it was crazy. All the chairs were special ones which were designed to break into pieces when you hit someone over the head with them… so every time you wanted to sit down, the chances were that the chair collapsed."[8]

The back cover features a Van Vliet painting and a poem, 'Lick My Decals Off, Baby', although it is different from the lyrics of the album's title track. Interestingly, Bob Krasnow's name crops up on the 'thanks to' list. Other dedicatees include benefactors Margaret Harkleroad, Sue Vliet and Grannie Annie in particular, and The Whales in general.

After *Trout Mask Replica*, Dick Kunc, who had struck up a friendship with Van Vliet, was told that he was going to engineer the next album no matter what. When Zappa disbanded the original Mothers Of Invention, Kunc was also dismissed from the set-up and moved to New York. But he was soon back on the scene, albeit briefly. He takes up the story: "When *Decals* came around, Don called and hired me to fly out and do the engineering. When I arrived, I lived in the band's house, where we rehearsed prior to the sessions. Herbie Cohen, who controlled the purse strings, made it very clear to me that I was to make sure Don wasted as little studio time as possible. Now I was caught in the middle. Herbie was signing my cheque, and I was going to be held accountable.

"During one of the first sessions, after Don had spent hours fooling with some microphone effect he wanted, I gently – and I mean gently – suggested that we 'move along', or something like that. Don detonated, accusing me of trying to tell him what to do and take control of the project, or whatever. At the end of his totally unexpected tirade he said, 'You're fired!' This was the guy with whom I'd been close friends for many months before this. The band just looked at each other, but no one said a word. That was typical. I collected my money and hit the road. To this day I don't really know what that was all about, but it was the last contact of any kind I ever had with Don."

Phil Schier was drafted in as a replacement, while Van Vliet produced. They didn't do a very good job, managing to flatten out the group's thunderous power. On some of the *Trout Mask* tracks the drums were damped with cardboard; here they sound as if they were made of cardboard. It's unusual to get two percussionists of the quality of French and Tripp in the same group, and the production does their formidable playing a disservice.

Harkleroad: "I don't know if Phil Schier was a real educated engineer at that level. Don was totally in control but he didn't have enough studio knowledge and he was probably using elliptical terms. When you tell them it's got to sound like a 'blue baby's butt', what does that mean to anybody? So I think a lot was lost in translation. I don't think that it was intended to sound so puny."

With Harkleroad now the sole guitarist, the group sound became more focused, and individual lines breathe more freely than in the mayhem of *Trout Mask Replica*. Boston's magnificent bass playing is pushed up to take a more prominent place in the sound field. The album rocks with an oblique ferocity that often transcends its illustrious predecessor. Harkleroad's guitar has a more distinctive sound, although in common with his approach to the material on *Trout Mask Replica* that was partly accidental: "I never spent much time worrying about the tone," he says. "Plug the thing in and play the shit! A tall skinny guy with a Telecaster. How could it get more trebly and thin and weird anyway? It just grew that way."

The songs are more direct, although paradoxically some of the musical structures are even more extreme than before. The only song that was mixed down and not included on the album was 'Well, Well, Well', a curious and rather ugly little pop song, featuring Boston's vocal début. He sounds bored out of his mind as he makes the assessment, "You don't taste so well."

The title track opens with busy drums, cowbells and percussion scrambling along in pursuit of the guitar and bass. In the skewed verse section, dropped beats and prehensile bass motifs frame the lyrics, which are as sexual as 'Neon Meate Dream Of A Octafish'. Van Vliet eschews romantic niceties and makes a sly reference to The Beatles' 'I Want To Hold Your Hand', with tongue-in-cheek – and in other fleshy places, no doubt. He's looking for more licentious pleasures. "I wanna lick you everywhere that's pink," he enthusiastically proclaims. He later claimed the album's title had nothing to do with sex, but rather with the gaining of freedom via the removal of labels. But here he has lost his mind in a sexual delirium. He comes back round for long enough to warn us not to lose these self-same impulses, explaining that the song is about the birds and the bees "and where it all went wrong".

Despite fierce competition, 'Doctor Dark' is arguably Van Vliet's most remarkable composition. The introductory section finds the group playing their lines in a finely choreographed shambles. A common rhythm is hinted at, and for a few precious heart-stopping seconds the song stands on the brink of disintegration before the threads are pulled tight and the musicians snap into a rolling, tumbling groove. Van Vliet bellows out a warning as the daemonic figure of Doctor Dark gallops in on horseback, the "hooves makin' sparks".

Then comes what Fred Frith described in *New Musical Express* in 1974 as a "unison passage plucked out of nowhere".[9] It sounds like alien currents have suddenly swept in, knocking the musical convoy off course. As on many of the *Trout Mask* tracks, Van Vliet's massive high-in-the-mix voice races away, pulling against the music so strongly it further distorts its pattern of musical shapes. When one listens to the vocals-less dubs from the original master and picks over the bones at leisure, that passage sounds only slightly less magical. As *Trout Mask* refuses to be demystified, so closer scrutiny of the *Decals* material reveals hitherto unnoticed instrumental intricacies and correspondences, especially in the way Boston's bass guitar obliquely relates to all around it. His playing throughout the album is literally peerless, as no one else was even attempting these sorts of lines. After a unison guitar and hi-hat interlude played over flailing drums and bass, the track saunters to a close, with Van Vliet's soulful voice sounding uncannily like Van Morrison *circa Astral Weeks*.

The two guitar instrumentals on *Decals* share common ground with the succinct 'Dali's Car', but substitute that track's harshness with a new-found lyricism. Harkleroad recalls Van Vliet being excited at the way 'Peon' became transmuted into a guitar piece from his initial piano recordings. The guitar and bass are locked in unison throughout, even though the timing is strange and hesitant. It sounds like one player is playing the two instruments with four hands. The end result is an exquisite guitar and bass vignette, quite unlike any recognised guitar style. In his *Melody Maker* review of the album, Richard Williams tentatively deduced a method that eluded many journalists. He wrote that "the guitar and bass play together so perfectly that I can't believe the piece wasn't written out. If it wasn't, there's an umbilical between the musicians' brains."[10]

'One Red Rose That I Mean' was originally conceived as a similar duet but ended up as a solo guitar showcase for Harkleroad. Again interpreted from a piano tape, it marks the apogee of the composer's liaison with the guitarist. The piece is both angular and reflective, running through a number of lyrical motifs and into a brief flamenco-like passage before the close.

Like its predecessor, *Lick My Decals Off, Baby* has its moments of comparatively orthodox rock. 'I Love You, You Big Dummy' is dominated by Van Vliet's wheezing harmonica and a simple vocal line based around the title, which consists of him leering, cajoling and laughing, while the Magic Band play some angular figures before sliding into a mutant boogie. 'Woe-Is-Uh-Me-Bop' hinges around a simple chord sequence with Van Vliet's voice even more massive than usual as he chants a four-line mantra based on the rock'n'roll parody of the title. Instrumentally, it comes across as a fractured R&B tune, with Art Tripp's marimba dancing against the guitar beautifully.

The ecological messages of *Trout Mask* take on a renewed urgency here. A feeling of impending doom runs through the brief 'Petrified Forest', a furious, astringent composition with the guitars locking horns, circled warily by the marimba. Here the human race is compared to the dinosaurs and looks to be heading for the same fate. Dinosaurs are also used here as a metaphor for species that have been driven to extinction by human beings. The law of the jungle is swinging back and the "Breathe deep, breathe high" exhortations of 'I Love You, You Big Dummy' have become apocalyptic portents. Life is being breathed back into the dinosaurs, who return bent on revenge and destruction. Petroleum is the fossilised remains of these ancient creatures and their environment, and its usage brings pollution. Van Vliet longs to breathe healthily, heartily, but is aware he inhabits a world on the brink of ecological disaster.

'You Should Know By The Kindness Of Uh Dog The Way Uh Human Should Be' is included on the lyric sheet but was never recorded, though the text was occasionally recited in concert. With such a title it's no surprise that Van Vliet is here praising nature at the expense of the oppressive human "fatman", rating the snake's diamonds over any jewellery and appalled that the whale can be slaughtered to "oil some bitches lighter".

In 1971 Langdon Winner wrote a second major Captain Beefheart piece in *Rolling Stone* ('In Search of America: Captain Beefheart and the Smithsonian

Institute Blues'). He and Van Vliet are looking around the Smithsonian Institution, Washington D.C., which was, somewhat ironically, promoting an appreciation of wildlife through its stuffed exhibits: "At the next exhibit, 'Extinct Birds', Beefheart began to get angry. Dozens of feathered creatures were displayed in what had once been their native habitats. A sign next to each glass case told when the last specimen had been seen alive.

"'I can't believe it,' sighed Beefheart, peering in at the stuffed carrier pigeons. 'Look at that. It's paradise. Man had paradise and he blew it.'

"He repeated this idea several times and was reminded of the main purpose of his visit. 'We might as well go see how we're going to end up,' he groaned, and headed towards the dinosaur fossils."[11]

The obvious inspiration for Winner's trip to the museum with Van Vliet was 'The Smithsonian Institute Blues (Or The Big Dig)'. The themes of 'Petrified Forest' are reworked, but in a more humorous way, "dinosaur" being punned with the Fifties singer Dinah Shore. The scene is the La Brea tar pits, Los Angeles, where myriad prehistoric mammals (which actually lived millions of years after the dinosaurs, to be pedantic) like sabre-toothed tigers and mammoths got stuck in the lakes of naturally occurring bitumen, drowned, and were discovered remarkably well preserved by palaeontological excavations early last century. Interviewed in 1980, Van Vliet recalled being taken to La Brea (now within Hancock Park) by his parents as a child: "I'm told they brought me down here and as soon as the car door opened I ran out to go down and see an actual dinosaur. I wanted to see one and I tried to actually go in there."[12]

Word associations tumble over each other in 'The Clouds Are Full Of Wine (Not Whiskey Or Rye)', and the rushed vocal melody sounds as if it was grafted onto the convoluted instrumental track from another song entirely. A guitar, bass and marimba trio open the song with a minute or so of dazzling unison ensemble playing. The zigzagging, linear format is like the pattern of a line following coordinates on graph paper. So well drilled were Tripp and Harkleroad that they actually recorded this piece in different rooms, with Harkleroad able to see only Tripp's right elbow. Richard Williams may have been closer than he realised with his umbilical brain-connection theory.

'The Buggy Boogie Woogie' gently swings along like a fractured version of bar-room jazz, with unassuming guitar and bass seeking out strange corners to the song, and a rhythm track consisting of French and Art Tripp actually playing brooms, metaphorically cleaning those same corners. Van

Vliet's soft baritone erupts into a holler as he sings about a boarding-house lodging, a "two-dollar room", which he is cleaning up with a "two-dollar broom", disturbing a "Momma spider" and her nest in the process, ending up with a room full of baby spiders.

'Space Age Couple' finds Van Vliet's voice racing away over the group's galloping backing track, with a brief, elastic bass solo before the group dive in once more. This is an example of his enthusiasm for the group to play the songs faster and more intensely until it reached the point where he only just managed to cram in his words. The lyrics are a brilliant critique of early-Seventies post-hippie solipsism. Van Vliet's scurrilous and unpatriotic view on the moon landing, voiced in the Meatball Fulton interview, was no doubt at the back of his mind. The Space Age Couple, meanwhile, are an example of people cutting themselves off from nature. Van Vliet exhorts them to act through his relentless questioning: why don't they just flex their "magic muscle" and ditch their "cool tomfoolery" and their "nasty jewellery"? In another environmental warning, the couple are told to cultivate the ground. But time is running out and the crops are polluted with pesticides; the moisture on the leaves "ain't dew no more".

The convulsive music of 'I Wanna Find A Woman That'll Hold My Big Toe Till I Have To Go' plays host to one of Van Vliet's more light-hearted lyrics. His vocals race in on the tentative, tangled introduction as he runs at the world with delirious enthusiasm, shouting out an absurd romantic wish list which includes activities like serenading sweet potatoes with a gigantic blue-swirl plastic ocarina. The instrumental 'Japan In A Dishpan' finds his elliptical soprano sax spiralling over a group performance that wanders into new territories of unorthodoxy. The oblique non-rock drum patterns canter around the guitars with tangential tattoos and frantic open and shut hi-hat work.

Lester Bangs admitted that even he had difficulty with the "sonic hurricane"[13] of *Decals*, although he considered the album brilliant. On 'Flash Gordon's Ape', the hurricane hits town with a vengeance. Both the vocals and the band's playing are all but blown away by a double saxophone cacophony mixed so high, it sounds like the backing track is being played on a portable cassette player during feeding time in a monstrous aviary. Feathers fly as the occupants caw, squawk and call. Half-way through, a cursory, cascading marimba interlude gives brief respite before the mania renews itself. It's one of the few tracks in Van Vliet's canon where all but the most stoic listeners will find themselves pleased when they've had enough.

Without the vocals and sax, it sounds like a completely different piece of music, and a particularly intricate one too. The sax that was almost charmingly naive and capricious on 'Hair Pie: Bake 1' achieves blanket obliteration here.

Moris Tepper, Magic Band guitarist from 1975 to 1982, gives this assessment of Van Vliet's method, with specific reference to 'Japan In A Dishpan': "[The sax is] mixed too loud, always too much quantity. He wrote the music and then he hears the band do the track and it sounds amazing and he doesn't feel he's part of it. He feels, 'Oh, my God, I'm not on it.' He doesn't realise it's all him everywhere. That's how big that ego is. He wants to be there, not the band. That is the honest truth. I think he covered up a lot of great music, but at the same time watching him take out his big fire hose and spray was real boss!"

John French shared his views on Van Vliet's sax playing with Justin Sherrill in 1998: "His successful solos were 'trial and error' and though some of his sax and bass clarinet solos were extremely innovative (such as 'Wild Life'), he could never come close to reproducing anything he did, because he had no idea how he did it."[14]

It's difficult to compare Van Vliet's playing to that of any other saxophonist. Ornette Coleman's name has been brought up in this context, but he was completely in control of his playing. And comparisons with free-blowing sax colossi like Archie Shepp and John Coltrane are no more accurate than comparing his piano ramblings to Cecil Taylor. Van Vliet didn't call his saxophone his "breather apparatus" for nothing. When questioned by Connor McKnight on his views on Coltrane in 1973, he said: "Fish take care of the scales; as soon as I saw a fish, I realised that they had the scale department sewn up completely. I think I sound more like a whale or a dolphin than I do John Coltrane."[15]

As with his piano playing, Van Vliet experimented in that he tried things out, but there was no experimental game plan. He just curled his lips around the mouthpiece and blew. Consequently his saxophone style showed no development whatsoever during his career. It's difficult to intellectualise "going to the bathroom" after all. Perhaps he was being less than disingenuous when he told Lester Bangs nearly a decade later that although saxophonist Eric Dolphy was good, he didn't move him as much as a goose. "A gander goose could be a hero," he said, "the way they blow their heart out for nothing like that."[16]

At live shows from 1970 onwards, his alto sax took the spotlight on

'Spitball Scalped A Baby' and 'Earth Angel' (also the name of the song by The Penguins, which topped the R&B chart in 1954). These titles were ostensibly different names for similar sax and drums improvisations. The results were by nature variable, but a performance on September 18, 1970 at Pepperland, San Rafael, California, was utterly staggering. Van Vliet announced 'Earth Angel', dedicating it to Jimi Hendrix, who had died that morning. In a ritual exorcism of grief, he blew about three minutes of the most intense, scalp-raising saxophone imaginable – an untrammelled torrent of rage, agony and ecstatic joy.

On occasions like this, when he played way beyond himself, he could eclipse players who were technically far superior. But because of his lack of technique, his sax excursions often came over as incoherent and distracted. At the Bickershaw Festival in 1972, on 'Spitball Scalped A Baby', after a full-blooded start, he noodles along vaguely and might have continued to do so had someone not started tampering with the group's gear. Interrupted, Van Vliet remonstrates with them, then marks out his onstage territory with ferocious warning calls.

Although "going to the bathroom" is a primal act, at some times it can be more difficult than at others. In 1977, Van Vliet gave the best summary of his playing style to John Orme in *Melody Maker*: "The first time I came to England I played at the Middle Earth [1968]. I played my horn for two and a half hours and it was the first time I had played it on stage. I just could not stop. I did not know where the notes were or anything and I'm proud to say I still do not.

"I produce sounds that other players do not get. I get sounds out of myself as opposed to getting them from a formal scheme of playing. I have never yet heard people play the horn like me. Do other people like it? Well, they didn't complain at the Middle Earth. For me it is an escape valve, another paint-brush.

"I am always looking for new mouthpieces for my horn. I have just got one that is really big, so big I can almost feel my tongue coming out of the bell of the horn. I am really looking forward to coming over to England and blowing my paint at everyone from my horn."[17]

The Ornette Coleman comparisons are interesting in that there is some coincidental overlap between the music of the Magic Band and Coleman's ensembles. On *Free Jazz*, the album which had blown Van Vliet's mind years before, Coleman used a double improvising quartet with the musicians playing lines that were unencumbered by more traditional jazz chord structures. This gave a blurring effect, similar to that achieved by Van Vliet's overlay of musical lines on *Trout Mask Replica*, which he had hoped would stop the listener's mind from fixating. Coleman had refused to be held back by tonality or bar length and developed his ideas into the concept of harmolodics in the Seventies, which can be (rather sketchily) summarised as a method of improvising which attributes equal value to harmony, melody and rhythm. This echoes Harkleroad's assessment of the equality within the members of the *Trout Mask* group, in that they all played melodically and all played rhythmically. The important difference is that Coleman was an exploratory musical theorist, the antithesis of Van Vliet, the intuitive – although one unifying factor is that both were accused at points in their careers of not being able to play the saxophone.

Lick My Decals Off, Baby was credited as being "produced by Captain Beefheart for God's Golfball Productions". As well as being a tongue-in-cheek description of Planet Earth, it was the name Van Vliet had given to a mini corporation set up by himself, Gibbs, an attorney and an accountant. The group had signed a contract with God's Golfball and were in effect now signed to Van Vliet, who also owned the copyright on their new names. Far from being the basis of some new Magic Band commonwealth, Harkleroad was now charged by accountant Al Leifer for having his yearly accounts calculated, even though he had made virtually no money.

Reactions to the album were positive, with *Rolling Stone* running four separate reviews in the issue of December 1970. Ed Ward gave these views: "I had the rare good fortune to talk to the Captain recently about his music, and noted that I hadn't really understood *Trout Mask*. 'That's OK,' he said, 'just put it on and then go back to doing whatever it was you were doing, and it'll come to you.' Well, what I was doing was sweeping the floor, so I had my doubts, but I did it anyhow. Damned if it didn't push the broom. You ought to get *Lick My Decals Off, Baby* and see what it can do for you!" Mark Boston puts it this way: "A number of people tell me that they either hate it or love it first off. Or they might listen to it once or twice and about the third time they say, 'Wait a minute, let's hear that again', and then pretty soon it starts growing on you – like a mushroom, I guess."

Richard Williams in his *Melody Maker* review wrote: "Much of the playing consists of that odd, jerky out of sync style, with the lines weaving and crashing so right it can't be accidental, and it's too complex to be purely intuitive. I can't think of anything wrong with this album; it's got fine rock and roll, insane blowing and singing, and some of the most amazing lyrics (or perhaps I should say word-progressions) in the world."[18]

Writing in *New Musical Express*, Charlie Gillett was not so sure, opining that "Captain Beefheart has chosen to reach us through ugliness" (which, considering he was trying to break up the catatonic state, is fair comment), but that deep down he was "a corny old ballad-singing crooner", which reads as a journalistic escape route to avoid confronting the music head on. But although Gillett doesn't fully 'hear' the music, he perceptively points out: "He knows that most of us will turn him off, but hopes that the few who stay to listen will get more from him than do the millions who listen to (but don't hear maybe?) those big bold stars."[19] Looking back in 1986, John Ellis bemoaned the fact that *Trout* and *Decals* were commercially unsuccessful in America and were largely relegated to the status of "pot party novelty records".[20]

But enough people were listening and buying for *Decals*, released in January 1971, to reach number 20 in the UK album chart, one place higher than *Trout Mask Replica* had achieved. In a feature for *Circus* magazine published in May of that year, Ben Edmonds asserted that *Decals* "is easily his best work to date. A distillation and refinement of the *Trout Mask* approach, it is also showing exceptionally fine sales." Edmonds took the time to mention Van Vliet's painting and sculpture, and the still-elusive volumes of prose and poetry, which were apparently then set to be published. Van Vliet must have stockpiled a lot of material, as some of the lyrics from *Trout Mask* had been written years before – but then there was the alleged burning the previous year. He continued, "The success of Captain Beefheart the recording artist will undoubtedly pave the way for the recognition of Captain Beefheart the complete artist." Edmonds was obviously excited that Van Vliet's abandonment of standard rock form and tradition and replacement of it with the "process of discovery" were released on a major label. "His music, with its child-like spontaneity and free-form implications, is perhaps the most real now being produced on any front," he enthused.[21]

Van Vliet still views *Decals* as his best album and came up with the best recommendation on how to listen to the music a couple of weeks after his fiftieth birthday. To Lars Movin: "What the music is going at is complete absence. That's the way I did it. You can't think about that music. That music is moving so fast that if you think about it, it's like watching a train go by and counting the cars. It's better to hear it without the mind so active, because the mind is active naturally, and if you don't try and think about it, you get a lot more fish (*laughs*)."[22]

In my late teens I bought a second-hand copy of the double reissue of *Decals* and its successor, *The Spotlight Kid*. The latter was the most immediately satisfying in a blues-rock way. *Decals*, meanwhile, lay disturbingly in the other half of the gatefold cover and playing it jarred me as much as it did Charlie Gillet. At first it sounded like an oppressive jumble, but then came the moment when the clouds parted – I actually realised what the group were doing. Then I couldn't stop playing it. Still reeling from the shock of the new – which has never fully left me – I felt I had to spread the word.

Despite the lubriciousness of the title track, Van Vliet was still adamant that the album wasn't principally about sex. A couple of years later he reiterated that view to the Jeff Eymael from *Aloha*: "With *Lick My Decals Off, Baby* I wanted to tell everyone that they must throw away those labels which divide people into categories, lick those decals away like a mother licking a baby to life."[23]

A short commercial was made to promote *Lick My Decals Off, Baby*. It only received US distribution and so a few years later Van Vliet described it to Vivien Goldman in *Sounds*: "A minute long and it's adequate. I mean it says what I want to say. I'll tell you it's good. It only cost $1,400 to make."[24] Conceived by Van Vliet and shot by Larry Secrest and John Fizdale, the commercial is a mixture of the banal and the sinister in a pre-David Lynch kind of way, with very weird black and white footage, and the cheesiest possible voice-over by Fred May, an announcer from LA TV station Channel 13. A hand flicks a cigarette butt while 'Woe-Is-Uh-Me-Bop' plays. It hits the wall with a thud and the music cuts out, then restarts. Then another cigarette is flicked at the wall and so on.

There follows a series of black and white tableaux of Van Vliet pointing at his foot ("In full view, Captain Beefheart," says May), then Boston, his head wrapped in black cloth, shuffles across the screen manipulating an egg whisk, then Harkleroad, similarly masked, mimes playing guitar. The visual *pièce de résistance* is a shot at floor level where Van Vliet walks across the boards and upturns a paint tin with his shoe. The viscous white goo oozes out of the pot and moves towards the camera in a grotesque lava-like flow. "It's *Lick My Decals Off Baby*," May concludes unctuously.

Considering the limited resources available, it's a brilliant miniature. Warner Brothers were pleased with the result to the extent that they bought some advertising space in the *Los Angeles Free Press* to plug the dates that the commercial was going to be aired. But it also caused controversy. KTTV's manager Charles Young checked out what the fuss was about, with the result that his station banned the commercial. Young was reputed to have said, "I wouldn't even show that at a stag party."

But he told Warner Brothers' media buyer "I just don't like it. I think it's crude and don't want it on my air. Let's say I find the commercial unacceptable and let it go at that." When pressed for specific reasons, Young declared the album title was "obscene".[25]

KTTV pulling out had a domino effect on a number of other broadcasters and the National Association of Broadcasters stopped the commercial being shown on their member stations. Again the reason was that the album's title was giving them problems. The NAB reckoned that 'Lick My Decals Off, Baby' was a "take-off on a well-known phrase",[26] which therefore rendered it offensive to a family audience.

Ed Baruch, station manager of WCDA-TV, recognised the film's merits. He was happy that it was aired on his station and featured it twice on Barry Richards Show, *Turn On*. "It's a terrific bit of film and beautiful advertising. It's a stopper. Of course there's nothing obscene about it. It's just that it's pure Beefheart, black and white, and different from anything else on television. We'd be happy to run it every night here in Washington."[27]

Interviewed by Elaine Shepherd in 1995, Ry Cooder gave these views: "It was very funny. And they showed it a couple of times on local TV and got hate mail, got hate calls right away: 'Take that off, we hate that.' People just couldn't take it. Now you would think nothing of it, you would assume it was a commercial for toothpaste, but in those days nobody knew and people were scared. You know the guy had a vibe out there. You either loved it or hated it."[28]

The controversy pleased Warners as it gave their product more publicity. The commercial was ultimately accepted on its artistic content by the Museum of Modern Art in New York, who acquired it for their permanent collection.

Shortly after *Decals* was released, the group played a few dates in the US (they had been pencilled in to play the misleadingly titled Hollywood Music Festival in Newcastle-under-Lyme in England, but failed to appear). They started off at Pepperland in September 1970, playing almost exclusively *Decals* tracks. Matt Groening saw them at the Paramount Theater in his home town of Portland, Oregon.

"All 75 of the weirdest of the weirdos... showed up. There was one guy had a helmet on with a light bulb that went on and off, on his head, and everybody tried to dress weird. We went in, sat there, filled up the first three rows of the theatre and the lights dimmed and Ed Marimba came out, one of the drummers. And he stood there in this long cape and of course he looked weirder than any of us in the crowd. And he held out a little toy children's ray gun and he pulled the trigger and it went Vzzz... Vzzz... Vzzz... and he said, 'Raygun, Raygun' Vzzz... Vzzz... 'Ronnie Raygun'. Vzzz... Vzzz... And he went over and sat at the drum set and Drumbo came out on the other side of the stage and they did this big drum duet and then the whole band came out and completely blew us away."[29]

In late 1970, Elliot Ingber joined the group and was given the name Winged Eel Fingerling. Ingber was another ex-Mother, having played on their 1966 début *Freak Out!*. More recently he had been a member of The Fraternity Of Man, whose drummer, Richie Hayward, went on to join Little Feat. The group had released a couple of albums but were best known for their single 'Don't Bogart Me', which later featured on the soundtrack to *Easy Rider*. Ingber was a talented blues guitarist and with hindsight, his joining signalled the beginning of a change in musical direction away from more avant territory and back towards the blues.

In January 1971, the Magic Band embarked on a six-week tour, starting on Van Vliet's thirtieth birthday at the Eastowne Theater in Detroit. Warner Brothers swallowing up Straight seemed to be working out well, as the record company funded the tour to an estimated level of twenty thousand dollars. In an attractive if ironic billing, Ry Cooder was booked as the support act. Unfortunately Ingber decided to fly home two weeks into the tour, allegedly because he had difficulty finding organic food. But he was soon to return.

There was a general air of speculation in the music business as to whether Captain Beefheart & His Magic Band were going to be able to – in rock parlance – "cut it" live. The group were shrouded in mystery and they had only played about fifty gigs (apart from early local shows around Lancaster) since their inception. And these were usually on the West Coast. A few shows had recently been blown out when Van Vliet felt that he had been misled as to the terms of his appearance. It had been commented upon in certain quarters that the band were loath to travel east of the Rockies, but lack of finance had been the predominant factor in them working nearer home. The deal with Warners gave them more exposure and the tour found them making their New York début at Ungano's club in New York City in January.

At the beginning of the Seventies, rock music was still opening up and the more adventurous entrepreneurs within the industry were looking to tap new markets, lest they missed out on something. The potency of the group's image and music and their elusiveness helped create a powerful mystique. Now the demand was beginning to outweigh the supply, from both the burgeoning Captain Beefheart fan base and the curious-minded wanting to check out this phenomenon. They became a big draw, regularly attracting capacity audiences on the tour. Boston University was a sell-out, with fans queuing outside in the snow.

Not all of the venues were as prestigious, though. John French: "The booking agent booked us in like a Country Club in Florida, for all those folks who wore plaid trousers and golf shoes and caps in their 50s, 60s – retirees. And here's Captain Beefheart & His Magic Band playing in a Country Club. I mean ten seconds, they were just gone. So that was kind of interesting. I don't think the booking agent had a clue as to what was going on."[30]

Although the ageing country club audience found the Magic Band's "sonic hurricane" too much, the live performance was always leavened with humour, with French and Tripp adding a pat-a-cake routine to their dual drum solo.

Van Vliet seemed in a relaxed mood at the start of a campaign which promised to win over a significant chunk of American youth. The music may have been extremely *outré*, but in concert it was well drilled and powerful. In a move that would become a staple of Van Vliet's live shows for years to come, Boston came out for a solo rendering of the bass guitar line to 'Hair Pie' from *Trout Mask*. And after the set finished, Van Vliet obliged the crowds' calls for more by coming back and whistling the song 'More' from the film *Mondo Cane*, that had been popularised by Perry Como in the Fifties.

In the spring, towards the end of the US tour, the Magic Band made a couple of TV appearances, on *Turn On*, and broadcast on a Detroit programme, *Tubeworks*. The programme featured the group performing 'When Big Joan Sets Up', 'Bellerin' Plain' and 'Woe-Is-Uh-Me-Bop', with links from 'Flash Gordon's Ape' and 'Hair Pie'. Van Vliet, looking rather well fed, manages to delay the entrance of the vocals on 'Bellerin' Plain' and is out of sync for the rest of the song, looking quizzically at some kind of cueing device. The musicians just carry on playing, as accommodating a missed cue would have been impossible. The rest of his performance was excellent, particularly 'Big Joan', on which Tripp's marimba adds a wonderful new colour. So as not to clash with the timbres of Tripp's drums, French had a couple of giant congas mounted on the bass drum rather than standard tom-toms. Odd one out is Ingber, who hangs around in the background, not doing much but nonetheless looking cool in his shades and vast expanse of hair.

The programme is brought to a bizarre end by a collective 'interview', where they all sit barefoot at a table in complete silence. The only action came from the camera panning across the group members, cut with shots of their wiggling toes. Just a typically surreal way for the Magic Band to approach an interview – or so it seemed. In fact the intra-band atmosphere was particularly tense and, fearing that someone might speak out of turn, Van Vliet decided that no one would speak at all.

9

APHORISMS, EPIGRAMS AND LUGUBRIOUS BLUES

"I could have made it many times, but I had to make my creative contribution, you know?"
Don Van Vliet to Patrick Carr, *Crawdaddy*, 19 March 1972

"I hate that album. It sucks."
Bill Harkleroad on *The Spotlight Kid*, Hi-Fi Mundo, 1998

At the turn of the decade, Van Vliet looked set to realise his ambition of success on his own terms: he was playing his uncompromising music to full houses and becoming a bona fide rock star in the process. *Decals* was, and still is, the most avantgarde album to enter the UK Top 20. And his admiration for the giants of the jazz world was beginning to be reciprocated.

Ornette Coleman came to see the Magic Band in action, was impressed enough to refer affectionately to Mark Boston as 'Superman', and was interested in getting Art Tripp to come and do some recording. In 1998, Harkleroad recalled meeting Coleman and listening to him playing "some old blues licks on the horn" and that later, "him and Don became big-time friends".[1] Van Vliet revealed to Caroline Boucher in *Disc and Music Echo* in 1972 that one of the reasons he disliked the perceived "freak tag" (a label he was slapping on himself far more than anyone else was) was because he wanted to tour with Coleman, whom he reckoned was "a great painter with that horn".[2] But he also admitted that neither of them needed such a venture. On a similar tack, he told Patrick Carr of *Crawdaddy*, "I'm not trying to put my name beside Ornette Coleman, because you can't put your name beside Ornette Coleman."[3]

One of Van Vliet's favourite proclamations – which had already baffled some interviewers – was that his music was "music without a lullaby". He had tried this idea out on Coleman. To Caroline Boucher: "The first thing I said to him was, 'Do you like lullabys [*sic*]' and he said, 'No, I don't like them, they're dangerous.' And that was it. Lullabys are dangerous, you know."[4]

In *Coast FM & Fine Arts* magazine, Van Vliet expanded on this idea, getting unusually tied up in his own word plays in the process: "I'm tired of lullabyes [*sic*], like The Beatles. I heard 'Lullaby of Broadway' when I was a baby, and I still hear it now, and I'm still a baby. We're the only people doing anything significant in modern music. I haven't heard anything else that gets away from mother's heartbeat. All I've heard is a rebelling against parents, and I'm tired of hearing that.

"I hope that people who come to see me come in without any attitude, or latitude, or longitude, or altitude… There's no competition with our music. It can't be compared or impaired, or impaled with point or justifications… It means absolutely nothing, just like the sun."[5]

Roland Kirk and fellow saxophonist Pharoah Sanders came along to Magic Band shows, and another jazz luminary who was spotted in the audience – bringing with him both attitude and considerable latitude – was Charles Mingus. Harkleroad describes an after-show meeting: "It was obvious this was Charles Mingus. I knew exactly who this was. I said, 'What did you think, Mr Mingus?', like a little puppy dog. He kept staring at the stage and his wife leaned around his belly and said, 'He liked it very much.' And then she pulled back into single-file line and we're all standing shoulder-to-shoulder looking at an empty stage. I thought, 'Wow, he must be cool, he won't talk to me.'"

Van Vliet had met Jimi Hendrix around 1968–9 and, although usually less than magnanimous towards his contemporaries, he was happy to admit that Hendrix was a genius. Hendrix was also an admirer of Harkleroad's playing. The two guitarists had met and Harkleroad described him to John Ellis in 1994 as "a nice guy. What was cool about him was he was low key".[6] According to Van Vliet, Hendrix had told him that with his guitar and Van Vliet's voice they could have really achieved something. Although it would be churlish to argue with that assertion, no one can vouch for the veracity of the story. It's best filed away alongside the rumours that surrounded Van Vliet's alleged unreleased collaboration with Miles Davis.

Again the two had met, but their 'lost' album, which supposedly languishes in the vaults at Columbia, is purely fictional.

Van Vliet was proving himself to be the master of the aphorism and the epigram (in the days when the word "soundbite" had yet to be invented) with utterances such as "All roads lead to Coca-Cola"; "A psychiatrist is someone who wants to die in your next life"; "Everyone's coloured or you wouldn't be able to see them"; "There are forty people in the world and five of them are hamburgers"; "Everyone drinks from the same pond"; "The ocean takes all day to wave"; and "You don't want to get into the bullshit to find out what the bull ate", often to the interviewers' amusement and/or incomprehension. And although he had been dismissive about being labelled a child prodigy, it was not for reasons of modesty. He was now happy to admit to being a "genius", claiming that he couldn't help the fact and that he really needed a new art-form.

Rock music had been gaining a greater cultural significance for a number of years, and the more literate practitioners were increasingly seen as guru figures. At least by the sorts of fans who hunted for meaning in the most flippant Bob Dylan lyric, and for whom John Lennon wrote the aggressive and deliberately meaningless gobbledegook of 'I Am The Walrus' in 1967. (Lennon's strategy backfired as some fans then applied themselves to breaking that song's "code", so he unequivocally attacked that mentality with the sneering 'Glass Onion' on *The Beatles*, the following year.)

Van Vliet took his own music very seriously. He also felt that it was of itself and carried its own message. He was conscious that some potential listeners would find it repellent, some would approach it on its own terms and others would try to analyse the life out of it. He was also horrified at the idea of being seen as a "rock guru". If he had a "message", it was of personal empowerment and enlightenment through the dismantling of the mental barriers, thus breaking down the obstacles that stood in the way of independent thought. He admitted that some tracks, like 'Space Age Couple', for example, had a more specific meaning, but he was rarely willing to offer a linear explanation. He was aware that to *hear* his music, the conscious part of the mind needed to be put on hold to allow it to come in, rather than the listener getting in a sweat trying to figure it all out. Then you could reach the state of "complete absence" that he'd tried to encourage with *Decals*.

His comments on the subject were, one feels, often overlooked in favour of the more quotable, far-out fripperies that peppered his conversation.

But this subtext showed that he was single-handedly determined to make the rock audience listen to music differently. To *Coast FM & Fine Arts Magazine*: "I don't think there's any way you can know music. The minute you 'know' it you stop playing, and the minute a person stops playing, the [act of making] music isn't playing any more... I think most people try to get others to see through their eyes. And if you look through enough eyes, like in books, you end up not knowing how to use your own."[7]

And to *Los Angeles Times*: "My music isn't that much different from the music that's in their minds. Because I conceive it so naturally, it's bound to be in their minds. Sooner or later they'll catch on; they'll learn to understand it without asking why. Unless they're so far out they can't get back. I don't really think they are. All tongues are connected, you know – we all drink from the same pond."[8]

Somewhere along the way Van Vliet had become aggravated by the seemingly harmless John Lennon lyric "I'd love to turn you on" from The Beatles' 'A Day In The Life'. Lennon was already on Van Vliet's bad-guy list as he hadn't responded to the telegram of support he had been sent during his post-marital "bed-in" with Yoko Ono. Despite having lampooned Lennon on 'Beatle Bones 'N' Smokin' Stones', Van Vliet was still annoyed at this snub, saying to one journalist: "I'll tell you one thing I didn't like – The Beatles saying they were going to turn you on. I've never heard anything so ridiculous in my life. No man or woman can turn another person on. The minute you hit the air you're on. Like I said on 'Flash Gordon's Ape' – "Jump in the air and hit your eyes/Try to go back and there wasn't none." The idea of trying to turn someone on, that's the biggest concession stand I've ever heard."[9] Van Vliet claimed to have met McCartney, whom he thought of as "a nice person" and whom he lauded as the creative force in the group. McCartney was certainly aware of Van Vliet and Harkelroad remembers hearing a number of stories about them meeting. McCartney, however, has no memory of such a meeting taking place.

Something more serious was brewing up in Van Vliet's mind – that "freaks" were inevitably perceived as voracious consumers of drugs. He was determined to put a distance between himself and any such connections. His antennae picked up danger signs that pointed to his output being lazily compartmentalised as that of a 'drug artist'. Having largely, but not completely, left that behind him, he didn't want to be tagged like a piece of luggage. He told Andrew Weiner of *Creem* in 1972: "The idea of being called a genius because someone thought me a really heavy tablet is kind of horny… all of a sudden my whole being is put into a capsule and thrown over and put under a set category."[10]

In the early Seventies it would have been difficult to find a musician who hadn't taken drugs. The hip cachet associated with drug consumption was compounded by the Establishment's paranoid reactions to this insurrection in their midst. Suggestive use – or indeed any use – of the word "high" could get you into trouble, as The Doors famously found out when they were told to edit the line "Girl we couldn't get much higher" from 'Light My Fire' when appearing live on the *Ed Sullivan Show*, on US TV, in 1967. Jim Morrison conveniently 'forgot' to do so, much to the horror of the show's director.

In the UK, even the apparently wholesome Mungo Jerry had their 1971 B-side 'Have A Whiff On Me' banned from BBC airplay because of its references to smoking hash. But their number one single, 'In The Summertime', with its jovial references to having a drink and a drive was deemed suitable for public consumption. This kind of stupidity was kicked against to the extent that fans would search out any drug innuendo precisely because the straights were against it and it was therefore cool. Times have inevitably changed from those formative counter-cultural days and now drug outlaw chic carries far less kudos.

There were druggy mutterings that 'Sugar 'N Spikes' on *Trout Mask Replica* was about the ingestion of sugar cubes spiked with a drop of LSD. This encoded 'knowledge' divided the pack into "Us" and "Them", albeit on the most superficial level. Drugs had a big role to play in the pop culture of the Sixties, especially when they helped fuel the destruction of stultifying musical conventions in the heyday of psychedelia. But when some dopey "head" would evaluate music along the lines of "Hey, man – he must have been *really out of it* to record something like that", it was time to start asking where it was all going.

Van Vliet had sailed close to the wind with 'Ah Feel Like Ahcid' and was occasionally accredited – with reference to the sleeve of *Strictly Personal* – as having a "5000 microgramme personality". He was prepared to admit that he had smoked dope at an early age – hardly a remarkable admission – and wasn't ashamed of it. He had been *really out of it* himself in the past, but if anything he was now too *in it*, unable to switch off the flow of ideas through his head.

All this seems to warrant a big "So what?", but Gary Marker, who had been stoned many times with Van Vliet in the past, reckons it was a deliberate way of adding to his uniqueness by separating himself from prevailing trends. It also seems clear that Van Vliet, to his credit, could see that drugs were ultimately no more than a palliative. Aside from his own dalliances he was aware that as a template for a lifestyle, smoking pot or dropping acid was a non-starter.

He would claim, with good reason, that his imagination was better than the off-the-peg pseudo-imagination of an acid trip. So to eradicate all this from the complex equation that was his music, image and personality, he became uncompromising on his anti-drug stance. In the true spirit of licking off his own decals, he simply didn't want the labels.

Langdon Winner was present at a number of post-concert, meet-the-fans sessions during the Magic Band's 1971 tour. A typical line of inquiry would be to verify Van Vliet's claims that no one in the band used drugs: "Beefheart would suddenly wax very serious. 'No, we don't use that stuff. Our music comes from merely breathing in and breathing out, do you know what I mean? You aren't using it any more, are you? God, you don't need it. It's just another trap. Don't kid yourself. You're not as hung up as you'd like to think you are. They're [*sic*] too many people these days who wear their afflictions like a badge. Their little marry wanna speed afflictions.' The Captain would sigh and make a badge sign with his thumb and forefinger. 'It's just too corny.'"[11]

As someone who had given up wealth, psychedelic drugs and most earthly pleasures to sweat blood realising the Magic Band's music, Harkleroad would be dismayed when cornered by fans asking what type of acid he had used to get a particular effect.

In subsequent years, Van Vliet's interview banter was full of put-downs of drugs and drug culture. Marijuana made him feel like "a fly with a wing trapped in honey",[12] and LSD was summed up thus: "I would say that it's an awfully overrated aspirin and very similar to the old people's Disneyland."[13] With scant regard for the truth, Van Vliet admitted just one mind-expanding experience to Andrew Weiner: "I did have lysergic acid slipped on me ten years ago in Honolulu. I don't want to lie about it. And I thought I had a horrible temperature and that I was really ill. It really didn't feel like real to me. It was corny, man. Really like a cheap movie, like one of those American movies where all of a sudden the woman feels faint and the walls go wooor, woooor. But I'm a painter, so I got better imagery than that. It's a dead scene, man, I think it's over for that stuff and I wish it had never begun."[14] It's surprising that all this weighty sermonising failed to provoke even a single press reaction along the lines of – to paraphrase Shakespeare – "The Captain doth protest too much, methinks". But in Van Vliet's case, attack was an effective form of defence. He had written a significant number of the lyrics for *Trout Mask Replica* after the group's hash smoking rituals, but that didn't make him a drug artist. But still he continued with these paranoid denials. He was also now in the position where he was keen to be taken seriously and not just as a musician. He felt he was coming into his own as an artist and was looking for outlets to exhibit his paintings, and still apparently writing a novel.

The Magic Band had moved en masse to rented accommodation in Santa Cruz, then towards the end of 1971, up to the north Californian coast above Eureka when they began work on the new album, *The Spotlight Kid*. After the uncompromising and surprisingly popular *Lick My Decals Off, Baby*, Van Vliet backed away from its musical furnace and revisited his blues roots. Despite his bluster, it seems with hindsight that he may have lacked the confidence to continue on this uncompromising path. But Harkleroad doesn't think this was the case: "The determining factor for me was the fact that he'd married Jan. When we got into this, the dollar sign probably became a way to facilitate that domestic situation. He was changing his focus to 'I want a car and I don't want to live in a dirty house with you guys any more.'"

John French says that dating back to the post-*Strictly Personal* era, he had tried to convince Van Vliet to make enough money to at least keep the group financially solvent – a strategy that might have kept Handley and St Clair on board: "I tried to talk Don into doing a couple of blues albums. I said, 'Can't we do something to make some money, so that I'm not living off your mother and feeling like a terrible person – something that people are going to listen to and pay money for and get some radio airplay?' I wanted to do that. Don did not want to do that. He was in strong competition with Frank Zappa as far as I knew – trying to be farther out.

"I think that somehow Don conceived that being farther out would get him a bigger audience and make him money. It gave him a more specialised audience but not a bigger audience. He was considered in America as the best white male blues singer at the time of 'Diddy Wah Diddy'. I thought that he should capitalise on that for a time and then when everybody was financially comfortable, where we wouldn't be so insecure about our finances and our future, we could explore and really concentrate on business."

The Spotlight Kid was a definite step in that direction. Van Vliet had a new manager, Bill Shumow, having let Grant Gibbs go. "That man was just too hip,"[15] he cryptically explained to Patrick Carr. This was the first album to be exclusively released on Warner Brothers/Reprise, and he said that he was happy with the label and the complete artistic freedom they had given him.

On the new album, the new musical structures were far simpler and looser than might have been expected. But this stylistic shift had not been forced upon him by his new masters. And although he had changed his position, he was not about to concede any ground, as he made clear to Patrick Carr: "No, it's not a compromise. I got tired of scaring people with what I was doing. I mean, people were backing away. I realised that I had to give them something to hang their hat on, so I started working more of a beat into the music. It's more human that way."[16]

Elliot Ingber had abdicated during the 1971 tour, but returned for the recording, introducing a new timbre to the group's sound with his incisive and imaginative guitar style. He was enthusiastic about the group, later claiming that as long as there was a Magic Band he was happy to be a member. He did, however, encounter some difficulty in navigating the more complex parts. Although Harkleroad was fond of Ingber, he resented the fact that he had been drafted in as the hot-shot soloist. Harkleroad himself had been an explosive blues player in the recent past, but now found himself stuck in his designated role: "Improvising had been taken out of me on purpose, and Elliot, that's all he could do, because it was hard for him to repeat parts. I was the 'musical custodian', let's say, for the whole thing. I had been pushed into this place of part-reproducer and I could have soloed at any time within a month of getting the shackles off, maybe played free enough to have been appealing. But the shackles had been on so long, that became my place."

Ingber was one of the very few musicians in the history of the Magic Band to be given a licence for free playing. Harkleroad gives his opinion on why Van Vliet wanted to introduce this new element: "I think in the bigger picture, there was always somebody coming and going. The essence of that was as soon as Don got comfortable with the people in the group, something else had to happen. He needed new energy."

The musicians who had pulled off the magnificent *Decals*, applying their formidable talents to blues/rock forms, should have yielded a classic, but *The Spotlight Kid* fell short of expectations. When Van Vliet joined in the band's rehearsals in Arcata, north California, the pace of the music was slowed down so that he could fit his vocals in comfortably. He wanted to be a blues singer again and avoid the sort of situations on the *Decals* sessions (and even farther back to the *Safe As Milk* demos), where he had excitedly forced the pace to the point where he couldn't keep up and the take would fall apart. Harkleroad: "Because he'd never rehearsed with us he couldn't get all his words in – they were just free superimposed things anyway. He didn't have control 'cos he was never there." After the musical euphoria of that album, the atmosphere within the group was at a new low.

Harkelroad to John Ellis: "*Spotlight Kid* was really great music but a horrible time for the band. Performance-wise it was one of the worst experiences for the band. We were just emotionally beat to death by his particular environment… the stress started to show… we were playing really anaemically and it sucks because of that."[17]

Harkleroad recalls that although the idea was to "get more commercial, get more money and some girls in the audience", he equates the result with the schlock-horror flick *Night Of The Living Dead*. Although Van Vliet's more relaxed vocals were some of his best, the songs became "zombie tunes", hobbling off into a "mummy land".

The Spotlight Kid has some brilliant highlights but, overall, the end result serves as a pointer towards where it *could* have gone. The album was recorded at The Record Plant in LA and again Van Vliet's production, in tandem with Phil Schier, was sub-standard, the dull playing reflected in the boxy sound. The group had reached the apogee of their eccentric orbit, and rudely crash-landed back in the Delta mud.

For the cover photograph Van Vliet tapped back into his heritage, looking every part the young Southern dandy. He is depicted clad in a suit from the Los Angeles Rodeo Tailors, Nudies, whose list of clients included Hank Williams and Elvis Presley. A jacket with red piping fits snugly over an ostentatiously frilled dress shirt with black bow-tie. His left hand is casually inclined towards the viewer, displaying an equally ostentatious ring on the index finger. His hair is coiffured and his expression is cool and intense. Given his expensive taste in footwear, one can only wonder how he'd treated his feet. Rumour has it that he blew a considerable amount of the advance for the album on the suit, much to the chagrin of the group, whose economic position was far from comfortable – they were still having to queue for welfare food. And ironically, Van Vliet was still relying on money from his mother to make ends meet. Harkleroad: "I really believe it was a controlled move to becoming more star-like. I mean, look at the album cover. I could have lived off what it cost for his jacket for two months' food." The back cover features a Van Vliet sketch or painting of each band member with an accompanying poem – all except John French.

French plays drums on most of the tracks, although Rhys Clark plays on 'Glider' and Art Tripp features on 'I'm Gonna Booglarize You, Baby', under the name Ted Cactus. He also plays piano, harpsichord and marimba. Boston and Harkleroad assume their usual roles, alongside Ingber. The opening number, 'I'm Gonna Booglarize You, Baby', which was spawned from a group studio jam, is as lustful a sex song as any Van Vliet wrote, punning on the American slang term 'burglarise'. The track assembles itself loosely at the outset: Harkleroad's slippery chords skid around an implied rhythm; Ingber revs up his slide guitar; Boston's bass rumbles like nearby seismic activity; and Tripp's hi-hat snatches and on-beat snare drum whip all the components along into a licentious groove.

Van Vliet incants the lyrics in his most lascivious man-beast voice, tapping the tradition of sexual euphemisms that has perennially fuelled the blues, like 'Dust My Broom', 'Rollin' And Tumblin'' and 'Wang Dang Doodle'. He tells of a couple, Vital Willy and Weepin' Milly, driving in a car, the moon reflected on the hood, in a scenario that crackles with sexual tension. The lyric uses the car itself, driving and even parking as sexual metaphors. In an exchange that invites comparisons with the dialogue between the characters Fast Talkin' Fanny and Razor Totin' Jim in Willie Dixon's 'Wang Dang Doodle', Milly urges Willy to get down to business, warning him: "If you keep beatin' around the bush, you'll lose your push."

The drug detectives were again on the lookout and 'White Jam' was singled out for scrutiny, as a woman comes bearing gifts including flowers, yams and the mind-scrambling "white jam". That particular line of inquiry is about as exciting as the song, which starts in a promising way with Tripp's pretty, yet atonal neo-Baroque harpsichord. But after locating its rut, it plods along until the close. The elongated coda finds Van Vliet blowing harmonica and scat-singing "I don't know where I am" as if he really means it.

The track that finally put them off the trail was 'Blabber 'N Smoke'. Jan Van Vliet wrote the lyrics and the couple's views seem in accordance in this wake-up call for the sort of person who just sits around and acts like "ah dope", who can't be bothered to tackle important issues like pollution and wildlife conservation, or anything else for that matter. Their only concern is how much is going to be packed into the next spliff. The song is based on a pedestrian blues lope decorated with marimba so chunky and delicious it feels like you could sink your teeth into it. But the pace of the song is uncomfortably slow, with French uncharacteristically dragging his heels.

In the *New Musical Express Encyclopaedia of Rock, The Spotlight Kid* is described as "manic depressive".[18] It's not quite that far down, but there are few of Van Vliet's usual flashes of lyrical levity, and a menacing presence stalks its borders. Around this time Black Sabbath were being touted as 'The Dark Princes Of Downer Rock', but their cartoon Hammer Horror doesn't come close to the brooding malevolence of some of these songs.

'When It Blows Its Stacks' finds Van Vliet calling a warning to look out for the mysterious stranger encroaching on the edge of town. Snake and wolf imagery builds a picture of a lycanthropic monster, a feral presence who "don't pussy-foot around". Van Vliet cries out to hide all the women in town, like an animal caught in a trap. The music is powerful and extraordinarily dark, with Boston playing a bass line taken from part of 'Hair Pie'. Guitars lock into the riff and Ingber cuts loose from the gloom with some quicksilver runs. After a brief, beautiful, dancing unison passage played on marimba and guitar, the group are inexorably drawn back to the monstrous riff.

'There Ain't No Santa Clause On The Evenin' Stage' is monomaniacally grim. Even the sleigh bells – presumably kept from the *Trout Mask Replica* recording sessions – sound ominous. Anyone who doubts their capacity to toll funerally should listen to this song. As simple as any of the material on the record, it staggers along on a lugubrious bass line and simple, abrasive guitar motifs. Van Vliet has explained this track as a reminder that there's no safety net and no John Wayne figure coming along in an eleventh-hour cavalry charge to grant salvation to all. Latterly he claimed that it also alluded to the ruthlessness of the music business. The overriding feeling is of utter hopelessness, with the protagonist a slave to basic human requirements like food and shelter. The subject of the song is bled dry of the vitality that Van Vliet wrote into his hobo characters and instead rides off on a moribund journey through a bleak, pitiless landscape.

'Glider' features Rhys Clark on drums. He was drafted in to replace French, as Van Vliet suddenly decided that French wasn't up to playing the drum patterns (which, given his proven ability, makes it clear that there were other more personal factors involved). Clark was initially nonplussed by the track, but eventually managed a fairly creditable impression of French. In another ironic twist, the solid drum sound here is by far the best on the album. Guitar and bass lock into a twisting pattern, garnished by harmonica. Van Vliet's vocals struggle to break free from their worldly shackles, off and up into the stratosphere, circling towards the sun in the silent, peaceful blue. The glider is a metaphor for unfettered spirits, but Van Vliet's vocals tinge the song with melancholy, pleading, "Don't you bring my glider down."

Some humour is found in amongst these creepy duskscapes. 'Grow Fins' borrows the bass line from 'Blabber 'N Smoke', and features incisive slide guitar and harmonica lines over a marimba and piano counterpoint. In a humorous account of a failing domestic situation, Van Vliet describes a man and his slovenly wife living in the sort of squalor that would disgrace a student house. He informs her that "Yah got juice on yer chin" – and then there's the pie on the wall, eggs on the draining board and filthy carpets to take into account. Van Vliet makes a droll reference to Howlin' Wolf's 'Tail Dragger', but where the Wolf was out on the prowl, dragging his tail to cover his tracks, here it's his wife's "tail draggin the gravy", dragging more detritus into his life. He is drowning his sorrows in drink and, in a tongue-in-cheek denouement, his answer to his predicament is to devolve, grow fins and return to the water with a mermaid in tow, leaving 'landlubbin'' women back on terra firma.

'The Spotlight Kid' epitomises the timelessness of much of the material on the album, which is blues-based, but stays clear of contemporary blues rock mores – there are no standard twelve-bar sequences, for example. Consequently the song sounds both modern and unfathomably ancient. In this case the main repeated figure is the 'Shortnin' Bread' melody from 'Pachuco Cadaver' played at half-speed. Van Vliet dusts off his higher-register blues holler, sounding like a wheezy old man in a rural backwater as he begins the song a cappella. He describes a rural nativity scene: a mother in the cornfield addressing her first-born child and giving her the name of The Spotlight Kid, as a rooster calls in the dawn and an onlooking cow weeps tears of joy. A marimba melody line played in unison with guitar leads into the old blues device of slide guitar duplicating the vocal line towards the close. The track would swing deliciously if only it wasn't so slow.

The instrumental 'Alice In Blunderland' was written as a showcase for Ingber, partly because Van Vliet reckoned that he might not be in the group for too long. It starts with a brief introductory passage of guitar, marimba and drums and leads into a gorgeous repeated marimba motif. A cue for Ingber to come in, gliding over the top for his razor-sharp blow-out blues solo. He was, according to Harkleroad, much admired by Jimi Hendrix and here gives evidence of the way he could stretch blues styles and scales way out of shape. The piece had been a live favourite since Ingber joined the Magic Band for the 1971 tour, and some lengthy workouts were played on tour in the following year.

The stand-out track on *The Spotlight Kid*, 'Click Clack', also became a perennial live favourite. One of Van Vliet's most brilliantly realised songs, it encompasses decades of blues influences, yet is rhythmically unique. A three-note bass and piano line introduces the song, but the down beat isn't where it first appears to be, as French motors in with a baffling locomotive drum pattern – 'inside out' is the only way to describe it. After the initial thrill of this confusion has subsided, it starts to become clear how the elements are locked together. Until, that is, the beat is turned outside in. Harkleroad's slide patterns weave in and out of this relentless forward motion and Van Vliet blows a harmonica solo like a giant clucking rooster.

His girl had been threatening to go to New Orleans to get herself "lost 'n' found", and true to her word has left. There were two railroad tracks, Van Vliet tells us, "one leaving, another one coming back", and she chose the former. She waves her handkerchief in a poignant farewell. As the train draws away, the onomatopoetic 'Click Clack' of the train on the tracks thereafter elicits a Pavlovian response: "My ears stand up," he tells us. In a concert in Paris in 1977, Van Vliet augmented the line to let the audience know that he was still remembering the good times: "My ears stand up, *'n somethin' else stands up*, when I hear that sound."

'Click Clack' derives from the symbolic position of the train in blues heritage, which itself reflected the nomadic life of the blues artists and migrant black labourers in the South in the early twentieth century. The train line was potentially a conduit to carry them to pastures they hoped would be greener, as Giles Oakley explains in his book *The Devil's Music*: "Some pianists spent the whole time in one place but endless others were on the move, some as hobos, some finding work on honky-tonk trains –

excursions run on the railroads with pianos provided by the company to entertain the passengers. Just as the country guitarist would sing of movin' on, or the harp player would blow his train imitation, the stock-in-trade sound of the blues pianist was the sound of the railroad. Blues piano is mainly based on bass patterns in the left hand, sometimes but not all times walking basses, set against endless variations and improvisations in the right… Played fast, the rolling, on-rushing impetus of the piano gives the sound of a train rattling on the lines, clicking over switches, or thundering over bridges and plunging through tunnels."[19]

In a radio interview with Michael Tearson shortly after the album's release, Van Vliet gave his opinions on *The Spotlight Kid*: "I like this album better than any of the others I've done really for feeling, although I like *Trout Mask Replica* and *Lick My Decals Off, Baby*. I like them all, it's just that I think I'm getting more into − err − getting it together on clarity, you know. I have a hard time focusing my mind: all of a sudden it's studio day, and all of a sudden the sound gets cut into quarters and, you know, it's ridiculous."[20]

Released in January 1972, *The Spotlight Kid* was nominated as *Melody Maker*'s album of the month. Richard Williams compared the group to the Larry Young/John McLaughlin/Jack Bruce/Tony Williams jazz-rock supergroup Lifetime. He also echoed Van Vliet's own views when he continued, "They both seem to be able to do things which would be patently impossible for anyone else to emulate at this moment, although their standard departures may well become standard practice in ten years' time."[21] The unfortunate irony was that being less far out didn't equate with more sales, and *The Spotlight Kid* only reached number 44 in the UK charts and didn't trouble the scorers in the US.

Looking back on the album when it was reissued in 1977, Phil McNeill in *New Musical Express* reckoned that what separated it from *Trout Mask*, and *Decals* (with which it was repackaged) was that "with practice flesh and blood could play this".[22] Many reviewers picked up on its grounding back in the blues as opposed to its predecessors' more avant-garde tendencies. Van Vliet apparently mailed a copy to the boxer Muhammad Ali, whom he was fond of citing as "the heaviest percussionist in the world" around this time, but unfortunately received no response.

Van Vliet was less enthusiastic about the album when interviewed for *New Musical Express* by Ian McDonald the following year. McDonald reckoned it sounded "melancholy and slightly untogether". Van Vliet agreed and blamed the group: "I know what you mean. The band wasn't into what I wanted to do at the time. They wouldn't let me be there, you know what I mean? They failed miserably on *The Spotlight Kid*."[23]

But there was more to *The Spotlight Kid* sessions than met the eye or ear. Van Vliet told Jeff Eymael of *Aloha* a few months after the album had come out what appeared to be a typically tall tale: "For *The Spotlight Kid* we recorded 35 songs in the studio, ten of which were put on the record, but actually I'd written 400 songs to get those 35. At home I still have some 1,000 songs on tape, but they're not of studio quality."[24]

Without wishing to contest the exact quantity of songs that Van Vliet had stacked up in his library of cassettes, or that were still in his head, he got the musicians to commit a number of works-in-progress to tape during this period. Some were tightly composed but unfinished, others find the group playing some of Van Vliet's basic ideas. The lengthy 'Pomapadour Swamp' is a mixture of strictly composed sections with some looser passages, with Ingber again given the nod to blow his own stacks in extemporisation. These sketches included 'Suzy Murder Wrist', 'Your Love Brought Me To Life', the serene 'Flaming Autograph', 'U Bean So Cinquo' and 'Dual And Abdul'. Some of the pieces dated back to the Sixties; some were abandoned completely; some would pass on their content – or just the title – to new songs. It was a reservoir of raw material that Van Vliet would dip into for the rest of his career.

Harkleroad explains the genesis of the mass of unfinished material from this era: "We had a blocked amount of time [for *The Spotlight Kid*] and we had an cache of tunes. We just went in there in the typical way that we worked. Just take it, keep it, move on. Don was trying to use the studio more. [He thought] here we are, they're paying for it, let's get the most out of it and put some things down – unfinished licks and riffs that he thought were songs. It was a very incomplete, uncontrolled situation, like 'What the hell's going on, what are we playing and where does this go?' Even with tunes that were 'done', and that people think are great, a lot of them were unfinished ideas with a part missing here and there."

The only tracks that were mixed down to two-track for possible inclusion on *The Spotlight Kid* but were discarded were 'Harry Irene' – which crops up later on in the story – and 'Funeral Hill'. This uncompromisingly grim tune is as slow as the slowest tracks on the album. The railing against mortality, the fist in the face of death that hallmarked 'Fallin' Ditch', is itself ditched as the protagonist of the song is actually deceased. The only advantage of this state is that it avoids life. The boss man of 'Plastic Factory' is again recast as the "fat man", the oppressor, but he can no longer "spat [*sic*] in your eye", as you've finally "paid your bill". There are two versions of the track: a shorter, tighter one and an elongated version where Ingber sets off on a berserker-style fretboard foray.

In May 1971, the past re-emerged in the shape of material from the original November 1967 *It Comes To You In A Plain Brown Wrapper* sessions, finally released as *Mirror Man*. These were the three lengthy blues tracks, 'Tarotplane', '25th Century Quaker' and 'Mirror Man', and an early (and longer) version of 'Kandy Korn'. Buddah had ended up with the tapes and the time was now right to cash in on the group's increasing popularity. The strategy worked and the album sneaked into the UK Top 50 in May 1971. The package failed to do the music justice. The sleeve claimed that the album had been "recorded one night in Los Angeles in 1965", which started the oft-repeated rumour that it was a live album. There are three Van Vliet poems on the back cover – 'One Nest Rolls After Another', 'I Like The Way The Doo Dads Fly' and 'Bleeding Golden Ladder' – and the front cover displays a totally inappropriate photograph of the 1970 group, without John French, superimposed on a shattered mirror.

Van Vliet was less than impressed by the way the whole episode was conducted. He told *Zig Zag*'s Connor McKnight in early 1973: "I think it was very vulgar of them to put that out. They told me that I was going to be able to mix it, but they lied to me... and they told me that since I was mixing it, would I mind giving them some poetry for the sleeve. Of course, I said 'sure', and sent them the poetry... and then they put it out. All the details on the cover are wrong... they don't care. But I like the music."[25]

To promote *The Spotlight Kid* the Magic Band embarked on a US tour, which again started on Van Vliet's birthday, this time his thirty-first, on January 15, 1972 at the Anderson Theater, New York City. Van Vliet could look out over the ocean and see his beloved whales from where the group were living up on the coast, but he was less than impressed with the big city, confiding to Patrick Carr that in his opinion, "New York is a slow turtle with diarrhea."[26]

To keep the Magic Band unique, Van Vliet categorically ruled out the concept of competition with his peers, asserting that there was no point in this sort of rivalry. His confidence in his own abilities and those of the band was high, but if this approach might have indicated a nagging insecurity on his part, it was cleverly turned on its head when he likened the 'Battle of the Bands' mentality to macho posturing, which he felt was the province of the older generation, was uncool and ought to have died out by now. "I see a war emulation in the youth," he told *Sounds'* Steve Peacock, equating it with the USA's lack of communication with China in the recent past.[27]

There was a new recruit to the touring line-up, Roy Estrada, who had played bass with The Mothers Of Invention from their 1966 début *Freak Out!*, through to *Cruisin' With Reuben And The Jets* in 1968, and who had more recently featured in Little Feat. He gained himself a new name, Orejon. Although Van Vliet was antagonistic towards Zappa, he still had an affinity with his musicians, and vice versa, later claiming that Estrada started the Mothers, not Zappa. Boston moved seamlessly to guitar, forming a three-pronged six-string line-up with Harkleroad and Ingber, and played occasional bass. The group toured fairly continuously through to the end of April, playing a set that relied more on *Spotlight Kid* material and more conventional tracks from the back catalogue, with occasional inclusions of 'Hobo Chang Ba', 'My Human Gets Me Blues' and 'Steal Softly Thru Snow', together with new tracks like 'When It Blows Its Stacks' and 'Grow Fins', the instrumentals 'Peon' and 'Spitball Scalped A Baby', and Van Vliet's a cappella rendition of the blues standard 'Black Snake' (the song had been performed by a number of artists, including Blind Lemon Jefferson and Victoria Spivey, but his version was closest to John Lee Hooker's). Attendances were high and the final show on the US leg at Fox Theater, Long Beach, Long Island, was sold out.

When the Magic Band came over to the UK in April 1972, they were interviewed in London for *Frendz* magazine by journalist Nick Kent. They were due to play at The Dome in Brighton the next day and invited him to travel down with them on the tour bus. Kent went on to become a legendary figure in music journalism through his work for *New Musical Express*, but at the time he was still 19 and this was only his second assignment. He remembers it vividly.

"He [Van Vliet] seemed fairly straight, he wasn't taking anything in front of me, he wasn't smoking a joint or anything, so when he told me he was completely drug free and that his music was not anything to do with drugs – moreover that his band didn't take drugs – I believed him. But frankly, looking around me, that guy Elliot Ingber was completely fried. I discovered later that he was on PCP all the time. Ingber was really a casualty; he was a space case. On 'Alice In Blunderland', Beefheart would just let him go and he would play a solo that was so far beyond anyone I'd ever seen play, including Jimi Hendrix: it was just amazing. He could do that one thing, he was there for that one solo. It's interesting, because years after, I would see Elliot Ingber in all these awful Hollywood hippy films, cast as a druggy hippy.

"I remember trying to talk to him and the rest of the band. One of Beefheart's managers – Carvalho, I think his name was – was there on the bus and he was managing Little Feat, and they had just released their second album *Sailing Shoes*. And of course, Roy Estrada had left Little Feat to join Beefheart. So this manager guy was trying to hype me to Little Feat. And I was saying, yeah, I'm interested in Little Feat. So this guy turns to Ingber and says, 'Hey, this English guy is really interested in Little Feat.' And, like, Ingber turns to me and says [drawls] 'Hey man… what about *big* feet?' That was the level of communication.

"Halfway along the journey we went into a transport café. And this middle-aged waitress came up to take our orders. Beefheart immediately pulls out some paper and draws a sketch for her. He turns to her and says, 'Look, I'm a genius. Keep this piece of paper and in about ten years you can sell this for $20,000'. I'm like Picasso, me. I could not believe it! It was just incredible. He had absolutely no doubts about himself, I'll give him his due.

"Beefheart would just talk and talk on any subject, and very persuasively. It wasn't bullshit he was saying. Half the time he'd do his stuff like how animals were superior to human beings, no saxophonist can play the scales like an armadillo; that would be half the conversation, but the other stuff would be very erudite. He explained to me very clearly why he was making his music and what he was doing it for: he liked Howlin' Wolf, he liked Albert Ayler, he liked Ornette Coleman, he wanted to put free jazz and Howlin' Wolf blues together.

"It's really simple when you look at it – that's exactly what he did. He liked those two forms of music and he was going to put them together. He wanted that slide guitar thing, but in a free jazz mould. That's what he was saying over and over again, and that's what he got. It makes total sense to me: this guy gets hold of acid, decides he's already a genius at a very early age, but just has to find the necessary format to make himself a genius. OK, I'll start with music. That's a good idea, so he does Howlin' Wolf. That works and then there's the acid derangement, and he's working towards this thing but it does work. What he did was totally brilliant, it was genius.

"I'll never forget when we got to Brighton and parked near the pier. It was a ten, 15 minute walk to the Dome and they were dressed in their stage clothes, these mad clothes, and the people were looking at us on the street. But the thing I remember most was when we got in the building and they started to play. I have never heard music before or since like that."

The English tour was also a sell-out at most venues, with extra shows being added to keep up with demand. Not only was their date at London's Royal Albert Hall sold out, but in anticipation of the sort of experience that had astonished Kent, fans were queuing outside hoping to get hold of tickets. Rather than being just a gig or a dry-ice-and-pyrotechnics rock concert, a Captain Beefheart performance was a show, which included absurdist theatrical elements. Fans at the Colston Hall, Bristol, were treated to a ballerina and a belly dancer as warm-up acts. Boston would come on first, wearing his printed suit, sporting either a hat or, his millinery *coup de grâce*, the electric toaster – 'a toast from Rockette Morton'. Brandishing a cigar, he would announce that he was going to smoke it – twice – then bopped through 'Hair Pie'. At the Albert Hall, Tripp (sporting a green moustache, a pair of panties on his head like a skullcap with his hair sprouting through the leg holes, and a monocle), then joined in on washboard and in amongst all this tomfoolery Van Vliet emerged dressed in a Chinese silk suit surmounted by a black cape with a pair of puff-cheeked cherubs embroidered on the back. He had gained a considerable amount of weight and wore the cape to disguise the fact. "I got extremely fat. But I got fat as an experiment to find out what people think at that weight. I mean, you have to know before you can say anything about it," he explained to Andrew Weiner.[28]

Harkleroad has described the start of the Albert Hall concert (with ex-Beatles in the audience) as one of his live highlights, albeit a harrowing one: "… I opened the show. I run out, start whamming some power chord and my amp's off. You run out in the Albert Hall, the biggest gig of your life, balconies, people hanging out, and I'm opening the show, heart beating clear through your chest, run out there and your amp is off. Mommy, I wanna go home! My life passed before me. So I hold up my finger, 'one minute', and then I go back, flip the switch, get back and go behind the curtain, run out again and pause a second, and start whamming the chord again, which of course brought down the house. I don't know where that came from… but I pulled it off somehow. And then, the bass player comes out, and his cord is wrapped around the amp, so he gets out there and BOOM! the amp falls and slides down the stage. The crowd thought it was totally choreographed. It was awesome."[29]

159

10

SINGING FOR WOMEN

"I should have made five million dollars in the seven years I've been in this business."
Don Van Vliet to Elliot Wald, *Oui*, 1 July 1973

"This is just right, just the right time for this. Just like this. Gets all that ego out of the way. You know that? It's true."
Don Van Vliet to Elliot Ingber, informal rehearsal tape, 1972

"There aren't too many men in this world. Too many of them believe in that Greek stuff, that Adonis crap. A nude man is not very interesting – believe me, I'm a man and I've been nude and seen what I look like, and it doesn't look anything like a dolphin, which is a beautiful thing. Women spend most of their lives babysitting little boys – I'm a man so I know this to be true. Woman is the superior sex, indubitably."
Don Van Vliet to Kristine McKenna, *New Musical Express*, 9 August 1986

The Albert Hall concert was proof that Captain Beefheart & His Magic Band were big business, in the UK at least. The group went on to perform at the Bickershaw Festival, in May 1972, famously coming onstage at 3 a.m.* Other live highlights were an appearance on the German TV show *Beat Club*, playing 'I'm Gonna Booglarize You, Baby', and a slot on a French programme, *Pop 2*, which featured footage shot at The Bataclan in Paris.

---

* The festival was organised by a young Jeremy Beadle, then in the business of promotion, but who would become a household name in the UK as the practical-joker-in-chief on the eighties UK TV show *Game For A Laugh* and later *Watch Out, Beadle's About*.

Nick Kent was in the audience at Bickershaw and saw it as a turning point, of sorts, in the leisure activities of the counterculture. "He took me out into the audience, and young English kids were coming up to him saying they discovered acid listening to *Strictly Personal* and *Safe As Milk*. He was saying, 'No don't take acid, don't rot your brain, it's not about acid at all.' But at the same time that was his main audience, people that were chemically altered – most of them from what I could see. At Bickershaw Festival, a bunch of acid freaks actually got on stage during his performance and started waving at him, trying to get his attention. He stopped the band and did an a capella version of 'Evil' the Howlin' Wolf song. He performed it directly at these people: he walked towards them and they walked backwards. I've never seen anything like it, the power this guy had onstage. He basically just freaked them out with his voice; they were literally being moved by the sound of his voice towards the staircase down and the exit. It was a fascinating thing to see. But that was the end of that era – 1972 was the last time you saw large scale acid-deranged behaviour at a festival."

Back in the US, Gary Lucas, a student and budding guitarist, had already undergone a teenage Damascene conversion when he saw the group's New York début at Unganos, back in January 1971. He decided, prophetically as it turned out, that if he did anything in the music business it would be to play with Captain Beefheart. The group were due to play at Woolsey Hall on the Yale University campus in 1972. He was then music director of WYBC, Yale's radio station, and was told by Bill Shumow that Warner Brothers wanted him to interview Van Vliet on air. He describes what took place: "They were playing commercials on the air that were cut by Don in the studio at Warner Brothers. He said things like, 'There are forty people in the world and five of them are hamburgers', repeating his own quotes from *Rolling Stone*. He was a nice guy in the interview. We chatted for an hour and they ran the whole thing live. He was the most jovial, friendly person in the world – like a Buddha."

The following week, Lucas met up with the group at the venue and noticed with some surprise that they didn't really bother with a soundcheck. In his opinion the concert, which featured material from the new album, was a disappointment compared to the Unganos show. "I was bummed out," he says. "The acoustics were atrocious. It sounded like mud or soggy oatmeal. The only thing that came across was Don's version of 'Black Snake Moan'." Opening the show that night was a monkey act, whichVan Vliet surprisingly sanctioned and later referred to as "really hip".

Lucas recalls meeting the group backstage: "I went up to Elliot – he was looking far away, completely spaced out. We talked awhile and I said, 'So what do you think of Jeff Beck?' He stared at me and went, 'You know, there was a record he recorded called *Truth*? Well… it was the truth.' I went up to Bill. He was very shy. I said, 'Listen, can you play some of those pieces?' He just started to roll off the guitar parts, like nothing, without an amp in the dressing room – I was very impressed. I also saw Artie apply his green moustache with a crayon. He winked at me and said, 'If the fans found out this wasn't my real green they'd be crushed.' Other people came by and Don was really smooth with them. One guy came in with some sort of papier-mâché gift to give to Don. It looked like a brain and he said, 'This is for you to paint on.' He was always getting gifts."

Even when the Magic Band were playing the music of mere mortals, it was still sufficiently different for confusion to continue to reign amongst press and punters as to how they actually did it. One of Van Vliet's occasional onstage comments was along the lines of, "We have no leader in this group. The only leader is the one that runs down the back of your leg and makes your foot work." Misinterpretation of this cryptic comment gave rise to the rumour that Van Vliet was giving information to the instrumentalists through his leg movements onstage.

Some journalists who had backed away from his music felt safer with the uncovering of his blues roots. As Van Vliet had deliberately set out to imitate Howlin' Wolf in the Sixties, he was acutely aware of the need to play down any similarities – although play 'Evil' back to back with, say, 'Flash Gordon's Ape' and the differences are pretty fundamental. With *The Spotlight Kid*, Van Vliet's blues influences were plain to hear, but his defences were hastily erected against a line of questioning that he perceived as searching for his Achilles' heel, the weak spot of his uniqueness, the thing they could use against him. As he didn't want to be labelled a heavy tablet and put in the bathroom cabinet, he didn't want to be casually filed away as a blues artist with free-jazz influences. "The largest living land mammal is the absent mind" was by now another of his stock phrases. It could have been amended to include the "closed mind". In this situation, attack proved the best form of defence.

Alain Dister from the French magazine *Superhebdo* got a typical rebuff when he brought up the subject of blues as an influence: "No, no, no. I have too much respect for the people who already have done the blues… I respect them too much to steal their music. They have their music, and I have mine. It is the same, only played differently. I sing a John Lee Hooker song and I announce it as a song by John Lee Hooker, but I sing it in my way. It's just like revolution: it never is the same thing."[1]

As he says in the poem 'You Should Know By The Kindness Of Uh Dog, The Way Uh Human Should Be', "uh monkey wouldn't shit on another's creation".

Van Vliet asserted to Steve Peacock in *Sounds* that it was just too convenient for a journalist to make such facile comparisons: "I want the writer to be, well, realistic, it's not that easy to write about me, and the thing is, it wouldn't be easy for me to write about you, but those alternatives and concessions, shouldn't be made in cases like this. There should be art put on top of it."[2]

In promotional radio interviews, Van Vliet was treating listeners to some blues – playing a harmonica solo, or singing a cappella versions of 'Black Snake' or Howlin' Wolf's 'Natchez Burnin'.' Harkleroad's view that Van Vliet never quite did justice to his singing on his records was given credence by scalp-raising performances on WBCN, Boston. Here, Van Vliet is relaxed and totally lets rip. On 'Black Snake' he explores his entire range from basso profundo to tightly controlled, hushed tones, then climbs up through astonishing melismata to stratospheric falsetto hiccups. He then politely tells the studio engineers: "This is no offence, but I can't get through this microphone, it's too little." He then overloads it with a ferocious version of 'Natchez Burnin'.'

His defensiveness was a waste of energy. Van Vliet had so successfully personalised the blues, he didn't really have anything to worry about. Writing in 1994, Luc Sante put forward this view: "The white fascination with the blues, especially the country blues, has always been vulnerable to accusations that it represented a kind of colonial sentimentalism. While perhaps unjust, this notion was certainly borne out by some of the grotesqueries of the Sixties and the Seventies, when pimply devotees of 'de blooze' misunderstood the music in a colossal way, unable to distinguish between tribute and ridicule… There were exceptions of course. The white musicians who did the most honour to the blues were often those, like the great Captain Beefheart, who took the largest liberties with the form."[3]

In a French radio interview from April 1972 (which also featured some live recordings of the Magic Band), Patrice Blanc-Franquart got his comeuppance when he put this blunt question: "But in your music, and even if you don't agree, there are a whole lot of influences from blues and free jazz. Do you listen to people like Albert Ayler or Sun Ra?" Van Vliet audibly bristled: "No. I myself am an artist too, you see… I'll tell you once again: I have i-ma-gi-na-ti-on… it isn't polluted, and believe me, people have always tried to put labels on me… what's the story with that 'blues' and 'jazz'? The more often people say it the more difficult it gets for me to come here. It took five years to play here in Europe, because the critics had written I was sort of avant-garde, jazz, blues and such… It's wrong: I am an artist; just like Albert Ayler is one, like Muddy Waters or John Lee Hooker. I know John Lee Hooker, and even in my boldest imagination I can't see myself using the music of Hooker, Ayler or anyone else. Why should I do that, when I have so much myself – you have heard it tonight… so why all those classifications? Tell it to The Rolling Stones, to The Beatles, to Jefferson Airplane – but not to me!"[4]

Aside from the contentious topics of blues, jazz, and music entirely, Van Vliet's first ever one-man art exhibition took place at the Bluecoat Gallery in Liverpool, UK, from 4 to 22 April 1972. Lucy Cullen, the gallery's director, had seen a Van Vliet interview on TV which featured his paintings. This prompted her to contact his agents and make a request for some work to be brought to Liverpool, as the London galleries would not have enough time to organise an exhibition. Cullen only saw the paintings that would form the exhibition when Van Vliet arrived in the UK, a week before the start of the European tour. "I was a bit frantic because I had not seen them in colour and thought they might be awful, but they are very good indeed, rather stark and strong,"[5] she admitted.

Her request was made at unusually short notice, but Van Vliet had no problem in putting the material together. In a typically maverick display, he ignored the easy option of selecting examples of his past work. Instead he primed thirty small canvases white and then set about his task with uninhibited, gestural enthusiasm. His claim to have painted thirty canvases in one day appears to be a typical exaggeration – in the gallery press release two days is the time stated, and he himself later puts it at three.

More importantly, his spontaneous approach to painting mirrored his spontaneous methods of composing music. This time he side-stepped any analogies about going to the bathroom, and used a more poetic simile to describe the process: "I was just exercising my arm, like an ass swishing his tail." He also told Caroline Boucher: "It's just like combing your hair really, you can't get interested in it otherwise you'd just end up watching yourself. I run away from mirrors."[6]

A gallery press release gave this description of the paintings: "Beefheart executed various gestures, suitably untamed, in black and white paint. In some of the paintings, the image is confined to a single swift brush stroke almost as if the canvas were a detail from some enormous composite work, and in others the paint swirls and mixes to greys, practically spilling over the unframed edge of the canvas."[7]

Van Vliet was interviewed on Granada TV to tie-in with the exhibition:

Q: Why do you paint?
DVV: I need exercise. I don't get that much exercise physically being on the stage and what not. Just on the stage and sitting around waiting for this job and that job, so I exercise this way, exercise my arm.
Q: Why are all the paintings in white and grey?
DVV: 'Cos I think they leave more imagination to the person observing them. I don't like colour television. I think that Kellogg's cornflakes and television are the same thing: coloured. Black and white television or grey and white is more dramatic for the observer. They can put their own colours in. If somebody got mad and saw red, they could make a red background.[8]

Half of the thirty paintings were exhibited. The response to the exhibition was positive. Rather than being viewed as the product of a dilettante rock star, the paintings were taken seriously and assessed as having style and intrinsic worth. They were described, a little tenuously, as 'Zen art' by some critics. But Van Vliet's sparse gestures and speed of execution were more indicative of his hyperactive mind demanding an immediate outlet than waiting calmly to execute the telling line, the "one breath, one stroke", that characterises Zen calligraphy. The *Guardian's* Merete Bates appraised them thus: "His paintings – great black and white daubs, some that catch, some that miss – are left like a trail behind him."[9]

Van Vliet was also keen to share some of his idiosyncratic views on architecture. He specifically wondered why there weren't a greater number of female buildings. He felt that the preponderance of high-rise buildings throughout the world was less due to cultural percolation from the ideas of Le Corbusier and his followers, and more from architects who built up towards the sky because they were afraid of women – which implied that female buildings had not been built

165

because of some sort of Vagina Dentata castration paranoia within that predominantly male profession. He told Bates: "They're afraid they won't get out. That's why they build all those red, male, blood, phallic buildings. You know what an architect is? A man who crawls up his own penis to pull up a shade and design all night…"[10]

There was more to this idea than obscurantist mischief. In the late Nineties, sculptor Anish Kapoor was working on what he called a "female fountain" in a water feature outside the new law courts in Bordeaux, France. Instead of jets of water ejaculating at the sky, underwater motors would create a vortical effect, giving a pre-whirlpool indentation in the surface of the pool.

Van Vliet was planning a new album and he gave *Creem*'s Andrew Weiner a taster: "I am a superstar. As a matter of fact I'm writing an album called *Brown Star*. I have it done now and it will be the next one out. At the end of the poetry or whatever you call it, it says, 'You ask a child if he's seen a brown star around, and he'll laugh and jump up and down and say, I found a brown star right on the ground.' I think this planet is as bright as Ceres [Sirius]. But I think it is the other side of the fence, the grass is greener element that is ruining this paradise."[11]

Brown Star was also set to include a song by Jan called 'Happy Blue Pumpkin', and was reported as an album of music and poetry, or interview recordings. The poem of the same name was printed in its entirety in a record company circular. The charming, child-like text of 'Brown Star' disappeared, however. And although poems 'The Beep Seal' and 'Sun Dawn Dance' had been published in *Rolling Stone* two years previously, and there was a contemporaneous claim for an imminent book entitled *The Night My Typewriter Went Daaaaa*, all remained quiet on the publishing front.

Brown Star was 'aborted' around May 1972, with news via a Warner Brothers circular of a new project, *Kiss Me Where I Can't*. Although a lot of material from the previous year had been recorded and left unreleased, this was no lost album. As it turned out, all the projects were alternative titles for what became *Clear Spot*: no spoken word and no 'Happy Blue Pumpkin', just Captain Beefheart with his most commercial album, reckoned by many to be his best.

On *Clear Spot*, Van Vliet intended to travel further down the road towards success, and write music for women, taking him away from the competitiveness and "red-faced erections" of his hung-up peers. He wanted to talk to women in a language they could understand. 'Neon

Meate Dream Of A Octafish' may literally ooze sex, but it's more surrealistic biology textbook than seduction soundtrack. Inviting the object of your desire back to your place for the first time, pouring some drinks, dimming the lights, then switching on the stereo and playing a sonic approximation of a thorn bush, with a guy sounding like he had painfully snagged himself on it bellowing about "Syrup and semen", "Dungdust" and "Mucus mules" would surely be the precursor to another night spent alone.

Van Vliet chose to blame one person in particular for his perceived image as an asexual weirdo. To Steve Peacock: "You ask them what they think about the Captain having sex, because they've always thought of me as a eunuch – a far-out lunar eunuch, due to my brief association with Zappa. I mean I'm a sexy, healthy male, and I'm not in captivity so I haven't regressed in my organs – I've got blood running everywhere. I wonder what they'll think now that I have a group of men who play men's music to women. Other men can enjoy it too, but it is definitely to women, because I'm playing to a receiver. I'm not playing to a phone company or an operator."[12]

He was, however, no hollow-cheeked pretty boy and was never going to be pin-up material, especially during his periods of corpulence. His singing conveys a sexuality which at least one female friend finds engaging. And on seeing his handsome depiction on the cover of *The Spotlight Kid* cover, she exclaimed, "Ooh, he's all man". Although Van Vliet was now a devoted husband, Gary Marker remembers him having success with women in his bachelor days: "Weird was cool then, and he had a headlock on weird. He has the attention of a gerbil, unless he's in hyper-focus, when he's relentless. Then he'll go after something and won't stop, like getting his hambone boiled, getting laid."

Gary Lucas recounted some of Van Vliet's later anecdotes, which contained some believe-it-if-you-will braggadocio, to Steven Cerio and George Petros in *Seconds*: "He had stories – 'I fucked Janis Joplin on the roof of The Avalon Ballroom. I had 23 women after I played the Whiskey in 1968' … He would say, 'My music is for women because they *know*.' Frankly it was for weirdos and intellectuals, mainly nerdy boys. Not your surfer types."[13] In *Lunar Notes*, Harkleroad recalls some (male) fans coming to shows dressed up as computers in home-made cardboard costumes.

Van Vliet decided that all this had to change. Shortly after the release of *Clear Spot*, he explained his current physical and mental state to Dave

Rensin of *Rolling Stone*: "I'm lyrically less turbulent now. I'm like a woman because I have my periods, if you know what I mean. Every once in a while I get the cramps and do something far out. This album needs someplace to go, you know? So I sing with a definite woman in mind, not like those groups that have men on their mind."[14]

He claimed that he had written *Clear Spot* (or *Brown Star* as it was at the time) in an eight-hour car journey from Boston to Yale. Or on a coach journey in the UK, depending on which version you read in the music papers. The material from *The Spotlight Kid*-era work-in-progress sessions was left aside, apart from 'Little Scratch', which was re-recorded and mixed down for inclusion, but again discarded.

The album followed a new tack, but if commercial success was the requirement, *Clear Spot* could and should have been massive – and without compromise. All the squalling action paintings and nouveaux blues of his previous work were crystallised into a vivid, multicoloured set of songs that were soulful and way more melodic than anything since *Safe As Milk*. It rocked ferociously, and was as sexy and groovy as anything else around.

Even a cursory listen to *Clear Spot* points to a new style of song construction – Van Vliet would whistle or play lines on the harmonica and the piano was left unplayed. He would have the last say over the shape of the material, but some songs were born from the group's playing, in the same way that 'Booglarize' was formed. Harkleroad feels he should have got some credit for working out guitar parts for at least three of the songs – 'Crazy Little Thing', 'Clear Spot' and 'Lo Yo Yo Stuff' – although he is also keen to make it clear that doesn't mean he claims authorship. But in groups run on different lines he would no doubt have got both recognition and remuneration for his contributions. He explains: "I was told I was going to get writer's royalties. And that's OK, because I still don't think just a basic guitar riff is a song, even if it was the focal point of the tune. But it was cumulative. He should have thrown back ten per cent, or whatever."

Van Vliet was excited about the way the group were playing the new material, and claimed to be bringing an entirely new method of composition into the equation. He told Alain Dister: "The relations between the members of the band are more telepathic now. They are able to play without someone having to tell them how it has to be. That's the way I work."[15]

Van Vliet was also starting to publicly play down his role as bandleader, coming across as humble rather than dictatorial, and stating that the musicians were in effect more the leaders of the group than he was. *The Spotlight Kid* cover, with the star in focus, was credited simply to Captain Beefheart, with no mention of the group. Now there was a semantic difference. The group name that had first appeared on the sleeve of *Decals* was reintroduced: Captain Beefheart & *The* Magic Band. The difference may seem trivial, but he claimed that it was a better description of the group and he'd never wanted the adjunct *his* Magic Band anyway. All this appeared to point towards the group becoming a more democratic unit.

He praised their energy and willingness to go. It all sounded perfect. Van Vliet didn't want this talk of activity on superconscious planes to be perceived as another freakish element, but as a telepath himself, the whole idea was appealing. In any case, sympathetic musicians often find themselves coming up with unconscious, intuitive reactions to each other's lines which are only apparent when recorded and listened to later. The atmosphere in the group was more comfortable now and his attitude was more relaxed, although rehearsals were still far from easy.

For *Clear Spot*, Warner Brothers brought in producer Ted Templeman to oversee the recording. His track record included production work with some big acts on the label's roster – The Doobie Brothers' *Toulouse Street*, Little Feat's *Sailin' Shoes* and Van Morrison's *St Dominic's Preview* and *Tupelo Honey*. He later continued his very un-Beefheartian course by producing Van Halen.

During the sessions in Amigo Studios, Los Angeles, Van Vliet also let Harkleroad and Templeman collaborate on some of the instrumental arrangements, the latter working on the horn section charts with Van Vliet. Harkleroad told this to Chris Salewicz of *New Musical Express* in 1975: "The way that I did it is very odd. Don would expect me to know how each tune was supposed to be."[16] On the subject of arrangement credits, Templeman and Jerry Jumonville, the outsiders, got their mention, but Van Vliet was so entrenched in his role as bandleader that he couldn't bear to relinquish any credit to the group members. If he had done so, he might have staved off a later crisis.

Templeman was keen to stamp his authority on proceedings, or at least run the sessions professionally and cut any extra-musical shenanigans down to a minimum. But he had rows with Van Vliet about how the record should sound. Harkleroad: "Ted said, 'Do you want me to do the album? Then get the fuck out. I don't have to put up with this shit.' I think he [Van Vliet] realised, 'Wait. We have a budget, we've got this guy and I'm gonna get that pay cheque I want and so I gotta shut up.' And it was probably really hard for him." Van Vliet was mad at Templeman for a long time afterwards, even claiming that he hadn't done any of the horn arrangements, but they made their peace in the early Eighties.

Even making allowances for diplomacy towards Warners' star producer, Van Vliet seemed pleased with the products of the collaboration, as was quoted in a Warner Brothers/Reprise circular: "I've looked for someone like Ted for seven years. And the engineer [Donn Landee] is fantastic as well. I mean, I can't believe it."[17]

Art Tripp gave these blunt views on the venture: "We had him [Templeman] come in there and make it more commercial. We'd come up with a lot of new songs, and simpler instrumental parts and forms – and Don's lyrics, I recall, were a lot simpler and more tuned in with what other people were doing. There were a couple that were a little different, but then there were another half-dozen that were just like the normal crap you hear very time you turn on the radio. Except we had a kind of unique sound."[18]

Clear Spot was recorded in late 1972 and although dated that year, its release worldwide slipped into January 1973. The plan had been for the record to be on clear vinyl in a clear sleeve (which Faust had done on their eponymous début album, released in 1971), but expense dictated that although the sleeve was transparent, with a card insert, the record was pressed on black vinyl. It still looked great as long as one didn't mind the record getting scratched by the perspex cover.

Van Vliet was right about its contents, though. The currents on the record ran counter to the macho stud mentality that imbued some rock music – particularly its harder, more masculine manifestations. Zappa also took a different tack, but ended up producing the misogynist groupie put-downs of 'What Kind Of Girl Do You Think We Are' from *Fillmore East June 1971* (a source of material that he mined long after the sleazy seams ceased yielding anything of interest). Van Vliet, meanwhile, recast himself as a ladies' man; the dude who knew how to treat them well. He was up for all the fleshly pleasures, but didn't need to become a phallocentric monument to himself in the process – he was cooler than that.

The recent touring line-up formed the backbone of the album: Estrada was on bass, Ingber had departed again, and with French still *in absentia*, Tripp played drum kit as well as marimba and percussion, augmented by percussion from Milt Holland. Other guests included Ry Cooder's

170

brother-in-law Russ Titelman (who had played, with Holland, on *Safe As Milk*) on a guitar cameo and, most surprisingly, the female soul backing singers The Blackberries. Meanwhile Boston switched to rhythm guitar for the first time on record, and Harkleroad was credited with 'solo guitar, steel appendage guitar, glass finger and mandolin'. The difference in clarity and punch between *Clear Spot* and all of the preceding albums is massive. The sound is widescreen, with all the instruments given more space. Even the drums are up, sounding good. It's a rock'n'roll album, Captain Beefheart-style.

On 'Lo Yo Yo Stuff', we're invited to dance to the heady concoction of Holland's congas and cowbells and Tripp's deft, sexy beats and huge parade-ground drum rolls, which stretch the parameters of blues-rock playing. The guitar and bass are absurdly funky, with Harkleroad's sharp lead lines etching themselves on the main body of the song. Although too close a comparison would be spurious, some ground is shared here with the whole-band-as-rhythm-section ethos of Little Feat and New Orleans group, The Meters. Van Vliet's relaxed and powerful vocals stretch out into this new-found space. The music here provides a platform for his horny mating calls. He's girl-watching again, standing on the corner checking out the female traffic, with a bizarre lyrical twist that hints at masturbation, with the protagonist thinking about his girl while "away from home, all alone", doing the Lo Yo Yo Stuff "like any other fella".

Van Vliet's cacophonous saxes would have sounded out of place here and were left at home in their cases. But his free-blowing harmonica playing is at its best – although Templeman thought he was fluffing his harmonica intro to 'Nowadays A Woman's Gotta Hit A Man' until he was told that was exactly the way it was meant to be. The song is whipped along with New Orleans-style snare drum tattoos and a brass section that could have graced prime Chess Records material in the Sixties, with staccato stabs cutting into the track's clattering momentum. Harkleroad's guitar solo is one of the most brilliant rock solos – certainly the best generated from whistling. Harkleroad: "He would whistle and we'd be smudging it around and fixing it and [he'd be] pointing to the neck – 'go higher up there, no, no, go down now', 'cos he didn't know what I was doing. He would just chisel it on the spot." Harkleroad assesses some of his lines as sounding like "little nursery rhyme guitar parts", when taken out of context, harking back to the inclusion of children's songs and melodic snippets on *Trout Mask Replica*.

'Nowadays A Woman's Gotta Hit A Man' is a song about misuse of women by men, and their egocentricity, specifically the typical male trait of putting women down by ignoring them. Here they have to hit men to get attention – and do so. Van Vliet comes over as proto-New Man, but one who knows what women need, rather than just trying to appease them. In this kind of form, he's firing a warning shot across the bows of his rivals. The usual man/woman rock song scenario is turned on its head. And if you don't believe him, he says, just ask his women (note the plural), and they'll tell you exactly the same. Remarkably, and rather sadly, he was the first major rock artist to address sexual issues in this way: "I think it's important that there be some men who appreciate women for what they are: women. Not as some kind of extension of man. There's been a big ecological imbalance for years, what with women taking a back seat to men for so long. Their influence on life has been mutated, and, because of it, the men have been getting into wars and screwing things up. My inspiration comes from appreciating women for what they are."[19]

'Long Neck Bottles' finds Van Vliet hanging out with a woman who, rather than hitting him, throws down the gauntlet by drinking him under the table. There seems little doubt that the long necked bottle in question has another meaning. Writing in *Goldmine*, John Ellis asserts that 'Long Neck Bottles' actually "celebrates a legendary woman's erotic technique".[20] But this woman is empowered and emancipated and causes havoc with her booze binges. Van Vliet describes one incident: "I'll be damned if she didn't bring an airplane down," he sings with both wonderment and worry.

Van Vliet confides that he doesn't like to be the sort of braggart who talks about his women, but he'll do it anyway then he'll split – which sounds a good move given the option of this kind of hell-raising company. All this is set to a hard-edged R&B groove which visits the syncopated one-chord boogie introduced on 'Nowadays', and onto which Jumonville grafts some honking horns. Van Vliet's harmonica blows like crazy and Harkleroad carves out a brief, skidding, slide solo. The Magic Band had made the transition from three-dimensional sonic sculpture to butt-shakers *extraordinaires*.

'Sun Zoom Spark' first came into being on a rambling rehearsal demo, with Van Vliet improvising the words over Ingber's guitar lines. On the fully realised song, Tripp beats out a manic, agitated snare drum and cowbell figure, running into big, solid atonal guitar chords. Van Vliet says, as an aside, "I'm gonna zip up my guitar", and Harkleroad does the business for him with a keening, minimal solo: "He loved one-note guitar solos," he says. Lyrically the song is as playful as its title suggests, with Van Vliet at one point bragging to the listener, "I'm gonna *magnetise* ya."

The berserk boogie continues throughout 'Circumstances'. Van Vliet's harmonica is again forefronted, meshing with a dense two-chord opening motif before the group collectively step on the pedal. Van Vliet pulls off an ecstatic vocal performance, shouting about some huge universal love grinding around in the celestial wheels. The girl he's addressing is exhorted to look at the stars: "Don't you know that they're blinkin' at you?" he asks. The high point comes when the group drop out and, for a few seconds, Tripp shoots across the empty soundfield like a double-speed drum machine. Then back to the dramatic guitar and harmonica chords, and into the fray once more with overdubbed wah-wah guitar.

Van Vliet's mojo is up and working again on the title track, where he's left the city and taken sanctuary in a rotting, stinking, mosquito-ridden swamp. Shuddering chords start up like a heat haze leading into an on/off two-note guitar and bass with Tripp working all around the beat. He sweats out the words "I have to run so hard to find a clear spot."

'Crazy Little Thing' is another testosterone-fuelled groover, with Van Vliet wandering into the territory marked out by Muddy Waters on 'Good Morning Little Schoolgirl'. This is a deliciously tongue-in-cheek account of a Lolita of the bayou – low-talking, slow-walking, "the way that drives the men all crazy". His object of desire remains obscure, but she is playing havoc with his hormones and he is hungry to find out more. But he is bothered by nagging doubts about the legality of his intended activity, wondering aloud how old she can be. The Blackberries coquettishly coo back: "Won't find out from me."

Whereas 'I'm Glad' from *Safe As Milk* was pure Smokey Robinson, 'Too Much Time' is Van Vliet nodding towards Otis Redding. The horn section is again pure mid-Sixties Stax, with The Blackberries sweetly intoning behind his magical vocal performance. The sentiments are simple, even banal by his standards, but sung with such genuine feeling that they fit perfectly. All except for a bizarre, spoken middle-eight where he becomes dewy-eyed, longing for some decent home cooking, but having to settling for the unappetising bachelor-fare of stale beans, sardines and crackers. Then a lick or two from Titelman's sweet, mercurial guitar and back into the chorus, where Van Vliet has time on his hands. "Too much time to be without love," as he puts it.

So convincing was this sardine-and-cracker soul stew that when released as a single it won an *American Bandstand* contest. It was also a hit on a Boston soul station until they found out that Van Vliet was white. Warners spent a lot of money on the promo package, which included a quote from legendary DJ Wolfman Jack (a fan since 'Diddy Wah Diddy') explaining that Captain Beefheart's voice was so powerful it would fry your speakers.

There are two more very un-Magic Band love songs on *Clear Spot*. 'My Head Is My Only House Unless It Rains' is based on a relaxed guitar sequence with a blues-country feel, which Van Vliet decorates with a superbly expressive vocal performance. The train and bus references are a long way from mainstream love song fare but his confession that his arms are 'just two things in the way' until he can again wrap them around his loved one comes out as both absurd and poignant.

'Her Eyes Are A Blue Million Miles' finds restrained guitars and Harkleroad's silvery mandolin backed by subtly shifting drumbeats and Estrada's melodic bass figures. The lyrical sentiments are stated in just a few lines, hinging around imagery of blue eyes and the ocean, in a paean to his wife, Jan. It is far from original, but beautifully stated, nevertheless. And after all the multi-layered verbal conundrums that he had recorded in the years preceding this song, it comes as a shock to suddenly hear Don Van Vliet the vulnerable flesh-and-blood human professing his love simply, even admitting "I don't know what she sees in a man like me," in an utterly disarming performance.

Then comes the *pièce de résistance*: "Greatest of all, of anything, anywhere, anytime is the stupendous 'Big-Eyed Beans From Venus',"[21] wrote David Stubbs, when reassessing the album in 1995. The two guitars start with a call and response across the speakers as Van Vliet sings the opening address, warning, "Distant cousins, there's a limited supply", like a huckster hawking his wares, before encouraging the assembled crowd to let their wallets "flop out" and open their purses. Those who don't get one, he says, will be suffering from the "worstest of curses". Van Vliet alluded to the beans being part of a capricious tale of extraterrestrial infiltration into society. Some commentators thought they were an aphrodisiac or (inevitably) some kind of drug.

John Peel feels the joke is on the interpreter: "A lot of his things were little jokes. You look at something like 'Big-Eyed Beans From Venus', which obviously at some stage he must have read 'Bug-Eyed Beings From Venus'. He used to love all those little word-plays, little puns." Van Vliet later maintained that it was about TV sets. He makes some corny puns on "right track"/"(of) course" and "beam"/"been"/"bean". Roll up and try to guess the meaning.

The song is sonically huge and sounds, as Harkleroad puts it, more "Beefheart-y" than most of the album. There are echoes of his earlier tracks in its agitated structures, but it's full of rock'n'roll directness. Boston and Harkleroad are *in excelsis* here, drawing lines over each other, creating a powerful tension in the process. The drum patterns are erratic and Tripp keeps playing around with hi-hat snatches and disjointed rhythms until a pause when Van Vliet requests politely, but with authority, "Mr Zoot Horn Rollo, hit that long lunar note and let it float." Harkleroad agitates his 'steel-appendage' slide around the fret, then in comes Tripp's staccato snare drum beats, a cue for the guitars to launch into an unfettered slide-crazy extravaganza. Van Vliet hits full throttle and Tripp's thundering tom-tom rolls whip the music up into peaks, with Harkleroad's guitar and massed overdubbed mandolins up there on the summits nearly succeeding in dragging the whole thing up and out into the ether. On the last "Big eeeeyyyeedd beans from Venus", Van Vliet's scalp-raising yell sounds destined once more to blow the mike to pieces. And then guitars wind down before Harkleroad's steel-appendage hits that lunar note again, then slides up and fades into nothing.

Van Vliet's request that the music shouldn't be over-analysed should be respected here. The only way to deal with such thrilling intensity is to get back to primordial basics, and scream right into its centre, or roll around on the floor, mindlessly barking like a dog. Nearly thirty years later, it's almost impossible to comprehend how rock could have stayed the same after it was reshaped and fired off at the listener in this way. Unfortunately, it did.

After all that excitement, 'Golden Birdies' brings the album to a steady conclusion. It's a weird hybrid of a poem set to two instrumental sections from old songs: the bass line from the end section of 'Mirror Man' from *Strictly Personal* opens the track and the interludes that follow are a chopped-up version of the guitar and marimba unison passages that prefaced 'The Clouds Are Full Of Wine (Not Whiskey Or Rye)' from *Lick My Decals Off, Baby*. The poem is an obtuse affair, with Van Vliet as melodramatic orator weaving a tale of Obeah Men, snoring merry-go-round horses and a pantaloon duck that quacks the pay-off line: "Webcor/Webcor" (the brand name of the tape recorder that captured his recorded début, 'Lost In A Whirlpool').

Clear Spot was not as successful as expected. It's difficult to explain why it didn't commercially surpass the previous albums, but it failed to chart in the UK and made a lowly 191 in the US charts. Ian McDonald of the *New Musical Express* was impressed, writing, "This album is a kaleidoscopic primer of basic Beefheartian tenets – but it doesn't exclude the faithful."[22] In *Melody Maker*, RH* made the claims that the album was "too underplayed to be funky", "appallingly tame" and, amazingly, "it would have been downright spectacular if they"d taken off their gloves and *played* the thing".[23] Mick Farren, reviewing its reissue in 1975, opined that it was "still a magnificent work, but it lacks the raw insights of *Trout Mask Replica*".[24] Lester Bangs wrote in *Creem*: "It feels good to listen to *Clear Spot*, and it feels good to know that Van Vliet has finally become a bit less of a phantasmal, somewhat arcane father figure and come into his own as a flat-out, full-throttle rock'n'roller."[25] Bob Palmer, writing in *Rolling Stone*, hit the mark exactly: "The dada-dabbling surrealist has become the teasing, tantalising back door man who entices crazy little things with almost drooling gusto."[26]

In the summer of 1972, a Warner Brothers representative who was touring with Jethro Tull had mentioned to the group's Ian Anderson that he had previously worked with Van Vliet. Anderson and bass guitarist Jeffrey Hammond-Hammond had seen Captain Beefheart & His Magic Band play in London in 1968 and Anderson rated *Trout Mask Replica* as a "naive masterpiece". Anderson casually said, "If you ever come across him say 'Hi' from me." Jethro Tull were big business at the time, with their album *Thick As A Brick* topping the US charts. The message got through to Van Vliet and he decided to try to pull in a favour.

A couple of weeks later Anderson was still on tour and received a call which he thought a practical joke, when the voice on the other end proclaimed, "Hi, this is your Captain Beefheart." "He'd just got that band together and was desperate to get out on the road and do something," Anderson recalls. "And like I have done for many people whose music I have liked, I tried desperately to put him off, because usually it turns out to be a disaster. A couple of months later another American tour came by and they came out and toured with us."

Jethro Tull's *Thick As A Brick* had been intended as a tongue-in-cheek concept album, although musically it plotted a course into the farthest

* Roy Hollingworth

reaches of progressive rock. The joke backfired in the UK, where on the whole it was poorly received by the critics, although not by their fans. Tull's live shows were full of oddball vaudeville and Monty Python-esque humour, which the American audiences loved. The Magic Band's theatrics failed to elicit a similar response. Anderson's warning turned out to be prophetic: "We got away with doing that, but what Don did seemed to have something that was defying the audience to like it – and so they didn't. They got a rough ride because there was a darkness and a strange, defiant surrealism about them. There would be catcalls and boos and people would throw things. Most nights it was very uncomfortable for them. I wouldn't say they died a death but it was a close thing."

In interviews, Van Vliet said he thought Anderson was a "nice man" and they got on well together. But neither he nor the rest of Jethro Tull were affected by Van Vliet's charisma in the way the Magic Band were – Anderson saw other people on the tour "totally mesmerised" by him. Their working friendship was soon put under strain when Van Vliet, whose sleeping patterns were unusual to say the least, called up Anderson in the middle of the night, asking for a meeting. The request was turned down. Guitarist Martin Barre, meanwhile, was completely nonplussed by him. Anderson: "Don just washed over him like a big three-master schooner in full sail." Van Vliet struck up a friendship with Jeffrey Hammond-Hammond and even forgave him for making off with his *Trout Mask Replica* stove-pipe hat that had been on display in the Warner Brothers offices. But when Van Vliet tried to provoke a confrontation by saying he could take him away to join the Magic Band any time he wanted, the pragmatic Anderson refused to get into an argument: "If Don couldn't control people he became obsessed with the frustration of not being able to control them. There were people around him who didn't fall for it and that would drive him crazy. You just have to accept there's a bit of the Colonel Tom Parker, a bit of the Barnum and Bailey, a bit of the spirit that carved the route for the railways to the West, that drove the wagon trains. And behind that part of Beefheart's blustering character, that great ebullient apparent confidence, there's a small element of deep insecurity."

Anderson also got to know the Magic Band, and wondered why they were prepared to put up with Van Vliet's domineering control and their impoverished lifestyle.

"Boston and Harkleroad were the most disturbed," he recalls. "They really loved the guy but they were really hurt. On the other hand you couldn't help but wonder at the naiveté of them. I remember back then we thought these guys were really laying themselves wide open, because Don wasn't really ripping them off, there just wasn't any money. They were walking onstage every night and playing to all these people and they'd been promised money and food and clothes for so long and they had nothing. They had hardly a stitch of clothing between them and they had no real possessions, they'd been living rough, they were literally fed the crumbs from the table."

David Rensin of *Rolling Stone* spoke to Van Vliet at the end of the year as the album was being finished off. "Going commercial" was the next criticism he had to pre-empt: "Believe me, I'm not compromising one damn bit on this album. Sure, the changes will ruffle some feathers – but I'm fooling them all, because I enjoy playing this stuff more than *Trout Mask Replica*." He was understandably confident of the group's abilities, his pride in them surfacing in claims that they were "untouchable by anyone on this planet".[27]

Van Vliet was happy talking to people for hours on the phone or chatting with fans after the shows or striking up a conversation with a stranger in the street. But there was something in him that needed to get away from them and find his own clear spot away from the hordes of people whom he said he had to "babysit". He seemed happier communicating with the redwoods at the group's communal home near Eureka: "I tell you, those things are really saying something. You gotta work hard to hear what they're saying. On my place I have lots of goats, horses, cows, cats, dogs. A lot of other animals eat here too: raccoons, coyotes, even a badger – gorgeous, tough, funny little animal. There's a lot to be learned from animals. They learned karate from cats. The way they move their hands in karate is the same way cats move their tails when they encounter one another."[28]

Harkleroad gives his own description of where the group lived: "The property was absolutely stunningly gorgeous. It was a hundred acres on the cliffs overlooking Trinidad Bay. The houses were shanty, almost, but they were big and reasonably clean. They were funky. There were three or four all connected together and we had this horrible high rent of $400 a month. The woman who owned the place used to train horses and she'd actually had Mister Ed there, the talking horse from the early sixties TV shows. And we had this huge goat which became Mark and Laurie's. Those stories [of Don's]: it's nice that they go past the fact that there were a couple of goats on the property, but I wouldn't say there was a special bear that came down and said 'hello' to Don."

If it wasn't exactly as Van Vliet described, he certainly would have liked it that way. His quote echoes the deep wistfulness that runs through some of his songs, which could break out into sadness, or erupt into anger when describing how natural perfection had been sullied by human beings and how both animals and humans had to suffer the negative consequences *en masse*. On a similar tack, he told Patrick Carr from *Crawdaddy*: "I've seen man's heart in a large filing cabinet, I've seen the smile of the Buick Riviera. Modern man keeps wanting to graduate, but they graduate in the areas that seem to be so solitary instead of the kind areas, like dolphins graduating across the horizon into the sun. Man graduates with no sand and sun and water. I think more children should play with mudpies, but that's out now."[29]

In late 1972, after four years away, guitarist Alex St Clair was back on the scene. Perhaps the strain of being Captain Beefheart was beginning to tell, but when speaking to Elliot Wald from *Oui*, Van Vliet was unusually contrite. He made these comments with reference to the first Magic Band: "I'm an animal. A human animal, but the animal may be better than the human in my case. It's the animal that paints, the animal that makes music. The human part is me losing one of the best groups [the original Magic Band] that ever was by being an art-statement-oriented fool." He goes on to refer to himself as a "chump", explaining that the reason for his wanting to do avant-garde music – "the cold place where they sometimes find icicles in the clouds" – was that he had an axe to grind about having to quit art when he was thirteen. He regretted trying to "sculpt" the people in that group, he said. To round it off, he puts forward the view that St Clair was a big influence on Hendrix. One suspects St Clair may have been present during the interview.

He also made his most emphatic statement about not being in charge: "I'm in the group rather than being Captain Beefheart with the group hiding behind the cape of the mystery man. Now it's called Captain Beefheart & The Magic Band instead of His Magic Band – that was never my idea anyway – and I'm glad of it. I don't want to lead the damn group, I just want to blow."[30]

Ian Anderson had seen Van Vliet in action with the press on tour: "He was just amazing to watch. Just unbelievable. He would just nail them to the wall and get them completely terrified and then conduct the interview on his terms absolutely." But as John Peel has pointed out, it seems that he couldn't help being intimidating, as was exemplified during a phone-in with KHSU, the Humboldt State University radio station based in Arcata, California, in late 1972. Despite the disorganisation, Van Vliet is charm personified and incredibly patient. A listener introduced simply as Paco, phones in and is on the verge of laughing with excitement as he can't believe he's speaking to his hero. He tells him that when he saw him live at the Virginia Theater, Alexander, Virginia, adding "that's when my life started". Completely unruffled, Van Vliet carries on chatting, and after Paco hangs up, he says this to the host, Rich Studebaker aka Studebaker Hawk:

DVV: He's a nice fella.
RS: Yeah.
DVV: So are you, Studebaker.
RS: [*embarrassed*]: Well, I wish you hadn't said that, but, er, there's something, er, he just mentioned ...
DVV: Why do you wish that?
RS: What? Oh, I don't know, that's irrelevant.[31]

Over 30 years after the event, Frank 'Paco' Hebblethwaite explains his appearance on the show. "I suppose that the reason C.B. [Van Vliet] was a no-show on the night of the radio interview scheduled to take place in the KHSU studio, is that it was a very stormy night. When Rich conducted the interview over the telephone with me in the studio and C.B. on the other end of the phone line, C.B. offered to play 'Old Black Snake' for us. He explained after he had finished with a short rendition of this old blues number, that he had cradled the telephone receiver in his lap while playing the harmonica and singing. This was, of course, way before any practical portable phones or cell phones. After C.B.'s rendition of 'Old Black Snake', Rich invited listeners to call in with questions. Since no one called in, Rich was given an opportunity to say, "We have a question here from somebody who has wanted to talk to you all of his life". When I asked C.B. a few questions I sounded like a stupid, 22 year-old who had just drunk five beers in rapid succession, because I was a stupid 22 year-old who had just drunk five beers in rapid succession."

At one point Van Vliet makes a reference to "not making his note" on the day of the interview. Although he didn't like to practise, he had a daily vocal ritual where he made sure he could at least get his highest and lowest notes. Van Vliet was convincing everybody that he had a seven-and-a-half-octave range, the number of octaves encompassed by a piano keyboard, even though the most outstanding trained singers are unlikely to reach even six. And as no one was arguing, he then claimed he could reach eight if he gave up smoking. Michael Smotherman, who played keyboards with the Magic Band in 1974, offers these views on Van Vliet's range: "If you put up a graph and he sang the lowest and the highest notes he could hit, that I guess would technically be three or four [octaves], which is pretty decent. But the thing is, he's cheating in a way, because he can't *sing* across that range. The noises he can make are low to high, from a grunt to a squeal."

Captain Beefheart & The Magic Band commenced a four-month tour in late February 1973 which took in Canada, the US and the UK. Alex St Clair was back on guitar and Ingber had left again. Van Vliet was ambivalent about touring, during which time he wanted to keep his group away from too many distractions. His view of John McLaughlin's Mahavishnu Orchestra, for whom the Magic Band opened at Winterland, San Francisco, in spring 1973, for example, was entirely dismissive.

As someone who was sensitive to his environment, he was often uncomfortable onstage; the lights would bother him, the monitors would bother him and he would become irascible, in a replay of his teenage aversion to performing. These distractions often gave rise to missed cues. Harkleroad: "Obviously, earlier he could hold the line, know what the lyrics were and sing the melody of the tune. Later, if you listen to any of the live stuff, he's lost." He describes this onstage tension as being painful to watch sometimes. But paradoxically, Van Vliet was also a born showman and could make things happen.

The touring ensemble was a formidable unit. There was a new-found sexiness about the Magic Band, although it took a male writer to point it out. Andrew Means: "The Magic Band is intensely sensual. Why such bizarre characters should radiate such sexuality is anyone's guess." This was Harkleroad's favourite live line-up: "We started loosening up at the edges, there was more improvisation," he explains. "With Mark playing such over-the-top aggressive bass lines [before], there was nothing to hold it down. It was like a helium balloon. Art Tripp and Roy brought it down to earth. There would be a thundering groove happening which made it a lot more fun to play."

John Peel was reunited with Van Vliet after a fashion at a concert in London in April 1973. He describes the context: "As time went by we became reasonably good friends. I used to phone him from time to time and he would occasionally phone me. Then there was one strange occurrence when he phoned and I wasn't there, and he kind of expected me to know that he was going to phone. For some reason he was quite offended and we didn't speak for about two years. Then he did another tour and I went along and he somehow knew I was there. It was really odd. This was at The Rainbow and I'd bought my ticket and was way at the back. And he said, 'I'd like to dedicate this to our friend John Peel, who's here.' He didn't say exactly in row L, seat 14, but it was one of those things where [I thought], 'How did he know that?'"

11

YOU DON'T HAVE TO BE WEIRD
TO BE WEIRD

*TC: "His intuition will have caused him no end of problems. There's
been lawyers and everything in his life. Yes or no?"*
MB: "That's true."
*TC: "How did I know that? I knew that because he's intuitive, he's
psychic and he's got insight. It can be a beautiful gift if you're working
with it on your own. If you're working with it with other people in any
field and react to them... He reacts to what he sees from his inner eye
and that can create nothing but problems."*
Conversation between author and Tarot Card reader Tricia Carney,
Camden Lock, London, May 1995

*"A guy like Beefheart intimidates or awes almost everyone so much
that almost nobody is ever gonna figuratively kick his ass, which is too
bad."*
Lester Bangs, *New Musical Express*, 1 April 1978

Clear Spot should have broken Captain Beefheart & The Magic Band into
the rock mainstream and made them into an artistic-commercial force to
be reckoned with. It did neither. Van Vliet then left Warners/Reprise, but
he did so claiming that the contract had simply run its course and that
there was no animosity between the parties. Bill Shumow also decided to
quit, precipitating further change. Van Vliet secured a deal with Mercury,
who would release his music in North America. One of the reasons he
gave was that he was drawn to the company "because of those little fast
wings that are on the Mercury promotion men's feet". On the UK side, he
landed himself a contract with Richard Branson's nascent Virgin Records,

which had rapidly grown from a cut-price mail order firm to being the hippest record label in the UK.

Fortuitously for Virgin, one of their first releases was Mike Oldfield's 1973 début solo album *Tubular Bells* – which, from a slow start commercially, went on to become a massive seller. The royalties from *Tubular Bells* gave Virgin a financial cushion, enabling them to pursue an adventurous and at times risky policy. They quickly provided an outlet for progressive-experimental groups like Hatfield And The North, the politically radical Henry Cow and German synthesiser pioneers Tangerine Dream. They also reinforced their cool credentials by releasing both Faust's Krautrock masterpiece *The Faust Tapes* and *Camembert Electrique* by the eccentric Anglo-French rock commune Gong for forty-nine pence, the price of a single at the time. In addition, the head of Virgin Records, Richard Branson, was a long-time Captain Beefheart fan (reputedly he had also tried to sign up Zappa to the label, which would have no doubt moved their rivalry to even higher levels of intensity). The set-up seemed the ideal launching pad for a productive new era in his musical career. Instead the venture proved to be a disaster.

In an attempt to get the success that had so far eluded him, Van Vliet decided to put himself in the managerial hands of Andy DiMartino and his brother Dave, a.k.a. Augie. They had come to prominence as producers of The Cascades' single 'Rhythm Of The Rain', a group whom they also managed. Another of their former managerial charges were Gary Puckett & The Union Gap, famous for the single 'Young Girl', a thinly veiled tale of a man sexually tormented by a minor to the brink of committing an illegal act, set to a great pop tune. It topped the UK chart in 1968. The brothers were also known as being wide-boy, hustler types, but Van Vliet was happy to go along with virtually anything at this point. The group, who were still effectively signed to Van Vliet via God's Golfball, were, if not content, then at least willing to go along with whatever came up. They had been working on the set of mediocre songs which would comprise *Unconditionally Guaranteed* with a distinct lack of enthusiasm. Bill Harkleroad gives this blunt assessment of the period: "The stuff was really bad, but it wasn't as bad as it ended up in the studio. There was a tune or two or a moment that might have gotten OK, if there was a decent groove happening. But it was sick. We all wanted pay cheques. Don was driving round in his new car and we were living in our little hovel."

Van Vliet was subdued and distracted, and musically it seemed like he was losing the plot. He even relinquished his totalitarian grip on the music, giving credits on each track to Andy DiMartino. Jan was also in on the three-way writing credits split, allegedly so Van Vliet would still be able to keep his hands on two-thirds of the composing royalties. Both Andy DiMartino and Van Vliet told the group – who were helping to arrange the music – that they would get some writing credits at last, but in the complexities of the unfolding story, they missed out yet again.

Seldom has an album by a major artist been so ironically titled as *Unconditionally Guaranteed*. The album is generally, though not exclusively, dismissed as an attempt at commerciality gone completely awry. On his sleeve notes for the CD reissue of *Safe As Milk*, Nigel Cross joins the small band of apologists, writing: "A lyrical white soul ballad like 'I'm Glad' [from *Safe As Milk*] proves 1974's *Unconditionally Guaranteed* with its mellow straightforwardness was no deliberate sell-out, just an experiment with ideas that had been swimming about since the early Sixties."[1] Ben Watson, in his book *Frank Zappa: The Negative Dialectics Of Poodle Play*, describes the album as "a brilliant distillation of hypnotic pop generally dismissed as a sell-out".[2] He expanded this view in *The Wire*, arriving at the conclusion that those who dismissed it were "deaf cretins".[3]

In 1993, Van Vliet – then a decade out of playing music – was asked by Co De Kloet, if there was any of his music he didn't want played on the show. He was keen to exclude anything produced by the DiMartino brothers. "They screwed with those,"[4] he explained.

After the interlude – Van Vliet's commercial break – in which he produced *Unconditionally Guaranteed* and its shoddy follow-up, *Bluejeans And Moonbeams*, he never again had a good word to say about the two albums. In later interviews he made light of the whole affair by telling fans who had bought them to go back to the record store and ask for their money back – and that if they couldn't get a refund he would come and play a concert for them in their home. He also proffered the explanation that he had just been trying to make money for the band. "I didn't want to do it," he said to John Gray from *Sounds*, looking back on the episode three years later. "I did it for them for lending me their fingers."[5] Whatever Van Vliet's motives for temporarily jumping ship from his own craft during this mercifully brief period, one thing was certain and that was that everyone involved was screwing up.

Van Vliet later deflected some of the negative criticism by accusing the Magic Band of refusing to allow Elliot Ingber to play on *Unconditionally*

Guaranteed – but it is inconceivable that he would have made a difference. With Roy Estrada departed and Alex St Clair back on rhythm guitar, Mark Boston reverted to bass. Mark Marcellino played keyboards, and the two other musicians who weren't credited as actual Magic Band members but contributed to the album were Andy DiMartino edging into the frame on acoustic guitar and Del Simmons, a "featured soloist" on tenor sax and flute. Simmons was an interesting addition to the music, not least because he was fifty-one years old. He was also a schoolteacher, was conservatoire-trained and had played with Glenn Miller, although Van Vliet preferred to remould him into something cooler, saying that he had played with Charlie Parker, and refuting his Glenn Miller connections.

In the spring of 1974 Bill Gubbins was backstage with Van Vliet and Simmons when they explained to him how the latter had joined the group. He noted down their version of events in *Exit*:

DVV: We were walking down the woods and he was playing his clarinet and I was playing the harmonica and a cosmic particle went up the bell of his horn and illuminated his mind. Isn't that what happened?

DS: Yeah, that's what happened. I wouldn't kid that thing, man.[6]

In fact, Andy DiMartino had brought him into the group because he led a cosmic particle-free Benny Goodman-style swing band. He'd had plenty of time to get used to Simmons's style as they regularly played in one of his favourite restaurants.

Unconditionally Guaranteed was released in the UK in April 1974. Adverts in the music papers featured a photograph of a slimmed-down Van Vliet holding fistfuls of dollars and leering camera-wards. Doubtless this was meant to be an 'ironic' statement, proactively making fun of his 'selling out', but unfortunately irony in pop music has a history of being misunderstood – and anyway, he actually *was* trying to sell out. "You don't have to be weird to be weird" read the accompanying caption. Just as well, because this record wasn't.

The album opens on a respectable note with the svelte swamp-pop of 'Upon The My Oh My', with Harkleroad cutting loose with a brilliant, searing solo. His playing is one of the album's few redeeming features. All the other musicians play workmanlike lines; not that the material demanded much more from them. Del Simmons's tenor sax and one-man overdubbed horn section sounds fine, but his breathy flute lines are rather run-of-the-mill Roland Kirkisms. The group were still the Magic Band but the magic was in short supply.

Don at work, Sound Castle Studios, Burbank, California, *Doc at the Radar Station* sessions, June 1980 *(Gary Lucas)*.

Don at the drive-in, Burbank, California, *Doc at the Radar* sessions, June 1980 *(Gary Lucas)*.

Don and Gary Lucas, Sound Castle Studios, Burbank, California, *Doc at the Radar* sessions, June 1980 (*Gary Lucas*).

Don seated in front of his drawings, with Gary's French horn, at Gary Lucas' apartment, New York City, September 1980. It was taken at photo a session for a *Newsweek* profile. (*Gary Lucas*).

The 'Trout Mask' house, Ensenada Drive, Woodland Hills, California, in the mid-1990s (*BBC*).

Don and Jan Van Vliet, Mojave Desert, Lancaster, California, February 1980 (*Gary Lucas*).

Don with his keys, outside Sound Castle Studios, Burbank, California, *Doc at the Radar* sessions, June 1980 (*Gary Lucas*).

Don in front of a Wyndham Lewis self portrait, Manchester City Art Gallery; Wyndham Lewis exhibition, Manchester, England, October 1980 (*Gary Lucas*).

Don, Dagmar Krause, Jan, and Eric Feldman, outside the Manchester City Art Gallery; Wyndham Lewis exhibition, Manchester, England, October 1980 (*Gary Lucas*).

Don Van Vliet onstage at The Venue, London, November 1980 (Rick Snyder in bottom left) (*Ian Sturgess*).

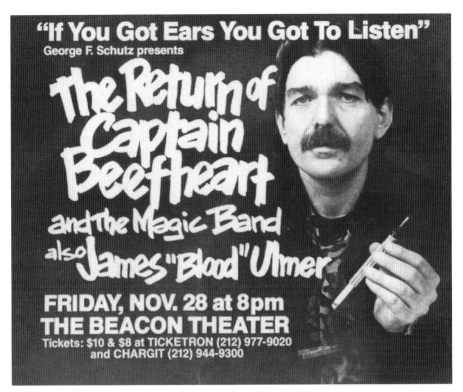

Concert flier for the Beacon Theatre, New York, 1980.

The last Magic Band line-up, circa *Ice Cream For Crow*, 1982. (left to right) Rick Snyder, Morris Tepper, Gary Lucas, and Cliff Martinez.

Don Van Vliet, 1982.

Jan Van Vliet's lyrics to 'Blabber 'N Smoke' from *The Spotlight Kid* were acerbic and pithy, but here the Don and Jan love song co-operative – if indeed that is what was taking place – sounded trite and insincere. The Carpenters they most certainly were not. 'Sugar Bowl' is a knockabout pop song, little more than that. And the lyrics, about little boys and little girls who "know they're being naughty" but "love that sugar bowl", are spectacularly inane. Rumours abound, however, that the song was about cocaine. Eyewitnesses recall that on stage during the subsequent tour, Van Vliet would recite the lyrics prior to performing the song in a manner that strongly hinted that the bowl in question contained something stronger than sugar. If that was the case, then it's simply one of the worst drug songs of all time.

Harkleroad again graces the funky but slight 'New Electric Ride', which, bizzarely, features a bass guitar line taken from 'Fallin' Ditch' from *Trout Mask Replica*. It throws the problem of the album into sharp focus. A collection featuring Van Vliet singing ten good-quality soul and blues-infused pop songs would have been an exciting proposition – he'd proved on songs like 'Call On Me' and 'Too Much Time' that he could carry off that requirement with aplomb. But the half-baked songs on *Unconditionally Guaranteed*, each based on a few obvious chord changes, failed to get anywhere near that ideal. "The vinyl equivalent of cheese food product"[7] was how John Ellis summed it up.

Compared to the disarmingly direct soul-baring on 'Blue Million Miles' from *Clear Spot*, 'Magic Be' is truly bathetic. 'Magic be, I'll hand you a magic flower' is a sample of the level of word play and sentiments on offer. Van Vliet's vocals are average throughout, and here he sings the song with a sincerity that is doubtless well meant, but sounds false and awkward. He flexes his larynx to greater effect on 'Happy Love Song', which is essentially lumpen sub-Stax, from the Otis Redding-style vocals to Simmons's multi-tracked horn section. Again, there's something forced and uncomfortable about the delivery on 'Full Moon Hot Sun'. The music is stilted and seems an age away from the super-confident swagger of *Clear Spot*. As well as Van Vliet's muse sounding like it was running on empty, the songs are played with a tangible lack of enthusiasm.

'I Got Love On My Mind' is a successful exercise in crushing banality, the most uninspired song that Van Vliet ever wrote. He proclaims he's got love on his mind and can't make up his mind who to love, over a four-chord sequence that runs on and on, with Harkleroad trying in vain to instil some interest. Art Tripp comes up with a few neat drum figures, but Mark Boston plays the sort of clumping, brainwashed bass lines that any also-ran of the time could have negotiated. The group that had been untouchable by anyone on the planet a year ago suddenly sounded like a bunch of complete losers.

'This Is The Day' and 'Lazy Music' are so vapid that it's not worth going into too much detail, except to say the latter lives up to its title. But if all the tracks had been up to the standard of the closing 'Peaches', then it would at least have been a worthwhile second-division release. It's a straightforward R&B stomper, but the band kick some life into it, with St Clair and Harkleroad's guitars striking sparks off each other and the rhythm section awaking from their torpor. Simmons's contribution is impressive, his one-man Tower of Power horn section firing up towards the end, and Van Vliet blows some bluesy harmonica too. Thirty-one minutes and twenty-two seconds and it's all over.

Up to this point, Van Vliet's creative processes had been spurred on by his avowed desire to make music "that extended rather than cared".[8] Superficially, that sounds callous, but it also makes perfect sense. To care too much about the audience's needs can encumber an artist. First, you have to guess correctly what those needs are. And if you keep on giving them the same music, you cannot develop, and they are just as likely to get bored and move on. There is plenty of room for error in this tactic. Any musician who is more than just a commercial product will want to keep to their path; to not care or to only care about yourself, your group, your art, at least allows unfettered expression. On *Unconditionally Guaranteed*, Van Vliet's music had the veneer of caring, but it is not clear for whom. One could say it has a generosity of spirit, but it feels forced. Interviewed by Jim Brodey of *Rolling Stone* shortly after the album was released, Van Vliet explained his new approach: "I haven't changed the message of what I'm saying, this is just a friendly extension."[9]

Anyone who follows a musician's music for its inherent personality or uniqueness – not as a transient fad or because they've been duped by a marketing strategy – can intuitively tell when they are being sold short. Aficionados of Van Vliet's work are drawn by its unique qualities and most looked on *Unconditionally Guaranteed* as at best an aberration and at worst such a turkey that it would be gobbling nervously in the run-up to Christmas. The potential fan base that the album was aimed at capturing was unimpressed and uninterested.

The press reaction was by no means purely negative. Some critics tried to understand it, others hated it and some were pleased with the results. *Melody Maker*'s Rob Partridge went for it in a big way, coming out with the astonishing assertion that, "Beefheart's last album, *Clear Spot*, signalled the changes but this time, with *Unconditionally Guaranteed*, he's really made it. The Magic Band have seldom sounded better than this…"[10]

Steve Peacock was more circumspect when reviewing the album in *Sounds*. He felt that if the Magic Band hadn't been on good form it would have been an unexceptional album, though he preferred it to *Clear Spot*. But he wondered whether it would appeal to the public at large. Ian McDonald writing in *New Musical Express* compared it to Bob Dylan's poorly received *Planet Waves* due to its "disconcerting lack of substance".[11] Lester Bangs was characteristically more direct, later opining that the album "conked out his music just short of total death".[12]

Unconditionally Guaranteed failed to chart in the UK and the US and so the plan backfired in every respect (although Van Vliet claimed that the album made him more money than its predecessors – quite possibly, because the contractual side was now less complicated). It was also the first artistic failure of his career.

Van Vliet and Andy DiMartino's notion of what a commercial product should be like amounted to no more than bad second-guessing. Their strategy was similar to those of the management company chancers who perennially place adverts in the back of music papers in a hasty attempt to put a band together to ride on the back of the latest big thing. In the early Eighties, Yazoo – the synth and female vocals duo who notched up a series of hit singles – prompted advertisements with wordings like "Wanted: Male synthesiser player and female singer to form Yazoo-type band". That duo – if it was ever assembled – disappeared without trace. One feels the music on *Unconditionally Guaranteed* could have been achieved by placing an advertisement stating: "Wanted: Bland version of Captain Beefheart & the Magic Band for pizza-house residency and possible recording".

Van Vliet's much-touted breaking up of the "catatonic state", his "music without a lullaby", was ditched in this major ideological volte-face. In his own terms of reference, this was his homage to catatonia. In a mixture of magnanimity and arrogance, he was now extolling the virtues of people like Mick Jagger and Rod Stewart – whom he perceived as the new opposition – but ultimately reckoned that no one had *really* done rock before because no one had the voice. He even admitted to liking the airbrushed soul music of The Stylistics and the pleasant pap of David Essex. Something was definitely up.

Van Vliet had always wanted to be a star on his own terms but it appeared that the self-belief that had pushed him the point of self-confessed tyranny had withered and died. Why shouldn't he make some money now rather than be both the music press's pet artist and a pauper? He claimed that he had invested $400,000 into the Magic Band and now couldn't even afford to buy canvases on which to paint. He wanted a piece of the action. His dilemma was summed up succinctly by John Ellis: "This 'I want a Rolls-Royce' attitude damaged his career in a way that has only recently been completely repaired; it is unfortunate that a choice between financial stability and free expression ever had to be made. Most American artists of any originality face it daily."[13]

Even though the album had been poorly received, the upcoming spring/summer tour of the UK and US was still eagerly anticipated. The Magic Band's shows for the last couple of years had generally been of such a high standard that the *Unconditionally Guaranteed* tracks would surely yield more when played live. But at the eleventh hour, the entire Magic Band quit, their mutiny coinciding almost exactly with the album's release. Harkleroad and Boston were now in their mid-twenties and their growing defiance of Van Vliet allowed resentments that had been simmering for years to finally rise to the surface. The financial situation had long been intolerable and although the group had not been paid for the 1973 tour, they felt they had evidence to suggest that money had been withheld. Whatever the exact truth of the situation, they'd had enough.

It was a dramatic exit and was made more so by the group's silence for a number of months before they went public with their grievances. In a press release circulated just before *Unconditionally Guaranteed* was released, Van Vliet asserted that Harkleroad was so good that if he left, he would follow him. Neither Harkleroad nor the others would have let him back if he had tried. He was in effect sacked by his own group, who went on to play and record as Mallard. He was devastated. In a letter to *MOJO* in 1994, John French recalls seeing him virtually "a broken man".[14]

With the benefit of twenty-five years' hindsight, Harkleroad explains their final abdication at the end of the "dirty little road" that led to *Unconditionally Guaranteed*: "It happened because we were getting stronger, he was getting weaker and it took a transitional period for the band to break up. You don't just wake up the next day after seven years of being brainwashed and go, 'Oh, I'm not here any more.' It actually created a natural transition of, 'The music sucks, these guys [the DiMartinos] are creepy weasels and Don doesn't have any power any more.' It made a nice slippery slide to get out of there. There were parts of that situation that were really wonderful: the creativity, the power of the person, what I was learning in an artistic mentality, not in a musical way. If it had been a more humanly considerate, compassionate environment, it probably would have been great to stay. [But] it probably would have been healthy for me to leave because of how much of myself I had given up on an emotional and personal level."

Van Vliet may have been on the ropes but he came back fighting. To Nick Kent of *New Musical Express*: "Five days – *five days*, man! That's all they gave me. Just before we were due to go out on the road. I knew it was going to happen though. I told them after *Trout Mask Replica* that it would happen... I taught them every note they've ever played, choreographed every move they ever made, and this is how they repay me! Five days, man – *five days* to find a whole new band.

"Like Zoot Horn Rollo – he was good. In fact he was getting to be one of the best, but when you get wickedly good, you not only get wicked, you get just like a wick. Y'know what I mean? Don't you? And he'll never be able to play like that again without me to look over him. No way.

"I mean, if they were concerned about being puppets they should have spoken up about it instead of leading me on to believe otherwise. But then again, who the hell's a better puppeteer than me? Huh?"[15]

Rather than cancel the tour, Van Vliet went out to promote *Unconditionally Guaranteed* backed by a hastily assembled pick-up Magic Band. One of the new group was keyboard player Michael Smotherman, now a writer and producer in Nashville. His group, Buckwheat, which had been managed by Andy DiMartino, had just broken up and he was desperate for work. He takes up the story: "They [the DiMartinos] were two Italian guys from Brooklyn who wore leather car coats and leather fedoras. They were just total street guys. I was living in a storeroom above a recording studio in Hollywood. Andy DiMartino had a little office a few doors down. He was a producer/publisher/writer/house painter, just anything and everything. He was well known in Hollywood for being a kind of hustler type. He was a good guy. He came down and said, 'I've talked Captain Beefheart into letting me manage him and produce him and we're going to go commercial, and I want to put a band together.'"

Smotherman and Dean Smith, also from Buckwheat, had just got an agency gig with some other musicians backing up singer Billy Joe Royal. He'd had some hits in the Sixties, but was now playing lounge gigs. The deal with Billy Joe Royal turned out to be so poorly paid that Smotherman persuaded the musicians to come along to meet DiMartino. "At least this thing with Don was paying a little better, so we told Billy Joe we'd see him down the line somewhere. I took those same guys over and they hired us to be the new Magic Band – the *faux* Magic Band."

Smotherman is still amused by the way events unfolded. "It was just a circus, man, the asylum in the hands of the inmates, just crazy. I knew who he was but to be honest I don't think I'd heard any of his songs. And Don was really uncomfortable with the whole thing. Seriously, to make Don Van Vliet commercial in the sense that we know commercial was just ludicrous, because he already had his own thing going."

The group learned some of the new material and also some older favourites like 'Mirror Man', 'Big-Eyed Beans From Venus' and 'Electricity'. Smotherman: "He was just singing them to us and we played what we thought went along. And after we learned them in our own fashion, years later I heard the albums they were off and we weren't playing them anywhere near what the other guys were doing."

The new *faux* Magic Band were: Del Simmons; Smith and Smotherman; guitarist Fuzzy Fuscaldo, fresh from Baby Huey And The Babysitters; Paul Uhrig on bass guitar, from Bobby Gentry's band; and Ty Grimes, who had played with Rick Nelson's Stone Canyon Band, on drums.

To his credit – and also out of pride – Van Vliet sang the praises of the pick-up band. He told Nick Kent that they had only had four rehearsals for the tour, but it had been really good. He said he would teach the new band everything that he knew and that the slide-guitarist (Smith) could be "one of the best". Still feeling wounded by the desertion, he reckoned that the new band "want to learn", whereas the original "didn't care".[16]

In Andy DiMartino's office, Van Vliet was interviewed by Jim Brodey of *Rolling Stone*. Typically enthusiastic about who he was working with at any given point in time, he seemed upbeat about the new Magic Band. He said that Del Simmons's saxophone playing "demands imagery" and that he could now explore some oboe and piccolo ideas he'd been working on. He was also enthusiastic about the "new band sound". He explained how it had come about: "Since the release of *Clear Spot*, I've been working on getting a form of music everybody could listen to. I must admit I feel I was being quite selfish about that other music I was playing. But I've never had a producer, really, until now… I wanted to be *produced* this time.

"I've been stuck in some weird fantasy-category out of someone else's need to explain what it was that we did. Like I did *Lick My Decals Off, Baby* to tell people to tear all those false labels off themselves and everything around them. Like it's crazy to say so strictly, 'This is old and this is new.' Like reggae isn't new to the Jamaicans. It's all something somebody in an office thought was threatening them. So they stamped a decal on it. I'm not a big bad bogeymen – nope, not any more."[17]

Sadly, Van Vliet seemed like the performing bear prodded into performance by his unscrupulous owners – except that he was going along with the whole charade. Having relinquished his studio control to Templeman on *Clear Spot*, he had now acquiesced to the inevitability of putting his career in the hands of others if he was to reap the dividends he thought this strategy would yield.

It's no wonder, then, that in their presence he seemed subdued, cowed even. Whereas virtually every Van Vliet interview had been a heady mixture of aphorisms, good sense and nonsense, a joint radio interview with the DiMartinos, in Massachusetts, during the 1974 tour, found the brothers squeezing business-speak and projected sales figures into any lull in the conversation, even making the outrageous claim that the new Magic Band were currently the best group in the US. Van Vliet listened quietly in the background, waiting to be told to continue.

The tour began in Toronto in April 1974, and reached the UK the following month. Van Vliet gave a particularly revealing interview to Steve Lake of *Melody Maker* in London at the start of the UK leg. He reacted angrily to criticism of his recent live performances in the US and Europe.

"Listen, they did the same thing to Dylan, didn't they? I'm changing all the time. They don't want me to have any money. They want me to be their little house poet. The only people that ever liked that band, I think, were writers. It was a writers' band. The average person treated it as kind of a novelty, like an ashtray made of diamonds. But I want a large audience. I want to hug the world. Why not? Why can't I be a blond?"[18] He also said that he was abandoning his sax solos because they were driving people out of his shows and that he had at last discovered the 4/4 beat – something that had previously been anathema to him.

For the UK shows, Captain Beefheart & The Magic Band were

supported by Virgin labelmates Henry Cow. Van Vliet would sometimes start live performances with a disclaimer of sorts, saying that Henry Cow had done the weird stuff tonight and the Magic Band were going to deliver the rock'n'roll. Bizarrely, the concert at the Royal Albert Hall – where the group had played in spring 1972 – was banned by the hall authorities after hearing the tapes of the new album, according to *Sounds*.

The group quickly gelled as a half-decent rock'n'roll outfit. Some journalists were impressed. Steve Lake, writing in *Melody Maker* in a review headed "White Hot Beefheart", describes the show at the University of East Anglia, Norwich, on the last day of May as a "riotous party" and says that the new band were so good that "you'll forget about Zoot Horn Rollo, Rockette Morton and the rest of those illustrious gents". He continues: "'Peaches' became an instant classic, the audience to a man on its feet clapping and dancing."[19] But then a rock'n'roll band minus the old angularities could always get a crowd going. Straw poll research among long-term fans who went to see them has yet to yield anyone who was impressed.

Sounds writer Martin Hayman, a long-standing fan himself, wrote an emotional, despairing review of the Paris show of 24 May during which he coined the subsequently much-quoted epithet the "Tragic Band" to describe the group. He reckoned that Van Vliet was "a shadow of his former self". In a bleak account of the show he asked rhetorically, "Who would want to write this?", before coming to the damning conclusion that the band were like pub rockers Brinsley Schwartz "on a bad night" and that "maybe the tour should have been blown out".[20] Lester Bangs thought it "boring mainstream blahrock, like bad imitation Bob Seger", that the band were "pathetic" and that onstage Van Vliet was both "half-hearted and petulant".[21]

A video documentary of the Paris show that had depressed Martin Hayman so much illustrates the alliance of Van Vliet and the Magic/Tragic Band in all their dubious glory. The set opens with 'Mirror Man', hammered flat into an average blues jam. They had played fewer than ten gigs together at this juncture and it really sounded that way. Unsurprisingly, drummer Ty Grimes wasn't anywhere near to reaching John French's syncopations on the original and the track is barely recognizable except for a few key phrases. It set the tone for the rest of the performance.

Van Vliet rated Simmons highly and enjoyed his playing, occasionally engaging him in a theatrical harmonica/saxophone exchange onstage. At Toronto he introduced Simmons, adding: "He sucked a cosmic particle into the bell of his horn and it illuminated his brain." But during the Paris set, a blot on the aural landscape was steadily growing as Simmons cut loose on 'Full Moon Hot Sun'. He had a respectable pedigree and his tenor sax work on *Unconditionally Guaranteed* was good, but here he introduces his live trademark of choogling along melodically for a while before biting the reed, gurning hideously and letting out a stream of elongated screeches *ad infinitum* – his "animalistic" style that he reserved for rock music. Given free rein, he indulges himself at every opportunity, no matter how inappropriate. His showcase, 'Sweet Georgia Brown', is a gimmicky, self-indulgent assault on the old jazz tune. Smotherman was surprised to note that, judging by the crowd's reaction, it was often the highlight of the show.

Van Vliet seems to be buzzing away and enjoying himself – probably because he didn't have too much to think about. He looked leaner than in the past and the rather hammy cape was ditched in favour of an old *Clear Spot* T-shirt with his own portrait on the front. He looks manically detached, waving his arms about, wandering up to players curiously as if he isn't sure who they are, and pointing his microphone at them. His voice sounds in good shape. A medley that includes 'Tarotplane' – or at least a few phrases of it – rambles on interminably. At this point it becomes apparent that, clad in purple Lycra top, bass guitarist Paul Uhrig looks uncannily like Derek Smalls, the bass player of the spoof heavy metal group Spinal Tap. Then, for some reason, Grimes boots his kit over and gets off his stool, attempting to look aggressive. At this point it's apparent that he's wearing platform boots. The footwear, the endless rock'n'roll jams and that final act of meaningless "rebellion" sum up the whole desultory Tragic Band affair, and a lot of the attitudes of the mid-Seventies. *Live In London*, a CD released in 1996, features highlights of their show at the Theatre Royal, Drury Lane, London, in June 1974. It is best left in the racks.

A young fan, Steve Riette – now a musician and artist, who has since changed his name to Ace Farren Ford – had often chatted to Van Vliet after concerts since first seeing him play live in 1972, but noticed that something was now seriously awry. "Don was so trashed drunk," he remembers. "At the Whiskey [A-Go-Go] show he polished off a bottle of Charteuse before he hit the stage. He was so tore up and I thought, 'Don never does this for a show'. And another thing, you'd go backstage and talk to him, and those manager guys would say, 'Oh, Don's too busy to talk to you right now' and Don would just look at you with this frustrated look, like, 'Hey I'd talk to you, but it's out of my hands. Sorry'. I was living with this bunch of Dada noise guys called Smegma and we made up this elaborate plan, that we would go to one of the shows, and I was going to bring a gun and kidnap him! Later, I told him of this plan and he said, 'God, I wish you would have done that'."

Smotherman admits he "had a ball" on tour, but is happy to agree with the bad notices: "The whole thing was a fraud," he says. "It really was. We were trying our best, but it was not the most stellar assembly. In the States no one seemed to give much of a shit, but in Europe, where they take these things a little more seriously, most of the time the audiences and the press were very hostile to the band. And rightfully so. Once in a while, someone would take pity on us and say we were trying as hard as we could with difficult material. But we'd get to France or Belgium and people would say, 'Hey, where's the Magic Band, who are these assholes?' But it was just like the blind leading the blind, man. It was just a strange deal."

The tour was organised on a low budget with the group travelling in what Smotherman describes as a metropolitan day-trip bus with bench seats. Sleep was difficult to come by and while Van Vliet was sipping from his bottle of Chartreuse, the musicians would share their contract rider bottle of Jack Daniel's and hope to pass out. He reckons that Del Simmons, a grown man with three children, must have wondered why he was there when friendly fist fights and general horseplay broke out in the back of the bus. He continues: "The tour was so slipshod. Until Augie came along as this tour manager, he'd been working on a shift line out of Boeing Aircraft. He knew nothing about anything. It was just a mess. The bookings were never quite solid and the hotels were never quite together and the money was never quite there."

Despite his blustering stage performances, Van Vliet was becoming increasingly uncomfortable with the whole situation. Smotherman: "I really enjoyed Don's company, he was very eccentric – I don't mean that perjoratively, he was just an eccentric and unusual dude. I personally felt like he didn't really care anything for us. We used to ask each other, 'Why is he doing this when he's already got his own little niche carved out?' I never did understand. But for all of his artistic bent… I never got the impression from him that he was venal, but he was very money-conscious and I think the idea of making more money was not an unacceptable concept to him."

Former Henry Cow drummer Chris Cutler recalls the atmosphere on tour: "Don spent the lion's share of his time with us. He treated them [the Magic Band]… it's hard to say, I just don't think they had very much in common and didn't have much to say to each other. Henry Cow were probably a bit more interested in the things that he was interested in. Musically it was a very bizarre experience. I don't think he was very happy. After the first concert on that tour, in some huge hall somewhere, while the public were still going crazy, shouting and cheering, I was going back to the stage from the room and Don was coming towards me from behind the stage. There was nobody around in the passageway and as he walked past – he didn't stop – he said, indicating the public, 'That was the worst gig I ever did in my life and they love it.'"

Van Vliet's anger indicates that his heart was sinking from this easily achieved popularity. The fact that the audiences went wild to a set which was simply his music done boogie-style proved that they were perfectly happy with the sort of good-time rock'n'roll that the Magic Band – and many other groups – were serving up. It was the price to be paid for the privilege of operating within the rock mainstream.

In all this the so-called Tragic Band deserve some credit. They had been put into a position that was not of their making, and with a minimum of rehearsal had at least got a presentable show together. If replacements for the "real" Magic Band had not been found, the cancellation of the tour could have been embarrassing and costly. It's amazing that grown men still become enraged at their mention, which is as perceptive as blaming Chuck Berry's hastily assembled pick-up bands for his notoriously scrappy live performances in the Seventies.

Chris Cutler: "'It wasn't their [the band's] fault at all. They were perfectly competent at doing what they were doing, but Don didn't even try, as far as I could tell, to direct them in the way that he directed the old Magic Band. Basically they played it pretty straight, the way that they were able to play it, and he just sang on top of it." Cutler also recalls Van Vliet telling him in all seriousness that he was planning to work with an orchestra in future. A tantalising prospect, but one that got no further than being mooted. Cutler: "Beefheart claimed he was ready to go but that Richard Branson wouldn't put up the money. Who knows?"

Despite receiving bad notices, on a one-to-one basis, Van Vliet still held the press in his thrall. Smotherman makes these observations: "The people who take the time to interview Don are either open or closet fans. And I think they want to believe that stuff he says is true. I think [it would be different] if you had a cop standing there interviewing him, going, 'Oh right, sure'… But most of the interviewers were going, 'Really? Oh, that's cool.'"

Before one of the shows at the Concertgebouw in Amsterdam, Smotherman saw this at first hand. He and Van Vliet were walking upstairs to the dressing room, just speculating about what food would be provided, and whether they were all going to go out for a meal together after the show. Smotherman describes what took place: "Then we got to the top of the stairs and saw all of these reporters. All of a sudden he'd become Captain Beefheart and goes, 'Er, excuse me, Michael, I have to go and meditate and levitate in my dressing room for a few minutes before the performance.' He could turn that on and you'd see all these reporters go, 'Ooh… aaah, Don is going to levitate.'"

Lester Bangs was a friend of Van Vliet's until his death in 1982. He was present at one of the shows on the 1974 tour. A microphone broke down at the end of the set and Van Vliet arrived backstage in what he describes as a "livid, almost frightening rage". Bangs wrote a brutally frank account of the ensuing spectacle: "For the first time ever I sensed something in him dangerous on a level consonant with physical fear. His tantrum was ridiculous and scary. Up in the dressing room he made the clarinet player [Simmons] tear off an extended solo in our honour, which was quite amazing, after which he talked, and talked, and talked. Almost all of it was bitterness talk, rage-spitting impotent frustration, seething endlessly, self-consumingly." The small party decamped back to the hotel. Bangs had talked long into the night with Van Vliet before then, but this time he sat for hours reluctantly listening to him "ranting" then snapping, and turning on Jan for no apparent reason, shouting at her to get out of her chair. Bangs described the situation as "gut-curdlingly ugly" and concluded, "I decided that he was a madman, potentially dangerous, that he probably had no artistic future, and that I did not want to see him again."[22]

During the interview with Kent for *New Musical Express* Van Vliet referred to a recent review of *Unconditionally Guaranteed* in the paper, in which he had been accused of "mellowing out". Although Van Vliet was keen to dispense platitudes at this time, if the new façade was pressured enough, it would crack and the dissatisfaction that was lurking just behind would spill out. Those two words touched a very sensitive nerve. Van Vliet to Kent: "Mellowing out? Did you say *mellowing out*??? But I'm not going to mellow out! I mean – look at my *eyes*! Aren't they *wild*? I mean AREN'T THEY?? They're psychotic!

"Listen, I'd like… you tell that guy that if he furnishes me with a soprano sax, I'll come over to his office and play for seven hours! And he'll hear the *wildest* music he's ever heard. Mellowing out – huh! Just look at these EYES!"[23]

For the first time in an English music paper, the whole tone of the article – entitled *Old Fart At Play* – erred towards making Van Vliet look ridiculous. The main photograph was a montage of Van Vliet holding a crude cutout of his own head, which was saying "Look into my eyes and repeat after me: 'I MUST buy Captain Beefheart's new album'." Even though Van Vliet was expert at manipulating journalists, on this occasion Kent was in no mood to go along with his spiel.

"I can take bullshit from people if they are making great music or great art, but not if they are making a record that is just a creative void, like *Unconditionally Guaranteed*," says Kent today. "I listened to that and thought: What happened? Where has he gone? And for him to just sit there and say this is the best music of his career, and that he wanted to be more commercial, it was just ridiculous. I went to Paris and saw [the new Magic Band] and Beefheart told me they were the best band he'd ever had, but he was just talking bullshit to me. He was being incredibly wrongheaded and it irritated me because he had fucked over this great band. I've seen bands as good in their own way, but never better. And for someone to reject that and not appreciate that enough, for me that was the failure of the guy. I never went to see him after that.

"If someone I admire really irritates me, I'm going to go for them, and I went for him. But such is life. It was sad to see. It's one thing to do it if you know you are going to make a lot of money there is a reason for this, but *Unconditionally Guaranteed* wasn't even commercial enough to be a money earning record. To make things worse he had a cult following that was building in this country and that record was not going to have a good effect on that or capture a new market.

"At the time he had this awful manager who was a complete crook, a real scumbag, who had no respect for Beefheart and was just counting the money, as I could see. I felt sorry for Beefheart. He was always with his wife, Jan, and he would always defer to her. It was a totally insular relationship those two had. They were inside themselves totally as an entity and it was obvious they were being taken for a really nasty ride by these managers."

Van Vliet was indeed sitting uncomfortably on the fence that separated commercial concerns from a self-image as an artist and a disrupter of musical mores. It became increasingly obvious that the writing was on the wall for the business relationship between Van Vliet and the DiMartino brothers. Steve Lake interviewed DiMartino and Van Vliet together. Van Vliet told him: "I'm not evacuating my old music, man. I've just got a few things to do and then I'll be right back. I have to do it. Because there's no one else that can do it right. No way!"

This prompted an interruption from Andy DiMartino, which contained some sales projections and this pronouncement: "Beefheart won't be back into the old music as a full-time thing. He'll continue to do both. They'll complement each other. I'd like to add, too, that where you might think he's deviating... how many other people have combined, in such a short space of time, rock with jazz and blues and avant-garde and an old-timer [Del Simmons] playing 'Sweet Georgia Brown' to a teenage audience? That takes imagination and it takes guts."[23]

Away from this farcical and tawdry circus, Van Vliet was still producing moments of his own personal magic. Two particular incidents remain strong in Chris Cutler's memory: "I remember we were on the ferry coming back to Dover at the end of the tour. Don suddenly started to point out tiny links and correspondences – the colour of that barstool and a child's socks, the shape of a shadow and a book on a table, that sort of thing – only a lot of them, and as if he saw the parts of the room and its occupants as a pattern or net formed by the positions of similars; a kind of topographical version of the internal rhyming stresses in a poem. And he did genuinely seem sometimes to be preternaturally alert. In the middle of a conversation in a noisy hotel foyer, I remember he suddenly stopped and commented on what a party of people over the other side of the room were talking about. None of us had heard anything of any other conversation – one blanks all that out – nor could we even after our attention had been drawn it. We did check. Don was right."

12

THE CAPTAIN'S HOLIDAY

"I wasn't smart enough at that time to see what a genuinely great artist he was. We would go into restaurants that had paper tablecloths and he would sit there and draw something with a magic marker that none of us had sense enough to pick up and take with us. We'd just walk off and see the waiter throwing it in the trash. And so many nights I've thought to myself: 'God, I wish I'd saved as least one of them.'"
Michael Smotherman (interview with author, 1998)

The pick-up Magic Band dissolved as soon as the tour ended in the summer of 1974. Michael Smotherman explains why: "That tour was just a one-shot deal. To be honest, I was struggling with it, but I was trying. The other guys couldn't wait to get paid and go home. We got back to California and did this *Moonbeams* album and then everyone went their separate ways. I never saw any of those guys again." If the tour was shambolic, the next instalment of the story, the recording of *Bluejeans And Moonbeams*, was farcical.

Smotherman and Dean Smith were kept on from the touring band and Ty Grimes contributed some "percussions". The new *faux* Magic Band also featured Ira Ingber (Elliot's brother) and Bob West on bass, Mark Gibbons and Jimmy Caravan on keyboards, and Gene Pello on drums. The dictating factor in the album's creation was expedience rather than aesthetics. The "Special thanks to the following without whose help this album would not have been possible" section on the album sleeve carries its own subtext. Unusually, it lists most of the musicians who play on the record, indicating how hastily it was thrown together. Victor Hayden, The Mascara Snake, made a return of sorts with his cover painting of a strange, gambolling, chamois-like animal.

The ensemble was rushed into a small studio, Stronghold Sound Recorders, in north Hollywood, to record the album. The budget, estimated with hindsight to be roughly $50,000, was allegedly not greatly dented by the events that followed. Smotherman remembers being desperate enough for more work to accept the $50 per song session fee that was offered, and that the recording took about two days. Andy DiMartino produced, although this time he is absent from the writing credits. Van Vliet later claimed that it was finished off and released without his approval.

He looked back on this era in 1977:"'It [*Bluejeans*] might have been good but for the fact that I was up north painting and writing a book and Mercury just put it out. And they had taken Winged Eel Fingerling [Elliot Ingber] off guitar and changed the drums to the way they wanted it. They took off a whole track of Winged Eel Fingerling on 'Party Of Special Things (To Do)'. Just took it off and didn't tell me. How ridiculous that is.

"What could I do? Go up the cement tower and say, 'Listen, little lawyer, STOP!' But they wouldn't do it. I haven't had a royalty statement on either of those two albums. Nothing. After I got rid of Virgin they should have sent it to me. They knew where I was."[1]

Van Vliet's assertion that *Bluejeans And Moonbeams* would have been good but for the DiMartino brothers taking guitar tracks off one song or even a number of songs is clutching at some kind of vindication for the exercise – the album is substandard and fundamentally flawed. Van Vliet said the pick-up band had been recorded against his wishes, but if so he had lost the spirit to make a stand. He was resigned to getting this particular chapter finished and filed away.

Events in the recording studio became embarrassingly comic. Smotherman: "Don was just as confused as he could be throughout the whole process. He would sit there in a chair and sing, and he had no idea when to come in or when to stop. Count-offs didn't mean anything to him. One time, about two o'clock in the morning, I had to go out and sit beside him in a chair. When it was time for him to sing, I had my hand on the back of his neck and I would push his face up to the microphone and he would start singing. And when it was time to stop I would pull him back gently."

The music on *Bluejeans And Moonbeams* is the sort of mainstream mid-

Seventies West Coast rock that could have been played by Eagles imitators. But ironically, although it finds Van Vliet even further away from his "true" music, it's a marginally better album than *Unconditionally Guaranteed*, if only because the vocals are impressive throughout. He might have needed physically reminding of his cues, but once he'd got them, it sounded as if he was trying to jettison himself out of his self-dug hole by sheer lung power.

Although Van Vliet used to jokingly describe his music as "So-real", the surrealism in the opening line of 'Party Of Special Things To Do' – "The camel wore a nightie" – sounds uncharacteristically half-hearted. Van Vliet goes on to describe the goings-on at the party, with references to "the mirror man" and to "distant cousins" – a lyric from 'Big-Eyed Beans From Venus'. He was now in the position of going for fame by association with his own past work. The song was co-written by Elliot Ingber, but the only positive thing to be said about it is that the group groove along pleasantly – an appropriately banal description of the music of a man who only a few years ago had composed with the express intent of shaking listeners out of their torpor.

The wild card in the pack is a surprisingly effective cover of JJ Cale's 'Same Old Blues', which finds Van Vliet easing past the snags of his mid-life rock crisis by temporarily borrowing Cale's mantle of grizzled troubadour. Whether or not the material was foisted upon him is unknown, but he sings the song with conviction. Smotherman: "All those obnoxious vocals that you hear in the background – that's me. There were supposed to be some other people singing background and then DiMartino thought he could get me to sing all the background for cheaper."

'Observatory Crest' is a languorous, bombed-out song, again co-written by Ingber (although featuring none of his guitar). Van Vliet has just been to a concert and "heard all the best", and then drives up to the hills – presumably to the Griffith Park Observatory, near his birthplace – and wistfully looks down at the city beneath. One wonders who had been playing at this mythical concert – not Ornette Coleman or Roland Kirk, for sure. Supertramp, possibly?

'Pompadour Swamp' (not the *Spotlight Kid*-era instrumental of the same name) was credited solely to Van Vliet, and finds him making the most of his own average material. He sings about a place "where the silhouettes dance" and the sun shines late at night, over swelling Hammond organ and a shuffling backbeat. He's circumnavigating the steaming bayous visited on

'Clear Spot', but this time seems afraid of getting his boots wet.

On the risible and appropriately named instrumental 'Captain's Holiday', Van Vliet was notable by his complete absence. The only other acknowledgement of his existence is the cheesy "girlie" backing refrain of "Oh, Captain, Captain" and some spirited harmonica, although it was not actually played by Van Vliet. The track is credited to the song-writing team Feldman, Richmond, Hickerson and Blackwell, which suggests that it was an abandoned song that would have otherwise gone to waste. But Andy DiMartino was even more pragmatic. Smotherman: "As a matter of fact, I think that track was on a 24-track reel in the studio that nobody had picked up."

'Rock'n'Roll's Evil Doll' sounds like a sketch for a good song, with some Art Tripp-style drum figures and clavinet adding chunky, funky sounds. Ironically, the group play with more grit than the real Magic Band managed on *Unconditionally Guaranteed*. If Harkleroad and St Clair been playing rather than Dean Smith, it could – just possibly – have been a fine example of rock'n'roll done Beefheart-style.

'Further Than We've Gone' is a soppy ballad capped by a long instrumental passage. Van Vliet's vocals nearly prevent it from sounding like a Barry White out-take. But not quite. 'Twist Ah Luck' again hits a funky R&B groove, vaguely reminiscent of 'Peaches' on *Unconditionally Guaranteed*. "Stitch in time, your path crossed mine" exemplifies Van Vliet's inability to imbue his lyrics with anything other than tired banalities at this juncture.

The closer, 'Bluejeans And Moonbeams', is constructed with a ballad-like architectural span. The first part houses a decent melody, but the lengthy coda peters out into a dreary drift. In *Melody Maker*, Allan Jones described it thus: "Spiralling guitars trace and swoop in delicate patterns over a synthesiser and acoustic guitar… it's almost worth the price of the album." What he fails to mention is that the synth solo is an indigestible garnish, hideous enough to hold its own against any other hideous synth solo. But in qualification, Jones's review was headed "Beefheart: No More Magic" and he went on to state: "This album has some difficulty in justifying its existence." He concludes the review diplomatically: "Beefheart has proven himself too vital an artist to be dismissed on initial reactions. He needs a little more time, perhaps."[2]

The album is a towering piece of art compared to the advertisement that appeared in the music papers. A grotesque picture of a baby in a sequinned suit holding a microphone is accompanied by appropriately shoddy text: "In 1965, when The Beatles' 'Help' was top of the charts, Captain Beefheart first began to delight the discriminating with his own wierd [*sic*] and earthy kind of rock music. The ironically titled *Bluejeans And Moonbeams* is the eighth album with the Captain's brand upon it. On *Bluejeans And Moonbeams* nobody plays at rock'n'roll, they just play."

How it was "ironically titled" is still unclear. *Bluejeans and Moonbeams* is a poor set of songs, but it isn't totally irredeemable. Those who had the time to do a join-the-dots extrapolation could see a half-decent album trying, but failing, to get out. But 1974 was indisputably Van Vliet's *annus horribilis*. *Bluejeans* had its UK release in November of that year, but a UK tour to promote the album, which was planned to run from February to March 1975, was cancelled. The sinking ship could be no longer be kept afloat and its flotsam – Andy DiMartino, his brother Augie and the musicians – soon drifted away.

Having sold himself short without even managing to sell out, and left with a couple of albums which he later pronounced "horrible and vulgar", the Captain's holiday looked like it might be permanent. He disappeared back up to his home on the northern Californian coast and left the whole sorry mess behind. What could he do now? Maybe he would take the time to concentrate on his painting and poetry. He was thirty-three, which at the time was old in rock business terms, and he needed to get some perspective on his career and figure out how he could make it progress.

Rumours began to circulate in the press that he was working as a lumberjack. This added to the myth, but Van Vliet's struggle with his muse didn't include feeling trees. During this period of self-imposed exile, a chance meeting with a teenage student, Jeff Moris Tepper, proved pivotal in getting him back on track. Coincidentally, Tepper (nowadays simply named Moris) was embarking on a college course in the area. Tepper was a long-time Captain Beefheart fan, and had met him once before, after a show in LA during the *Clear Spot* tour. He recalls the incident: "I just walked up to him and told him how much I enjoyed his music. He was wearing a hat that looked like a huge Dixie cup and I was holding a Dixie cup full of water. And I said, 'Look, I have your hat.' He laughed. And I said something like, 'Hey, will you draw me a picture?' and he gave me a piece of art right then and there."

On an expedition into the area to look for accommodation, Tepper noticed someone drive by in an orange pumpkin-coloured Corvette

Stingray. It was Van Vliet. He saw him park at a Corvette dealership and tentatively reintroduced himself.

"I walked up to his car and I went, very softly, 'Don?' and he fucking jumped. He hit his head on the roof of his car, and he goes, 'Man, you scared the shit out of me! Hey, man, I know you.' And I go, 'Yeah, you and I talked once at the Troubadour in Los Angeles,' and he said, 'Man, I gave you a piece of art, I don't *ever* do that.' This was all within the first ten seconds of talking to him, but he remembered me. It was really weird. He then said, 'People think I'm round here taking mushrooms and walking on rooftops, but I'm a pretty down to earth guy.'"

After a conversation outside his car, Van Vliet took Tepper to see a house next door to his own that was available to rent and within a couple of hours his accommodation was sorted out. Finding that they had a common love of art, music and wildlife, the two men soon struck up a friendship. Tepper: "He didn't know what he wanted to do. He was in a lot of pain and a lot of confusion. At that point he'd already done those horrible DiMartino albums and regretted them miserably. He'd actually quit music. I said, 'Screw that, man, you gotta get back into it.'"

Despite Tepper's intention to devote his attention to his studies rather than rock music, the attentions of his neighbour spurred him on to mess around with his guitar.

"For the rest of my two years up there, I was never left alone. Every day, he was banging on my window [saying], 'Come out, man, let's go get coffee.' I had this four-track and – I think just for the hell of it – started figuring out all the guitar parts to *Trout Mask Replica*. One day he came over and I played him 'Dali's Car', both guitar tracks, and his jaw dropped. A couple of days later I played him 'Fallin' Ditch' and 'When Big Joan Sets Up' and pretty soon I had 15–16 of the tunes fully down, both guitar parts. He couldn't believe it. He said, 'Man, I'm going back to LA, and you'll be my guitar player and we're gonna go back into the business.' It was really romantic and fun. It was very cool."

That time would come, but it was to be deferred for a good year. Van Vliet wanted to get back into playing music and was still under contract to Mercury and Virgin, but had no Magic Band. He had also got himself into a contractual mess, later explaining that whilst still with the DiMartino brothers he had signed away his power of attorney when drunk on cognac. The interim solution to these problems, although simple, was so unlikely that it took everyone by surprise: Van Vliet called Frank Zappa, explaining his predicament, and became a member of The Mothers Of Invention, touring with them throughout April and May 1975.

Zappa realised that the only way he could help him out was by giving him some paid employment. He told Nigel Leigh in 1993: "Don had the ability and the inclination to sign any piece of contractual paper shoved under his nose, without comprehending what these papers said and how they interacted with each other. So his career fell on evil days because he had signed papers with companies all over the place that all had conflicting claims on his services. And so he was in a position where he couldn't tour and he couldn't record. And it was at that time that I put him in the band to do the *Bongo Fury* tour – that was the only way that he could earn some money because he was just legally tied up all over the place."[3]

Van Vliet explained to Barry Miles how this collaboration began: "I hadn't spoken to him [Zappa] or seen him for five years. I was up painting and writing and doing all those things and I just happened to come down to southern California. The minute I came down there we went on a big tour. Ha, that was fun! I'd been with a group for so many years that it was nice to get away and be free again with a very intelligent person. A very old friend…

"I just called him up and told him I'd like to see him and he says, 'Well, great, come down and hear this album I'm working on,' and I said, 'Well, yeah, I'd like to, but I've gotten out of the business. I'm not gonna be in the music business any more,' and he says, 'Oh no you can't do that,' and I said, 'Well, I think that's what I'm gonna do.' So Frank said, 'Well, come down and hear some records, you know, we'll go on a tour!'"[4]

Zappa's version of events, as recounted to Miles, was completely different: "He apologised for all the garbagio and asked for a job. He flunked [the audition]. See, he had a problem with rhythm and we were very rhythm-orientated. Things have to happen on the beat. I had him come up on the bandstand at our rehearsal hall and try to sing 'Willie The Pimp' and he couldn't get through it. I figured if he couldn't get through that I didn't stand much chance of teaching him the other stuff.

"Although he still has trouble remembering words and making things happen on the beat, he's better. Just before the tour I tried him again and he squeaked by."[5]

Maybe this was Zappa's way of extracting his metaphorical pound of flesh after having been badmouthed for so long. Or maybe Van Vliet had blown the audition. Their relationship had become so complicated that none of their comments to the media could be taken at face value.

When Zappa's story was relayed back to Van Vliet, by Kate Phillips of *New Musical Express*, he shrugged it off thus: "Imagine there being an audition for people who've known one another for that many years. If he did audition me, I didn't notice. Maybe he thought he did. I don't know. I can't imagine myself being auditioned."[6]

Van Vliet wanted to break out of his creative trough and re-establish his reputation. He tried to smooth over his harsh criticisms of Zappa, claiming that he had said some unkind things but they had only looked so bad as a result of distorted journalism. And no doubt Zappa was happy to take the kudos for rehabilitating a legendary figure by featuring him in his group. A truce of sorts was declared.

In an interview backstage at the Capital Theater, Passaic, New Jersey, during the tour, Van Vliet gave a frank account of his conduct in the long-running feud with Zappa. To Steve Weitzman of *Rolling Stone*: "I said some silly things because I was a spoiled brat and I don't understand business to the extent that Frank does. I probably felt neglected. I'll admit it... and I told him so. I said, 'I'm sorry, Frank, and I don't mean that for an excuse.' We shook hands and that was that."[7]

Prior to the tour Zappa had been working on the album *One Size Fits All*, which was released in June 1975. Van Vliet guested on harmonica under the pseudonym Bloodshot Rolling Red. In a spin-off from this temporary liaison, Zappa and Van Vliet had a spot on a radio show on KWST during the tour. They ran through the story of 'Electricity', and Zappa played some old Studio Z material and backed Van Vliet on guitar on a live-on-air performance of 'Orange Claw Hammer' from *Trout Mask Replica*. They also introduced a track, 'You Will Drink My Water', by their tongue-in-cheek new group, The Smegmates, which included Van Vliet playing sax. During an interview on WABX, Detroit, Zappa was breezily antagonistic, informing the interviewer that Van Vliet had no natural rhythm and could hardly read. Van Vliet, meanwhile, was withdrawn and sullen, responding to questions in an out-of-it-sounding drawl.

Onstage with The Mothers, he sang and played harmonica and occasionally treated the audience to a blast of saxophone, most notably on the instrumental 'Echidna's Arf (Of You)'. The Zappa/Beefheart/Mothers tour was an intensive affair, with over thirty shows from April to May 1975. It yielded an album, *Bongo Fury*, a live document which also featured a couple of studio tracks. And typically, Zappa decided to augment the live material with some overdubs – "selected studio wonderment", as he calls it on the record sleeve.

Van Vliet is in excellent voice on the album and his timing is spot-on throughout. Zappa always ran his groups on rigorous lines and where Van Vliet might have got away with singing approximately in the right place on live versions of his own songs, here he had to come in on cue. Zappa had given him a chance to prove himself, revive his flagging self-confidence and earn some money. And to feature in someone else's band took away some of the pressure of performing live. He told Steve Weitzman of *Rolling Stone* that he "had an extreme amount of fun on this tour. They move awfully fast. I've never travelled this fast with the Magic Band – turtles all the way down,"[8] he concluded cryptically.

One of Van Vliet's idiosyncrasies is documented on the sleeve to *Bongo Fury*, where he is credited with "Harp, vocals, shopping bags". Back in the earliest days of the Magic Band he kept his lyrics on pieces of paper in a brown paper sack. On the *Bongo Fury* tour he carried around bags full of lyrics, sketch books and paraphernalia, which he had a habit of mislaying and would then frantically try to relocate. In *New Musical Express* Zappa told Mick Farren: "The way he relates to language is unique, the way he brings my text to life. Of course he has problems. He won't be separated from his sheets of paper that have his words written on. He clings to them for dear life."[9]

After Van Vliet ambled onstage with his shopping bags, he spent his time drawing when not performing, as recounted by Mothers' trombonist Bruce Fowler: "Don would sit on stage and just draw for most of the entire concert in his art books. Then every once in a while he would turn around and show it to us. 'Gotcha,' he would say."[10]

Van Vliet's contributions included 'Willie The Pimp', 'Orange Claw Hammer' and an early version of 'The Torture Never Stops' subtitled, 'Why Doesn't Someone Get Him A Pepsi', which later appeared on Zappa's 1976 album, *Zoot Allures*. Zappa would announce the track in this way, with reference to Van Vliet's teenage habit of shouting to his mother to bring him a Pepsi.

The in-jokes continued on the opening track and the best song on *Bongo Fury*, 'Debra Kadabra'. Zappa wrote the song around a stream of images from the pair's shared past which are cryptic to the point of impenetrability. Van Vliet, however, claimed it was about Grannie Annie. At points the subject matter becomes literally painful as well as personal, especially when Van Vliet recounts covering himself with Avon cologne and then having to be driven off to a relative's house until his skin cleared up.

This allergy, which had prompted Zappa and Jim Sherwood to pretend they had splashed cologne on the front seat of his car, produced spectacular effects on Van Vliet's skin. Zappa explained the story behind this song in 1991: "Don's mother, who sold Avon products door to door, had all this stuff from Avon stashed at the house, which everybody used. Y'know, it was free beauty aids. Don, being neurotic, and a bit of a narcissist, was quite prone to dumping any kind of beauty aid that he could find onto his body. He made the unfortunate mistake of taking some Avon cologne and putting it in his hair, one day, which made it start falling out. He also put some sort of Avon cream on his face which made him break out in this giant rash. His face looked like an alligator. He was losing a great deal of status at the high school, and he moved out of our little desert community, Lancaster, where we went to school, and moved down to east LA to live with his aunt for a while [till] he got his chops back together."[11]

Zappa tailored the song for Van Vliet, who navigated its serpentine complexity with ease. Musically the track is as much of a collage as the lyrics, starting with a Magic Band-esque boogie, then chopping around between moods and motifs. This was Van Vliet's first appearance on an official live recording and his voice ranges from a bellow to a peculiar constricted sound. Although it could have been a stylistic device to mirror the turbulent flow of the song – and having to relive the Avon cologne trauma – its roots were at a deeper level. Zappa echoed other people's observations of Van Vliet's onstage vocal technique, noting that the force of his singing and his tenseness increased his blood pressure and effectively closed his ears, making it difficult for him to hear the onstage monitors. This also accounts for a contemporary report of Van Vliet's face growing "flushed" during a concert.

'Poofter's Froth Wyoming Plans Ahead' was also written specifically for Van Vliet – a jaunty, sublimely dumb "sort of a cowboy song", as Zappa announces on the album. It was a predictive satire on the upcoming 1976 US bicentennial celebrations and the inevitable marketing of trash souvenirs. The use of the word "Poofter", English slang for a male homosexual, was picked up by Mick Farren when he reviewed *Bongo Fury* in *New Musical Express*. He noted that both here and on 'The Man With The Woman Head' it was used as if both Zappa and Van Vliet didn't know the meaning of the word. This proved to be the case. Van Vliet was shocked when given the derivation of the word by Vivien Goldman in an interview in *Sounds*: "Is THAT right?!? Y'see, Frank and I didn't know that that meant that. We're both naive."[12]

Following on, '200 Years Old' also taps the bicentennial vein. This bluesy studio cut finds Van Vliet's high-pitched harmonica opening proceedings and Denny Walley's slide guitar slicing through the dense sound. Van Vliet also plays harmonica on 'Cucamonga', which takes its title from the location of Studio Z. The song highlights a nostalgic, even sentimental, vein in Zappa's writing that only rarely surfaced on tracks like 'Village Of The Sun' (on the 1974 live album, *Roxy And Elsewhere*), which harked back to Sun Village, where The Blackouts played in the late Fifties. Zappa sounds close to wistful as he recounts the place where many years previously he and a couple of friends "began practising for the time we might go on TV".

From the outside, it looked like Van Vliet and Zappa's friendship was fraught with so many difficulties because they both had problems maintaining the selflessness required to make such a relationship run smoothly. Neither was prepared to open up – which necessitates putting oneself in a position of vulnerability – without qualification. Barry Miles spent a considerable time with them both and offers these views: "They always had this ego problem between them, which was ridiculous. Frank was obviously very insecure. That's where all that cynicism and aloofness came from. He had very few friends because he turned everything into a business relationship. I think they both had tremendous nostalgia for the days when they used to cruise around Lancaster and listen to R&B records together – theirs was a very, very deep friendship. I think that the business and Los Angeles got in the way. It's a horrible place [and] really fosters the worst sides of people."

Nick Kent compares their friendship with another he observed first hand. "It's a typical relationship in the music business. I've been around Iggy [Pop] when he's been not too complimentary about [David] Bowie, but at the same time, without Bowie he wouldn't have had *The Idiot* and *Lust For Life*. It's all very fucked up, but people who are helped are often so egocentric and paranoid they don't like to admit they have been helped. I think Zappa has always had a very decent and giving perspective when he has worked with Beefheart, I think he's always admired what Beefheart has done and just wants to have it expressed. I don't think he's wanted to make money out of the guy or turn him into a freakshow or to turn him into anything that he didn't admire. But Beefheart had a perspective that was not tied to reality and would decide on a whim whether to trust someone or not. He trusted a lot of people who let him down and screwed over a lot of people that, frankly, he could have trusted."

The bulk of the album consists of quality Zappa material, a bluesier take on his post-*Overnite Sensation* (1973) style – with the exception of 'Carolina Hard-Core Ecstasy', which marries an exquisite tune with a misogynistic, 'humorous' S&M lyric which is so crass, its most shocking aspect is that an intelligent man could have written such dross thinking it was funny. Van Vliet also joins in on the choruses to the closing track, 'Muffin Man', and plays harmonica on 'Advance Romance'. The two Van Vliet compositions on *Bongo Fury* are prose poems, recited over imaginative, semi-freeform backing by The Mothers: 'Sam With The Showing Scalp Flat Top' and 'The Man With The Woman Head'. Van Vliet had appeared to be in a state of creative bankruptcy, but these two compositions are individual, marvellously vivid vignettes, albeit dating from 1973.

The lyrics are stylistically removed from the ecological doomsday warnings of *Lick My Decals Off, Baby*, the hobos and the surreal relocations of the American mythos of *Trout Mask*, or the warped bluesology of *The Spotlight Kid*. They are word sketches with a vivid sense of place and character, the protagonists coloured by Van Vliet's extraordinary imagery.

As well as sketching onstage, Van Vliet would take his sketch-pad into cafés, bars and restaurants to capture interesting visual subjects. Similarly, the prose poem 'The Man With The Woman Head' reads as if the incidents that took place and the character's visual idiosyncrasies were being jotted down by the observer on a surreptitiously concealed note-pad.

Van Vliet recites over loose, backgrounded improvisation by The Mothers, with Napoleon Murphy Brock blowing some unpredictable sax. At the start he asks the audience, "Are you with me on this, people?", before describing a character who appears to be an ageing theatrical type in a drive-in Hollywood restaurant, an "early vaudeville jazz poofter" with a face "the colour of a nicotine-stained hand", opium-stained wooden teeth, wrinkled "map-like" eyes, lined from the excessive use of eye paint, and who casually lets cigarette ash fall on his "white-on-yellow Daks".

After the half-hearted fare of the last two records, it is a shock to find such a brilliant piece of work as 'The Man With The Woman Head': the vivid word associations, the faded low-budget theatrical decadence of the main character and the entrance of Ace towards the end carrying a tray and mouthing, "You cheap son of a bitch". He is portrayed as a jealous rival – an actor waiting tables to support himself.

'Sam With The Showing Scalp Flat Top' returns in part to the mood of 'Veteran's Day Poppy', but here the Vietnam veteran with the army flat-top (or a mental patient's crop) is stuck inside a scenario full of vivid, fleeting images like stills from a film. Then enters a trolley, with "hard, dark rubber wheels", Sam's self-propelled mode of transport. Van Vliet succinctly explained Sam's predicament to Vivien Goldman: "The fellow is obviously a war victim, he's deformed by the war and he's a basket case, y'see. You've seen those people selling pencils."[13]

The empathetic backing by The Mothers moves into a shuddering rock finale as Van Vliet roars, "I wish I had a pair of bongos", before exclaiming the title of the album. In the past, he had claimed that Zappa had commandeered his phrases and used them as titles. This time he was happy to allow the album to be named after his line.

Jimmy Carl Black was an original member of The Mothers Of Invention – and was soon to have a short spell drumming with the Magic Band. Looking back, he gives this view on the Zappa/Van Vliet relationship: "I think Frank was always very envious of him, because Frank could never be as avant-garde, as far out as Beefheart – though he tried really hard to. I don't think anybody can be. It was natural for him to be like that – that's where he was coming from."

Envious or not, Zappa's magnanimous gesture might well have helped save Van Vliet's career. But their mutual appreciation society was starting to disintegrate. Jimmy Carl Black remembers meeting them after the tour: "Him and Zappa never did get along. Never. In fact when they came to El Paso, Frank wasn't even talking to him any more... would not even acknowledge that he was around. Beefheart was drawing pictures of Frank as the devil with horns and a tail... Frank really didn't like it." Zappa's view on the rigours of touring together was simply stated to Nigel Leigh: "That was not easy but that was only a few weeks."[14]

The next episode after the *Bongo Fury* tour was a swiftly reformed Magic Band. Van Vliet had met up with John French when he was singing with Mallard in northern California and persuaded him to work with the Magic Band again, this time on guitar as well as drums. Although his friendship with Zappa was again in limbo, Van Vliet continued to make use of a throughput from Zappa's group. This time Bruce 'Fossil' Fowler – so called because of his enthusiasm for palaeontology – was drafted in straight from the *Bongo Fury* tour on trombone. Jimmy Carl Black, a.k.a. Indian Ink, was also on drums, while Elliot Ingber returned on guitar, together with new recruit Greg 'Ella Guru' Davidson. A suitable bass player could not be found, so at Davidson's suggestion, Fowler played his instrument through an octave divider, in which the note played is automatically doubled up with one an octave lower, giving a unique bass sound.

A long time Zappa fan, Davidson had gone backstage after one of the shows on the *Bongo Fury* tour to chat to the group, where he remembers meeting Van Vliet for the first time. "The Captain was standing backstage talking to someone. He was buzzing with energy, his eyes were glowing. I knew he hadn't had a band of his own in a few years, so I walked up and asked him if he was going to have another band after the Zappa tour. He said, 'Well yes!' I told him I could play both guitar parts at once – I guess I was enthused – and I'd like to play in his next band. He said come over to the hotel and play.

"I went to his hotel and for the next two nights. He didn't tell me what to play – we just played. After jamming only a few minutes he told me I was in the band. I didn't believe him. I thought he was kidding. But I had a great time with him playing and hanging out. He did odd things like smoking a cigarette while looking right at me and whistling with his mouth closed. I asked him how he did it and he told me the sound was actually coming through a small hole in the side of his nose. I left him on the second day after the sun came up. He took my number and I thanked him and told him I had a really great time, not expecting to hear from him again. Three weeks later he called me and said, 'Come to LA. We're going to England'."

In preparation for their transatlantic trip, the group decamped from El Paso back to California for seven weeks' work in the rehearsal room at Zappa's DiscReet Records on Sunset Boulevard, Hollywood – which indicates any residual animosity was soon brushed aside. French was running the rehearsals, back in his familiar role of musical director. The work regime was far from pressurised, as Jimmy Carl Black describes: "Most of the time was [spent] listening to him either talking, or [watching him] drawing pictures of somebody. We didn't really practice that much. We used to go to The Brown Derby, a very famous restaurant in Hollywood where all the movie stars use to go in the 1930s and 40s. He would sit and draw everyone that came in and the whole band had to go with him – we had to go everywhere with him. It was a twelve hour a day job, and we rehearsed about one and a half hours of those twelve."

According to Davidson the rehearsal regime was a little more taxing. Although the group were given some dispensation to improvise when playing live, rehearsals were still very strict. "The band would have never been able to function without John [French]," says Davidson. "Don's forte was to create it, but not to deal with the tediousness of going through the painstaking details in rehearsal. John was good at that. Some nights I would stay at Elliot [Ingber]'s and I would work on our parts together, often listening to the records over and over and dissecting the parts. Eliot called me 'Tweezer Head' because he thought I was good at picking out the details. The parts of Elliot's that were the ones he recorded on the albums were the hardest to learn, as they were just him being spontaneous. I would guess Don didn't have him do the note-to-note regimented parts he had other guitarists play."

Davidson fondly remembers a number of post-rehearsal jams with a relaxed Van Vliet joining in and "blowing some great harp". A keen documenter of these sessions on tape, he recalls one particularly remarkable recording. "Don, John and myself were up in Lancaster, California and went to see a band with Mark Boston in it. They were doing some cover tunes like 'Brown Sugar'. We were asked to play. In the parking lot Don had me whittle one of his reeds for his sax. So, it was John on drums, Don on soprano, me on guitar, no bass. I vaguely recall John and I briefly talking about what beat he was going to play. In this case I didn't have to worry about what key we would be in. But that was all we discussed as we stood on the stage before we went on. So, with barely any idea of what was to come out, it was, 'One, Two, And…' It was a wild tune. I looked out to the audience. They were in to it. The music had a jungle-like feel to it and I remember them boppin' and groovin' to it, with a few yelps from their mouths. Don only uttered one word during the jam and it sounded to me like he said 'Ahhhhhhh, Zimba!'"

This version of the Magic Band only stayed together for a short time and played a handful of concerts. They recorded some material for a national TV show, *The Sound Stage* – although none of the footage turned out to be useable, principally due to Van Vliet's increasing agitation in the studio environment – and played two nights at the Roxy in Hollywood. In between those dates they played the Knebworth Festival in England on

July 5. In an attempt to find a bass guitarist, Buell Neidlinger, who had played with Ornette Coleman, was auditioned. John French described what took place to Justin Sherrill in 1998: "Buell is renowned as a great studio bassist and has incredible sight-reading skills. I handed him the original transcription to 'My Human Gets Me Blues'. I explained the form of the song. Everybody else had been rehearsing it for several days. I counted it off and he played it so incredibly well that I thought Mark Boston had walked into the room! There are so many 'musical rules" broken in that song I can't count them all, and in the centre section, everyone is playing in different time signatures. Buell was able to grasp that on his first try, partially because he was a great reader to begin with, so didn't have to 'think' about what he was doing."[15]

Ultimately Van Vliet stuck with Bruce Fowler and his air-bass. The festival was held in the grounds of Knebworth House in Hertfordshire, a graceful stately pile situated in rolling countryside about ten miles beyond the outer limits of London's suburban sprawl, with the stage positioned in a natural amphitheatre on the estate. Pink Floyd headed an eclectic bill which also featured The Steve Miller Band, Roy Harper and Trigger, and members of the UK comedy troupe Monty Python, with John Peel as DJ. The set was powerful, if ramshackle, with old favourites like 'Abba Zaba' and 'Moonlight On Vermont' alongside a rarely played 'Beatle Bones 'N' Smokin' Stones' and chaotic semi-improvised pieces like 'Spitball Scalped A Baby'. On 'When It Blows Its Stacks', the group play with brutal power, behind Van Vliet's visceral singing. They hadn't had enough time to completely gel together as a unit, and the set was played without a soundcheck, but the performance was a vast improvement on the 1974 shows.

Contemporary reports of the concert remark on Van Vliet throwing things into the crowd. As he was once again having problems remembering his lyrics, Jan had been up late the previous night writing them out on giant cue cards. Van Vliet turned his amnesia into a spectacle. When he had finished each song he would spin the card from the high stage out into the audience. "It was so funny," recalls Jimmy Carl Black. "Couldn't believe the guy couldn't remember the lyrics to his songs." His performance of 'Orange Claw Hammer' was erratic, even with the cue cards, but to have heard it howled out over the Hertfordshire countryside must have been a moment to savour, especially when it was followed by 'Dali's Car'.

The *Bongo Fury* tour had allowed Van Vliet temporary respite from his financial and contractual problems, but when he came over to the UK at the end of 1975, they once again reared their multitude of ugly heads. *Bongo Fury* was released on Warner Brothers in the United States, but Virgin, who were still in charge of Van Vliet's output in the UK – and who had signed a contract with him in Los Angeles – put an injunction on its release. As he was on their roster, Virgin required a sleeve credit and a financial arrangement. An impasse was reached. A Warner Brothers statement said that the situation "might go on forever". So despite the good reviews and the fact that Zappa and Van Vliet were both pleased with the results – Van Vliet described it as a "happy album" – the only way to obtain a copy in the UK was to buy it on import.

It is tempting to attribute the outcome of this episode to Van Vliet's inability to get his head around the minutiae of business arrangements. But when the tour was announced, *Melody Maker*, who had anticipated these problems, were told by a record company spokesman that as long as Van Vliet fulfilled his recording commitments to Virgin, there would be no problems about the release of collaborations between himself and Zappa. After *Unconditionally Guaranteed* and *Bluejeans And Moonbeams*, Van Vliet was keen to get away from Virgin, but the company claimed that they tried to get in touch with him with a view to releasing more material and had got no response.

All this jiggery-pokery exemplified the contemporary problems that faced artists who were under contract to different companies. If they worked together, they often had to do so uncredited or under assumed names – as Van Vliet had done under his Bloodshot Rolling Red alias. He cut through all known business conventions when he told Barry Miles: "Francis Vincent Zappa and I have made an album together, but Virgin Records won't let it out! They have no right to stop the world from hearing Frank and I having fun. Who are they kidding with a name like that? There are no more virgins, we all know that. The dance of the seven veils is over!"[16]

The new Magic Band toured Europe and the US from October to December 1975. Davidson had temporarily quit to go to Chicago, and due, in part, to a "nasty confrontation" with manager Herb Cohen, he decided to stay there. In a bout of musical drum stools, Jimmy Carl Black decided that he wanted to remain in Texas rather than move to California and left the group, making it necessary for John French to concentrate solely on drums. Guitarist Denny Walley, who had featured on the *Bongo*

Fury tour – and who Van Vliet had known since the late Fifties in Lancaster – came in alongside French, Ingber and Fowler. "He plays in that Muddy Waters kind of style, and you can't get better than Muddy," Van Vliet told Steve Lake of *Melody Maker*. He went on to say that not only had he written new material but he had fifty compositions from around the time of *Trout Mask* that had never been played before onstage. He'd be playing saxophone again, and was "through with all that rock and roll stuff... I'm back into the free thing – and that's really all I'm interested in."[17]

In his review of Captain Beefheart and the Magic Band's show at the New Victoria Theatre, London, in November 1975 in *Street Life*, Angus McKinnon enthused: "Beefheart on the right track again. Almost too good and too right to believe."[18] In his review of the show for *New Musical Express*, Chas De Walley commented that Van Vliet "saved his flagging reputation" and, less than accurately, that he had "bid farewell to the hotch-potch band of gypsies we saw at Knebworth in the summer".[19] The set included old favourites like 'Beatle Bones 'N' Smokin' Stones', 'Abba Zaba' and 'My Human Gets Me Blues'. A teenage girl climbed up onstage and embraced Van Vliet at the end of the set. Perhaps his music appealed to women after all.

13

PULLED BY RUBBER DOLPHINS

"Everything they did I had 'em do. I mean I'm a director. I don't wanna boast or anything like that, but I am an artist. And the thing is that sometimes artists are considered horrible after they direct something. Y'see those guys, they fell too far into my role, and then they didn't like me after that. It happens in theatre and everything. But I can't think of myself as doing something wrong, because I asked them everyday, 'Are you sure you want to do this?' I said, 'You'll get to the end of the road and there's probably no pot of gold, y'know, in ART.'"
Don Van Vliet on the former Magic Band to John Gray, *Sounds*, 10 December 1977

Captain Beefheart and The Magic Band's sojourn in England for the Knebworth Festival coincided with a visit to the country by former Magic Band mutineers Art Tripp, Mark Boston and Bill Harkleroad and their new group, Mallard. They stayed near Newton Abbot in Devon, where they recorded a set of new material sponsored by an anonymous backer. As they were recording using Jethro Tull's mobile studio, the identity of their patron was not difficult to guess. They were staying at Jethro Tull guitarist Martin Barre's house, with Ian Anderson the man behind the venture. In fact Anderson's involvement had begun the previous year. Immediately after the former Magic Band had sheared away from Van Vliet, he had organised an impromptu session in the hope of keeping the momentum going. He explains: "I said to them, 'Look, not wishing him any harm, but as far as the world is concerned you are The Magic Band and he is Captain Beefheart. Now he may feel that there is a legal ownership of the name The Magic Band and he could make a play for it, but you should give it a go.' So I wrote them a song called 'Magic Band' and we went into the studio in Los Angeles. I said to Rockette Morton, 'Right, you're going to be the front man, Mark, you're going to sing.' 'Oh, I've never sung before.' 'You're going to do it this afternoon.' I was probably just as bad as his ex-boss! Anyway, we made this record with Barrie Barlow from our band playing the drums, because I think everybody else had legged it – it was basically Mark and Bill and Barrie and me sitting behind the desk.

"It was written very much around what I knew Bill Harkleroad would play. I never kept a copy of it, sadly. They took it [the name The Magic Band] some way down the wire to the legal front, only to get the impression that they couldn't afford to take it any further because Don was going to jump on it with big boots, through his lawyers. So that petered out."

In *DISCoveries* in 1988, Harkleroad said of Mallard: "It was the Magic Band without Don. We figured we had a career."[1] Initially, Mallard moved to Arcata, near Eureka, north California. John French was both drummer and vocalist and he contributed music and lyrics. Although barely twenty, keyboard player John Thomas had played with French in the group Rattlesnakes And Eggs and was already a relative veteran of the Lancaster scene. But work had been hard to come by; the group had no record deal and became dormant after Van Vliet persuaded French to go back to the Magic Band after the *Bongo Fury* tour. Harkleroad had been concerned that he was likely to get into the "same sort of drudgery" as he had with the Magic Band: working hard without making any money. Differences in musical direction had begun to develop. Boston had a leaning towards country and blues, whereas Harkleroad's tastes were significantly different. "I was listening to Weather Report and jazz things and I wanted to improve my playing," he says. He quit and the group fizzled out.

Anderson's reappearance on the scene, and with it Mallard's renaissance, came about via his friendship with Mark Boston. His investment in the group was a simple, altruistic gesture: "I brought them over to England and said, 'If you want to give it a go, I'll give you the studio for a couple of weeks.' It was on the grounds that if it works out I'll tell you what it cost and you can give me the money back. If it doesn't you can go home again and forget about it. It was that simple. I thought here's a bunch of guys that had some really good music in them if given the freedom to do it."

By mid-1975, Mallard were back at full strength. They found a vocal successor to French in Sam Galpin, a country singer who'd spent over a decade on the lounge circuit in Las Vegas and the West Coast. He had a weather-beaten, phlegmy voice that was later described as being like *one* of Van Vliet's voices. But such comments would have meant little to him as he knew next to nothing about their musical past. Art Tripp had been making a living selling insurance, and was tempted back to drum with the group only after he'd been guaranteed money in advance. The group were still working on a limited budget and as Thomas was not, in his own words, one of the "principals", he remained back in Lancaster. Galpin and John 'Rabbit' Bundrick took over keyboard duties. Connor McKnight of *Zig Zag* caught up with the group in Devon. Tripp spoke to him about his past employers, coming up with this blunt assessment of his career thus far: "Man, I've worked for two of the worst people in the business – Zappa and that fuckin' Vliet."[2]

Soon after the Magic Band had left him, Van Vliet was claiming, with some relish, that they had all given up music. He was also telling journalists that whereas the group had all enjoyed comfortable accommodation, he and Jan had been sleeping on the floor for the past six years. A year later, he was still fuming. To Steve Weitzman of *Rolling Stone*: "I did *Lick My Decals Off, Baby* right after *Trout Mask Replica*. The group wanted to be commercial and since they were so nice about doing those two I thought I owed them a moral obligation and I stayed. But I should have gotten rid of them then."[3]

With the two rival factions now agreeing to be interviewed, *New Musical Express* ran a typically irreverent double-page spread in July 1975. Harkleroad and Van Vliet put forward their respective cases in a feature billed as 'The Big Fight: Ole Swollen Fingers v's Duck Harkleroad'. It made a good public spat.

Van Vliet referred to Harkleroad as "a little squirt" and Mallard as "a bunch of quacks". He went on to claim that he had got Harkleroad and Boston out of the draft and that he had spent $400,000 on the group, barely having time to draw breath before upping that figure to one million. Aware that the question of authorship was about to be discussed publicly, Van Vliet brought along the original manuscripts of the *Trout Mask Replica* material that French had transcribed from his piano lines, in a bid to "defend his art".

"They made a big mistake, though. I mean a *big* mistake," he told Kate Phillips. "Because there aren't that many artists, and they aren't some of them, I'll tell you that." He then launched into a stream of vitriol, the gist of which was that the group's creative days were numbered. He then attempted diplomacy by saying that he wasn't mad at them. "I *am*. But not that mad. I mean, I know they're sick." Referring to what he saw as claims that they had composed some of the Magic Band's music, he said: "And they say they wrote all that stuff? Well, they better do a damn good album. And from what I hear, it's horrible…"[4] As Mallard were recording the album at the time of interview, Van Vliet had nothing on which to base his judgement. But this was war, after all.

From the opposite corner, Harkleroad confirmed to Chris Salewicz that the group had initially wanted to use the name The Magic Band, but Van Vliet held the rights to it and also to their pseudonyms. "It'll mean we have to start like a totally unknown, brand-new band," he complained. This was the first time that Harkleroad had had his say to the UK press and he had a lot to get off his chest. "The music was put together by the band. Not by him. It was *totally* arranged by the band," he asserted. He steered clear of claiming actual authorship and had some complimentary things to say about Van Vliet: "As a lyricist he's one of the best I've ever heard in my life. He's not a musician… He got a lot of credit for doing a lot of music that he never did. It came from the band."[5] Harkleroad felt that Van Vliet was "running scared", no doubt on the basis of his last record, *Bluejeans And Moonbeams*, and that some aspects of his 'genius' were in fact bullshit.

In October 1975, just before the start of the Magic Band's UK tour, John French joined in the debate. To Steve Lake of *Melody Maker*, he professed himself very surprised at reading some of Harkleroad's assertions. His own view was that the musicians had not been fully in control, at least around the time of *Trout Mask*, which was the only album he felt qualified to talk about as "musical director". He concluded, "Whatever Harkleroad might claim about his guitar virtuosity at the time – I was *there* and I would watch Don going over all Harkleroad's parts with him with incredible patience. Don's very musical. It's true that Don can't play guitar, but that never stopped him getting his ideas across."[6]

The explanation of who did what and how was complicated by the unprecedented methods of composition employed, and with hindsight one feels that the nuances of composition and arrangement within the Magic Band – so unlike any other – were still only partially understood by press and fans years after the music of *Trout Mask* and *Decals* had been forged. What took place has only recently been clarified. Both sides later claimed they received an apology from their contrite counterparts and both sides also subsequently tempered their own views.

Back to Mallard. Their eponymously titled album was mixed with overdubs at Morgan Studios in London and was eventually released on Virgin in autumn 1976. Harkleroad had been under the impression that it was a demo which was being made to secure a record deal and was surprised when the recordings were released. Speaking to Chris Salewicz he said, "The record we just did… I think when you hear that you'll hear the similarities because it came from the musicians."[7]

He had a point. *Mallard* carried echoes of *Clear Spot*, the album he claimed had the most obvious band input. This can be heard most clearly on the instrumental 'Road To Morocco' and 'Winged Tuskadero', both snaking, syncopated tracks with Tripp's marimba and drums evoking a recently expired era. Harkleroad's guitar is superb throughout, and echoes some of his articulations on *Clear Spot*. Boston's bass keeps clear of the elliptical orbits of the early Beefheart material and instead fulfils an anchor role. The material again invites comparisons with the rhythmic push-and-pull of Little Feat, although generally it is more taut and agitated. Their more relaxed, rootsier side comes out in a cover of Guy Clark's 'Desperados Waiting For A Train'.

Mallard's mixture of country, blues, rock'n'roll and more avant tendencies is finely balanced. The album closes with Harkleroad and Boston duetting on a tender, sensual version of 'Peon' from *Decals*. All the angularities are smoothed out, and their pastoral reading is ushered in by a short tape of birdsong. Maybe it was an olive branch offered to Van Vliet, or a homage of sorts, but the group put forward the explanation that it was just a piece they enjoyed playing. Harkleroad offered that it might make some money for Van Vliet as he was totally broke. The composer, meanwhile, dismissed this version precisely because it lacked the attack of the original. Ian Anderson is ambivalent about the overall results: "The Mallard record from what I recall was OK-ish. They brought in some singer [Galpin] who I didn't think was particularly up to the mark. It wasn't a bad album, it just didn't have that sparkle."

In May 1976 Mallard's manager Bill Shumow was quoted, with no apparent trace of irony, as saying that he was looking forward to the group coming back over to the UK to play some autumn shows because, "Beefheart's music has always been more appreciated here than in the States. People are much more open-minded to his music here."[8]

Rewinding, Captain Beefheart & The Magic Band's UK shows in late

1975 had been a critical success, but despite Van Vliet's hyperbolic assessment of the fifty unplayed *Trout Mask Replica*-era compositions he'd had at his disposal, the group had played old material exclusively. With the exception of his two recitations on *Bongo Fury*, he had not released any quality new music for over three years. But he had been busy composing on the piano in the house on Trinidad Bay. He and Jan were forced by penury to leave behind the high rent, the redwoods and the wildlife of the northern Californian coast and move back to Lancaster, making their home in his mother's trailer in a trailer park on the eastern margins of the town. He was keen to start work on transforming these piano tapes into new Magic Band material.

On a whim, Ace Farren Ford decided to go to the desert to reacquaint himself with Van Vliet. The only thing was that he didn't know where he lived. But this problem was not insurmountable. Ford: "I just got these guys to drive me to the desert, and when I thought I found the trailer park that was his, I thought, 'Well I can't just go and look for him wandering around in there'. So I went across from the trailer park, out into this big stretch of desert with an alto saxophone and I started blowing. In about three minutes he came out. Maybe he thought, 'Must be my people out there. Better go and round them up before the neighbours complain.' I never did ask what it was; maybe Sue said, 'It's one of your friends out there, better go get him'. But somehow he forgave me for that. From then I got to know him, got a lot of late night phone calls from him and would go around there all day and play records. Sue always kept back. She would be friendly and cordial, but she wouldn't sit in on conversations ever. It was very pleasant, but the whole time I'd be there, Jan and Sue would never come out, they would be in the other room talking. Jan was always nice to me, but I don't think she really liked me because Don and I would go drink coffee and he would be all animated and awake for five days. Jan would say, 'You hang out with him and I've got to deal with him for the next few days, baby-sit him.' He had a fairly serious case of insomnia."

True to his word, Van Vliet did take Moris Tepper to LA to do a record, the remarkable *Bat Chain Puller*. The album came about through another liaison with Zappa. Van Vliet had again found himself effectively without a record deal and, despite the personality clashes on the *Bongo Fury* tour, his friend was willing to throw him another lifeline. The original plan was that

Zappa would act as executive producer and put up the money for the recording of an album which would be released on his own DiscReet label, or they would try and get a licensing deal with Warners/Reprise.

Those assembled as the new Magic Band were Tepper, French, Denny Walley and, brought in at short notice, keyboard player John Thomas. The recurrent problem of finding a suitable bass player (the role that Bruce Fowler had recently fulfilled with his air-bass) was circumvented by Thomas using synthesiser to play the bass lines. On paper, his recent stint in Mallard hardly boded well for working with Van Vliet. But they had met a number of times in Lancaster and were on good terms, and Van Vliet was both intuitive and pragmatic when it came to sensing who would be good to have in the group. Thomas remembers finishing his pre-Magic Band bar gigs and going over to Denny's, the only twenty-four hour diner in Lancaster. This was its main selling point to one regular customer: "At two in the morning when all the bars closed, generally all the local musicians would go gather at this one place and have breakfast at two thirty because there was nothing else to do and no place else to go," he explains. "And very often I would see Don sitting over in a booth, usually by himself with a sketch pad, furiously sketching and looking around and drawing people who came in who looked interesting. He would leave his own home and just go sit somewhere to have this stimulus so that he could keep creating."

He describes Van Vliet as an "unstoppable fountain of sheer creative energy" and the most charismatic conversationalist he has ever met. Van Vliet had made extravagant claims that he had not slept for a year and a half, but he really didn't seem to be sleeping much at the time. Thomas remembers occasions when he went around to his trailer to listen to music and chat and would completely lose track of time, often emerging disoriented in the early hours of the morning. "He could talk endlessly about nothing and made you feel you were conversing with the gods," says Thomas. "It was amazing. He would call my house to talk to me and if I wasn't at home, he would get my wife on the phone and I swear he could keep her engaged for an hour, just in the course of discovering that I wasn't home and wasn't around. I saw him call operators to make a long-distance call. These are people who are trained just to get on with their work and he could keep them on the phone for fifteen minutes before the call was even put through."

Prior to his joining the Magic Band, Moris Tepper had proved that he could play some of the more knuckle-busting guitar parts from the

Beefheart back-catalogue. He also harboured ambitions of being a singer-songwriter. Van Vliet was innately suspicious of this and applied some unorthodox homespun psychology into the process of breaking down Tepper's potential "catatonic state". He reckoned the guitarist had been listening to too much of The Beatles and was consequently humming (the note) 'c' in the middle of his forehead. Despite Tepper's protestations that he didn't have perfect pitch and therefore wouldn't know what 'c' was, Van Vliet's solution was bizarre, but ultimately effective. Tepper describes one of the "very strange rituals" that were happening at this time: "He put me in this little bathroom closet that was the size of just the toilet – you couldn't move – and made me listen to this track called 'Red Cross Store' by Mississippi John Hurt over and over and over for three hours. I'd come out and say, 'I've got to eat, I'm starving,' and he said, 'No, you've got to hear it more.' He'd go, 'Did you really hear it, did you hear it?' and he'd look in my eyes and go, 'No, you've got to hear it more. You haven't heard it yet.'

"I was listening to it, thinking, 'Yeah. So?'… I couldn't dig it, I couldn't go, 'Fuck, yeah, I really hear this.' At the same time my psyche was saying, 'He's full of shit, this is a joke,' but I think deeper shit really did happen. I think it gave me a whole lot of respect for the uniqueness and the idea that he could infuse me with this other colour by forcing me through it and that then I'd be able to stop humming 'c'. All of it was great, magical."

Van Vliet had reached thirty-five, an age when many rock musicians had already sloped off into the twilight zone of semi-retirement and redundancy, especially if they had been in a creative trough as deep as the one he had recently dug for himself. *Bongo Fury* notwithstanding, there may have been no way back. Another way of looking at it was that a couple of bad albums do not suddenly make a genius into a loser. *Bat Chain Puller* has generally been acknowledged as a major Captain Beefheart work, and a startling comeback, but some writers have assessed it as a sort of poor man's *Trout Mask Replica*, a wishy-washy distillation of former glories. This misses the point completely and shows how expectations can be impossibly raised – to the detriment of critical judgement – when an artist's previous work casts such a long shadow.

There are fundamental differences between this new music and the tormented structures of *Trout Mask Replica* and *Lick My Decals Off, Baby*. And although the music shared some overlap with that ground-breaking era, it also showed a marked development in style. This subtle difference was closely linked to Van Vliet's increasing proficiency – in his own terms at least – on the piano. His intuitive outpourings on the instrument were far more fluent now, leaving behind the sonic pile-up of fragmentary lines that had hallmarked those earlier albums. He was still through-composing, but was now able to express himself coherently over a longer time-span. The songs were based on elongated, linear explorations of rhythm, and the instrumentation was more tempered than that on *Trout Mask*, which Harkleroad assesses as being "totally dictated by rhythm, and almost not at all by pitch". Ted Templeman had created a studio-enhanced ambient space on *Clear Spot*. But here, using his own idiosyncratic methods, Van Vliet had generated greater *structural* space within his purer music.

Rhythmically, the album is often quite different from its predecessors. The drums, which achieved equal importance to the guitars and bass on *Trout Mask* and *Decals*, are here given a different role, punctuating and conversing more subtly with the instrumental flow, or forming repetitive patterns against which the body of the music shifts – although the 4/4 beat was again out of bounds. He could fit his lyrics more easily into these wider spaces and went back to expressing himself in his semi-melodic, semi-spoken style – there are few developed vocal melodies on *Bat Chain Puller*. Now the listener's mind had more of a chance to fixate, perhaps, but only to be dazzled by an intricate mosaic of sound if it did.

The last four albums had involved varying degrees of compromise, whether from Van Vliet giving the group 'easier' material, using big-name producers, or desperately trying to grab a piece of the commercial pie. But that was all in the past now. It was time to move on. Tepper saw Van Vliet's compositional process at first hand. On one new song sketch, 'Voodoo Shoes', he combined two heterogeneous musical lines, singing "She wore bugs/Voodoo Shoes" over a guitar line that resurfaced a few years later as 'Telephone'. Tepper: "He often sang with the main guitar line, but he also wrote where he wasn't trying to get one line to talk to, or respond to, the other line. You're hearing several conversations at once and they're not necessarily relating to each other." His methods had always involved an instinctive juxtaposition of elements, but in this case it was impossible to get the ideas to work with or off each other and the song was abandoned.

Tepper again: "If you talk about Captain Beefheart, you can say he's experimental, but to me it sounds like someone just letting their soul come out, someone just letting loose. 'Experimental' brings up this very scientific, analytic, intellectual approach and having no soul or faith in letting go and letting the deeper sense of art itself come through – your balls, your heart, your blood, your eyes. I don't think Captain Beefheart ever played experimental music."

Despite his assertion that he could play piano "like nobody's business", Van Vliet again found himself in the position of having to convey abstract musical ideas to the musicians. Given the margin of error that would inevitably occur in the realisation of these unorthodox ideas, frustration often set in and, with it, bouts of irascible behaviour. Van Vliet may have mellowed with age, but there was no doubt that he had got his power back.

Thomas recalls the atmosphere in the Magic Band in the run-up to the recording of the album: "He was a tyrant, very demanding, very controlling. You couldn't really bring in anything from the outside world without it either meeting his total approval or his complete disapproval. It was like walking on eggshells working with him. Don was extremely paranoid. His whole genius might even boil down to a very extreme kind of paranoia. We're all able to appreciate the extreme creativity that it fed, but it also had a negative side and it made him very, very sensitive to nuance. If there was some little thing in what you said to him that he was unsure about, it could turn into a huge thing without you realising that you'd done anything. I was often in fear of saying or doing the wrong thing that would suddenly turn Don's negative focus on me."

Now fully back in control, Van Vliet asserted his unequivocal role as bandleader, sometimes, it seems, for no reason other than sheer bloody-mindedness. In one instance, he made one of the guitarists play the same motif over and over while berating him for making "mistakes" – this to the incomprehension of the other musicians to whom the versions sounded identical. Bandleaders are often dictatorial and respect is always due to musicians who are prepared to put themselves in the firing line to enable their music to be realised. Ten years down the line, the prerequisites for playing in the Magic Band remained the same: exceptional musical talent and a skin of rhinoceros thickness.

Tepper gives his views on the not-always-so-benevolent despot: "He's like an emperor, he's got a very commanding natural presence that demands an audience, and that struck me the very first time I met him. It's not the same thing as celebrity. It's not like you're in the same room as Mick Jagger – it's different. He's intimidating, at the same time he's like a small child, very gentle. He's got this tension, magic, specialness, and you just respect it. When you're around him you respect the space."

Most of the ex-Magic Band members, even the musicians who had a particularly harrowing time in the group, were willing to put in the hard work because the good times were unique. This trait was exemplified by French. Even though he'd received bad treatment, he was inexorably drawn back to the group, finding nothing comparable. The idea of slugging out a standard rock backbeat after playing in the Magic Band made his heart sink. And with the way his inimitable style of drumming had developed, there were few others whose music was geared to accommodate that type of rhythmic expression. Many of the musicians, especially from *Bat Chain Puller* onwards, still have fond memories of their time in the group. Twenty years on, Thomas rationalises Van Vliet's role as bandleader: "When you're in that position and it's your name and your reputation that's riding on it, you become more sensitive to the people who are working with you and how their expression affects you. Because you're the one that takes the fall if someone does something that's lame."

Genius, paranoid or both, *Bat Chain Puller* is an example of Van Vliet's "extreme creativity" in action. It found him both venturing into new territory and also dusting off and refreshing some of the sonic sketches from the library of material recorded in 1971 and 1972.

Considering the bad-mouthing that he'd had to endure almost constantly since his production work on *Trout Mask Replica*, Zappa wisely decided not to get too directly involved and left Van Vliet to produce, with Kerry McNab on engineering duties. He just dropped in from time to time to check on progress. After French and Thomas had written out the charts, the group rehearsed solidly for about six weeks in Zappa's studio in Hollywood then went into Paramount Studios, where they recorded *Bat Chain Puller* in a mere four days.

On the title track, the locomotive rhythms of 'Click Clack' are revisited and slowed down. Whereas that train was speeding away, the metaphorical vehicle that passes through the five and a half minutes of 'Bat Chain Puller' is a slow, enormously long goods train. When the track was being rehearsed, Van Vliet was frustrated that he couldn't convey his rhythmic ideas to the musicians. In an inspired move, he drove off to a nearby level crossing and waited for a train to trundle by. With his windscreen wipers running, he recorded the sounds on a cassette recorder, punctuating the field recording with occasional whistling. The story sounds like a generous helping of apocrypha, but it did take place and the tape successfully conveyed what he was trying to achieve. John French recalls that the exercise was a success: "He was sitting in his car and recorded it and he had me listen to it. We went into the studio, and I worked it out on the set. And it turned out to be a great, great beat."

French's hi-hat and tom-tom patterns faithfully replicate the rhythm. And unlike the music of *Lick My Decals Off, Baby*, the cars can be counted as they pass.

This phenomenal song finds Van Vliet at the peak of his powers both lyrically and musically. Drums and bass synth form a steadily moving conveyor belt, bringing first his harmonica and then mutated hoedown-style guitars into the picture. Van Vliet chants the title before bellowing out the word 'Bat', making it sound like it would have to be phonetically written with ten 'a's. The kaleidoscopic lyrics find him trying to describe the indescribable: a semi-mechanical, semi-organic train with "yellow lights that glistens like oil beads", limp, hanging wings, and bulbs that "shoot from its snoot" into the surrounding darkness.

The Bat Chain Puller sounds like a mechanised relative of The Blimp, with its own "trailin' tail" dragging behind, thumping over the sleepers between the tracks. The guitars then jag into the rhythm at obtuse angles as Thomas's synthesiser sends out flickering bleeps. As the intensity builds, Van Vliet belts out an ever more delirious account of the hybrid locomotive and the landscape through which it moves inexorably towards its unstated destination, pulled by a team of rubber dolphins and passing by "green inflated trees" and massive pumpkins grouped like land forms. Towards the fade he incants the title softly before shouting it out in a final series of affirmations. It trundles off into the distance, slide guitars coiling around each other and the synthesiser sending sonic tracers up into the ether.

Tepper was curious to find out more about the song: "One time I asked him, 'What's that song about? What did you mean? Just give me some clues, where are you coming from?' He said, 'Man, all songs that I write are about the same thing.' I said, 'What?' He said, 'You know.' I said, '*What?*' He said, 'Sex. Everything's sex.' I go, 'Come on, man, it's this thing that's been dragged out of a lake with hooks and it's got veins on it, you're telling me that's about sex?' And he said, 'It's *all* about sex, man.' But if you asked him on another day he would say, 'If you don't know, why do you ask?' Always. That was his line."

'Seam Crooked Sam' follows, a radical reworking of a rough sketch of the same name dating back to 1972. The only instrumentation on the spartan original was maracas, harmonica and the clattering of French doing his tap-dancing routine. Here the musical content is completely different. The song had become a chiming, crystalline construction with electric piano and guitar perambulating into a lengthy coda. French's talents extended to guitar here and on some subsequent cuts, underlining his crucial role in realising Van Vliet's music. The lyrics remain the same, but are recited rather than sung. They include descriptions of rooms available to rent in the "hat-rack hotel", where the walls are yellow, or more specifically the colour of "damp, dead chickens".

A lazy, swinging groove forms the basis for 'Harry Irene', the tale of a couple who ran a canteen. Their *modus operandi* sounds interesting: selling wine "like turpentine to painters" and, in a marvellously tenuous following line, taking to social life "like props to aviators". Although the song is a fairly slight work, it features some delightful accordion by Walley and a whistling solo by Van Vliet that demonstrates his skill and control. He was obviously fond of the song. It had been recorded in the sessions for *Clear Spot* and its genesis dated back to the late Sixties. "It incorporates four lesbians and a tavern. I get a kick out of those people – out of humans, period. I think they're absolutely hilarious," he told Richard Cromelin in *Wax*.[9]

Van Vliet often used idiosyncratic inflections when reciting his poetry. In his book *Frank Zappa: The Negative Dialectics of Poodle Play*, Ben Watson praised his unorthodox diction, but the prose-poem ' "81" Poop Hatch', spills out in a structureless stream, as if he is reading out a mass of ideas jotted down on a note-pad. It's also one of his most difficult texts to unravel. The "poop hatch" in the main character Biff's cotton undergarments is a peripheral detail in among "dust speakers", "raisins warped by thought", and all manner of flora and fauna in a teeming, twitchy microcosm of activity. Although Van Vliet was happy with his performance, he hesitates in a couple of places, as he often did when performing his poems in concert. He seems to have his sights set on the end by about half-way through and recites the remaining text in a flat and inflectionless way, with all the enthusiasm of someone reading out an extremely long shopping list.

Bat Chain Puller is such an eclectic compendium of ideas that it's difficult to guess what will come next. In this case it's the exquisite solo guitar vignette 'Flavor Bud Living'. Played by French, this piano-derived piece is a slow, sparse foray into the lyrical avant-guitar territory of 'Peon' and, in an ironic twist, is reminiscent of the gentle way Harkleroad and Boston approached that piece on *Mallard*.

'Brickbats' builds around a zoomorphic wordplay on bats and a lining of a fireplace at night with the 'window curtain ghost' billowing into the darkened room. The piece see-saws back and forth before the drums stagger in. In the middle section, the group hits some turbulent eddies before finally riding off on a beautifully tangled coda, with Van Vliet's sax both garbled and lyrical. Although the vocal performance is ultimately convincing, it starts off with a fluff on the first line, which was inexplicably retained.

The lyrics on *Bat Chain Puller* are generally rooted in contemporary observations and sketches. On 'The Floppy Boot Stomp', however, he delves deep into folklore, digging up an archetypal confrontation between a farmer and the devil. In this struggle between good and evil, the farmer emerges as the winner, drawing a chalk circle and threatening the devil that if he encroaches he'll "tan yer red hide" and "dance yuh on yer tale", but not before the "red violin" has played the "Hoodoo hoedown" and the farmer's horse has quizzically compared his hooves to Satan's.

Musically the song is driven by a drum pattern that at times turns itself inside-out on its Möbius strip-like course, and includes another appearance of the 'P-K-Ro-P' rhythm, but played at double speed. Underpinned by electric piano, the guitars take their partners in a transmogrified square dance, one keeping the rhythm, the other playing a sweet slide melody.

'A Carrot Is As Close As A Rabbit Gets To A Diamond' is a guitar and piano duet with a neo-Baroque feel, the two instruments unifying to give the piece a harpsichord-like plangency. The instrumental is a tightened-up version of an earlier piece entitled 'Ballerino'.

'Owed T'Alex' was dedicated to erstwhile Magic Band guitarist Alex St Clair, and his enthusiasm for motor bikes. The lyrics, co-written by Van Vliet and Herb Bermann, date back to 1966 and document the perils of that form of transport. With its roaring engine and white-hot pipes, the vehicle becomes a dangerous creature. The rider ruefully looks back after taking a "spill", admitting he thought he'd almost paid his "bill", as Van Vliet puts it, before pushing off to a party in Carson City. Van Vliet explained another facet of the track to Richard Cromelin in *Wax*: "I used to ride those damn things. I wasn't actually a biker, but I had an old Indian with a suicide clutch and all that stuff. But I'd never ride one now – unless somebody gave me one."[10]

232

French recalls that the original was an uptempo song along the lines of 'Dropout Boogie' but here it is transformed rhythmically. Its pattern of snare rolls and tom-tom thuds are another example of Van Vliet embracing the view that a repetitive rhythm pattern needn't be "corny". As on 'Bat Chain Puller', the drum figure is played continuously. Over that bedrock, the spiky guitar figures and purring synthesiser bass start off in the same rhythmic measure before slowly shifting out of phase with the drums. The guitars and vocals break away in a middle section, then it coalesces again. The lyrics sung, Van Vliet then caws and cackles maniacally, as the twin guitars rev up, leaving dust trials in their wake at the fade.

The hobo lifestyle depicted on 'Orange Claw Hammer' from *Trout Mask Replica* is revisited on 'Odd Jobs', Van Vliet's most poignant lyric. This particular hobo, an old odd-job man, is described as "a bag of skin and bones". Odd Jobs used to appear on his bicycle, with sweets to give the children – to them the contents of his bike basket were like a "whole candy store" – but he has disappeared. The women and the young girls all ask why he no longer comes around and the way this is sung – in a soulful lamentation – makes the listener fear the worst.

After the tale is told, the group lock into a stunning instrumental section, a linear extrapolation of a modal guitar motif, played with a plangent clarity by French, who finished the song off with Thomas. French's assertion that he was not really a guitar player is belied by his performance here. Just how much more competent Van Vliet had become on piano is demonstrated by the original piano demo of the track. In a display of intuitive brilliance, he switches on the tape, sits down at the piano and spontaneously composes the five-minute track in one take. Other than two or three notes that were altered, the musicians play it exactly the same.

'The Thousandth And Tenth Day Of The Human Totem Pole' finds the bright, keen guitars of Walley and Tepper snaking off together, tracked by Thomas's synthesiser bass. French punctuates the unravelling music with drum rolls, rim-clicking, tom-tom accents and yet another reappearance of the shuffling drum groove, 'P–K–Ro–P'.

On the "distemper grey" morning of the day in question, Van Vliet goes to inspect the pole and relays a darkly humorous depiction of human overcrowding. Representatives of all the races are piled on top of each other. There are problems getting food in to feed them, and they can only exercise by isometric flexing. The man at the bottom was smiling, we are told, because he had just managed to finish his breakfast uninterrupted – it hadn't "rained or manured" on him for a while. In the lyrical denouement a young girl approaches the pole displaying a Statue of Liberty doll. The Statue of Liberty cropped up as the subject of one of Van Vliet's earliest songs, 'Who Do You Think You're Fooling', where he criticised its use as a symbol, albeit indirectly. Now it is presented to the totem pole, its parodic reflection. The pole is also a metaphor for urban overcrowding, with its constituent human parts effectively prisoners of circumstance, brought face to face with the symbol of the liberty which is denied them.

The poem 'Apes-Ma', a home-cassette recording lasting all of thirty-eight seconds, is a stunning piece of work. On it, Van Vliet plays the role of incessant inquisitor. As the subject is an old caged ape, his questions will remain rhetorical. He recalls incidents in the animal's life story, asking if she remembers the little girl who named her – well, anyway, she's dead now. And then he reminds her about the time when she was young and used to try to break out of the cage – the cage that is now filthy and too small for the obese animal, which is overeating from boredom. Van Vliet states his case dispassionately and the primitive recording makes him sound like he's talking from behind a closed door, compounding the poem's disturbing atmosphere. Tucked away at the end of *Bat Chain Puller*, 'Apes-Ma' makes a powerful case against the maltreatment of animals in captivity and shows Van Vliet's poetry at its most disciplined and finely honed.

His enthusiasm at having assembled this excellent new Magic Band was palpable. In interviews he went back to extravagantly asserting that most of the group had no previous musical experience. To play Van Vliet's music, technical skill and the right attitude were essential, but technique was of little help. He was especially pleased to be working again with some young musicians. They were malleable enough to be moulded in the way he wanted – to be "his paint" – and bright enough to fulfil their roles. Walley was nearer Van Vliet's age, but was a technically excellent, empathetic player, and French was back as drummer, and facilitator *non pareil*.

John Thomas succinctly sums up the musicians' role within the group: "Don was very fond of saying something which kind of angered all the musicians: that he taught them how to play, that none of them could play until they worked with him. But what he was getting at was he virtually had to teach them how to play the music the way he envisioned it, because there was no precedent for it – so it was really that way. And he's such a powerful mental presence that you bowed your own will, lost your own individual will, in order to serve his vision. To be in the band took what pretty much amounted to a religious devotion, because you couldn't logically justify any of the steps we were taking to make this music happen."

Thomas left shortly after the album was recorded. When he accepted the offer to play with Mallard again, on their second album, *In A Different Climate*, Van Vliet made his disapproval clear. Thomas found the experience of being in the group overwhelming and was ultimately willing to leave. Although he laughs at the absurdity of the idea now, at the time he felt that when Mallard split and his career fell on hard times, it was because Van Vliet was "vibing" him from a distance, putting some kind of "jinx" on him. "Maybe I had an overestimation of his mental powers but certainly I felt influenced even when he wasn't around," he says. "His sheer will is so overpowering. It was frightening in a way. I was relieved when I wasn't working with him any more, because I was maybe too young and too impressionable."

By mid-1976 Van Vliet found a replacement for Thomas in Eric Drew Feldman, one of Tepper's best friends. Tepper: "Eric being my buddy and the person who turned me on to Captain Beefheart, I wanted to get him in the band. I was talking to Don all about Eric, and immediately I could tell he was very excited at the thought of the guy. We went over to meet Eric one night and being Don he was probably four hours late and by the time we got there – I think it was four in the morning – the light was out.

"I knew we couldn't go to the front door, we'd wake Eric's parents, so I took Don to the back gate and whispered, 'Be quiet, we gotta sneak into the room.' We went around the side of the house, and I opened up the door to Eric's room and he was asleep on his bed. Don crept in and I swear he walked over to the bed and said, 'Hi, little fella.' And I know by that point Don had made up his mind. It was obvious, like he had just found this really cute hamster asleep in its cage and he definitely decided that this was an animal that was going to be there. Being woken up, startled out of sleep, seeing Captain Beefheart in his bedroom, there was about five minutes or ten minutes of 'Uh, yeah, can I get you some water?' and that was it, that was the audition. And that's the honest truth."

Feldman recalls the actual audition being only marginally more based on his ability as a musician: "We met in a coffee shop and Don said, 'Do you want to blow?' I always thought there would be some sort of audition or something. I had been working really hard, learning how to play some of the songs. He came over to my home a few days later and I was trying to play him stuff and he was not even paying attention. He said, 'Yeah, fine' – he just decides."

Feldman's role was to play keyboards, synthesiser and bass guitar. The task incumbent upon him was to learn the material from copies of the master tapes held by Warner Brothers and from some of the keyboard charts that Thomas had made. He reckons the fact that he hadn't played bass before was a positive advantage: "I think part of the contradiction in his music is the mixture of people who are musically educated and those who aren't. I'm not even saying which one I was, but I don't think he cared. In one sense, any lack of expertise you have is a benefit for playing with him. In as much as I appreciated what he did, it took a while to wash some of the technique or musician's ego out of my hair when I worked with him. But he was always really nice and very patient."

French decided to leave yet again and was replaced by a friend of Feldman, Gary Jaye. French hung around long enough to teach Jaye some of the earlier material, and there was even talk of another double-drum line-up, but his relationship with Van Vliet soured and the drummer once more disappeared from the frame. Jaye was a skilful player but not as much of a Captain Beefheart aficionado as Feldman and Tepper. Consequently he found some of the more avant pieces like 'Hair Pie' too difficult and baulked at the task.

One unreleased song from this era is the mighty 'Hoboism', an impromptu song featuring Walley playing snaking R&B guitar and Van Vliet coming up with an off-the-cuff murder tale, a sort of hobo take on 'Hey Joe'. In this case the murderer takes off riding the rails to escape retribution after killing his wife with a "pocket knife". His freewheeling vocal performance is riveting, culminating in the demented yell of "It's not jazzm, it's not jism, it's railroadism."

Walley: "'Hoboism' was recorded on my little portable Sony tape deck in my house in North Hollywood. That music was my music and I started playing it and Don started singing it. I think I had a half pint of Jose Cuervo gold, and we drank that and we played, and that was the result."

In late 1976, Van Vliet spoke to Barry Miles, extolling the virtues of the new band – which now comprised Jaye, Tepper, Feldman and Walley. Victor Hayden was on alto sax and bass clarinet, and he had been learning cello, he said. He was upbeat, saying how the group was playing material from *Trout Mask Replica* and the old Soots number 'Tiger Roach', reckoning that they were "the greatest band in THE WORLD", adding: "It makes everything else seem like cough drops. D'you know what I mean?"[11]

Despite the tantalising prospect of the enigmatic Hayden once more added to the ranks, he slipped away unheard. Van Vliet had sent the tapes of *Bat Chain Puller* to Virgin three months previously and was waiting for the OK to be given for its release. It had come in too close to the Christmas release schedule and was slated for spring 1977 release. Inconvenient perhaps, but it turned out to be the least of his worries. By now, Zappa had already parted company with manager Herb Cohen, and DiscReet was in turmoil, with rumours of litigation and counter-litigation in the air. Thomas was aware that trouble was brewing: "From what I understood, Zappa looked over the paperwork and found that Herb Cohen owned 51 per cent of the assets [of DiscReet]. He went to work and was locked out of his own studio." Van Vliet told Miles: "Herbie got Frank really bad. When Frank left Herbie, he reckons [he] opened a whole can of worms – a whole new can of worms he didn't even know was there. It seems that over the years Frank has signed these pieces of paper, you know, signed in order to be able to keep on with his art."[12]

Van Vliet's typical vagueness as to the exact status of these "pieces of paper" – similar in content, no doubt, to those he was always happy to sign – was worrying. He was also involved in legal wranglings with the DiMartino brothers and was still in dispute with Virgin. As it turned out, all these pieces of paper combined to prevent the album from ever coming out. When Van Vliet blithely stated that he had "three managers and they're all nice guys",[13] a shudder must have passed through anyone with his interests at heart. He had faith that even if there was an impasse with Virgin, Warner Brothers would put the record out. Even that proved impossible.

Assuming that the situation would soon be resolved and that the release of *Bat Chain Puller* was still imminent, the group continued rehearsing and played some shows at the tail end of 1976 and early into the following year. Jaye's days were numbered, though. Feldman recalls the manner of his departure: "He did his best, but he really had a hard time with the idea of who Don was and how things worked. We were at a rehearsal and at some point he got mad at Don, and they got arguing about something and he [Jaye] said something to the effect of, 'Do you want to step outside and talk about it?' Don had said that he had never ever fired anybody, that mostly people just quit, but I think that may have been the one time."

The legal mess surrounding *Bat Chain Puller* became the most frustrating episode in Van Vliet's career. He had been written off as a has-been, but had returned with a come-back album comparable with his best work. But not only was the album destined to lie dormant, a tape was circulated. How it became available is a mystery. The most plausible explanation seemed to be that it had been circulated by Virgin as a pre-release promo, perhaps by an over-zealous press officer. Walley is not convinced. In the late Nineties he was allowed access to the original master tape by its owners, the Zappa Estate, who were planning on releasing it.

"The thing that gets me is all that other stuff pales in comparison to the two inch tape," complains Walley. "The tape that's being circulated in all these bootlegs, that was just a half-assed dub, a quick mix in the studio so that the guys could have a reference. It wasn't completed and there are also alternate takes that no one knows about. What really pisses me off is that original tape is sonically so much better. That's not a mixed master tape they got, but a second generation rough copy of the half-inch reel. Virgin got hold of the tape, and someone who was an engineer snuck off and got a copy of the half-inch, and then that was put out."

Worst of all, the half-assed version was soon readily available on bootleg stalls.

14

SEQUINNED WHALES AND SHINY BEASTS

"Some of the people over here on the papers said all that I do is come over here and talk about whales. As if I should say something new, y'know, a whale with a sequin or something. Such stupid stupidity."
Don Van Vliet to Vivien Goldman, *Sounds*, 22 November 1975

"I don't think I'm that artistic. I don't know if there even is such a thing, but I was always vomiting as good as I could."
Don Van Vliet to John Morthland, *Gig*, February 1978

Following Gary Jaye's departure at the beginning of 1977, John French agreed to fill in on a temporary basis. But he soon ceded his position to a brilliant young drummer, Robert Williams. Like Moris Tepper and Eric Drew Feldman, he was a long-time Captain Beefheart fan. In the autumn of 1972, while at boarding school outside Philadelphia, he disappeared one night, hitching into town to see the Magic Band supporting Jethro Tull at The Spectrum. "It was like hearing music for the first time," he recalls. One of the other support bands asked Van Vliet to give them a name, after which point they went out as Good God – a move they may well have regretted. With plenty of front and a dodgy English accent, Williams managed to convince security that he was with the band and blagged his way backstage to meet Van Vliet.

Two years later, the eighteen-year-old Williams was back home in Boston when Captain Beefheart & The Magic Band appeared at The Grange. He went down hoping to meet Van Vliet once again. He ended up getting a job, albeit temporary and manual: "His manager, Augie

DiMartino, was arguing with the owner of the club over who was going to move the equipment between shows. Evidently they had only one stagehand and he didn't know how to assemble a drum kit. That was when I offered my services for the week-long run. At the end of that week, on the night of the last show, Dr John was in the audience with his manager, and someone told me he was in search of a new drummer. I convinced him to stick around and hear me play before I packed away the drums and although I didn't get the gig, Don told me that if he ever needed a drummer, I was the one. Augie gave me twenty bucks for a week's work."

In the winter of 1975, Williams moved to LA. He was visiting George Duke at a recording session for one of his post-Zappa solo albums. During a break he was thumbing through a rolodex and found Van Vliet's phone number and thereafter became a regular phone correspondent. It was an expensive friendship, as Van Vliet's love of talking on the phone regularly extended the conversations to four to five hours. Eventually Williams got his break. Having heard on the grapevine from former Zappa percussionist Ed Mann that Van Vliet was looking for a new drummer, he called him up again. He was given the keys to the garage in Van Nuys, Los Angeles, where the group rehearsed. Williams recounts how he joined the Magic Band: "I spent all my time in that garage, practising the parts my every waking moment. It was early March 1977, on a Sunday morning before my afternoon audition, that Don opened the garage door to find me just waking up on a thin piece of foam rubber I laid out on the floor. He stood there in silhouette, the morning sun behind him, in his grey Fedora. He said, 'Good God, man! You've been sleeping here?' Don interrupted the first song we ran through to say, 'You've got the job! Let's go have some ice tea.' Tepper and Feldman asked to speak privately and advised him to at least try out some other drummers. His answer was simple: 'Why bother when I've already found my man?'"

Van Vliet was now in charge of a formidable new Magic Band, and working in tandem with a new manager, Harry Duncan, one of the "really nice guys" he had mentioned the previous year. Duncan also guested on harmonica onstage and occasionally turned in a solo version of 'The Blimp', sometimes donning a bizarre mask to mark the occasion. The first show featuring the new line up of Williams, Walley, Tepper and Feldman took place on Hallowe'en night, October, 31, 1977. After eight more dates – supported by Sunnyland Slim, the blues pianist, of whom Van Vliet was a big fan – they played a one-off show at the Paris Olympia in November, a benefit concert for the French Socialist Party. The extraordinarily diverse bill also included Gong and Buffy Sainte Marie.

The Magic Band's set started with Eric Drew Feldman metaphorically stepping into Mark Boston's long-vacated shoes, playing the 'Hair Pie' bass guitar solo. A revised version of the restless 1971 instrumental 'Pompadour Swamp' (renamed 'Suction Prints') followed. Van Vliet made his entrance and introduced himself via the cryptic announcement "The very same ass that carried man across the deserts of time also gave man the brainless hamburger." The group then grooved into 'Lo Yo Yo Stuff', Williams navigating Art Tripp's original swamp-funk patterns and towering drum rolls with ease. 'Bat Chain Puller' followed and the band's confidence was demonstrated by their successful navigation of the complex paths of 'I Wanna Find A Woman That'll Hold My Big Toe Till I Have To Go'.

Van Vliet assessed the show as a "greatest hits" set. Every era was covered. Mixed up with muscular versions of 'My Human Gets Me Blues', 'Electricity' and 'Click Clack' were curios like 'A Carrot Is As Close As A Rabbit Gets To A Diamond', 'Dali's Car' and 'China Pig'. He tackled the poems 'One Nest Rolls After Another' and 'The Dust Blows Forward 'N The Dust Blows Back' struggling on against a rising chorus of whistles and howls from the audience – which judging by the equally loud applause at the conclusion was a boisterous, but affectionate, variation on straightforward heckling.

Feldman linked this kind of audience reaction to the sort of venues the group had been booked to play: "A lot of times, especially in America, the venues were wrong. Small bars, let's say bluesy or rootsy places, weren't quite right and this was the early days of punk rock, and that didn't seem right either. He just had an aversion to being in dressing rooms with graffiti and deep-fat fryers in the corner. This didn't suit him – or anybody who has any respect for themselves."

Van Vliet was, however, in an expansive mood after the show. A few days later, his excitement caused waves of disruption when he treated interviewer Kris Needs of *Zig Zag* to an impromptu blues roar in a London hotel bar. A common complaint of people with intuitive or psychic abilities is that they aren't always able to filter out data, especially when surrounded by a lot of people. Duncan sat in on the interview with his new charge and was momentarily nonplussed when Van Vliet suddenly announced that he was getting too much of him in his psychic radar: "If that guy would quit thinking about me over there, he's had too much to think," he said. "He's just so focused on me it's incredible." He swiftly moved on, praising Williams's ambidextrous abilities and claiming he was so excited that he couldn't sleep. He was in good shape, which he said was due to his jogging six miles a night on a portable trampette, "in order to keep gravity away".[1] He'd been organising an art exhibition, claimed to have written forty songs since the end of October and talked about Project Jonah, the aim of which was to prevent the mass slaughter of whales. He had been an active supporter of the organisation for a number of years and had leafleted his audiences in the UK back in 1974. But the most exciting topic was his new group.

"I have a new band that's fantastic. The best band I've ever had. The nicest people I've ever met. I'm real happy now, REAL happy. I can go into way more dimensions than I ever could before. I played Paris and the people were dancing and everything to this far-out music. It's amazing, people dancing to this avant-garde music, or whatever they call it now.

"I want to make people happy, get smiles on the faces of the people in the audience. Break up all of that catatonic state that you get in! None of these people use poison while they're playing. Perfect, that is to say they are imperfect, but they're perfect... This group is it, the final glide pattern."[2]

He was just as effusive in his praise of the musicians to John Orme of *Melody Maker*, going on to inform him that Tepper "wants to be called Morras Tapir" after the South American pachyderm. "He likes animals too,"[3] he explained.

He had seen John Coltrane's quartet with Elvin Jones, McCoy Tyner and Jimmy Garrison in the early sixties and reckoned his own group played with the same "magic" spirit. To him, the music of Coltrane's group was like a living sculpture, and he had that himself now. Although the creative impulses were equally spontaneous, the important difference was the Van Vliet's quintet played a living sculpture that had been made beforehand by their leader, rather than creating one in the moment.

Just how good this group were was exemplified by Lester Bangs's reconversion to Captain Beefheart & The Magic Band at the Bottom Line, New York, a week after the Paris show. His friendship with Van Vliet had dissolved in acrimonious circumstances – Van Vliet himself said that Bangs had hated him – but he begrudgingly went along, worrying in case it might be "really pathetic".

His fears proved unfounded: "He walked onstage clamly, with the sober, knowing, probably more than a little resigned air of a man who has been

242

there and back, seen the whole cycle and ended up just about where he started out. You see lots of ageing musicians with that look: it's tired and very, very set."[4]

Bangs was beside himself with excitement as he found himself opened up – in another reference to Coltrane – to "a love supreme rekindled". He describes people hanging from the rafters in the packed venue, "tongues lolling out in ecstasy". His own table were showing their appreciation: "As we whooped and cheered and beat our beer bottles on the table – when we weren't agape in astonishment – we might have wondered how long it had been in these poisonously sterile times since we had seen a stage full of humans who played like beasts. Who threw themselves with such animal gusto into what they were doing that they fell out of themselves entirely and into a collective riptide with a momentum of its own.

"Here, take this, New York, and all you cats that sit around practising at raising one weary unflappable eyebrow because you think nothing can ever knock you off your cool high-chair again. Because this was it: the real raw-faced unalloyed hoodoo devil jive-drive – which felt even better because for some stupid reason we hadn't been expecting it at all. Yet here it was, naked and looking for nothing but trouble."[5]

Returning to the domain of hard-nosed business, any mention of either Virgin Records or *Bat Chain Puller* prompted mutterings about legal action from Van Vliet. Onstage in Paris, he had proudly announced certain songs as being "from the album *Bat Chain Puller*". But the misery caused by the contractual impasse was amplified by the fact that tape copies were being duplicated and circulated. Van Vliet was unimpressed that his creation had been leaked out into the world by the company that was partly responsible for it remaining legally shackled. He was "aghast" at what had happened to his creation: "They took my baby, my tape that we sent them to hear, and spread it all over – it's strewn half-way between here and probably Tibet. There's no way they should be doing what they're doing," he told Kris Needs.[6]

Duncan surmised that half of Europe probably had a copy of the tape. Van Vliet's views on Virgin were now extremely uncomplimentary and tinged with bitterness. He described the label's name as chauvinistic and imbecilic, and the way the company put women up as idols was disgusting. It annoyed him as much as people's mistreatment of whales. Unfortunately a news item in *Sounds* from August the previous year had correctly predicted events: 'This is the Beefheart album very few people are going to hear unless the record and management companies involved with the Captain get moving.'[7]

Already plans were afoot to circumnavigate the problems of the stillborn *Bat Chain Puller*. Van Vliet would get a new deal and either record a new album or release new tracks together with some of the material that was already in the can. Duncan chipped in with the opinion that Van Vliet should try to make an album that had *Clear Spot* quality and the appeal of *The Spotlight Kid* – in theory at least, his recipe for success. After the round of touring ended in February 1978, Van Vliet approached Warner Brothers with a proposal for a new album. But this time around, and with their view on the group jaundiced by all the legal shenanigans, the company insisted that he needed to prove himself to them, and asked for demos of new material before they would commit themselves contractually. Feldman remembers it feeling like a deliberate put-down at the time. The material recorded for the demos included songs that were left over from the *Bat Chain Puller* sessions like 'Candle Mambo', an old, but never recorded song 'Love Lies' and a number of reworked ideas from the past, including 'Dirty Blue Gene'. Art Tripp made a prodigal's return, adding some percussion and marimba to the demos. Warners were sufficiently impressed to offer a deal.

On the brink of this new phase, Denny Walley was sacked from the group. Closer to Van Vliet in age than the rest of the group, he had been outspoken in his criticism of the way the group was run. He had a family, little money coming in and was fed up with wasting time at rehearsals where not one note of music was played. Feldman was delegated to give him the bad news. Williams viewed his departure with regret. "He was the real shit," he says. "He'd been with Don for three years and was let go about a week before Don got his deal with Warner Brothers. It was easier to manipulate the other guys with Denny, the seasoned pro, out of the picture. Don's loss is how I feel about it." It turned out to be Walley's loss as well, as like John Thomas before him, he suffered from acute post-Beefheart syndrome after leaving the Magic Band. "I love Don," he declares. "I respect him so much. He's always been extremely gifted. I love his artwork, his poetry is magnificent, his voice unsurpassed. The things he's written musically - there's nothing I can say that hasn't already been said. But the impact that it had after playing with him... Who do you play with after that? Where do you go, what do you do? The guys go out and do their own thing or they just become a plumber. When I wasn't touring with Zappa I was touring with Don for several years. I was approached by a few people to be in bands, and the music seemed so pedestrian after that, I couldn't imagine myself playing the same three chords for 20 or 30 songs every night. I like flying by the seat of my pants and you definitely did that with Don and Frank."

His place on guitar was taken by Richard Redus, an old friend of Feldman's. Although an accomplished player, he had been confined thus far to playing in his bedroom and had never really harboured ambitions to be in a group. Bruce Fowler returned on trombone and air-bass, but as he had a number of other work commitments he was essentially a floating member of the Magic Band.

The group began to learn the new material which would constitute *Shiny Beast*, with Williams given an introduction to Van Vliet's idiosyncratic approach to rhythm. As well as playing drum parts himself, he was becoming interested in generating rhythmic ideas from found sounds and occurrences, some of which had no rhythmic structure whatsoever. Williams explains: "[Some] other beats were recordings that he had made of a set of keys hitting the floor or a five-gallon water bottle with the bubbles rising... 'bloop babloop budella bloop', or him singing into his recorder, 'Bum chicka a do bop dweep boing, diddley doop, plop plop fizz fizz.' And oh what a relief it was to see it come together, like pieces in a puzzle."

The group rehearsed with an inhuman dedication in a situation with little or no money forthcoming, simply to make sure that their parts were absolutely right. Feldman also feels this youthful enthusiasm also contributed to Walley leaving the group. The rehearsals were arduous and not made any easier when Van Vliet was present. The newcomers may have joined as fans but were soon subjected to the difficulties involved in working with, or more accurately for, him on a daily basis. Williams remembers reaching for something in rehearsal, accidentally closing his hi-hat and being accused of "putting tin foil in his radar". Although some former group members are reluctant to detail their own negative experiences, Williams is candid about being made the scapegoat: "Most of the time he'd pick on me. One day I pulled him aside and told him that I perform much better when he's nice to me and he said, 'Hey, man, I just do it to you because you can take it. These other guys would fall apart and shrivel away if I did it to them. Do you know what I mean, man? I mean, do you? I mean, I need that tension, man. Besides, I was only teasing.'"

Van Vliet's insistence on the existence of intra-group telepathy within the Magic Band had confused journalists from *Trout Mask Replica* onwards. Some were intrigued and took it seriously, while others were simply happy to add yet another eccentric tale to the burgeoning Captain Beefheart legend. Echoing past statements, he said: "True, they are playing what I have written, but they really are playing. This band is moving so fast that very soon I won't have to tell them anything."[8]

In reality, the material had to be learned without any embellishment. Feldman explains: "Everything had to be played exactly as written. He was the most strict person in that way. It would be an insult to him to do otherwise. I never had a problem with that. I felt like I was getting parts dictated to me from one of the best, especially when they were designed for me. You feel like a model in a fashion show wearing a really nice dress!"

Taken at face value, Van Vliet's own words could have rekindled the authorship debate. But Tepper maintains that while he did come up with some guitar parts himself, he didn't see fit to claim any compositional credits, for the simple reason that those lines were generated with the sole purpose of fitting within a musical landscape that had already been mapped out.

Tepper describes how the ideas that were welling up from Van Vliet's imagination could be used as instructions to stimulate his own: "He was very descriptive in imagery and metaphor when conveying musical ideas. At first it was baffling. Often he'd use colours, like, 'Play that like a smoky yellow room, make it more *sulphur* yellow'; or, 'Play it like a bat being dragged out of oil and it's trying to survive, but it's dying from asphyxiation.' He might go into it more and more if you were not getting it: 'The death struggle, the death clutch of an animal.' Or, 'Play like your arm's being ripped out.' Or he'd say, 'Play it like a trailer-park trash, inbred, monkey-headed cat.' The process took some time, but when I knew him more and more his language became very easy to understand."

Williams assesses Van Vliet's total contribution to the music as being about 85 per cent, but again he had to give 100 per cent approval before a piece was complete. He diplomatically refers to the presence of the group's "fingerprints" on some of the music and recalls how Van Vliet had reacted to his own particular prints being noticeable: "Don often said to me of my coming up with parts for his records, 'Man, you knew exactly want I wanted you to play and you read my mind! You're amazing! How do you do that? I mean with your mind, man. How do you do it?' It doesn't matter though. Besides, you can't copyright a beat."

The new Magic Band were also getting used to the tall-tales that peppered Van Vliet's conversation. In the media spotlight, he had already launched his Captain Beefheart *alter ego* to spectacular effect. But to add to the confusion, some of the stories that seemed the least credible turned out to be true. Tepper gives some examples.

"Don would say, 'Man, I had a wolf skull on my stickshift.' He'd say this shit and you'd be, 'Come on, man, get outta here,' and it would always be true. He told me he'd stayed up for a year and a half and I've met people who told me it was true – I know I never ever saw him sleep when I knew him. He always told these wild, weird stories and Eric and I would roll eyes at each other on the way home and 90 per cent of the time you'd hear the story from the guy he was talking about. Two years later you'd meet some weirdo in Lancaster who would go, 'Did you hear about the time that Don and I saw a spaceship?' And I'd be like, 'Oh, my God!'"

Shiny Beast (Bat Chain Puller) was recorded at the Automatt, San Francisco, from June 6 through to August 27, 1978. With only a few shows played that year and no other income forthcoming, the Magic Band members had been forced to find a source of money from somewhere. Given the truth of the matter, it's amazing that people still assume that groups they've heard of must automatically be making money. But just because you are in the same issue of *New Musical Express* as The Rolling Stones doesn't mean you share their glamorous lifestyle. Throughout his time in the Magic Band, Feldman had also been working as a runner, assistant engineer and night manager at a recording studio in LA, trying to juggle work commitments with rehearsing and the occasional tour. His absences put this work relationship under strain. "When it finally came around time to go and record *Shiny Beast* they really begged me to quit so they could hire someone that would be more malleable in regard to work time," he admits.

The album was co-produced by Van Vliet and Pete Johnson, who was an A&R man at Warners, a jazz musician and friends with French. A long time supporter of Van Vliet's music, he had championed the group as a journalist back in the Sixties, and the still-cautious executives at Warners saw him as a kind of insurance policy, in that he would oversee proceedings and make sure the recording was kept on track. Sandy Pearlman – who had made his name as producer and mentor of Blue Oyster Cult – was in the Automatt at the same time, recording sessions for The Clash's *Give 'Em Enough Rope* in an adjoining studio. Mick Jones and Joe Strummer – who had been obsessed with *Trout Mask Replica* in his youth – came in and introduced themselves as fans. Van Vliet was cordial but he had no time for their music. The Clash had left their studio door open during the protracted mixing of 'English Civil War', a song based on the American Civil War song 'When Johnny Comes Marching Home'. This irritated Van Vliet. Later, he would caustically remark that he'd had to endure them playing 'Go Tell Aunt Rhody' (the old American children's song) over and over.

The fact that the album was called *Shiny Beast*, but with the original title in parentheses, made it clear that Van Vliet still wanted to have some control over his musical offspring which had left the fold without permission. The front cover featured a fine Van Vliet painting of two anthropomorphic creatures, entitled 'Green Tom', with a colour sketch of conjoined animal forms executed on brown paper on the back. It was an impressive package, the first to feature all original artwork. And in case anyone wondered where he currently stood on the matter, the album is dedicated "To all conservation and wildlife preservation organisations everywhere".

Judging by the credits, Van Vliet was no longer so concerned with giving names to the group members, other than nicknames, like Robert 'Wait For Me' Williams. Feldman's alias was 'Eric Black Jewel Kitabu', coming from one of the few books that Van Vliet was willing to admit to reading, Jean-Pierre Haloat's *Congo Kitabu*.

Sloughing his Ed Marimba identity, Art Tripp rejoined the group at this point, or, more accurately, made a telling guest appearance. Feldman: "Don sang a part, he'd scribble it down and we'd record it. We were there for months and months, Art Tripp was there for all of three days. He was a warrior!" Bruce Fowler made his recording début with the Magic Band on trombone and air-bass, adding a vivid new colour.

The tracks from *Bat Chain Puller* that were re-recorded – and with identical arrangements – were 'The Floppy Boot Stomp', 'Harry Irene', 'Bat Chain Puller' and 'Owed T'Alex'. The home recording, 'Apes-Ma', appeared as on *Bat Chain Puller*.

Shiny Beast (*Bat Chain Puller*) lacks its predecessor's hard edge, but compensates for that with its warm, joyous sound. Production-wise, Van Vliet and Pete Johnson did an impressive job. The skeletal guitar undergrowth is garnished by a gorgeous amalgam of marimba, trombone and synth. Feldman's bass and synthesiser lines are sometimes doubled up with Fowler's air-bass to thicken the texture – on 'Owed T'Alex', for example.

The music, although hardly dance music, dances within its own soundworld and texturally this Magic Band sounded unlike any other. To those unable to get hold of the bootleg of the original *Bat Chain Puller*, and who had heard nothing new from the Magic Band for years, *Shiny Beast* emphatically proved that the previous two releases were the best-forgotten aberrations everyone had hoped they would be – as if they had never existed. Some commentators take the view that Van Vliet couldn't help but be different: that he could not make his music accessible and in effect his path was both a blessing and a curse. Although there is some truth in that notion, he had proved with *Clear Spot*, and on the lacklustre albums that followed, that he could be as accessible as anyone else. Now he decided to allow himself to do what he did best, knowing it would be different anyway. "I'd never just want to do what everybody else did. I'd be contributing to the sameness of everything," he said to Richard Cromelin from *Wax*. "Finally I got a completely perfect picture. These people I have now are playing it better than ever before. They're playing more of a spell, right where I want it. I was dealing with a lot of shapes, textures, releases, dissolves, all kinds of things. I've always tried to play spells. I don't think music gets enough of them."[9]

Sadly, Van Vliet chose to discard the superb 'Odd Jobs', but he was loath to waste good material and took the guitar refrain from the end of the song and employed it as the central riff of 'Tropical Hot Dog Night'. Here Art Tripp's marimba evokes the swirling, carnivalesque sound of the Mardi Gras – or maybe a mariachi band – while Fowler's melancholic trombone breaks loose with the sweetest of melodies. Van Vliet's mellifluous whistling towards the end of the track gives a window into his compositional techniques. It flits around the trombone line, which Fowler had derived from a whistled motif in the first place.

Van Vliet takes on the mantle of growling, whooping Master of Ceremonies for this party, with a scene-setting description of "two flamingos in a fruit fight", an image that matches the mood of the song. When he says that he's playing this song for all the young girls, one can picture a nymphet, done up Carmen Miranda-style, shaking her booty and squeezing out another drop of sweat on the sleazy bandleader's forehead. He continues with a bizarre hint at sex and sacrifice. He's wondering who will be the one to get lucky this evening. The prize? To spend some time in his company and also to be able "to meet the *monster* tonight". This tongue-in-cheek excursion was Latinate enough to be covered by ex-Kid Creole sidekick Coati Mundi on a single released in 1983 – which also featured Nu-Yorican singing star Ruben Blades. "The baby was South-of-the-Border that night,"[10] Van Vliet later commented to John Piccarella of *New York Rocker*, the baby being his inspiration or muse, which he also called "my artist". "Sweet jungle fever"[11] was how the song was described by Billy Altman in *Creem*.

'Ice Rose' is a vibrant update of 'Big Black Baby Shoes' from the *Brown Wrapper* sessions. Fowler's trombone arcs beautiful melodic lines above the skeleton dance of guitars and marimba. Van Vliet would probably dismiss the suggestion, but this incarnation does sound distinctly Zappa-esque. Yet its early genesis pre-empts any accusations of plagiarism. Fowler is again highlighted, playing a gorgeous, pivotal trombone melody. John Orme felt this track "could have come from a Zappa session, but succeeds where Frank tends to fail because Beefheart is trying to create and not parody".

'You Know You're A Man' comes over as a pastiche of a macho love song with Van Vliet's throat-rasping lead vocals backed up by his own comical, semi-convincing repetition of the word "Yeah", and startled yells, as he mixes up and extrapolates a series of cock-rock clichés. The song veers towards standard rock fare and its inclusion in preference to 'Odd Jobs' or 'Totem Pole' is a disappointment. But the band push and pull it around with vigour, the highlight being Redus's fretless bass solo.

This was the first time that most listeners had heard the track 'Bat Chain Puller', which although lacking some of the grit of the original version sounds massive. His voice is formidably intense. This time there are no fluffs and he opens up, hitting notes lower than any that he had managed before. Paul Rambali recounted how this track had helped to break up a rocky relationship between a couple whom he knew: "He stayed up long into the night playing one track over and over and over again. 'BAT CHAAAIAN… puller… puller, puller…' Beefheart's unearthly low moan seeped through the house and out of the chimney. The next morning there was a note on the table… 'Sod you, mate. And sod your Bat Chain Puller, Puller, Puller! Your dinner's in the garden.'"[12]

'When I See Mommy I Feel Like A Mummy' is a tale of desire and obsession. The twin guitars etch their way into Williams's absurdly funky drum rhythm, augmented by Art Tripp on cowbell, bell tree and marimba and Fowler's trombone setting up a strong counter-melody. When he finds the object of his desire he's going to "seize" her, and then "freeze" her. "I'm gonna wrap her up," he asserts confidently, but then her interest in him quickly vanishes, "like breath on a mirror". In the instrumental bridge passages, synthesiser bass and trombone weave together in a stately melody that evokes a Bach trumpet line.

'Candle Mambo', however, is an unashamedly romantic song, a paean to dancing in the flickering candlelight, with buoyant marimba and trombone sketching out sweet lines and Van Vliet tenderly caressing the melody. Lyrically, it hints at what he could have achieved on *Unconditionally Guaranteed*. The sensuality is apparent, although he slips in a mischievously sexual line in "Candle her".

Van Vliet wanders the streets, the jilted lover on the slow, soulful 'Love Lies', a song which originally dates back to the Sixties. He is rueful of his actions towards his lover, who has failed to turn up to their tryst as planned, and he is left there "with a flower", waiting in vain in the street under lamps with bulbs about to blow that "flutter like fireflies". Fowler's trombone is at its most dolorous here, a foil to the pained vocal howls as the track fades to a conclusion.

'Suction Prints', a substantially reworked version of 'Pompadour Swamp' from the 1971 sessions, was already a feature of the group's live repertoire. Again, this composition was compared in some quarters to Zappa's early seventies material. This super-tight, episodic instrumental allows the band to show off their chops. Robert Williams in particular stands out: his dexterity and timing are dazzling. It also features the first eruption on the album from Van Vliet's soprano sax, which blasts into the fissures of the rhythm and sprays randomly over the unison passages, sounding disconnected, like an instrumental karaoke, where the player has never heard the backing track before. But this time the instrument is mixed at a conservative level. 'Apes-Ma' brings the album to a conclusion. Not bad work for a group in which Feldman, Williams and Redus were making their recording débuts.

"I'm totally happy with this album," said Van Vliet to Billy Altman of *Creem*. "I just had a blast, and I mean a blast, doing it. Glen Kolotkin, the engineer, is just brilliant. This is the first time you can hear my voice the way it really is. Glen did Stravinsky's last record. I've always used my voice as an instrument but these people never realised that. What a job he did. When I heard 'Bat Chain Puller' it just knocked me down. He got my voice the way it is. You know what I mean?"[13]

Shiny Beast (Bat Chain Puller) was released at the end of 1978 in the US, ahead of the UK release, and hailed as an important new chapter in the group's career. *Downbeat* were enthusiastic, saying: "Now Beefheart fans who remember the past glory of classics like *Trout Mask Replica* and *Lick My Decals Off, Baby* can once again look ahead to recordings by the Magic Band."[14]

"The following band have a new album out on Warner Brothers, called *Shiny Beast (Bat Chain Puller)* and this is the first time they've ever done a radio concert, so it makes it an historic event to say the least. Could you please give a warm welcome at WLIR FM to Captain Beefheart and The Magic Band," said the presenter, his voice rising to an peak of agitated excitement as he spoke the group's name.

Cue: whooping, whistling and hollering and the group kick off with a steaming, funky version of 'Tropical Hot Dog Night'. The concert took place in the middle of a short tour to promote *Shiny Beast*, at My Father's Place in Roslyn, Long Island, New York, November 18 1978. The line-up was the same as the album, minus Art Tripp, and with Bruce Fowler's girlfriend, Mary Jane Eisenberg, on occasional maracas ('Shake Bouquet' as Van Vliet renamed them). She also performed a mime of domestic chores on 'When I See Mommy I Feel Like A Mummy'. The band replicate the atmosphere of the album, sounding less intense but more orchestrated than on their live performances the previous year.

The concert found the new Magic Band hitting top gear. Although the broadcast was a pressure situation, Van Vliet sounds relaxed and jovial throughout the show, getting virtually all his cues right, and singing with power. On 'Nowadays A Woman's Gotta Hit A Man', one of the guitarists breaks a string. Van Vliet sounds positively delighted at the end of the song, explaining to the audience: "He played that on a broken string. Which if you think about it is narrowing it down a little bit, 'cos there are six strings... and four fingers".

The crowd shout out requests at the start of 'Old Fart At Play', to which he inquires 'What is this Gatling Jukebox activity?... Oh, let's do it...' New material features strongly alongside older songs like 'Moonlight On Vermont'. One of the *Trout Mask Replica* tracks that caused a ruction was Van Vliet's a cappella showcase 'Well'. Distracted throughout by a member of the audience clapping along, he finally barks, "Cut it out, man, this is not in 4/4 time! Some things are sacred." On finishing the song, he defused the situation. "Thank you, thank you," he says, jovially over the applause. "Very difficult it is to do poetry in this world of constant... Denny's staying open all night... and McDonalds."

Feldman remembers an incident before the show: "It's really nice seeing him humbled by certain things that you'd be surprised about. I remember once we were in Long Island, New York, in some hotel on our way to a soundcheck or a gig and Count Basie got in our elevator and seeing Don get an autograph, him being [like] a kid and a fan, was very surprising."

The tour continued until to the end of November. Williams remembers a show at The Bottom Line, New York, exactly one week after My Father's Place, which was attended by a host of celebrities including Woody Allen, Diane Keaton, David Byrne, Meatloaf, Willie DeVille, Chrissie Hynde and John Belushi.

Meanwhile, back in the glamour-free zone of Basingstoke, in the late summer of 1978, the young author was on the look-out for records. The town, situated about forty-five miles west of London, was designated in the Sixties as "expanding" for the purpose of creating new business and housing the influx of migrants from London – "overspill", as they were collectively labelled. Now redeveled, New Market Square was one of the most prosaic, utilitarian urban retail complexes in the UK, designed by architects who, one surmises, put aesthetics way down their list of priorities. But one of the market stalls was a haven. It sported a strange mixture of souvenir football scarves and mugs emblazoned with team crests and colours, hideous fake silk scarves displaying names of pop groups, plastic Spielbergian sharks and scratched, second-hand copies of Genesis, Foreigner and Jethro Tull albums. The vendor, a down-at-heel middle-aged character, used to proclaim his wares with the cry: "All yer teams, all yer stars, all yer Jaws."

He also had a section of bootlegs hidden at the back of one of the racks, the sort of stuff that you'd normally have to go to London to find. During one visit I unearthed what was treasure trove to a neophytic, yet already ardent Captain Beefheart fan. While thumbing through the racks I found and bought an album that I didn't see again for a long while – an American import copy, on Warner Brothers, of *Shiny Beast (Bat Chain Puller)*. To the few friends who knew anything about Captain Beefheart – or if they did, didn't hate the music – this was a real find. I was the first to get it. It had just appeared. It seemed strange that there had been no music press fanfare, no pre-release hoo-ha, nothing at all. I kept looking at it, as if I couldn't believe it actually existed. It hardly did. Imports would soon dry up and it disappeared into obscurity.

With heart-sinking inevitability, the exhausting and tortuous legal processes creaked into action once again. Rumour has it that Van Vliet had signed something on a napkin with Virgin which he had then forgotten about. But whatever the minutiae, being under contract to two companies was definitely a bad idea. All this was making it nigh on impossible for him to start work on any new project with a clean slate; the consequences of some previous dealing were always about to catch up with the group and put a halt to their activities. This time the release on Warners of *Shiny Beast* was followed by a Virgin lawsuit after it had been in the shops for about six weeks. This is exactly what Warners didn't want to hear. They dropped the project and Van Vliet's career hit another brick wall. Feldman feels they were a little half-hearted about Captain Beefheart anyway: "He was dropped because although they thought, 'Hey, we would love to have him on our roster and add prestige to it,' he wasn't worth any particular money to them and they just said, 'See you later.'"

The UK reviews of this scarce commodity were complimentary. In *New Musical Express*, Paul Morley summed it up as "Syncopation, freedom, flickering vigour, colliding rhythms, odd connections, security, intensity, sweetness – this in some ways an accessible sampler of Beefheart's first fourteen years on record. The four major curves show up consistently: country-blues, avant-garde, rock and the straightforwardly whimsical shaped by an apprehension of reality. If the album is one huge Van Vliet grin, it isn't a particularly comfortable one, nor how could it be?"[15]

Away from these business problems, Van Vliet had been involved in a couple of extra-curricular guest activities over the past year or so. The Tubes had featured Captain Beefheart material in their shows since 1976 and eventually the group's Bill Spooner asked Van Vliet for the rights to record 'My Head Is My Only House Unless It Rains' for their LP *Now*, recorded and released in 1977. Spooner also asked him if he'd like to play on the album. He reckoned it might be fun to do so and made his way down to the Record Plant in Hollywood. But having Van Vliet feature on your track was quite different from hiring some super-session musician who would come in, play a perfect part and disappear from whence they came – as The Tubes were soon to find out. Getting his harmonica take down on 'Golden Boy' proved to be more difficult than expected as he kept getting distracted by Harry Duncan also playing the instrument. Not so unusual, except Duncan was in another – soundproofed – room at the time. Bill Spooner recounted the story to C. Linstrom in 1999.

"He was sitting there [in the control booth], honkin' a few things every now and then, and Don would go… 'God damnit, I can't play now, there's someone in there playin' harmonica. God damn.' And we'd been tryin' for hours just to get him to play a simple little part. But I wanted that sound, so I had to go out and say, 'Harry, could you please put away the harmonica so Don can play his part?' So we tried it about ten more times and he would just not play what you wanted, and then Don said, 'God damnit, someone's thinking harmonica in there!' So we said 'OK, Harry could you wait in the hall?' At this point Van Vliet asked that they rewrite the song to accommodate his playing, an impossible request. After they had got something down and Van Vliet left, they secretly got Duncan to overdub the harmonica.

Van Vliet's saxophone on 'Cathy's Clone' went more smoothly and he liked the track, but he was anything but predictable. Spooner: "[There were] coloured lights all the way around the room, somebody's screwed in these little bulbs – about seventy of 'em – all the way around the room. Don said, 'God damnit, one of these lights is drivin' me crazy! I can't play! One of 'em's drivin' me crazy!' OK, so the assistant engineer goes to the storage room and gets a ladder – comes back, goes up the ladder, starts right in front of him, unscrews the light, moves the ladder, unscrews the light. Half an hour later he comes all the way around and does the last light and Don goes: 'That's it! That was the one!' Getting the part out of him for 'Cathy's Clone' was easy. I just had a couple of tracks and first I played him the song and I asked him, 'What do you want to hear, bass and drums, or…' 'No, I don't want to hear anything, just start the tape.' So I just started where I knew it was going and I just pointed at him and he wasn't listening but he just went crazy on the track. But he didn't want to hear the track, he didn't even want to know the key. He's not so good at playing along with things, y'know?"[16]

Van Vliet ultimately felt that the saxophone was mixed too far down and, after the event, had reservations about getting into a situation where he had been governed. But this session was plain sailing compared to another with an old friend, Ry Cooder, in 1978. Cooder had worked on film soundtracks since the late Sixties – notably on *Performance*, when he worked in conjunction with producer and arranger Jack Nitzsche. Cooder and Nitzsche were working together again, this time on Paul Schrader's film *Blue Collar*. Cooder told the story of their collaboration to Jonathan Romney in *The Wire* in 1998: "We wrote the tune and I don't remember a whole lot about it except that [I wondered] who can sing this? Well, only

Beefheart's got that kind of crazy low voice to put this across. I got him to come down out of the desert – it was the last time I saw him. Locked him in a room and went through all kinds of hell to get him to sing the whole song once. He's the most incorrigible, difficult guy in the world. (*Conducting imaginary dialogue with Van Vliet*) 'I hate Hollywood… Those lights – I hate those lights… Who's that guy?' That's just the producer, leave him alone… 'I hate producers.' Just sing the song. 'I have to go to the bathroom.' Just *sing* … *the song*. Jesus Christ! We locked the door. Actually did. 'Get me outta here,' he was yelling – banging the door with his fists. I said, 'You sing – *then* you can come out.' (*Laughs*) He put me through a lot of hell during the *Safe As Milk* days and I got off on that. (*Laughs*) I got him now! We got Beefheart now. But it was good."[17]

The song in question is a minimal blues, based around an incessant steamhammer beat topped off by an intense vocal performance. It was released as a single on MCA. There also exists an "obscene" version which has appeared in bootleg form where Van Vliet sings "I'm a hard working *fucked-over* man" in the choruses. As well as Van Vliet being the right choice of vocalist, the song fits comfortably into his oeuvre. Whereas 'Plastic Factory' from *Safe As Milk* found a young man railing against what he perceived as a potential trap, the character in 'Hard Workin' Man' comes across like the same guy ten years later and still working at that same factory. Time is no longer on his side and he is stuck in the hell of never getting anywhere, cursed by the knowledge that that's the way it's going to continue. His world view has crumbled from defiance to bitter resentment. This time the "boss man" or "fat man" is the "shit-ass foreman". The protagonist can rue his failure at school all he likes, but he's still stuck in the same hole. Fucked-over indeed.

For Captain Beefheart & The Magic Band, 1979 was a lost year. Van Vliet had somehow scraped together the money to buy some land on the north Californian coast, near Eureka, but with no house built as yet, he and Jan were obliged to stay in Lancaster. The group was in limbo and played no shows whatsoever. *Shiny Beast* had yet to be released in the UK and Van Vliet had decided to fire Harry Duncan. Yet another deal had gone down the pan and Van Vliet, wounded again by the sharp end of the music business, was feeling pretty down as well. He disappeared back to his trailer, away from the spotlight, to mull over the inflexibility of the industry, which, combined with his own lack of business acumen, had once again brought proceedings to a standstill.

15

ROCK AT THE DADA STATION

"Fifty years from now you'll wish you'd gone, 'Wow'."
Don Van Vliet to Paul Rambali, *New Musical Express*, 1 November 1980

"I don't pay any attention to people who misunderstand me because I don't want to misunderstand what little I understand about myself."
Don Van Vliet to Tom Pompasello, WBAI phone-in in 1984

If anyone had made a bet in 1974 that six years later Van Vliet would produce an album that rivalled his best work, they would have been considered either psychic or stupid. But they would have also been right. The recent portents had been ominous, with the Magic Band in a state of strength-sapping paralysis. There had been no official news on new material, but as the decade began there was plenty of activity behind the scenes.

Things began to pick up again at the end of 1979, coinciding with Gary Lucas's arrival back on the scene. Unbeknown to him, he was soon to take on a vital role. After his radio interview with Van Vliet back in 1972, Lucas had kept in contact. During the *Bongo Fury* tour in 1975, they met up in Boston, where he auditioned for the position of guitarist in the planned new Magic Band. He passed, but Van Vliet was unsure what else might happen with Zappa, and was vague about his future plans in general. Without any firm assurances, Lucas took up an opportunity to work in Taiwan.

In early 1977 he returned to the United States, got a number for Van Vliet and called him. They then met up again, Lucas and his wife Ling, accepting an invitation to see the Magic Band play at the Keystone Korner,

Berkeley, in April. Lucas moved to New York and got a job as an advertising copywriter at the CBS press office: "I stayed in touch. I had access to CBS's Wide Access Telephone Service and I started to talk to him nearly every day. I must have spoken to him for an hour a day, sometimes two hours, sometimes several times in one day about art, politics, culture, movies, everything. He was the most erudite, magical conversationalist. We got really close on the phone." In spring 1978, Lucas went over to California to discuss some advertising concepts with The Boomtown Rats and at the group's request drove Van Vliet down to meet them.

During these long calls, he told Lucas that he was planning an album. In autumn of 1979, he sent him a tape of the *Bat Chain Puller* guitar piece 'Flavor Bud Living' to learn for the record. But Lucas and Ling got more than they bargained for when they went to visit Don and Jan in January 1980. He takes up the story: "We spent a week out in the desert in Lancaster and had a really good time. He said, 'I don't trust anybody. Will you guys help me, because I need a manager?' Ling's attitude was, 'We'll help you, Don,' and I was willing to try to help him in whatever way I could. I was a bit of a disciple and wanted to expose the world to his genius as I thought he'd had a raw deal. I was something of a reluctant manager as I'm not a businessman. It was out of love and certainly I was getting psychic rewards out of playing with him. The management thing was a loose rubric. We never signed any papers."

While working on 'Flavor Bud Living', Lucas found out that Van Vliet had lost none of his uncompromising – or wilful – approach to the treatment of his own music. He explained to Andrew Bennett: "Don said that he hated the way French played it on record, that it was 'too religious', and it 'put the whole thing in heavy syrup'. I learned it from that version originally and went out to the desert and played it for him. He critiqued it by saying that it was all wrong. I told him that's how French played it and Don said, 'Well, obviously he must have done it all wrong. I want you to play it using my exploding note theory.' 'What's that?' I asked. 'You play every note as if it has only a tangential relationship to the preceding note and the note that follows.' In other words, a very staccato and disconnected phraseology."[1]

The good news on the business front was that the deadlock between Warners and Virgin was at last broken. Van Vliet's lawyer, Brian Rohan, secured an exclusive deal with Virgin, which had successfully negotiated with Warners for the rights to *Shiny Beast (Bat Chain Puller)*. The album was given its official UK release on the label in February 1980 – nearly two years after it had been recorded – attracting a second round of generous critical praise. The new album, whose birth Van Vliet had been plotting since the previous autumn, was to be entitled *Doc At The Radar Station*, after one of his friends who worked as an air-traffic controller in the desert. At one point it was mooted that 'Doc' might be spelt 'Dock', to give more of a science fiction vibe.

About half of the album is based on the reworking of old ideas. On the face of it, that could be taken to indicate a lack of inspiration. But put in context, big-bucks rock acts typically make their money by recycling their one or two ideas over and over again – via the corporate product conveyor belt – as technically new material. Van Vliet may have been reworking old material but he was still more interested in breaking up the 'catatonic state' than in contributing to its preservation.

Any ecologist worth his salt would ensure appropriate recycling, but it's hard to reconcile Van Vliet's still-prolific output of new ideas with his enthusiasm for revisiting old ideas, be they motifs, melodies or entire unrecorded songs. It was a trait that went way back to the early Magic Band. Bill Harkleroad thinks the explanation could be very simple: "My idea, at least from my time in the band, was that a lot of tunes were built off a guitar riff and he'd fall in love with it. And two years later he would say, 'You remember that riff. Play that riff,' and it would turn into a different tune. He would fall in love with ideas, he had a reservoir of licks and vocal ideas. How he internalised those things nobody knows, but they just got recycled all the time."

Importantly, most of the revamping work built on skeletal ideas and fragments that would have mouldered away in the vaults had they not been exhumed and transformed into full-blown, totally convincing new material. They didn't sound old, and only the most dedicated aficionados were aware of their origins anyway. No one sees fit to dismiss "serious" composers when they rework and develop earlier ideas but rock musicians are expected to keep coming up with new ideas, or it's suspected their creativity is on the wane. In 1998, Beck Hansen, talking to *MOJO*, defended his plan to record material some four years old by explaining that "they're songs which have aged for a while".[2] By the same token, the older songs on *Doc* had obviously reached their optimum state of maturity.

The recording sessions for *Doc* ran for a couple of weeks in June 1980. Engineer Glen Kolotkin persuaded Van Vliet that the album should be mastered at the CBS studios in New York, where a brand-new piece of technology, the disc computer cutting lathe, was installed. In an echo of the mike-blowing events of the late Sixties, this piece of technology was not immune to a potent mixture of Van Vliet's vocal power and human error.

The mastering engineer Stanley Kalina had the group all go out for a meal in the middle of the cutting process. When they came back, a chip fire had broken out on the cutting lathe and the waste vinyl from the groove that was being cut in the master had melted over the stylus, freezing it in its track. It had been caused by the friction from Van Vliet's voice because the level had been set too high.

Doc At The Radar Station was released in the UK in August 1980. It arrived in a cover sporting a Van Vliet painting on the front and on the reverse a photograph portraying the Magic Band in formal garb, looking like hip accountants. Rather whimsically, Van Vliet uses a clothes peg as a tie-pin on his flamboyant tie. Moris Tepper, Robert Williams and Eric Drew Feldman are present from the previous incarnation of the group, as is Bruce Fowler (although he plays on only one song). At the back of the pack, looking like he'd just run in, stands John French.

In a sense this is what he had done. Richard Redus quit shortly before the recording was scheduled to begin. Feldman recounts his friend's departure: "Redus just lost interest in it and said, 'I want to go do something else,' and just left. There was no animosity. He was the kind of guy that didn't even wear shoes, a mountain man kind of a guy. He didn't really have any ambition, or care about the reality of being in a band, going on tour and staying in hotels."

Fortuitously French had made contact with Van Vliet when he was most needed. He explained his final return to the Magic Band fold to Marc Minsker of *Ptolemaic Terrascope* in 1998: "I had been running into Don here and there. We were on good friendly terms. I was really following my Christian faith, going to church, reading the Bible a lot, but I was having trouble finding a job. I was walking along praying, and I asked God what I should do. I was under the impression to go see Don about working in his band. This was completely against anything I wanted to do, so I figured it had to be God speaking."[3]

Call it divine intervention, synchronicity, telepathy or whatever, but French went over to Van Vliet's trailer, arriving when he was in the middle of a phone conversation with Redus, who had called to tell him he was leaving the group. French's last stint in the Magic Band was characteristically crucial – as guitarist, marimba player, bass guitarist on one song and drummer on two.

Even taking advances in technology into account, the production of *Doc*, like *Shiny Beast*, was so much better than some of the earlier albums that it begs the question what they might have sounded like if they had been produced in this way. The musicians' playing demands superlatives on what is unarguably Captain Beefheart & The Magic Band's most focused, powerful album. And on its own terms, it's comparable in quality to any of its predecessors.

A mention of the forthcoming album in the news pages of the music press caused ripples of excitement among the cognoscenti. Looking back I can still remember the excitement one night in August 1980, when, shattered from the daily toil of a summer vacation job working on a farm, I tuned in to John Peel's show on Radio One to be treated to a selection from the album: 'Sue Egypt', 'Hot Head', 'A Carrot Is As Close As A Rabbit Gets To A Diamond' and 'Ashtray Heart'. Equally excited, Peel previewed the selections by saying, "Wait till you hear the tracks, there's some fantastic stuff."

Although the sound is clear and punchy, Van Vliet, on sole production duties this time, steered away from anything he considered gimmicky or corny. Reverb, a standard part of studio enhancement, especially on the voice, was viewed suspiciously as another brand of "heavy syrup" and was thus used very sparingly. In cahoots with Kolotkin, the musicians would occasionally risk Van Vliet's wrath by adding some reverb or other effects to make the sound warmer and more vivid when he was out of the control room. A number of groups were being compared to Captain Beefheart & The Magic Band – The B-52s and Devo, for example – and the group members wanted some of those groups' production values, to help them compete on equal terms. But Van Vliet would have none of it and always noticed any tampering when he returned.

Some group members reckon his line of reasoning was that the old blues artists whose work he so admired didn't use effects, so why should he? But without any sonic enhancement, digital technology flattens out the 'liveness' of the recording environment, whereas earlier methods of recording achieved more of a live sound from a combination of the equipment, the room acoustics, the microphones and the tape almost sounding like it had its own active EQ. Reverb was also a standard part of the recordings on the Chess label, for example. But in the final analysis, he wanted his musical aesthetic to be "two-dimensional, like a painting". Feldman: "I think of Don as being somewhat sceptical about technology. Anything that's going to possibly 'enhance' the music, he doesn't feel in control of – everything should be done by the playing and singing. However, you couldn't actually have a linear discussion with him about it."

'Hot Head' canters off on a heavily accented R&B groove, like a flattened-out reworking of the classic Bo Diddley rhythm, but full of shifting elements. In his review in *New Musical Express*, Charles Shaar Murray summed it up thus: "In the Beefheart Universe, you see everything you see in other places, but it always seems different."[4] Feldman plays a squelchy bass line on keyboards, while the guitars twist and turn around each other until one hits on an oriental-sounding slide figure. Williams's drum pattern keeps turning the beat back on itself and he fits in a few martial inflections he'd been asked to add at the last minute. Van Vliet fans the licking flames of lust, singing of a woman who can "burn you up in bed". References to fire, roasting and spits culminate in a unique addition to rock's lexicon of sexual imagery when he describes her as "a red hot pig".

'Ashtray Heart' is based on a swung boogie rhythm with astringent guitars and atonal bass gnashing their way into its structure. French's drums, meanwhile, thump along like an alien trying to play rock'n'roll. The lyrics seem to be a chronicle of deep hurt inflicted upon the singer. But Van Vliet claimed the song was "Getting it all out. Like an illness... or a fever burning off... In nature, a fire burning everything away and then coming back with new things", when talking to John Piccarella of *New York Rocker*.[5]

We have probably all felt discarded and as stale as a stubbed-out cigarette butt at one time or another, but Van Vliet vivifies the situation when he exclaims, "You crushed me when I was burning out", also telling us that he feels like a "glass shrimp", in a voice that veers from wheezy shocked surprise to an embittered snarl. Then he comes up with an order to break away from parental attachments in "send your mother home your navel", followed by another of his favourite phrases: "Somebody's had too much too think." And in a brief nod to rock's New Wave, he issues a command to open up a "case of the punks", although he later denied he was specifically singing about them.

The track drops away for a brief interlude with Eric Drew Feldman on Mellotron (a keyboard instrument developed in the Sixties, which utilises tape loops of violins, voice, flute or brass, activated when the keys are depressed). This inspired use of the instrument reclaimed it from its former role as a pseudo-orchestral backdrop to the classical conceits of progressive rock groups like Barclay James Harvest and The Moody Blues. Van Vliet was taken by its "abused throat" sound, as he called it. Feldman recalls that once as a joke he played the intro to The Beatles' 'Strawberry Fields Forever' on the instrument, much to Van Vliet's annoyance. But here he willingly casts himself as melodramatic orator, backed by the instrument's icy sheets of sound.

'Run Paint Run Run' propagates a germ of an idea from 'Drink Paint Run Run' from the 1971 *Spotlight Kid* sessions, although the semantic overlap is about the only thing they have in common. Both rhythmically and in its one-chord groove, it's a not so distant cousin of 'Nowadays A Woman's Gotta Hit A Man' from *Clear Spot*. Bruce Fowler's trombone parps along with the guitars, then breaks loose, fluttering off like a disappearing shadow. Over its irresistible momentum, Van Vliet declaims a tale of paint as a sensual medium, running by its own volition, and the artist painting all day until the sunset, spurred on by the group chanting the title. Then he hits on the pivotal line "You got hot paint 'n yer havin' fun". When the song was played back in the studio, one of the speaker cones was faulty and buzzing. Van Vliet insisted that this was itself recorded and mixed in with the track, although it is barely audible.

'Sue Egypt' takes its main guitar line from the version of 'Pompadour Swamp' that was played live on the 1973 tour. The slide guitar line skids around the scale, underpinned by delicious synthesised bass and decorated with flurries of Mellotron flute. The music and the poetry fit together like a glove. A semi-sung, semi-spoken vocal line refers obliquely to those people who have used Van Vliet as an influence or have done him a disservice; people "who ride on my bones", as he puts it. Or who, in a manner of speaking, have fucked him over. The old sketch is reworked to such a dazzling effect that it sounds unlike anything the Magic Band recorded before or since.

A Mellotron section, driven like a wedge into the centre of the song, was composed spontaneously by Van Vliet in Feldman's lounge. Luckily his host had the good sense to have a cassette recorder to hand to capture the moment: "I remember that my housemate had a cat and when Don started playing the organ, it started really acting strangely, dancing wildly around the room. So for a long time we referred to it as 'the music that made the cat go crazy'. I just transcribed what he played as exactly as I could and used a Mellotron – it sounded much more dark."

'Dirty Blue Gene' is another example of material released at last after a lengthy metamorphosis. Its thirteen-year transmutation saw it progress from a good title (which Van Vliet obviously loved) for an instrumental piece recorded in 1967, to completely different music complete with lyrics in 1971 and then a version close to this one from the 1972 *Clear Spot* sessions. With a few minor changes it became the thunderous song on *Doc At The Radar Station*. From the new, convoluted guitar and drums introduction, the band blaze away in a tricky stop/start creation, fast and furious – bulbous, even – with guitar lines bursting out in bloom all over its surface and French yelling the lyrics behind Van Vliet's ecstatic vocals. Charles Shaar Murray opined: "Something like the intro to 'Dirty Blue Gene' literally could not be the work of anybody else."[6]

Another song originating from the 1971 sessions is 'Best Batch Yet'. Again, the rearranged version blows holes in the original rough sketch. Robert Williams claims that his "fingerprints" were on the drum part and he is certainly at his best here: brutal, delicate and, to add to the paradoxes that define his style, an ever-shifting bedrock. In a bizarre detail, Gary Lucas contributes an eight-note French horn line that Van Vliet had whistled to him over the phone. The labyrinthine rhythmic connotations are made flesh by French and Tepper's guitars, revelling in their glorious lines.

This song exemplifies how Van Vliet approached the realisation of his songs on a number of different levels. The lyrics are typically image-rich and cryptic. He gave a detailed explanation of their meaning to Lester Bangs in *Voice*. In a manner of speaking, that is: "Actually, I was afraid to sing on that track. I liked the music so much, it was perfect without me on it. And so I put those words on there, you know, they're just cheap cardboard constructions of balls of simulated pearls floating through, and it's an overwhelming technique that makes them look like pearls. 'We don't have to suffer, we're the best batch yet' were these pearls talking to themselves... I'm, uh, ahm, whaddya call it, it isn't schizophrenic, but it is, uh, what people in the West think of people in the East, you see, meaning that in some instances they think that people are crazy who think multifaceted, that there's many ways of interpreting something. I mean 'em all. I can't say I don't know what my lyrics mean, but I can say that, uh, yeah I know what they mean, but if you call it you stop the flow."[7]

No doubt if he'd been asked on a different day the meaning would have been quite different. But then what does a tree mean? Or the patterns of ice spicules in a snowflake's structure? Or the sun, to which he compared his music nearly a decade earlier? Still, as a unifying theme, "cardboard" is about as un-rock'n'roll as it gets, but it prompted Van Vliet to instruct Williams to scowl like a cat when he was playing the song, as one of the tom-tom-based drum parts was meant to approximate the sound of "a cat trying to get out of a cardboard box".

If all these cross-references weren't enough, when the group were playing the song in the recording studio, Van Vliet decided to put more fire into their collective belly via some provocative mind games. At first his strategy seemed simply perverse rather than alchemical, but in the case of 'Best Batch Yet', some last-minute psychological sculpting of the group members added the missing ingredient: aggression. Feldman takes up the story: "We were all playing it really stridently and boldly and enjoying it. Don was the one with the talk-back button in there [the control room]. He says, 'Wait a minute,' and came out and said, 'I just need to make some changes', and made the drummer play it [differently], probably with the equivalent of tying one foot behind his back. Then he said something like, 'OK, take everything you're doing and play it upside down.' Everybody was trying to do it – you didn't talk back to him about stuff like that – and hearing this thing fall apart.

"We did that for about fifteen minutes, trying to get what he was talking about. The adrenalin and anger come up in you. I wasn't the only one – everyone was seething, but not saying anything. Then he says, 'OK, good, now go back to the way you were playing it before.' So he was totally manipulating us. We were playing it too smooth, not angularly enough, so his way to do that was to get everybody pissed off, angry. And then we went in and everyone played it like they hadn't played it for quite a while."

'Telephone' is a bizarre comment on telecommunications paranoia, especially as Van Vliet was so fond of using the apparatus. The lyrics, which accuse it of being "a plastic horned devil" waiting at the end of the hall, are recited with an air of panic as the band churn away for under a minute and a half.

The new versions of tracks from *Bat Chain Puller*, 'Brickbats' and 'A Carrot Is As Close As A Rabbit Gets To A Diamond', are virtually carbon copies of the originals. Meanwhile Lucas had re-recorded 'Flavor Bud Living' according to the 'Exploding Note Theory', resulting in a clipped and much faster version. It was to Van Vliet's liking now. He commented that they would have to dust the hands off Big Ben to keep up with that timing.

The lyrics to 'Sheriff Of Hong Kong' were written with Ling Lucas (who is Chinese) in mind. It was Van Vliet's longest song since 'Trust Us' from 1968, weighing in at a hefty six minutes twenty-two seconds. The intricate bass/guitar/electric piano ensemble playing follows a serpentine path which only repeats itself with a recapitulation of the opening lines right at the end of the song, where Tepper uses his slide guitars to open the throttle with redoubled intensity.

At any given point in the song, the instrumental lines roam around a benchmark chord on electric piano. Van Vliet was telling journalists that he liked to compose on grand piano and synthesiser now, and this was originally a piano piece called 'Tight Kite Blues' (although it's hard to imagine a Steinway grand fitting into his trailer). The left-hand line became the bass guitar, the right was the lead guitar and Feldman's electric piano filled in the middle. Van Vliet had come up with the lines on the spot as he had done on 'Odd Jobs'. But whereas that track was beautifully poised, 'Sheriff' became a blast of stormy weather. Van Vliet gave Williams a drum pattern, then decided that he couldn't play it. As on 'Ashtray Heart', he got French to come in, this time to improvise a pattern. French was complimented that he knew exactly what Van Vliet wanted. Williams was unhappy about being temporarily ousted from the drum stool in this irrational put-down by his bandleader

French had been the recipient of Van Vliet's undermining of his own abilities on the *Spotlight Kid* sessions when his "inability" to play 'Glider' resulted in Rhys Clark being drafted in. Here he gives a bravura performance on both bass and drums, his clumping tom-toms and hi-hat snatches tracking the guitars. Although it had a sour birth, it stands as a late masterpiece.

The pseudo-oriental feel is compounded by Van Vliet playing Chinese gongs provided by Ling. Their arrival in the studio was a special, almost ceremonial occasion. They were apparently a female and a male and were introduced to the group "like visitors he had brought in", says Tepper. They add a metallic sheen to the song and were played with such vigour that during the recording, one audibly crashed to the floor.

The lyrics are feisty, full of puns and oblique imagery and a whiff of mercurial sex, bellowed out at such force, you can almost feel his hot breath on your cheek – if you were the recipient of the sentiments, that is. "Sheriff" and "chef" are punned, with the multi-talented female in question never making "a taste mistake". Van Vliet tries to hold on to her, in an erotic mating ritual, biting the "end of her sash", but she's back off to Hong Kong "in a flash".

Adding to the cod-Chinese atmosphere, he incants a few lines in Mandarin: "Er-Hu" and "Tsing-Hu" (both stringed instruments used in Chinese classical music), culminating in "Wo eye knee shau jay", which means "I love you, young lady".

A radical departure from previous styles is found in the astonishing closing piece, 'Making Love To A Vampire With A Monkey On My Knee'. 'Neon Meate Dream Of A Octafish' from *Trout Mask Replica* exemplified his poetry splashed over music with the sonic action taking place in independent but coalescing planes. But here Van Vliet's vocal style is closer to narration or monodrama, the subject matter extending the atmosphere of Anne Rice's book *Interview with the Vampire*.

In the mind-boggling scenario that unfolds, a dry pond is likened to "a lady's compact", while the monkey, attendant to this sexual act with the undead and smiling "needles", is like a witch's familiar, a mercurial "fur shadow" with a curling "soot tail". All this is set to a stuttering group accompaniment and melodramatic Mellotron fanfares that loom out of the murk like rock faces. Van Vliet wants to break open the dank, rotting, claustrophobic environment he has delineated, shouting to God to fuck his mind. The recitation ends with a verbal wooden stake hammered through the heart of the vampire he has ravished, with the Shakespearean plea "death be damned – life", as the song meanders to its conclusion.

The album itself was like a Beefheartian stake, or flagpole, hammered into the post-punk music scene of 1980. Press reaction was heavily stacked in favour of the album. There were few dissenting voices, although Dave McCullough began his review in *Sounds* by referring to the "loony hysteria" of the original Magic Band – which hardly inspired confidence in his critical perception – and continued with a damning appraisal; that it was a "Lazy parody of former genius... What remains is Beefheart fighting against the bric-à-brac pastiche with his own dwindling persona. The magic has gone. There's nowhere left for it to go."[8]

Everyone else, from cognoscenti to casual listener, was hailing the album as one of Captain Beefheart & The Magic Band's greatest achievements. Lucas managed to get a number of the top US music journalists over to his apartment in New York for salons to listen to the album, and both the dailies and the music press lavished praise on the record: "Captain Beefheart's most meditative, heroic album"[9] was the headline of the review by Ken Tucker in *Rolling Stone*; a four-and-a-half star rating in *Downbeat*; number eight in the year's ten best albums in the *New York Times*; "As brilliant an album as anyone has released this year,"[10] said *Musician*; "Prime Beefheart like you haven't heard in years,"[11] said *Creem*.

This return to top form was timely. In the late Seventies, the groups corralled together in rock's New Wave – and their fans – had spontaneously decided it was time to kill the kings; to destroy the hegemony enjoyed by redundant, bloated rock stars and replace it with an essentially younger, more vital – and basic – musical force. Of course it wasn't quite that straightforward – Mick Jagger, for one, failed to hand in his resignation and in 1977, progressive rock *bêtes noires* Emerson, Lake & Palmer scored a hit single in the UK with 'Fanfare For The Common Man'. But in this social and musical upheaval, focus was being significantly shifted away from the passive spectacles of big rock shows to the democratisation of the stage and the realisation that grasping the means of production, at least in the music business, was something you could do, and *now*.

Many of these avenging angels had cited Van Vliet as a major source of inspiration. He was a hip name to drop. In this climate of iconoclasm, musicians like Rod Stewart and Elton John were examples of old farts whose statues were metaphorically kicked over. These were Van Vliet's words, wrenched from their context on *Trout Mask Replica* and directed against the new enemy – which was ironic, as he was older than both of them. But he was held in reverence and his statue was left untouched and, if not worshipped, then at least respected. In 1977, The Sex Pistols' John Lydon was at the height of his *enfant terrible* Johnny Rotten notoriety. He was called into London's Capitol Radio for an interview and to play some of his favourite music, where he surprised listeners by including tracks by Can, Peter Hammill and Captain Beefheart's 'The Blimp'.

After the initial Punk Rock New Wave shake-up, the best groups – those whose imagination extended beyond mere attitude – became part of a vanguard which broke down musical boundaries and created exciting new forms, in an eruption of creativity the like of which had not been witnessed since the late Sixties. Groups like Wire and Television managed that in style, but by 1980 record companies which had been anxious to buy into this new phenomenon were becoming more selective in their signings, and both the US and the UK scenes were fragmenting. The more radical elements were driven underground, and those left on the surface were the ones more readily acceptable to the record-buying public.

In this post-New Wave milieu of the new decade, the epithet "Beefheartian" was being used to describe groups playing more angular *outré* music: The Pop Group, The Birthday Party, Devo, XTC and Père Ubu, to name five. Andy Partridge of XTC was a huge fan, and had spent long teenage hours in his Swindon bedroom attempting to learn the guitar lines to *Trout Mask Replica*.

The man himself was less than magnanimous towards the whole scene. Even if you hated the music of Blondie or The B-52s, for instance, it was a different reaction to the one Van Vliet wanted to provoke by his own heavy-duty musical irritant. And it was certainly not living sculpture. John Lydon's praise of Captain Beefheart & The Magic Band was left unreciprocated. Lydon had been invited to dinner by Van Vliet's friend, journalist Kristine McKenna, in order to meet them both. He failed to appear. This was just too casual in Van Vliet's estimation, and certainly no way to treat a lady.

Lydon's music was subsequently pilloried in a musical 'blindfold' test conducted by Jim Miller for *Vanity Fair*. When Van Vliet was played 'Swan Lake' from Public Image Ltd's 1979 album, *Second Edition*, his comments gave short shrift: "That beat that loud — that's what makes the money. Who's that? John Lydon? They're copying my drum sound. How corny of him. I thought he was better than that."[12]

Van Vliet saw this new radicalism as little more than rehashed rock'n'roll. He succinctly summed up his view to Paul Rambali of *New Musical Express* with a subtext that harked back to his own "heart attacks" in the Sixties: "I'm trying to do all I can and I have been all my life. And I thought there would have been more happening by now. I thought that *Trout Mask* might do something to break up that catatonic state. That's why I did it, to take the labels off... get rid of the labels and let's see what's going on. But they do more bom... bom... bom. I'm so sick of that mama heartbeat! Hey, listen... I don't want my heart to attack me! I would never treat my heart that way. Never."[13]

Lester Bangs had made his own views on New Wave groups clear during his account of the Magic Band's show at the Bottom Line, New York, in 1977, when he wrote the following: "What was that I heard about a 'new wave' of something or other that was supposed to be such a challenge to the existing order, such a brave stand? Yeah, right, tell me all about it when even the best of them aren't really gonna even barely catch sight of the Captain's flying boot-heels for years in terms of sheer audacious originality of lyrics or music."[14]

Talking to Bangs, Van Vliet was equally dismissive on the subject: "I don't ever listen to 'em, you see, which is not very nice of me but… then again why should I look through my own vomit? I guess they have to make a living though."[15]

Van Vliet's universe was a solipsistic one. As always, he had to feel, and be seen to be, unique. This dislike of *anyone* impinging on what he perceived as his territory was exemplified by his reaction to the Charlie Daniels Band's 1979 hit, 'The Devil Went Down To Georgia'. He felt that their version of the farmer-versus-the-devil story was too close to his own song 'The Floppy Boot Stomp', even though the tale probably came over to the States with the Pilgrim Fathers. He was even muttering about litigation, a course he sensibly chose not to pursue. He knew he was in a field of one and wanted to keep it that way. It is hard to imagine that if *Trout Mask Replica* had opened the field in the way he reckons it could have, he would have been any more kindly disposed towards musicians who had actually discarded their 'labels'. Père Ubu, for example, had got rid of a few labels themselves, but were coming from a totally different direction to the Magic Band. About the only points of overlap were that Ubu had a singer, David Thomas, with a highly unusual voice and a synth player who also played action-painting sax in a similar way to Van Vliet. Thomas also viewed the initial punk movement as "reactionary and arch conservative".[16] The subject of Ubu was brought up by John Piccarella in an interview in *New York Rocker*. Van Vliet's arrogance became overbearing, extending to his perceived right to criticise a group he had never heard because someone was feeding him with the erroneous information that they played music similar to his own. He was asked if *Doc* was a response to all the people who claimed to have been influenced by him (that rode on his bones). "Not at all. No, I couldn't care less,"[17] was the answer.

In the extensive round of interviews Lucas had arranged to take place in his apartment in the autumn, Van Vliet was far more effusive when steered onto other subjects. He summed up his perception of his current role to *Rolling Stone*'s Kurt Loder: "I'm not Chuck Berry or Pinky Lee, I'm right now, man. If I wanna do something, I do it right. Look how long I've been at this, my tenacity. It's horrible. It's like golf – that bad, but that's what I do."[18] The upcoming tour, when the Magic Band would be playing Europe, was discussed. Van Vliet sounded enthusiastic: "My favourite wine I ever had was in Brussels. This stuff was *old* – seventeenth century. There was a petrified spider in the cork. I thought it was about time we had some good wine, so I bought everybody in the band a bottle and charged it to the room. I did – charged it to Warner Bros. It was *good*. And it was snowing in Brussels, and the snowflakes were like white roses falling in slow motion. *Ooh*, it was wonderful – especially on that wine."[19]

During an interview in *Musician*, Bangs cut to the core. After fifteen years of Van Vliet running the show in interviews, he was the first journalist to question him directly on the personae that he suspected he adopted in conversation to confuse the questioner and keep him (this applied largely to male journalists, who, he reckoned, often came with a subconscious agenda rooted in male rivalry) at bay. Never one to let friendship get in the way of his lines of inquiry, Bangs wrote rhetorically: "What good is being an artist, creating all these beautiful things, if you can't just throw down your defences *sometimes* and share things on the common level of other people? Without that, it's barren and ultimately pathetic. Ultimately, without some measure of that, it can never matter as art. 'Cause art's of the heart. And I'm talking about the heart that flies between two or more humans, not to the ghost of the great auk, or a glob of paint, or any of his other little friends."

Having set out his stall, Bangs then engaged him in a revealing exchange:

LB: Why do you almost always talk elliptically?
DVV: Due to the fact that probably it's very difficult for me to explain myself except in music or paint.
LB: But don't you think talking that way all of the time is kind of impersonal, a distancing effect?
DVV: It probably comes out very personal in the music. That's where I'm truthful and honest. I don't know how it happens exactly, but my mind becomes the piano or guitar.
LB: What about when you're alone with Jan?
DVV: We don't talk too much. Because we trust each other, and we don't have that much faith in the spoken word. I guess it's true that I do talk selfishly as a conversationalist.
LB: Well, don't you think you're missing something you might get

from other people by being that way?

DVV: Sure, but they usually won't accept me anyway. I'm comfortable talking to you. Not many people seem to have things in common with me. I guess what intrigues me the most is something like seeing somebody wash my windows – that's like a symphony.

LB: But if you and I are friends, and you trust me, we should be able to have a reciprocal conversation.

DVV: We're talking without talking. I mean that in a good sense. We're saying things that can't be put into the tongue. It's like good music.[20]

During an interview at Lucas's apartment in December 1980, Van Vliet's psychic receivers were twitching. The critic Robert Palmer had recently been present when he had walked over to the telephone to answer it before it rang, although he would laugh about this ability, as it wasn't something he could control. But this particular night he picked up something astonishing. Lucas: "In the middle of an interview, at eight or nine o'clock as I remember, Don said, 'Wait a minute, man, did you hear that?' He put his hand over his ear, but we didn't hear anything. He said, 'Something really heavy just went down. I can't tell you what it is exactly, but you will read about it on the front page of the newspapers tomorrow.' We said, 'Well, what?' and he said, 'I dunno.' Then the guy left and another journalist came. We were in the middle of another interview and about eleven, the first guy called me and said, 'Did you hear the news? Something just happened, John Lennon was shot.' And I couldn't believe it. It really seemed like Don predicted this. So I told him and he just looked at me and went, 'See? Didn't I tell you?' That was really eerie."

Back at CBS, Lucas was somehow managing to juggle his work duties with co-managing the Magic Band. He and Ling organised an intensive tour of the US and Europe to run from October through to January 1981. Gary concentrated more on press, publicity and looking after Van Vliet, whereas Ling sorted out the details of the shows with the promoters in conjunction with Virgin.

Although all the elements appeared to be in place, the situation was plunged into chaos shortly before the start of the tour. The official line given in the music press was simply that French didn't want to play live. That was true, but what it failed to convey was that French's aversion to the activity had been caused by Van Vliet himself. He had been put under pressure to learn an enormous number of songs for the upcoming tour –

far more than would eventually be played. At the eleventh hour, he made his final exit from the group. Lucas: "He [Van Vliet] called up, reversing the charges, two weeks before the tour, with French sitting in a bar in the desert saying, 'Gary, tell French about how excited you are that he's playing.' I said, 'Yeah, John, it's really a thrill that you're going to play guitar and I always loved your drumming.' He said, 'Thank you.' I said, 'I've been telling the English writers that you're coming over and it's the first time Drumbo's been with Beefheart on guitar, and they're all really excited.' And in the middle of it he ran out the door, Don went, 'Holy shit, man. Wait a second. The goddamn guy he left, hold it.' He drops the phone, I'm on a dead phone for five minutes, long distance.

"Then he comes back and he goes, 'The guy just split. He jumped in his car. I gotta go after him, man. I'll call you back.' He calls back later that day and says, 'He quit, man. I snapped him like a rubber band.' He gave him a list, this impossible task and French just bolted. This is what I had to worry about as the so-called manager. It was really out of my hands. I was in New York fretting."

Luckily no one had to fret for too long. Enter Rick Snyder, a Captain Beefheart fan since the age of twelve. Snyder had been a bass player in a band called Ace & Duce in the late Seventies. They played free jazz workouts, Beefheart-inspired originals and some cover versions like 'Click Clack' and 'Sugar 'N Spikes'. The group were even inspired by the Magic Band in their choice of instrumentation, occasionally using marimba and musette. When Ace & Duce split, Snyder continued to work out parts to Van Vliet's music. "I only hoped to be able to take his musical puzzles apart and piece them back together. Very little more ambition was there to this exercise," he told Justin Sherrill in 1995.[21] A spell as a psychiatric nurse and a gig with a power-pop band, The Shake Shakes, followed, with Snyder wondering whether to put his psychology degree to better use.

The Ace part of Ace & Duce was Ace Farren Ford, who was still in contact with Van Vliet, and told Snyder that he was auditioning guitarists for the forthcoming tour. Snyder already knew some of his songs and had played for him during a visit to his trailer in Lancaster years before. Before his initial audition with Moris Tepper, his work colleagues at the hospital helped by covering his work for hours at a time while he honed his parts to perfection. The audition went well, but Snyder, essentially a bass player, didn't feel too confident. He was more or less resigned to his few minutes of fame-by-association, and even offered his services as a roadie. When recruiting new group members, Van Vliet usually made up his mind very quickly. He wasn't always so efficient with formalities, though. In this case he didn't actually tell Snyder that he had got the job. That fact came up in the course of a conversation when he phoned him a few weeks later. Snyder was thrown in at the deep end. His Herculean task was to learn the whole set in quick time, again helped out by his work colleagues

"I had to adjust to the unusual directives that Don insisted his guitarists follow which added just a bit more 'task' to the task at hand. For instance, the use of very heavy-gauge strings to aid in achieving a purer slide tone and the requirement that we use metal fingerpicks – which, after the bleeding and blistering subsided, became almost second nature in their use."

Van Vliet was amazed by Snyder's dedication and his ease in slipping into this most demanding of groups, and moulded his story to underline how pleased he was. "I had just a few days to find a guitarist and he called me on the phone and said, 'Let's do it.' I said you gotta learn 29 songs in three weeks, and he did it! I can't believe it. He's the best there is with Jeff [Moris] Tepper. Incredible! I've got it now. I've been looking for 15 years for this. It's that good."[22]

"He [Snyder] was a hero, man," recalls Lucas. "Then I hear: 'Gary, we got to dress him, man. You know, the way he looks, I'm gonna "kook" him,' that's what he [Van Vliet] used to say. So he called me up and said, 'I just had a vision, man, a little hat with red felt and a ribbon on the front.' Snyder called Lucas up late at night to give him his hat size for the "kooking" process. Forgetting the time difference between Los Angeles and New York he woke Lucas up around midnight. Ethnically, Snyder was also part Winnebago Sioux. Putting all these factors together, Van Vliet gave him a new name – 'Brave Midnight Hatsize Snyder'.

"You'd go crazy trying to fulfil all these things," says Lucas. "He told Eric Feldman once, 'You gotta get this,' and he ripped off a lampshade from a fixture in some European hotel, gave it to him and said, 'OK, you gotta get a strap made and it's clear plastic chemistry tubing with little red cinnamon hearts going through the tubing, just placed so, with two straps here.' Yeah, right, you're gonna find this in the middle of a tour! He once got Eric to wear a red fireman's helmet during a live version of 'Hot Head'. He loved putting everybody through changes – impossible demands to fulfil Don's art visions of surrealistic folderol."

16

A KIND WHIP, A KIND QUIP
(OR OFF ON AN AVANTANGENT)

"I live in a trailer up in the Mojave Desert, the high desert. And my neighbours are coyotes, rattlesnakes, ravens. And the desert is so subtle. No, I mean if you really delve into how subtle it is, it's subtle. Too subtle to... I don't know, it's hard to pay that much attention."
Don Van Vliet to David Hepworth BBC Radio 1, 1980

"I'm an only child. A tyrant. Irascible."
Don Van Vliet, *Eyewitness*, TV show, 1980

Writing in *Rolling Stone*, Kurt Loder had rather optimistically assessed that Van Vliet was "itching to get out on the road", which he qualified with the observation that recommitting lyrics to memory wouldn't be an appealing prospect with such a complex and lengthy repertoire. Van Vliet agreed with him, the vomit, metaphor itself being regurgitated: "I have to learn all of that vomit, you know? It's like reaching back in a toilet, bringing it back. God, that stuff is so far back to me at this point. I mean, Jesus Christ, I can't even remember where my keys are in my pocket." He was also complaining that the group would have to play for an hour and a half, which was too long, an insult to the audience. "But after the Grateful Dead and Zappa what can you do? I mean, if you don't *have it*, man, you have to play longer."[1]

When Paul Rambali was taken to the group's low-rent rehearsal studio, The Stone Fox in Burbank (a run-down building and, in common with many Californian studios at the time, crawling with drug dealers), Van Vliet typically declined to sing with the group, telling them to wait until they all got onstage. He felt the exercise was an imposition. He'd maintain that the initial recording had been a spontaneous splashing of poetry over music, an art statement that he couldn't or didn't want to replicate exactly. He'd done it once in the studio already and was bored by the exercise. Not even the promise of some more of the mythical 300-year-old wine in Brussels, where they were due to play in November, could get his enthusiasm firing.

This was soon proved to be a bad strategy, but bass and keyboard player Eric Drew Feldman puts Van Vliet's absence into context: "It is not as if Don didn't want to be there. We encouraged him *not* to be there all of the time. There was a lot that needed to be rehearsed. Like how to play along with and simultaneously ignore the musician next to you, and how to play the right wrong notes. Don had a lot of patience for this in the writing process preceding recording. But in the rehearsals for live performance, his constant desire to update the arrangements of his compositions could be hazardous to our mental health. It was easier for us to try to get somewhat solid before Don showed up, or else we would still be there rehearsing today."

Tepper offers this appraisal of the start of the tour: "All those shows were pretty bad. It wasn't like in the States where we'd be touring for six weeks and really begin pulling into the shit, getting really heavy. I was so excited and nervous being in England. Even though I'd been in the band for a long time, they were like first gigs again, 'cos they were on wholly foreign territory. But from what I heard, for most audience members, it was wonderful to see him again, playing music that was not [from] the DiMartino records.

"I was very aware of comparisons to Zoot Horn Rollo," he admits. "I had both the consciousness of that original *Trout Mask/Decals* band and I knew that we weren't them, and in my mind we didn't have the uniqueness and the weight that they had developed over many years of playing together. I remember Don being very supportive and bolstering us, saying 'You guys are better than that band ever was. They are going to love you'."

The tension that Van Vliet had claimed was essential to his music came back to haunt the instigator. Just before the opening Magic Band show at Cardiff University, their under-rehearsed leader was far from relaxed. Gary Lucas describes trying to give him an encouraging pat on the back: "He recoiled and howled 'Don't touch me!', and Jan was beaming and saying, 'Oh he's going to be great tonight, he's all worked up'."

Once onstage, the lack of cohesion between The Magic Band and their leader was obvious. During stage announcements, he would even forget from which albums particular songs came, and despite the cue cards propped against his vocal monitors, he didn't seem quite there. In common with most tours, the first date was also beset by technical problems: the monitors weren't mixed properly, Snyder's equipment cut out on him at one point and guitar strings broke.

Lucas had been watching all this from the wings with increasing concern. But he had his own problems when he played the solo guitar piece, 'Flavor Bud Living'. "I was given a pair of sunglasses to wear by Jan and I started to sweat profusely under the lights," he recalls. "They started to slowly slide down the bridge of my nose until they were dangling by a molecule of sweat and then just completely fell off. I never attempted to wear sunglasses on stage again."

Snyder has vivid memories of the new Magic Band's first performance together in Cardiff: "Both Jeff [Moris Tepper] and I made 'clams' during the show. During 'Dropout Boogie', I believe, things started to fray and mistakes started to fly on my part, which, in turn, threw off Jeff's performance. It was just one of those anomalous moments that takes you over – and though it only happened once during the entire tour, it just *had* to happen on my maiden voyage. I would've gladly consented to doing a second free show for the Wales audience just to assuage my guilt.

"After the show, the both of us offered not to accept any pay for our performance that night, but Don was nonplussed and very kindly re-assured us that it was not only not as bad as we felt, but that it was sure to get better – even by the very next time we got on stage. Sure enough, Don was right – and, if only by the way of the rather shrewd psychological approach that he had just employed with us, he managed to get better performances out of us the next time out."

Tepper had his own aftershow problems: "I remember getting offstage and there was a fan who wanted to take my picture. I was in such a bad feeling, 'cos the show went so bad and I told the guy 'fuck off', or something like that, and he wanted to fight me. He was yelling at Don and at Jan, 'What a pussy! Why is he in rock 'n' roll if he doesn't want to get his picture taken?'"

The next show at the Colston Hall, Bristol was no great improvement. Lucas: "Afterwards, Jan marched Don into his room saying 'You've *got* to concentrate', forcing him to improve the delivery of his lyrics. And when we hit Birmingham and Manchester it was a lot better."

Whatever Van Vliet did on stage, the group were under strict instructions not to deviate from their predetermined parts, or to try and compensate for any missed cues. On some tracks like 'Old Fart At Play', where Van Vliet played at raconteur, he would have to replay a coincidence to get it to gel exactly as it had done on the recorded version. And that wasn't necessarily the point. But on more structured songs there could be problems. At The Venue, London, Van Vliet sang a whole rhythmical measure out on 'Dropout Boogie' and stayed that way, lagging behind the band for the entire song.

That was a minor blemish in an otherwise excellent show. Starting with Feldman's bass solo to 'Hair Pie', the set encompassed 'My Human Gets Me Blues', 'Doctor Dark', 'Electricity', 'Safe As Milk', 'One Red Rose That I Mean', and a selection of tracks from *Doc At The Radar Station* including an awesome 'Sheriff Of Hong Kong', which Williams played with no difficulty, and with Van Vliet whacking his Chinese gongs. By now Snyder was meshing with Tepper to stunning effect. Lucas featured on 'Flavor Bud Living', and added occasional guitar and bass. Each night he was on poem-recital duties: either 'Untitled', 'Hey, Garland, I Dig Your Tweed Coat', 'One Man Sentence' or 'You Should Know By The Kindness Of Uh Dog The Way Uh Human Should Be'.

Onstage, Van Vliet was becoming more relaxed and charismatic. "I hope you don't get Reagan-face," he said as a precursor to 'Dirty Blue Gene'. "I'll tell you what Reagan is, man – he's a bad actor," he said, later followed by "Reagan saddle-soaps his hair" and "Reagan and Margaret Thatcher should do a tango. And their palms should be napalmed," making plain his disapproval of the political leaders of the United States and its satellite state across the pond.

On their UK tour, The Magic Band drove from show to show in a van that Jan nicknamed the Goldfish Bowl. The tedium was relieved and the mood of the group – especially Van Vliet himself – would be elevated by some story telling. "At times he had me reading from this book by Wyndham Lewis called *Snooty Baronet*, which he loved," Lucas says. "It would send him into raptures, saying: 'Old Snooty. Oh, man that's so hip!'. He'd be quoting from the book and chuckling backstage."

Although they had secured some pot, the Magic Band was some way below Aerosmith on a scale of rock'n'roll debauchery. When the group played in Manchester they made a special detour to the Manchester City Art Gallery to see an exhibition of Wyndham Lewis's paintings. When they got to London, Tepper and Feldman accompanied Don and Jan to look at work by Francis Bacon at the Tate Gallery.

For someone who was not keen to play for too long, Van Vliet's schedule at the major London dates was punishing. Two sets on the same night in London followed by a set in Guildford, followed by two more in London the next day. At the second show of the second night he took a tape he had made of the noisy plumbing at the group's Bayswater hotel and played it to the audience. This was the same hotel where he had hurled an ashtray across the room and as it landed spinning on the floor had exclaimed, "Oh, man, this is something I have to give Williams as a drum part."

"Don was such a surprising individual," says Snyder. "He was the prototypical 'adult child' – full of wonder at the simplest things. On one occasion, in a hotel hallway area in Manchester, Don introduced me to his 'good friends', Pyrene, Pyrene Junior... and Bell. The first two friends were two different types of fire extinguishers that were mounted on the wall. Bell, of course, was the fire alarm bell. He proceeded to tell me of a conversation that he had had with Pyrene, Pyrene Junior and Bell in his previous stay at that same lodging facility. He deemed it only a matter of politeness that I be properly introduced to them. It was just another in a series of delightfully abstract moments with Don that seemed to come at you from only Don-knows-where."

One of Lucas's coups was to get Captain Beefheart & The Magic Band an appearance on the hip American TV comedy show *Saturday Night Live*. Hal Wilner, the producer and impresario – and music co-ordinator for the show – booked them for an appearance in November 1980. The host that night was actor (and Captain Beefheart fan) Malcolm McDowell and the group played 'Hot Head' and 'Ashtray Heart' in among sketches with titles like 'Leather Weather' and 'Serf City'. They were also featured in concert on Chorus TV in Paris. It was originally intended that they play The Bataclan, but it had shut because of noise complaints two weeks before the show. The rescheduled venue was a *Folies Bergère*-type theatre in Montmartre. The show was broadcast live on a Sunday afternoon and as The Magic Band finished, the girls filed into the dressing room to get ready for the evening striptease show.

Van Vliet's fondness for the mellotron occasionally led him to play an impromptu solo onstage. At Boston in December, he went from mellotron to mini-moog to electric piano – sometimes two of them simultaneously – in a jagged collage of sound. The first solo was well received, the second less so, and was curtailed by an angry outburst from the player. "If you're going to talk, forget it," he barked, before tempering his annoyance and mildly stating, "They didn't do that in New York, by the way".

"He's been called the Father of the New Wave, one of the most important composers of the last fifty years, a primitive genius. Don't know who he is? You're not alone. He's never really had a hit record. He lives reclusively in a trailer somewhere in the Mojave Desert. His name is Don Van Vliet and he dedicates his music to animals and children," was the autocue eulogy stated by the presenter of a profile piece, *Eyewitness*, on a Los Angeles TV station.

In between clips of the group in rehearsal, Van Vliet chatted about his lack of schooling – "If you want to be a different fish you've got to jump out of the school," he said, and explained the essence of his music: "I don't like hypnotics. I'm doing a non-hypnotic music to break up the catatonic state. And I think there is one right now. I just wanna play, I want things to change like the patterns and shadows that fall from the sun." He claimed that he taught the music to the musicians with "a kind whip; a kind quip" and admitted they didn't get paid enough. At the end the presenter looked the camera in the eye, earnestly concluding, with a compliment of sorts, that although Van Vliet "came off like a wacko", he really knew what he was saying.

Back at the wheels of industry, Lucas had split up with his wife, Ling, and was, with some reluctance, the sole manager. One of the first things he found out was that Virgin had lost their distribution deal with Atlantic in the United States the same week the group were on *Saturday Night Live*, which meant *Doc* disappeared from American record shops for a while. In the UK the situation wasn't much better. Lucas: "I remember complaining at Virgin during that UK tour. We had done spot checks of the Virgin Megastore in Oxford Street to find no product there. I said, 'How the hell did you allow this to happen? Here we are killing ourselves, like hamsters in a wheel, travelling around the UK, and you don't have the record on sale.'"

When they returned to the States, Jim Farber, in his review of a New York show, wrote: "The most revealing moment of the evening came during a number from 1967's *Safe As Milk*, when Beefheart asked the crowd if they recognised the guitar tunings. 'Do they remind you of anyone who performs now?' he asked, oh-so-cleverly. 'DEVO!!!' shouted back the crowd."[2] Touché.

On January 15, the group played at The Showboat, Seattle, on the occasion of Van Vliet's fortieth birthday. The mixture of the group's power and the birthday boy's intense, authoritative vocal performances made this a thrilling show. He complains about the "urine-coloured lights", then admonishes someone in the audience for smoking something particularly pungent. "I'm not a complainer but what are you smoking? It's *horrible*. That's the worst-smelling cigarette I ever smelled. What is it? It's horrible smelling tobacco... Yeah, it's got something. It's got *me*. Something one-dimensional. It reminds me of Ray-Gun."

There is a spectacular fluff on 'Bat Chain Puller' where, after unleashing a feral roar at the beginning, Van Vliet attempts to come in a minute later, obviously totally lost. The Magic Band have to restart. "One more time. It's my birthday. It isn't the musicians' fault, it's just that I forgot," he jovially informs the crowd.

Feldman recalls that although Van Vliet needed his trusty cue cards onstage, he could recite any of his lengthy poems or lyrics to order when out of the spotlight. He speculates that he may still have been affected by some kind of stage nervousness. Or maybe it was just down to distraction caused by the constant flow of ideas through the Van Vlietian cranial cavity. He recalls one extraordinary incident: "One night I was playing this song on stage, one that was very difficult for me to play – I don't even remember what it was. I'm in the middle of doing it and it's very loud up there. And he comes up to me and just starts yelling this stuff in my ear, a title and the first couple of lines of some song he was thinking of and saying, 'You gotta remember this, it's going to be worth a lot of money to you and a lot of money to me.' And two hours later when we were back in the dressing room, I didn't even remember it – much less what he said, but him even saying it. And he comes back to me with his book and says [sternly], 'OK ...' And still to this day he'll say, 'So. What *was* that?'"

The last ever Captain Beefheart & The Magic Band concert was at The Golden Bear, Huntington Beach, south of Los Angeles, on Saturday, January 31, 1981. It wasn't a full house, Van Vliet was obviously unhappy, and Jan was telling him that he should stop touring. A sad anticlimax. Snyder had been learning the parts in his spare time, earning him a reputation as the 'square' of the group, but his strategy paid dividends. At the end of the tour, Van Vliet even sprang a surprise on the musicians with the inclusion of songs not played thus far. But they passed that test and, in Snyder's words, now had "the level of synergy required to bring the hammer straight down on the spike that Don put in place for us".

Robert Williams decided to quit the band after the tour to pursue a solo career – he had already recorded an album, *Nosferatu*, with Hugh Cornwell of The Stranglers, the 'Eazy Teeth' single and a solo album, *Buy My Record* (with guest appearances from Feldman and Tepper, ex-Doors guitarist Robbie Krieger and the Mothersbaugh brothers from Devo, among others). There had always been an undercurrent of friction between the outspoken Williams and Van Vliet, which again broke out on the *Doc* tour. Even though he gave one of his drawings to be used on the cover of 'Eazy Teeth', Van Vliet was jealous of his drummer's extra-curricular activities and had been irritated when Williams had slipped his records to the DJs at venues on the tour. Financial strictures, a constant factor in being a member of the Magic Band, played the major part in his decision. And in common with most exiting band members, his departure from the tough regime was tinged with regret. He explains: "Back then I was under contract with A&M Records and the two schedules were conflicting. It was a difficult choice to make between playing with Beefheart or doing my own record, but the money to be made from playing with Don was nothing compared to what I'd make with A&M so I indulged myself in my own music. Don was a genius when it came to getting us to do what he wanted and what he wanted was often very demanding. On the other hand when it came to paying us he automatically turned into an idiot who couldn't count to three. It makes me laugh to think of it now. I may sound bitter about some things but deep down inside I wish it weren't over. Those were some of the happiest times of my life."

Van Vliet took a break for a while, but in the summer of 1981 he was keen to start work on a new album. While still working at CBS, Gary Lucas found out that Virgin had a new deal with Epic in the US. He knew Greg Geller, who was then head of A&R at Epic, and found out that the UK Virgin office hadn't sent over Captain Beefheart & The Magic Band's details. Geller wasn't even aware that the group were still with Virgin. Once alerted to the fact, he was keen to get to work and suggested the recording costs for a new album be split between Epic and Virgin.

Although Van Vliet was one of the 'difficult' artists on the Virgin roster, at least the head of the company, Richard Branson, was a big fan. Lucas sums up Van Vliet's relationship with Branson: "There was a really funny time when we brought him to do publicity and took him to the offices of *Record World*. Branson showed up, and the two of them got into a very weird competitive little joking thing. Branson took his shirt off. Don was like, 'I can't believe that. How silly. Can you believe the guy?' There was always this competitive vibe between the two of them. He loved Branson because Branson believed in him. But Don was always bitching that they hadn't done enough for him. It was just a typical adversarial artist vs. record company relationship."

The first thing to be done was find a replacement for Williams. First choice was virtuoso drummer and percussionist Ruth Underwood, who had played with The Mothers in the Seventies. Underwood recalls that Van Vliet spoke to her a number of times about the possibility of her joining, but although very flattered, she ultimately didn't think it appropriate – she was essentially a percussionist, not a kit drummer. Van Vliet was meanwhile making contingency plans, auditioning for a reserve drummer. One of the hopefuls was Cliff Martinez. In the late Seventies he had played in cult LA punk group The Weirdoes and had already made contact with the Van Vliet camp. Having found John French's number in the Union Directory he tracked down his mentor. He had learned some earlier Magic Band drum parts, and recorded them as an audition tape purely and simply for the purpose of meeting Van Vliet, unaware of Williams's impending departure. The tape reached Van Vliet via Tepper.

At the time Martinez was drumming in the group 13–13 with confrontational singer Lydia Lunch, formerly of post-punk shock troupe Teenage Jesus & The Jerks. The group decamped to the East Coast to play some shows in New York before touring Europe. But the tour fell through and six months later Martinez was back in LA. He read that Van Vliet was recording a new album and called Tepper for details. The news was far more exciting than expected. Martinez takes up the story.

"He [Tepper] said, 'Don is auditioning drummers and he wants to hear you Wednesday night.' That was probably the biggest thrill of my entire life, I could not believe it. I didn't sleep for three days. I didn't use any drugs, any coffee. I just stayed up day and night rehearsing, practising drum parts. The day of the audition, I went over to this really ramshackle building in South Central [Los Angeles], where I used to rehearse and started practising early in the morning, and as it got towards the evening time I began to get kind of screwy. I hadn't slept, I hadn't been eating that well and I began to forget everything.

"I heard him [Van Vliet] come in downstairs. He was two hours late, which made it even more of a nail-biter. I could hear his voice resonating through the upstairs and instantly it felt like I was in yet another plane of consciousness. I heard him coming down the hall and I opened the door to greet him and the first thing he said was, 'You didn't really like playing with that little girl [Lydia Lunch], did you?' And as I started to answer he said, 'You just did it for the money, didn't you?' and I felt compelled to agree. And he said, 'I know what you really want. You want Gretsch drums with leather heads.' I thought, 'Great, at least here's something I can talk about.' Then he says, 'You know, I was the first guy to use rubber drumsticks and cardboard cymbals?' I'm sitting there nodding like a dummy.

"He was with Jeff [Moris] Tepper, and his cousin Victor [Hayden] but no one's saying anything, Don's got his sketch pad and he's doing all the talking; it was a hard conversation to dive into. He said, 'You know you were lucky that you didn't go to England. You see that' – and he points to this black hole in the side of his nose [from an earlier nose stud piercing]. 'I did that with a number two lead pencil and not because I wanted to look like a Picasso painting – I was bored, man.' It was unreal. It was just like I had been pushed out of a spaceship and landed on another planet.

"He will really pour it on in the presence of a fan and he knew he had a huge one with me, so he was giving me the full throttle Beefheart act and it was awesome. He was funny, he was brilliant, I didn't know what he was saying half the time and I was delirious anyhow. So finally after a long monologue he says, 'So are you going to play "I Wanna Find A Woman That'll Hold My Big Toe Till I Have To Go"?' And I said, 'Yeah, Yeah.' So I started to play and he stands up in front of the bass drum, facing me eye to eye as I'm playing. No musical accompaniment, just me and Beefheart face to face. And I made it through, somehow. I was just on automatic pilot at that point. I played about three or four different tunes. There wasn't much of a reaction from anybody in the room; they were all poker-faced. But I thought, 'How many guys in town can do this?'"

The enigmatic trio then went off to hear Don Bonebreak – then with X – and Dennis Keeley (who had played on David Byrne and Brian Eno's *My Life In The Bush Of Ghosts*). Several days later, Martinez got the good news. Van Vliet called him up and during the course of a lengthy conversation mentioned that he was now in the group. Martinez's entry into the Magic Band was part of a considerable reshuffle of personnel. Gary Lucas now had plenty on his plate, as guitarist as well as manager. Rick Snyder, meanwhile, was happy to switch from guitar to his first choice of bass guitar, also playing bass marimba and viola. The reason for this swapping around was that Eric Drew Feldman was unavailable for the sessions.

In the period of post-*Doc* inactivity, he had moved to San Francisco and met up with The Residents. "I was starting to have ambitions by then," he says. "I wanted to produce things and had co-produced a record [*Manual Of Errors*] with their guitarist Philip Lithman, a.k.a. Snakefinger, and agreed to do some live shows." The album had been out for a couple of months and with nothing much happening on the Magic Band front, Feldman committed himself to a tour to promote the record. Although he never officially left the group this move effectively spelled the end of his five-year tenure.

Coincidentally, after numerous delays, Van Vliet was getting ready to record *Ice Cream For Crow*. He initially agreed to leave it a month, but then gave Feldman an ultimatum – the recording couldn't be delayed further. But Feldman, feeling "caught and stubborn", opted to do the Snakefinger tour. Van Vliet had said, "It's cool, do the next one", but was surprised – and none too happy – when Feldman actually jumped ship. He explains: "I think that he intended that I would do it and there was, I felt, a little tenseness about it for a while, like I should have been there – he didn't understand why I didn't come."

As the *Ice Cream For Crow* project approached, Lucas contacted Frank Zappa's manager, Bennett Glotzer, asking to use some of the *Bat Chain Puller* tapes. Van Vliet's concept for the album was that it should be half new recordings, with the rest of the album consisting of tracks from *Bat Chain Puller*. Van Vliet felt that they couldn't be bettered and wanted them, finally, to see the light of day.

After the legal wrangles between Zappa and Herb Cohen that had resulted in the original album remaining unreleased, Zappa retained the tapes – he had, after all, originally put up the money for the project. Initial phone calls to Glotzer indicated that there wouldn't be a problem using the tapes. Later, calls weren't returned and attempts to speak to Zappa personally were also thwarted. Van Vliet was furious, sensing that something was up. They finally managed to speak to Zappa's wife, Gail, and found out that he was rehearsing a band for an upcoming tour of Europe at Francis Ford Coppola's Zoetrope Studios in Hollywood. Van Vliet and Lucas drove over. Zappa's son Dweezil was hanging out there, as were a number of ex-Mothers and some ex-Magic Band members, forlornly hoping that Zappa would give them the nod to step up and play. Gary Lucas recounted the confrontation to Steve Cerio and George Petros in *Seconds*: "From the corner of his eye, Frank saw Don and he kind of whirled around to confront him. Don said, 'Frank, you know what we want, don't you?' in an authoritative voice. Frank said in a hostile voice, 'No, Don, what do you want?' I was thinking, 'Oh, man… I thought these guys were childhood friends.' Don just said, 'Gary,' and I went into my spiel, which was, 'Frank, we've been trying to get a hold of your manager because he promised we could get these tracks that you have the rights to for our record we're doing for Virgin.'

"He said, 'That's right. I heard about that… I changed my mind. Unless you buy all the masters back from me, it's not worth it for me to split up the set. It won't be worth that much in Beefheart-land.'"[3]

The derisory way in which Zappa referred to Van Vliet's musical constituency was not well received. It rekindled memories of his perceived treatment as a "freak" a decade before. Zappa was becoming embarrassed by the confrontation, but held out, agreeing to allow them to use a track that they had recorded together, 'Do You Want A Pepsi?', with Van Vliet singing over Zappa's music. The insult gave rise to a bizarre, uncomfortable scenario: Lucas and Zappa arguing while Van Vliet started to chant the lyrics to 'There Ain't No Santa Claus On The Evenin' Stage' – its fatalistic references to the bleak side of show business coming through clearly. After sarcastic farewells were exchanged, the two got back into the car. Van Vliet was pleased with Lucas's attempts, remarking that Zappa couldn't even look him in the eye.

Not that the exchange did any good in the long run. And the feud between Zappa and Van Vliet was once more in full swing. Van Vliet had a high opinion of Ruth Underwood's musical abilities, but a few months after this confrontation, he gave his opinion of her spell in The Mothers to Kristine McKenna from *New Musical Express*. It was difficult to look at Zappa in the same way again: "She was in one band that was just atrocious. She was just used as a kind of hood ornament – and you know who I'm referring to. That guy who looks like a fly's leg, Zappa. He's not even as hip as a fool."[4]

To prepare for the album, The Stone Fox was rented for two weeks' intensive rehearsal in May 1982. It was situated next to Amigo Studios, where *Ice Cream For Crow* was to be recorded the following month – the same studios, though not the same room, where *Clear Spot* had been recorded ten years earlier. Denny Walley hadn't been in touch with Van Vliet since being ousted from the band, so he decided to drop by and say hello. Van Vliet had a novel way of defusing any potential awkwardness there might be in meeting his old friend again. "Don acted like, 'Hey man, where have you been?,'" recalls Walley. "Like he didn't know anything about me not being in the band. 'So, the band fired me and you knew nothing about it, and rather than find out why, you didn't ask?' And he was like, 'Hey man, I didn't know, I had to do something. You weren't there - I had to get a guitar player'."

The fifteen-minute hole in the record was a potential problem, but Van Vliet came up with the goods. He had some ideas laid aside, including 'The Witch Doctor Life', a piece dating back to the *Brown Wrapper* sessions in 1967. The night of the Zappa incident, he went back to the rehearsal studio and immediately set to work. Fuelled by a few hits of pot, he spontaneously came up with all the music for the closing track, 'Skeleton Makes Good', in one evening, giving the guitarists instructions and scatting parts for Snyder. The song, one of Tepper's favourite Captain Beefheart tracks, finds his guitar tangling with Lucas's National Steel Duolian. It's one of the highlights of the album and was recorded only one week later. The speed of its conception and execution gives it what Snyder regards as its "certain cantankerous charm that months of rehearsal would have stripped away from it". The same could be said of 'Cardboard Cutout Sundown', a track quickly built around an astringent piano piece, 'Oat Hate'.

Tapes of the rehearsals for the album are illuminating from a fly-on-the-wall perspective. One incident gives an insight into Van Vliet's buzzing creativity. Snyder is talking about his "slight case of narcolepsy" and the danger of falling asleep driving a car, becoming hysterical in the telling. Van Vliet says, "That's so childish... You gotta get that right on bass when we do this album... *That's* what I want on bass, the parts the way I wrote them, but that feeling in it."

Two weeks wasn't long to rehearse an entire new album. A number of tracks were learned from old tapes, but some of the newer songs on *Ice Cream For Crow* were as complex as anything Van Vliet had written. Some of the parts were translated in a way that Martinez had never encountered in his previous groups. He knew a lot of Van Vliet's music backwards – which was useful, as in common with his predecessors, he was occasionally asked to play the drum parts that way. Van Vliet was becoming more and more interested in using found sounds to generate musical ideas and his descriptions of what he wanted were beginning to sound like a verbalised equivalent of a section of graphic score. Martinez: "Sometimes descriptions would be hysterical, a lot like his lyrics: 'Make it like Fred Astaire dangling through a tea cup'; 'Like BBs* on the plate'; 'Babies flying over the mountains', things like that. I have to give credit to myself and a lot of the other players. Occasionally you were asked to do something that I would call creative interpretation because I couldn't really tell what he wanted to hear.

"One time he gave me a cassette at the end of rehearsal and said, 'Cliff, take this home and learn this beat.' And it sounds like he and Jan in the kitchen, talking and doing the dishes and the microphone is placed really close to the running water – 90 per cent of the sound is rushing water, but in the background you hear pots and pans being clinked together, so there is percussive activity, but I never would have described it as a beat. And it was really long, the whole side of a tape.

"I tried to imagine some other Beefheart stuff that I heard that reminded me a little of what I was hearing on the tape. I came back to rehearsal the next day and Don said something like, 'That's it, man, you knew that's what I wanted, that's the beat.' And then Jeff [Moris] Tepper, who had seniority in the band – he was a bit of the musical director and translator – said, 'But, Don, I don't hear the water. Where's the water?' Don says to me, 'He's right, where is the water?'"

Martinez occasionally played duets with Van Vliet, laying down a rhythm so he could come up with inflections and accents. Martinez reckons he was "a pretty interesting drummer". And a powerful one. He continues: "I'd had this steel cowbell for like five years – really heavy steel, hard as a rock. You could run over it and it wouldn't budge. He was playing that for ten minutes or less and bent it. It was weird – it was almost it had to be something other than just the force of hitting it. It had to be brain waves or something. I looked at it and I just could not believe it."

Rehearsals were far from easy, with group members trying to avoid being the one "in the barrel", which meant they were the scapegoat, the bad guy that day. Once in the group, relationships between the musicians and the leader inevitably became more adversarial. Martinez reckons that there was a method to all this. Van Vliet sensed when a player became comfortable, deliberately adding difficulties to make them play with more

---

* Metal pellets used in children's guns.

aggression. The music was meant to disrupt and he wanted the players to feel that way too, as he did when recording 'The Best Batch Yet'. During the recording of 'Skeleton Makes Good', Van Vliet wanted even more aggression, instructing Martinez to hit a fire alarm bell that he had mounted on a cymbal stand harder and harder, for take after take.

"It would vibrate your whole arm and it was actually unpleasant to hit it. I was playing very angrily and as hard as I possibly could using the biggest possible drumsticks made, '3S' drumsticks [extra long, heavy sticks used in parade drumming]. And I finally hit it so hard that this stick snapped in half and it hit me under the eye and broke the skin. I started bleeding. And he comes out of the control room and he goes, 'Man, my music's not worth an eye… Why weren't you wearing those sunglasses I gave you, man?'"

From a listener's point of view, it's a relief that Zappa was so uncooperative. *Bat Chain Puller* remains unreleased to date, an obvious loss to the inhabitants of 'Beefheart-land'. But the mooted inclusion of some of its tracks would have given the new album a schizoid split. It's impossible to see how it would have stood up as a coherent piece of work. The material would have come from two eras, two studio sounds, two almost completely different Magic Band line-ups. The main reason for trying to salvage the old tracks was purely and simply to save money. Van Vliet reckoned the budget that Virgin were offering him was not enough. He was right in that respect, as prolonged mixing made the cost run over budget by $15–20,000. The company baled him out but were none too happy.

A combination of Virgin's budget and Van Vliet's obduracy denied the world a recorded collection of his poetry. Virgin were promoting their 'Twofer' line in the early eighties, where you could buy an album by XTC, for example, and get the dub version or the remix version thrown in for the same price. They were hoping that Van Vliet would take the bait when they suggested that if he included a free give-away poetry album it would help him sell 10,000 more copies. He wasn't impressed by the idea. Lucas recalls: "Don got on to the phone to the guy and said, 'How dare you, sir, think that with your frowzy little recording budget you can get me to just give you my poetry like that? Forget it. You can pay me.'" Lucas also confirms that Van Vliet was sitting on an enormous amount of material stashed away in his trailer, including a proposed collection of written work entitled *The Sand Failure*.

So, no poetry album and *Ice Cream For Crow*, released in September 1982, turned out to be the swansong of Captain Beefheart & The Magic Band. The title track is another take on the archetypal "train-kept-a-rollin'" boogie. Here it becomes the framework to a crazy dance ritual dealing, from the title down, in the contradictions of black and white. The guitar line originates from 'Drink Paint Run Run' from *The Spotlight Kid* sessions from 1971, and a few ideas for the lyrics from its contemporary, 'Two Rips In A Haystack'. Martinez muscles into a boogie beat which spills out into a plethora of delicious inflections – hits on his newly dented cowbell, big pressed rolls, tom-tom fills and Chinese cymbal crashes – while the guitars play around each other, occasionally letting out avian squawks.

The lyrics can be seen as a precursor to some of Van Vliet's 'Crow' paintings. The 1990 painting 'Cross Poked A Shadow Of A Crow No. 2' evokes the multiple shadows cast by the flight paths of these enormous birds on a bleached desert terrain – a perfect visual companion piece to the lyrics, which are full of descriptions and wordplays on the blazing heat and the bitterly cold night of the Mojave Desert. "'It's so hot, looks like you got three beaks, crow.' I thought it was so bad," says Tepper. "I get it now. I think it's the funniest thing, it's like Jimmy Durante or something. That's how cool it is. He would say to me, 'Man, it's so cool you can't even see it.'"

'The Host The Ghost The Most Holy-O' is a surprise addition to Van Vliet's canon. It finds him airing his thoughts on the state of play in the world, circa 1982, and getting involved in the eternal tussle between good and evil. While steering clear of a Billy Graham-style address from the pulpit, he uses Jesus as a focal point for man's inhumanity to man.

His views on religion were far from orthodox, though. "Religion's OK as long as it doesn't get too lively," he said a few years later. "People believe the Bible and all that damp bedsheet crap, but I'm not convinced. I think it was a real thoughtless hot night in the sheets that put me here. The world is pure biology and we're just deluding ourselves with all these spiritual notions."[5]

The music has an ominous tolling and Lucas recalls that his guitar line was a transcription of Van Vliet's sax solo on 'Wild Life' from *Trout Mask*. Tepper and Lucas, the "Jewish Guitar Army", sing backing vocals here. Lucas: "It was like trying to get us to eat pork or something!" Aware of the irony, Van Vliet joked, "Some people think it's hip to have blacks in the band but I've got Jews, man. They know all about suffering."

The instrumental 'Semi-Multicoloured Caucasian' is, title-wise, a take on one of Van Vliet's oft-repeated quotes: "Everyone's coloured or you wouldn't be able to see them". It dates back to the *Spotlight Kid* era and dances like 'Suction Prints', although it is slower and more melodic. Tepper's and Lucas's guitar lines mesh beautifully with some country-ish slide laid on top. Snyder's dollops of bass buoy up Martinez's drumming and they roll along together polyrhythmically. Van Vliet decided to change the version the band had learned as he suddenly decided that it would be hip to start the piece with a false beginning. Just before the group were due to go into Amigo to record, they made a reference tape and Van Vliet took a copy for Jan to listen to. She was horrified that he had ruined one of her favourite pieces. He came back apologising to the group, saying he didn't know what he'd been thinking and asked them to revert to the original arrangement.

Hypothetically, 'Hey, Garland, I Dig Your Tweed Coat' should be a classic. It marries an astonishing poem – which dates back to at least the early Seventies – with a backing track that thrashes around like an octopus being dragged on board a ship. The music was assembled quickly, with Tepper playing a transcription from one of the sax solos from *Trout Mask* and the other musicians receiving parts that were made up at the session. The structure of the track was formulated on the hoof but the musicians dived headlong into its maelstrom.

In his review in *New Musical Express*, Richard Cook reckoned that "[it] has the parties blindly going their separate ways, two levels of intense activity never bridged".[6] Van Vliet's style of half-singing and half-reciting over thematically abstract music always required bravado, an intuitive leap into the void. It was the sort of trick that you by now expected him to pull off, but the crucial difference here is that he sounds significantly less sure of himself.

The lyrics are a free-flowing stream, where image follows image in a torrent. "Hot silhouettes", applauding in a car, are like characters giving approval to the song in which they are encapsulated, as if they were watching a wild, freewheeling drive-in movie full of frantic activity provided by creatures such as the "rubber turkey", "wiggle pig" and the reappearance of Pena, all under "red thyroid sunsets". When the "rainbow baboon gobbled fifteen fisheyes with each spoon", it evokes a connection, probably unconscious, with Federico García Lorca's poem 'The King of Harlem'.

With a spoon
he scooped out the eyes of crocodiles
and slapped monkeys' bottoms.
With a spoon.

The music on 'Hey, Garland' is as extreme, or 'pure' perhaps, as anything on *Trout Mask Replica*; with its contemporaneous lyrics it could even *be* a track from that album. Rough mixes highlight Van Vliet wrestling with his sax in the background. The instrument was taken out for the final album version, but on 'Light Reflected Off The Oceands [*sic*] Of The Moon', the B-side of the 'Ice Cream For Crow' single, the vocals are removed and the sax reinstated.

Even as Van Vliet's guitar instrumentals go, 'Evening Bell' makes daunting demands on the player. Although it carried on the deftness and delicacy of 'Flavor Bud Living' and 'Peon', it is even more convoluted and complex than either predecessor. Rhythmically, its non-repetitive, constantly flowing nature is analogous to an excerpt taken from a skylark's song, although it substitutes harshness for mellifluence. It was Lucas's task to learn. He explains the painstaking process: "'Evening Bell' took about six weeks to learn. He sent me a cassette tape of him playing the piece on the piano to learn on guitar. I struggled with it. I did it by ear, incrementally. Every day I would try and memorise five seconds of music and pick out the notes on the guitar as best I could and he would shape it and say, 'Yeah, this is good,' or, 'You've got to attack this differently.' And then when I figured out what I thought was the complete piece and proudly sent it to him, he said, 'Yeah, that's really good, but that's only half of it.' I said, 'What do you mean?' He said, 'I'm sending you another piece, just tack on this music to where the other one finished.' I learned the second half in the same discrete way, but the bitch for me was trying to join them together. I learned a lot of how the memory works in trying to paper over the crack in that piece."

'Cardboard Cutout Sundown' is built on another convulsive instrumental track in different but interlocking metres. The lyrics, recited by Van Vliet in a sandblasted voice, read like a sort of superimposition of frames from the movies *How The West Was Won* and *Blazing Saddles*, all fake Western town movie sets and snapshots of deserts complete with cacti, cross-cut with rolling prairies. The humorous tone of the lyrics is counterbalanced by the aggressive energy of the group's playing.

After the recitation finishes, the band lurch through a series of stop-start passages, cued by Van Vliet in the studio while the tape was running. Meanwhile Lucas played his 'Oat Hate' guitar piece all the way through. This could have been a recipe for disaster, but Van Vliet's mercurial intuition enabled him to weave the trio and solo guitar into a spontaneously realised entity and the ensemble suddenly find themselves locked into unison passages in the second half of the song. Elements of chance or coincidence no doubt found their way in, but they had their place too, and however strange the methods appeared, importantly they worked.

'Little Scratch', discarded from both *The Spotlight Kid* and *Clear Spot* sessions, resurfaces as 'The Past Sure Is Tense', a much tougher version than its predecessors. Van Vliet sings in his higher exclamatory register with a range of puns on the title. He squeaks out a melody in an asthmatic harmonica line and intermittently scat-sings while dirty, distorted guitars latch on to the main riff before the fade.

As a title, 'Ink Mathematics' resonates in a number of ways. Van Vliet was on record as appreciating business because it was 'good mathematics'; his lyrics were published under the name 'Singing Ink Music'; and musical notation was, to his mind, 'black ants crawling across white paper'. His word-plays go into a new area, often consisting of completely made-up words, like 'Branium domics', as he plays with language in an attempt to describe these mathematical conundrums. The song lurches and rocks and the breakdowns are dark and shattered, with his vocals tightly locked into the music.

'The Witch Doctor Life' was a long time in the pipeline, Van Vliet working on it then abandoning it over fifteen years. At last it made the grade. The delicious bluesy syncopation, punctuated by Snyder's marimba, frames a tale of the throwing of bones for the purpose of divination; in Van Vliet's words "the bones that sing of silence".

Martinez: "We had gone to 7-Eleven to get some snacks, and we're carrying these sacks full of potato chips and peanuts and soft drinks and Don goes, 'Get the tape recorder running, I've got it. I've got the part for "Witch Doctor Life".' He steps up to the microphone and he's got these two shopping bags and he starts swinging them back and forth. They were brushing up against his thighs, going 'Fssh, fssh, fssh, fssh', and he starts whistling on top of it. It was great – classic Beefheart melody. Then there was a big thud. One of the bags slipped and he dropped it and everything went flying out and he goes, 'Fuck. I blew it'. Lucas remembers Van Vliet's instructions of how to approach one scratchy guitar line. He was told to imagine he was a murderer writing on a mirror with lipstick: 'Stop me before I kill again.'"

The poem '"81" Poop Hatch' is the same recording that appears on *Bat Chain Puller*. Although Van Vliet hadn't got the master tapes of the album, he had a copy of the poem on a ¼-inch safety master – hence the slight drop in recording quality – and decided to use the self-same version. It fulfilled two purposes. First and surprisingly, he reckoned that he couldn't do it any better and second, it stood alone as a single-finger salute to Zappa.

In Richard Cook's lukewarm review of the album in *New Musical Express* he felt the recitation "sounds like a man abruptly woken up from an afternoon nap".[7] Far more disappointing is a reworking of 'The Thousandth And Tenth Day Of The Human Totem Pole', from *Bat Chain Puller*. Here Van Vliet's multi-tracked saxes and "prop horn" daub it in a cacophony that sounds both half-hearted, and far too loud.

The track had been re-recorded at the tail end of the *Doc* sessions with John French on guitar and Robert Williams on drums. Having left, they both ended up out of favour with Van Vliet, so he erased their respective tracks. Martinez later faithfully replicated the drum part and Tepper's guitar and Feldman's keyboards were left on. Tepper comes up with this appraisal: 'God, was that horrifying. The original was really good and the re-recording totally sucks. The first one I spent months learning, it was one of my first pieces and I was really in it. Imagine the momentousness of putting it all together to make it happen where it had the beast of beauty in it. And then five years later it's like, 'relearn that piece and play it again' and you know it just can't happen. It just seemed like an enormous waste of time and [I thought], why aren't we doing something different?"

'Skeleton Makes Good' closes the album on a grim note. Snyder had broached the idea of using the sort of monstrous fuzz bass that featured on 'Diddy Wah Diddy'. Here it sounds even nastier, clashing with keening guitar lines as the musical patterns churn around and around in the Magic Band's most abrasive musical moment. The protagonist is stranded in a hypnogogic landscape that threatens to develop into a full-blown nightmare. Van Vliet had jokingly referred to his own musical style as "avantangent", as a riposte, of sorts, to Ornette Coleman's concept of harmolodics, but it perfectly describes the musical correspondences that are going on here. Tepper: "I thought 'Skeleton Makes Good' was amazing, with Gary on the National [Steel Duolian] and me on the other. That song sounded great, had a great vibe." The song and the album end with Van Vliet hitting his Chinese gongs.

He claimed, "This is the best record I've ever done." But again the group, who had done their best with a rushed rehearsal and recording schedule, were somewhat disappointed by the flatness of the sound. Van Vliet and engineer Phil Brown had been at loggerheads over certain issues in the studio. Brown had some ideas of enhancement, like putting ambient mikes in the studio, to get cathedral-like sonics on 'Evening Bell'. Van Vliet was less than impressed by the idea, which he saw as another big spoonful of heavy syrup about to pour in on his two-dimensional painting. His rigorous aesthetic inevitably won through.

Rolling Stone gave the album a four-star write-up and it was generally well received, but without the stampede for superlatives which had accompanied *Doc*. David Fricke, reviewing the album in *Musician*, commented that it was "a spirited successor in the recent *Shiny Beast* and *Doc At The Radar Station* line of *Trout Mask Replica*-rooted experiments with some bold distinguishing marks."[8] Writing in *Sounds*, Edwin Pouncey assessed that "there are initially few surprises", but praised Van Vliet's lyrical dexterity. "A veritable gourmet of words, he relishes the sounds they make in his throat and chews them over before releasing it all in a gush of Fleischer cartoon imagery that bobs and weaves effortlessly and free."[9]

Ice Cream For Crow is a fine album, and contains a few of Captain Beefheart & The Magic Band's best moments. But considering that the most original and vital tracks are the newer ones, it is ultimately frustrating that he was content to dip into the bag and include the lacklustre version of 'Totem Pole', for example, when his muse was in as good a shape as ever. Ultimately it feels like an *hors-d'œuvre* for a main course that never came. There's certainly a nagging lack of *something*. Snyder: "Most of the *Ice Cream For Crow* material had been gleaned from the loose ends of his career – the unreleased and/or undeveloped ideas that he wanted to tie up once and for all, if not for posterity, then for the closure of some personal Gestalt."

Martinez gives his perspective: "Had we had more time as a band together and toured, and then done another album, it would have been great, but under these circumstances we were all new to each other and it had to be done in four weeks, and for Beefheart music that's really fast."

17

EXIT PURSUED BY A GIANT MECHANICAL BEAR

"You know, I never felt the desire to communicate with any music audience, so why did I do it? The entire process was torture."
Don Van Vliet to Kristine McKenna, *New Musical Express*, 9 August 1986

Q: *Do you like being on the stage?*
DVV: *I did, yeah, I did when I was there.*
Q: *Are you going to be going on tour now?*
DVV: *No, no. That's why I did that video actually, because I would rather paint…*
Amateur video, 1983

Don Van Vliet's assessment of the experience of playing live had veered between that of pain and pleasure according to his mood at the time of asking. But by now he had wearied of the process and when a series of live dates were pencilled in to promote *Ice Cream For Crow*, he pulled out before anything could be finalised. The show at The Golden Bear, Huntington Beach, in February of the previous year was to remain the last time that Captain Beefheart & The Magic Band played in public. The notion of touring had become anathema and he baulked at the idea of going through his vomit yet again. Before the album was recorded, Van Vliet had been persuaded, reluctantly at the outset, to make a video for the single 'Ice Cream For Crow' and maybe, just maybe, relaunch his career. In the early Eighties, MTV was gaining in popularity and videos had become less of a luxury and more a prerequisite for any major label act. And with no live work forthcoming, an alternative promotional vehicle was needed to prevent *Ice Cream For Crow* from sinking, commercially, without trace.

Once committed to the idea, Van Vliet began to come up with visual concepts. He had already sketched out an outline for a TV commercial: he would be driving his Volvo estate down the freeway with a bird flying alongside, trying to get his attention. When he rolled down the window the bird would say, "Don't buy *Ice Cream For Crow*." Unfortunately, this piece of reverse psychology was never realised.

While the album was being recorded, a cassette tape left running captured Van Vliet verbalising his ideas to the group over a rough mix of the title track: "Gary [Lucas] with a red cowboy hat. Strings come down, he's wearing a little red cowboy hat while he's playing the part right there. Then Jeff [Moris Tepper] goes off the side, walks out of the picture playing his part. We'll get a nice in and out. And then the hat will go whoff! – off your head. Strings. Strings. *White* string.

"And I want Mr Martinez to be doing that [background laughter], the great spaghetti tie-up. The apron flies off like that and the elbows are really nude and high, like a denuded birdwing on both sides – as he goes out and he comes in, and the hat goes whoff! And [*to Snyder*] you're doing an outrageous dance with your new haircut. 'Cos I can't take it, man. You can't be on video with your hair like that. What do you want to do – bring back the peace sign?"

These tantalising sketches were a long way removed from the dark, claustrophobic commercial for *Lick My Decals Off, Baby*. The video was shot over two days in the Mojave Desert in early August 1982, with Daniel Perle, the cinematographer who had worked on *The Texas Chainsaw Massacre*, behind the camera, and Ken Schreiber from CBS Creative Services producing and sharing directing credits with Van Vliet. On set he asked Schreiber how much it would cost to make the powerlines walk? But with a budget of $7,000, split between Virgin and Epic (which was small even for the time), it's a wonder it got made at all. Every possible favour was pulled in, with some people agreeing to work for free. And although the editing took place in top studios, it was done surreptitiously during periods of downtime.

A slightly more feasible idea was to have the Magic Band playing in front of a wall of boxes of Hartz Mountain birdseed. Rick Snyder had been allocated the job of prop manager and was sent off to the store to make his purchases. But too short of funds by far for a whole wall, he returned with six boxes. If one knows where to look, these can just be made out behind the group in a few sequences, but the effect is far less dramatic, even, than Spinal Tap's 'Stonehenge'. Snyder: "The only time you notice that they're even there is when Jeff picks up one of the boxes in his teeth while he's playing his Mello-bar guitar. Don obscured some of his references in the video so much that they become the equivalent of inside information, if not inside jokes. Many things were left on the cutting-room floor, including, but not limited to, a papier-mâché igloo around which I danced and several small plastic spiders being launched from Cliff's drumheads as he played."

Making a video in the desert was arduous; Van Vliet later claimed the daytime temperature had reached 114 degrees Fahrenheit. Being, by his own admission, "photophobic", he found the exercise particularly uncomfortable. At the opening line, "It's so hot", he wipes his brow with a Kleenex plucked from a foam rubber boulder and discards it. Soon a tumbleweed ('Sir Tumbleweed', or the 'Ecology Officer' as he called it) rolls beneath electricity pylons, picking it up along with more discarded tissues and detritus. The red cowboy hat flies off Lucas's head, and as requested by Van Vliet the group cavort around on a dust road like marionettes, as if the white strings, though invisible, were controlling them all. These scenes are juxtaposed with monochrome night-time shots of the group playing in front of brooding rock outcrops under the full moon, highlighting the song's black/white/night/day imagery. Cut into this visual narrative are brief tableaux where the musicians hold up some of Van Vliet's paintings, which, unfortunately for them, indicated the way his career was heading.

In keeping with the prevailing atmosphere of absurdist humour, Van Vliet casts himself as a shamanic, good-humoured desert creature, gesticulating and grinning mischievously. His lip-synching lagged slightly behind the music, but at a constant rate. The film and soundtrack were thus easily adjusted, although this had the effect of making the band appear to be playing slightly out of time *en masse*. Martinez also found it frustrating trying to mime to the sound coming out of the small monitor speakers on set. Although he is proud of appearing in the video, he was disappointed that the budget inevitably put the lid on Van Vliet's flights of fancy. "For me, making the video was a minor experience and a bit of a letdown," he says, "because I was just in the mood for something that was as wild and as artsy as the music, and it ended up being pretty much a straight performance."

The video is by no means ground-breaking, but any lack of innovation is compensated for by its humour and oddball charm – it was far removed from the narcissistic exercises in self-aggrandisement favoured by the pouting pretty-boy bands of the era. The following year it was deemed worthy of joining the *Decals* commercial in the permanent collection of the New York Museum of Modern Art. More importantly at the time, it was rejected by MTV. Glenn O'Brien, writing in *Artforum*, appraised it thus: "In 1971 Beefheart's language was considered obscene; perhaps MTV rejected his 1982 tape because it contains no sex or violence. It has been suggested that MTV considered Van Vliet to be too old; at 41 he looks great."[1]

When Lucas was a radio DJ at Yale, his producers' damning appraisal of the music of Captain Beefheart was that listeners would tune to another station when they heard Van Vliet's voice blasting out of their sets. That was back in the early Seventies, but a decade later, the prevailing culture hadn't changed much. Lucas: "The technical reason [for MTV's refusal] was, 'It doesn't fit our format of music.' I also remember going around New York with a single of 'Ice Cream For Crow' and DJs refusing to play it in clubs. The New Romantic stuff had just started up and Haircut 100 and A Flock Of Seagulls were what they were really happy with. Their reaction was, 'Oh please, take this away', especially some of the gay club DJs. I was saying, 'I think this would fit on Hardcore nights,' but [they said], 'No, we couldn't play it.' It was very frustrating."

Van Vliet said he didn't want to do anything much for a year after the album, but Lucas pulled off a scoop by getting him a spot on *The David Letterman Show* in October 1982. It was, and at the time of writing is still, a high-profile TV chat show – a good market stall for promotion if you are able to deal with Letterman's sharp line of questioning.

The appearance necessitated a trip to New York. When in an urban environment, Van Vliet became subject to stimulus overload. He had described the effect to John Piccarella when he was in New York to promote *Doc At The Radar Station* two years previously: "I don't live in the city because I don't need all those extraneous noises. I mean I feel like a puppet, y'know... my ears. I've developed my ears, or they were developed and here I am with 'em. Look at that! Three and a half inches long, man!... So it traps a lot of... trouble."[2] Consequently, the walk from his hotel in Manhattan to NBC studios, which would normally have taken five minutes, took half an hour. "He'd stop on the way, marvelling at every occurrence," Lucas explains.

When he first came on set he looked nervous, and when Letterman asked him if he would like a glass for the bottle of water he'd brought with him, he replied with a spectacular *non sequitur*: "No, but the war is a pimple on the pope's pet dragon" (perhaps an oblique reference to the pontiff's penis), then mumbled: "What did I mean?" Once settled down, his oblique witticisms were perfectly suited to the snappy soundbite format of Letterman's show, where the conversation is never far from being broken up by musical interludes and station identification pauses.

Letterman asked him what the album's title meant, to which he replied: "It has a lot to do with Ray Gun. He saddle-soaps his hair and tosses jelly beans through rope tricks. He's a bad actor. What it has to do with [is] black and white. A raven, vanilla ice cream." He also mentioned the MTV ban, turning its slogan on its head by concluding: "I don't want my MTV." Lucas: "He was great. He was concerned that Letterman was going to be his usual nasty self. Somebody had obviously told him, 'You'd better show the utmost respect for this guy or you're gonna look like a jerk.' He was nice to Don and Don really liked him."

There was a run on tickets when Van Vliet was asked back on the show in July 1983. He was again sporting a Fedora, and Letterman asked him if he always wore his hat. "Well, I don't shower with it," he replied, and with a pause of consummate timing added: "And I don't shave with it." They discussed Van Vliet's teenage art scholarship and his claim to have never been to school except for a half-day at kindergarten. He sounded so assured and confident that even Letterman didn't pick him up on this fabrication. He was asked to demonstrate his vocal range and made a strangulated noise, apologising and saying that he really needed something like "a bongo" for accompaniment. Clips from the interviews were later repeated on 'Best of' shows.

Virgin had the option on another record, and Van Vliet had some vague plans to continue recording, but ultimately nothing was produced. He wanted to concentrate on painting now, and realised that if both he and the art world were to take his art seriously, he would have to cut his ties with the music business or run the risk of being labelled a rock star dilettante. Jan was also well aware of this and was instrumental in persuading him to turn to painting exclusively. While he was in this state of flux, Virgin were itching to get him onto other promotional platforms in lieu of touring. They even tried to persuade him to be flown to Eastern Europe to appear in *Grizzly II*, the sequel to the tacky horror film about a giant killer bear.

Captain Beefheart & The Magic Band would be playing at a mock-up rock festival, into which the bear would gatecrash and wreak havoc. Virgin assured him there would be top special effects people working on the mechanical bear, but their main selling point was the assurance that there would be a spin-off TV show, *The Making of Grizzly II*, which would feature the Magic Band playing a couple of numbers. It would have been the perfect stage on which to resurrect 'Wild Life' from *Trout Mask Replica*, where the song's protagonist finds a cave and persuades the bears to take him in. But Van Vliet reckoned it was just about the lamest thing he'd ever heard and refused to have anything to do with it.

The career of Captain Beefheart and his various Magic Bands lasted for over seventeen years, but had no clean ending. Tepper: "It wasn't like 'Boom – today the band's done.' After *Ice Cream For Crow* was released, Don had people who would have still gone on the road with him and worked with him. We all kept in contact, but it was not plausible for him to put out a record and tour because no one was going to give him money to do that, at least not enough money. After a year of trying to get something together, he finally gave up. He said, 'Forget it, I don't want to do it, it's not happening. I'm just going to do painting for now.' So that was the slow death of the band."

Van Vliet maintained that the small budget Virgin were offering was the main factor in his decision to quit music. But it is likely that he was glad for an excuse to justify his dwindling enthusiasm. If he agreed to continue recording he would be expected to tour, and the financial rewards would not be great. Adverse economic factors had always impinged on the stability of the Magic Band and the will to keep pushing on with the ever-present prospect of financial adversity simply evaporated. He was past forty, tired of the music business and unwilling to summon up the energy for yet another round of cajoling, supervising and controlling the musicians, which, as the Captain at the helm of every Magic Band, were duties he had perennially imposed upon himself.

"I always told him that I thought he could earn more money painting than he could making music," says Tepper. "And when he finally started doing that he made a comment to me like: 'Man, you're the one who made me change careers.' Obviously that's a decision that he made on his own, but I had been suggesting to him for years that he spend more time trying to sell his art, rather than just sitting around drawing in books."

Martinez had only been in the band a short time but realised the writing was on the proverbial wall: "Beefheart used to say things like, 'Man, what do you want with music? I use music as an irritant.' Things like that made me know he was on his way out of music. It took a huge amount of effort to make the record and I'd never experienced the disappointment of doing what I thought was a milestone and getting critical recognition but no record sales, no tours. But I think he's a brilliant American artist and maybe in fifty years he will be considered something great. To be a part of his music and to have the record sink like a stone as it did was a bit of a heartbreak."

Snyder had told Van Vliet that he would be in the Magic Band for life and still feels disappointment that the last incarnation of the group was denied the necessary time to realise its potential. At the time he had the highest regard for the musicians and is still certain that if those musical resources could have been properly tapped it would, quite possibly, have been the best Magic Band of all. Tepper had been in the group for seven years straight and ultimately felt some relief when its course was terminated. But the neophytes found difficulty in coming to terms with the fact that the Magic Band – the membership of which had been their ultimate musical goal – had effectively ceased to exist. Lucas went through a period of "decompression" and Snyder had trouble adjusting to musical life after being a member of his all-time favourite group. The musicians would call Van Vliet from time to time to see if anything was happening. Some calls would not be returned, and sometimes the answer would be vague enough for them to realise that they wouldn't be playing with him again.

The French poet Arthur Rimbaud gave up writing completely in 1873, aged nineteen, to become – among other things – an explorer and a gunrunner and thereafter had no interest whatsoever in his past work. Van Vliet's abdication from his rank of Captain Beefheart was not so total, but it was still unprecedented that a rock musician would slip out of one creative field in which he had excelled and into another. Many burn out, repeat themselves to ever-diminishing effect, or attempt to go into acting when inspiration bids adieu and sneaks out of the back door. His view towards the rest of the rock world was becoming increasingly dismissive. In a 1982 interview with Barry Alfonso he said: "Literature has gone so much farther than almost all music. Most of what's out there has been ripped off from somewhere else. I have none of that guilt – there's no guilt in what I do. The public likes to hear dead stuff. They listen to the same stuff over and over, like a fish in a bowl who's feeding on its own excretum. How do they do it?"[3]

But although his recording career was effectively over, he was still keen to keep a grip on his musical franchise, even if it amounted to no more than talking up his act with defiant bluster. "I just wanna keep doing records," he told Tom Pompasello in 1983, but admitted that he was busy painting. "I'm moving my tail with a brush tied to it like a jackass," he said. "Hopefully I'll be able to paint some funny things. I'm gonna hit New York big time. I'll be there. I'll sure as hell be there. I'll be laughing at those women making their faces up in the reflection of the paintings." He was still living in the Mojave at the time and explained why. "I wanna be where it's real hot. It's extremely cold in the night and extremely hot in the daytime. I just like to be with musicians and I like big squares that drive me crazy that I have to paint."[4]

Tepper gave these views on the hostile environment in which Van Vliet had chosen to live and create: "I remember Don living in the desert all those years and I never understood it. There is something about being an artist and being miserable, and I don't mean that as a joke." Van Vliet admitted to Letterman that he didn't like living in the desert. At the time he was there by economic necessity, but in an echo of the psychological rigour that he had always tried to impose on the Magic Band, he said: "I love the tension. It's good for painting."

In the year of his retirement he was still in a fighting mood. Lou Stathis of *Heavy Metal* asked him if there was any room left for the avant-garde. "There better be room for those of us doing exactly what we want, 'cause that's what I'm going to do anyway. It's like in the record industry – they're totally desperate. The only way they're going to get out of their hole is to start paying attention to real artists." Although he reckoned that he had accomplished what he set out to do, his innovations never met with the commercial success he was sure they warranted. "It was only a few people I played to, anyway," he continued. "I mean, all the time that I was playing there were only a few people – small pockets of people really listening."[5] But it's easy to get bound up in this residual bitterness and forget that all his music was released on major labels and he would have had a far easier ride had his career not been robbed of momentum by the largely self-imposed contractual chaos of the Seventies.

Van Vliet's *alter ego*, the name Captain Beefheart, needed to be ditched before it became a millstone. He used his real name – with the added Van – as his working name as an artist. His new path may have been mapped out in his DNA. Back in 1970 he told Langdon Winner that he was descended from a Dutch painter of the same surname, who was a contemporary of Rembrandt. He explained that his forebear had been exceptionally talented but could never finish anything, and that Rembrandt had written to him saying: "I'm pretty good, but if you ever got it together… wow!"[6]. Although this tale prompts the raising of a suspicious eyebrow, Hendrick Cornelisz Van Vliet did indeed exist. He was born in Delft, Holland, in 1611 and died there in 1675. Even removing the 20th century American vernacular from the above quote, it's unlikely that Rembrandt would have said anything of this nature to Van Vliet. As they were contemporaries it is technically possible, of course, but Van Vliet was not in Rembrandt's league. That said he was a respected painter, although certainly not one of genius. He was a member of the Delft School – whose most famous member was Jan Vermeer – and specialised in paintings of churches and other buildings, such as the Ode Halles in the town, as well as typical Flemish family group portraits.

Relaunching himself as an artist could in itself have been fraught with difficulty, but fortuitously some of the heavyweight figures in the New York art scene were fans of his music as well as admirers of his painting. Lucas was still acting as his manager and was keen to get him an introduction to the art world. "Julian Schnabel had contacted me about meeting Don," he says, "and right away the light bulb went off: 'Wow, now we can maybe use this connection to get Don into an art gallery seriously.'"

Schnabel was both a Captain Beefheart fan and a hip and controversial artist. They met and got on well. Schnabel was represented by The Mary Boone Gallery, which at the time had the hottest young neo-expressionists on their books. Boone was also married to Michael Werner, whose main gallery is based in Cologne, Germany, with a subsidiary in Manhattan. A meeting was arranged between Werner and Lucas at the latter's New York apartment. Werner, himself a fan of Van Vliet's music, was impressed by the work he was shown. But he also knew that Van Vliet would have to concentrate exclusively on this new creative course; that if he was to be respected in the art world it would have to be as a painter, rather than as a musician who paints.

The meeting threw up the strangest of potential liaisons. Werner represented German neo-expressionist AR Penck, a Captain Beefheart fan and a drummer too. Despite Werner's view that he should leave the music business behind, there were moves afoot to get Penck to play with Van Vliet. Lucas felt uncomfortable about the way things were going. As well as the mooted Penck connection, Schnabel also wanted to make a record with him. Lucas recalls a jam session at Schnabel's house.

"Schnabel played a little guitar. He also had a sculpture in a gallery in New York that had a bell inside it. He had encased it in papier mâché, so it resembled a giant turd hanging from the ceiling. But when you shook it you heard a very dull thud of the clapper of the bell inside. He'd engaged me to record him playing the bell and I brought a tape recorder down. And he said, 'Let's do a single and I'll play the bell and I'll put my daughter Lola singing on it. Don can sing on it and you can play guitar.'"

"I was happy to do all of this but I warned him, 'I don't think Don will go for this.' And he said, 'Let me decide what I can and can't do.' That's when I saw the writing on the wall – the art on the wall. I thought, 'If he's not making records any more I'm happy to get him into this art milieu, but it's not for me.'" The home recordings with Lucas and Schnabel, during which Van Vliet sang 'Little Tomato' as a parody of 'Pretty Flamingo' by Manfred Mann, were by all accounts best left unheard.

These signposts towards a furtherance of his career ultimately led to nothing. But he continued recording ideas on his portable cassette recorder. A provisional album title, *War Milk*, was verbally committed to tape in 1983, accompanied by tantalising fragments of songs sung a cappella, which sounded well up to scratch. Lucas remembers another song sketch, 'Stork In Pyjamas', which was whistled to him over the phone one night. And then there was 'Varmint Mart', inspired by his account to Van Vliet of a particularly bad-smelling meat market in Taiwan.

The flow was something that couldn't be completely turned off. In 1980 Kurt Loder from *Rolling Stone* asked where all his creative works came from. His answer went some way to explaining his artistic discharge, excretory imagery and all: "Probably from a tortured only child. It just all comes out of my… sometimes cesspool, sometimes not. It's always there. I just hope it doesn't stop. *And* I hope my water doesn't stop – wow, can you imagine that? I'm more afraid the water'll stop. God have mercy: all of a sudden you can't go to the bathroom."[7]

Through saving and borrowing money, the Van Vliets had amassed enough to have a house built on the land he had purchased many years before in the idyllic location of Trinidad Bay on the northern Californian coast. Building work completed, they moved there in the summer of 1983. A number of group members and associates were sworn to secrecy as to where he lived, but in recent years Trinidad has appeared in articles and catalogues and Van Vliet has himself mentioned it by name.

Prior to this more relaxed attitude, he threw up a few smokescreens to keep the sequestered location a secret. For example, around the time he moved there, he told Lou Stathis that he was moving to Arizona from his trailer in Lancaster. "Why the hell are you doing that?" asked Stathis. "It's hotter – it's not hot enough in Lancaster," Van Vliet replied. "I want it as hot as it can get. I like the extremes and the extremes in Arizona are *fantastic!*"[8] For a photophobic who hated the "tyranny of the sun", as he put it, and whose skin didn't deal too well with sunlight, this seemed perverse in the extreme. It would have been if it had been true.

Kristine McKenna, a friend of Van Vliet, appeared to be complicit in this spread of disinformation when she wrote that he was living in Arizona in an article for *Spin* in January 1988. It's hard to believe she didn't know. Van Vliet also told Letterman that he was moving there because it was hotter, before admitting that he had made it up. He is the sort of person, by no means unique, whose love of being with people is cut with a profound desire for privacy, which became paramount with the passing of time. It was no doubt exacerbated by unannounced visits from fans to his trailer in Lancaster. Marginal or avant-garde music, especially when garnished with the far-out lore that surrounded Van Vliet's, tends to exert a magnetic attraction on obsessives and weirdos, drawing them out of their own personal woodwork to come and seek out their obscure object of desire. To engage a complete stranger in a lengthy conversation in the street, or in a bar or café, could be fun, but to have some pilgrim track you down and peer in at the kitchen window unannounced was becoming disturbing. He wanted to get away from that sort of greedy attention and into anonymity.

Back in 1972, as an enthusiastic teenager, Ace Farren Ford had tried to set up a Captain Beefheart fan club. Although he received plenty of promotional material from the people at Warners as a result of his telephone "bombardment", there was one major stumbling block: the indifference of the Captain himself. Years later, when he had become friends with Van Vliet, he broached the subject again. Ford: "I said, 'Hey, you know, whatever happened? I could never get anybody to get that fan club thing happening?' Don said, 'Oh yeah, wasn't that lame? What were you trying to do? There's nothing lamer than a fan club; what the hell did you want that for?' He always told me that he definitely made a distinction between someone who appreciated his art and someone who was a fan. He said, 'You understand what I'm doing, whereas a fan just thinks I'm neat.'"

In January 1984 Van Vliet decided that he was going to record an album of new material, which would include the a reworking of the song 'Hoboism', spontaneously created in 1976 with guitarist Denny Walley. Lucas went to his house to work on some ideas, but he remembers that Van Vliet seemed "unfocused" and nothing was realised beyond rough drafts. While he was there he noticed a sculpture in an alcove in his kitchen, one of the first things Van Vliet had created: "It was this cute little animal that looked like a Shmoo, which was an animal in the Li'l Abner cartoons," Lucas recalls. "He said, 'Do you know what this thing is? The Rumpabeep.'" Having introduced Van Vliet into the art world and realising that there would be no more music – which for him was the basis of their working relationship – he had no desire to hang around and become his "art pimp" and so he finally quit. Lucas felt uncomfortable after leaving Van Vliet's employ and, like John Thomas back in 1976, he felt haunted by his presence for some time.

When a musician ceases to record and his or her output suddenly becomes finite, any enthusiast will wonder what might be left unheard. In Van Vliet's case, many studio out-takes and sketches were eventually used on later albums, but many are still, at the time of writing, languishing in the Warner Brothers' vaults. The creator seems happy with the extent of his output, but as he had come up with so many claims of new songs and poems – most of which never saw the light of day – even those fans who don't rest until every last stone is turned can be excused for their curiosity. They were promised a lot that was never delivered. In the final analysis, it was a line of inquiry that he himself initiated.

For anyone interested in his work, it is irritating to think of such a loss to music caused by the hiatuses in his musical career and the non-appearance of his novels and books of poetry. But that in itself is consistent for an artist whose best and truest work eschewed any sentimentality, and would, he hoped, act as an irritant, "like sandpaper on a shrimp". The same "sandpaper", perhaps, that ultimately wore him down. In the past, he had quipped that he needed a new art-form. His appraisal of his departure from music came from a typically idiosyncratic angle: "I retired. I had too," he told John Yau in 1991. "I got too good on the horn and I got to the point where I thought I was going to blow my head right off. So I started a second life."[9]

Tepper looks back with particular fondness on some earlier pieces that never got past the rehearsal stage, which were, in his opinion, some of Van Vliet's most tender and most affecting musical moments: 'Your Love Brought Me To Life' – originally from 1971 – and later pieces like 'Rhino In The Redwoods' and 'Child Ecologist'. The time needed to realise his more complicated pieces, together with the loss of momentum in his career, had left a lot still stuck on the drawing board.

Such was the dedication of the latter-day Magic Band members that even now many of them admit they would be there for him if he needed them. But that is the unlikeliest of scenarios. Tepper has remained close friends with Van Vliet to this day and remembers that the interest in his music from outside parties continued long into his retirement, but was never reciprocated. "He'd get an offer from an independent record label every year or two after that [his retirement], but it was small money," says Tepper. "Up till about five years ago [1993], I talked to Don a lot about making a record on his own; playing piano or smashing on water bottles or taping rain wipers on his car – the same sort of tapes the band was given to learn. Just him on top of him, so people could hear the way he worked. I think it would have been the best, purest record of all, but he declined. He said, 'Man, I couldn't do that. No one even wants to hear it with the band.'" Another offer came from Bono, singer with U2. He wrote to Van Vliet offering him a support slot on an upcoming tour and allegedly said that he would like to write with him. Far from being flattered by this invitation, Van Vliet disingenuously asked friends: 'Who is this *Bongo?*'

Another interested party was Vivian Stanshall, formerly of The Bonzo Dog Band and author of the *Sir Henry At Rawlinson End* radio plays, which were subsequently made into an album and a film. Stanshall had met up with Lucas before in New York City and, out of the blue, he called him in 1988 with an extraordinary proposal which amuses Lucas to this day: "He said 'Gary, Gary, old man, I have an idea for a supergroup of myself, Don Van Vliet and Doctor John – old Mac Rebennack.' So I said, 'Vivian, knowing Don as I do there is no way that he'd ever consent to such a thing' and he was like, 'Let me handle that, old boy,' and he talked to him. But nothing came of it. I couldn't enable him, I'm sorry to say."

In the winter of 1984/85, Don Aldridge met Van Vliet again in circumstances that brought their friendship back full circle. "The last time I saw Don was upon the release of *The Legendary A&M Sessions* and it was pure happenstance. My girlfriend at the time lived in a mobile home park in East Lancaster. I was bringing her home early one morning, about 3am. As we pulled into the drive, she casually mentioned that Captain Beefheart's mother lived there and that he was visiting. I stopped my Blazer and said, 'Get out'. She was shocked when she saw that I was heading straight for Sue's place. She was scurrying behind saying, 'You're going to get us arrested!' I said, 'C'mon', and proceeded to climb the steps and knock on the door. The lights were on, and I knew Don was nocturnal. He greeted me at the door as if not one day had passed since we'd last seen each other. It had been nearly ten years.

"'Geez, man. Come in. It's cold out there. What have you been doing, man?' And so on. He almost immediately slipped a Cuban cigar in my pocket, from a box someone at A&M gave him. There were a few canvases around the room. He said, 'I'm opening in Cologne, next week, man.' I'm thinking, 'Opening?' He nodded at a canvas. 'A show, they're showing my work.' He also had a box of vinyls from the Sessions and handed me one. I said, 'Hey, I was at some of these sessions!'

"Sue walked in, dazed from her sleep, from the commotion, but smiled and said, 'Hi,' as always. Same ol' Sue. A sweet lady. Then Don, seemingly as an afterthought, said, 'You got a stereo? I wanna hear this, and Sue hasn't got one.' So, we piled into my truck and went to my place. We partied until dawn, drinking Jack Daniels, listening to the record, whiffin' dust off the coffee table, and talking about old times. He was really impressed with the sound the band got on those tracks.

"We met the next day at The Britisher, a bar in Lancaster, and started all over. When Don walked in someone said, 'Hey, man! It's Leon Redbone!' Don replied, 'Geez, I know that cat. No, really, man. I know him.' I bumped the bozo on the arm and said, 'This is Captain Beefheart – Don Van Vliet. Allow me to introduce you, dummy.' Then the bar went into whispers.

"Anyway, we spent all that night together as well. And, you know, all of the intimidation was gone. I was totally one-on-one with him. Maybe I had grown up, or he had mellowed – maybe a little of both. He signed my album, Luv Don, Luv Don. I'll always remember him standing in my living room in his long-sleeved shirt and brown fedora. When we were playing the tracks, I asked him, 'Will you ever come back, Don, with the group?' He said, 'Oh, yeah. Sure.' But I knew somehow he wouldn't. He was older and seemed tired, or maybe just introspective. He was not Captain Beefheart anymore. That man was gone.

"A month or so later, I received a call from Dennis Allen, the leader of a local band called BBC. He told me that he and Don had looked for me everywhere one night. I love Don and always have since we first became friends on that autumn afternoon in 1965, but I thought, 'I'm glad they didn't find me'. Things ended just fine."

Once a deal had been struck with Werner, Van Vliet's first major US show was at The Mary Boone Gallery in Manhattan in 1985. The exhibition was a success, with luminaries like Richard Gere and Diane Keaton – who had been present at Magic Band shows – in attendance. Gere even collared Van Vliet and quoted some of his lyrics back to him. It was a world apart from The Golden Bear, Huntington Beach. Interviewed by Kristine McKenna in *LA Weekly*, Van Vliet claimed he wasn't surprised. "They're pretty smart so they're probably as bored as I am,"[10] he said.

Mary Boone explained to McKenna why she had given Van Vliet his initial break: "I hadn't shown a new artist in three years when I decided to show Don. The artists I've always liked are the ones who have had enough courage to question accepted rules, and for the past 20 years Don has been doing figurative painting based on a consistent vocabulary of his own forms and images. For me, that made his work important and worth showing."[11]

Spring 1986 found him in London, having secured his first major UK exhibition at Waddington's Gallery. Schnabel came over to London to help him with the hanging and John Peel was reacquainted with him in the street outside the gallery. "It was raining slightly and he was bending down tying up his shoelaces," he recalls. "I walked up and said something like, 'Hello, Don' and it was as though he was picking up on a conversation, as though we had driven there together and I'd just gone and parked the car and had come back. About ten years had elapsed since I'd seen him last, but he just picked up as if it had been seconds before."

Peel reviewed the exhibition for *The Observer*: "He was standing in Cork Street, clutching the iron railings, with his wife, Jan, because he was ill at ease about facing the gallery goers within. 'I was never like this before with music things,' he claimed with notable inaccuracy.

"Over the years Captain Beefheart's reputation as an eccentric has been developed to an absurd degree. His jokes and wordplays, isolated from their natural context, are reproduced with great solemnity, with the consumer being invited to read profundity into observations which are often deliberately meaningless. The real Don Van Vliet is a good-natured man, quick to laugh, with a deep mistrust of the record industry and an appetite for words and, on the evidence of his paintings, colour."[12]

Peel opined that anyone who gave his songs such titles as 'When I See Mommy I Feel Like A Mummy' is not someone who wants us to take him totally seriously. One of the paintings in the exhibition had the same title. Other titles included 'Red Shell Bats' and 'See Through Dog With Wheat Stack Skirt'. "In my head I can hear Captain Beefheart singing that,"[13] Peel wrote of the latter.

Mary Rose Beaumont, gave this appraisal of the Waddington's exhibition in *Time Out*: "The relationship between the various protagonists [in his paintings] is impossible to unravel, but there is a complexity in his private language and a forcefulness in the application of paint – harsh expressive brushstrokes or finger marks and great sweeps of colour laid on with a palette knife – which compels the attention of the viewer."[14]

By 1986, The Magic Band hadn't played together for four years. Lucas, for one, had completely lost touch with Van Vliet, who, however, was appraising his current status as good. "Which is not to say I've finished with music," he told Kristine McKenna. Frank Zappa's imagination had been captured by Edgard Varèse's quote, "The present-day composer refuses to die," which Van Vliet echoed when he continued, "The only thing that stops a composer from thinking about music is rigor mortis, and I still compose all the time. I've been writing some pretty wild stuff too. But I'm definitely finished with the rock star scene... I haven't worked with my band for a while so people seem to think that they've split up, but they keep calling me and saying, 'Let's ride.' And I tell them... soon. I have no idea when I'll get around to making a record though. For the time being I'm really enjoying painting."[15]

As the eighties were drawing to a close, his artistic career took off. Following exhibitions in Cologne, Amsterdam and Zurich, Van Vliet was exhibited as part of a prestigious show at the San Francisco Museum of Modern Art. Although the exhibition was entitled *New Work*, it was a big break for such a 'new' artist – which in terms of his career in the art world he still was. The San Francisco exhibition ran from November 1988 to January 1989. A familiar face from the past, Gary Marker, bumped into him at the exhibition. When he asked if he was intending to do any more music, Van Vliet simply said that he'd done enough.

The gallery director John Lane gave this opinion of his work in the exhibition catalogue: "The essence of Van Vliet's sensibility is a longing for an artistic expression that is direct, intuitive, and bewitching. In the philosophical tradition of the eighteenth-century French writer Jean-Jacques Rousseau, he is critical of the current, corrupted state of society... Van Vliet advocates embracing nature and relocating man in a position that stems from natural order rather than an imposed hierarchy. His paintings – most frequently indeterminate landscapes populated by forms of abstracted animals – are intended to effect psychological, spiritual and magical force."[16]

Despite the backing of the gallery director, he was essentially self-taught and his inclusion in the San Francisco show aroused suspicion among some members of the art establishment. Considering the literal meaning of Abstract Expressionism, this seems ironic, even absurd, especially as he had been a practising artist since he was a child. But now his instinctive approach marked him out as coming from an area away from the established scene. Lane shaded in the difference between Van Vliet and more established artists of the Abstract Expressionist genre like Franz Kline and Willem De Kooning when interviewed by Elaine Shepherd in 1995: "It is certainly not a manifestation of it that comes through an art school. He is a self-taught artist and the handling of the paint is not in any traditional technical way beautiful. It has that same kind of edge the music has."[17]

Normally an artist doesn't get exhibited at such a venue until they have had a recognised lengthy career. Thus Van Vliet was viewed by some sections of the establishment as an upstart riding in on the wave of his notoriety as an avant-garde artist in the music field or, heaven forbid, a rock star. He arguably wasn't ready for that kind of platform, though his subsequent success has vindicated him being exhibited in that space.

In 1993, Michael Werner maintained that it was still appropriate that Van Vliet be more or less viewed as a 'young artist', explaining how the establishment perceives him. "He's been painting now for 15 years or so, and the first three or four years don't even count because he was also making music. It only counts from the time when he painted exclusively – and a young artist needs a ten-year time frame to start a career." And although there is a lot of interest from Captain Beefheart fans when Van Vliet has an art exhibition, the people who buy his paintings are just as likely to be unaware of his career as a musician. "Very few of the music lovers buy his paintings, because most of them don't have money,"[18] was Werner's succinct assessment.

At the time of writing, David Breuer is chief executive of the Royal Academy in London. He curated the UK leg of Van Vliet's travelling exhibition, 'Stand Up To Be Discontinued', at the Brighton Museum, which ran from September to November 1994. He gives these views: "His style is definitely not hip at the moment. His means of producing art, designs on canvas and paper, is quite old-fashioned. Artists in general don't think that's enough to do to surprise people now. However, when he started, people who championed him in the early eighties were artists like Anselm Kiefer, AR Penck and Julian Schnabel. They were then right in the vanguard of modern art and fetching millions of pounds for each of their pictures. And they primarily worked with paint on canvas in the same sort of way that Don Van Vliet does. So in that sense he wasn't old-fashioned. Now he is, but things move on. In five years' time he probably won't be – these things are cyclical.

"In the early Eighties, people were beginning to get fed up with brutal abstraction and were going back to, if not figurativism, then some kind of message in the art they were presenting. It might be figurative, abstract, or just textural, but it had a motivation behind it that was a narrative one. Very painterly people like Ron Kitaj were starting to get really important. They had a message to tell in their pictures. That's like Don Van Vliet painting 'Pig Erases A Statue In Passing'. It's telling a story that instantly makes the picture move for you, it vivifies it."

One of the essential and acknowledged influences on Van Vliet's early painting was the archetypal Abstract Expressionist Franz Kline. Although Van Vliet's work from the Sixties and early Seventies was particularly influenced by Kline, Kline's own background and *raison d'être* couldn't have been more different from his own. He painted only in black, occasionally on bits of newspaper over consciously selected grim headlines. He was fuelled by the adrenal thrill of the urban environment, but exemplified that if that flow was dammed up it could turn poisonous and become a reservoir of urban angst. Van Vliet was driven by a different muse entirely but arrived in a visual territory similar to Kline's. Breuer clarifies this difference: "Abstract expressionists are like man's imposition on nature from inside, saying, 'Life is shit, but we've made it so and now we're going to make it more so.' Don Van Vliet wouldn't do anything like that. He's saying, 'I'm living at the other end of life. I see what man can do, I don't like man, I don't want to live in an urban jungle, I appreciate the raven and the crow for clearing up man's mess and I'm going to stick them in my paintings.'"

In the catalogue for *Stand Up To Be Discontinued*, Roberto Ohrt highlights how the geographical difference between Van Vliet and Kline affects their paintings, making them, at least in part, products of a kind of environmental determinism. He also homes in on the essential confluence of ideas expressed in paint on canvas: "Kline makes an unexpected prototype. His painting was entirely dominated by the megapolitan reality of New York, by its traffic and by the colours of its industrial landscape; whereas you never even get to Don Van Vliet except by crossing the American continent from east to west, discarding as you go all memories of cities, its technology, its modernism, its topical concerns, and its contemporary history. All that remains, clearly, is the painting."[19]

Van Vliet simply compared New York to a "bowl of underpants"[20] and chose to stay away. He also assessed Kline's work via completely different criteria: "I like the way Franz Kline handles space. It's pretty easy to breathe in the universe he paints."[21] As a musician, Van Vliet jealously guarded his uniqueness by refusing to acknowledge influences, especially the more obvious ones. As an artist, he is more magnanimous in his appraisal of other painters, admiring Van Gogh, Matisse, Léger, Modigliani and Man Ray. His favourite painting is the early Mondrian 'Broadway Boogie-Woogie'. "It's so good you can hear the horns honk,"[22] he told John Yau in 1991.

But he was still circumspect about how much these painters had influenced his work. He had this to say to John Rogers in 1995 on Van Gogh and De Kooning: "They're not really an influence on me, though. No one is. I just paint like I paint and that's enough influence,"[23] which suggests that for exactly the same reason, *everything* is an influence.

Van Gogh was certainly an influence on Van Vliet and whereas his technique is not the equal of Van Gogh's – and they are stylistically poles apart – some of his canvases display a similar intensity of colour. Van Vliet's photophobia was amplified by seeing Van Gogh's ecstatic canvases first hand. He has often mentioned that after going around the Van Gogh Museum in Amsterdam, he emerged into the street to find the sunlight disappointing.

Van Vliet's painting, like his composition of music, was a product of his spontaneity. It was unsurprising, then, that he likes Kline's work. He explained why to Lester Bangs:"He's probably closer to my music than any of the painters, because it's just totally speed and emotion that comes out of what he does."[24]

He added another bodily metaphor to the repertoire when asked by Lars Movin of *Copyright* in 1991 what he wanted to achieve through his painting:"I'm trying to turn myself inside out on the canvas. I'm trying to completely bare what I think at that moment, yet I put a lot of thought into what I'm doing… it sounds like a contradiction, but…"[25]

On a more philosophical tack he told John Yau what painting was to him: "Fulfilling the absence of space between the opposite meanings. I think that's essentially what I think. That came the other night. It came blasting into my head. I quickly wrote it down. Yes, that's what painting is."[26]

18

BEYOND THE FINAL GLIDE PATTERN

"I feel like everyone else's been asleep. All along. And they'd better wake up."
to Lou Stathis, *Heavy Metal*, August 1983

BT: *"What was the first picture you can remember painting, and how do you feel about it now?"*
DVV: *"It probably doesn't even remember me."*
interview with Ben Thompson, *Independent on Sunday*, 21 August 1994

Don Van Vliet now finds himself in the position of being unequivocally important in each of his creative areas – painting, music and writing. Few, if any, twentieth-century artists can claim the same. No one area is subordinate to another and the inspiration which drives everything, from his writing to playing the shenai, travels along the same creative channel. Like his music, his painting resists categorisation and he sits at ease with himself outside the confines of any recognised movement. His geographical isolation and reclusiveness add to this feeling of separation.

The romantic notion of the "driven artist" has become corny through overuse. But the inner drive that prompted his all-night sketching sessions in Denny's diner in Lancaster has been a constant throughout his artistic life. The engine room of his creativity has always demanded a kinetic outlet for its energy, and he has attempted to cultivate a state of mind that enables it to escape without an inordinate amount of conscious interference on his part; just enough so that he avoids catching himself "in the wink". Years before, Elliot Ingber used a similar catch-phrase to describe the process of music–making when he said that to "call it is to stop the flow". He clearly defined this mercurial process to Lars Movin in 1991: "I think that most people would like to think they've got an idea. Well, I'm sure that my mind thinks that I have an idea, but sometimes I fool it and get my best stuff."[1]

Some of his poems and lyric texts – the free-verse streams of 'Hey, Garland I Dig Your Tweed Coat', for example – sound and read like a catalogue of images captured at the point of flash. More conscious consideration was involved in the semi-spontaneous 'The Dust Blows Forward And The Dust Blows Back' where he held down a tape recorder pause button while he was thinking of the next line. In contrast, lyric texts like 'Hobo Chang Ba' and 'Sweet Sweet Bulbs' are his most inherently personal and conventionally structured forms of expression. But it would be wrong to explain away his more spontaneous outpourings as a sort of *idiot savant* splurge.

Artistically, Van Vliet has been called a "primitive", but maybe "primal" is more apposite as his creativity is the fulfilment of a fundamental need. And importantly he has the ability to structure these bursts of creativity, even though in his music the big picture was usually coloured in with a little help from his friends. "It's very difficult to discuss in words what you do with a brush," he told John Rogers in 1991. "Usually you sound like a naïve artist, which is not what I am. Everything I do is on purpose."[2]

In the catalogue for his one-man exhibition at Knoedler & Company, New York, in November and December 1998, the biographical note described him thus: "Critically recognised as a composer, rock musician and author in the mid-Sixties, the artist has devoted himself to drawing and painting since the late 1970s."[3] Apart from the obvious inaccuracies in the chronology, the epithet "author" seems questionable. But that depends on whether one insists that the prerequisites of authorship apply only to work published in a bound volume. In his foreword to the compendium of the writings of Lester Bangs, *Psychotic Reactions And Carburetor Dung*, Greil Marcus picks up on one of Bang's self-eulogies, concluding, "Perhaps what this book demands from a reader is a willingness to accept that the best writer in America could write almost nothing but record reviews."[4] Similarly, the case for Van Vliet to be considered one of the best American poets of the twentieth century rests on almost nothing but the lyric sheets to his albums. The lyrics to the song 'Safe As Milk' from *Strictly Personal* are among his best, but due to his idiosyncratic vocal delivery, they are difficult to decipher, and are not found on any lyric sheet. Poems have been published here and there, but even the expensive, rare and disappointingly brief book *Skeleton Breath, Scorpion Blush*, published in 1987, consists of some colour plates of his paintings and transcriptions of his lyrics, but precious little new text. Considering how much material he must have written, that it remains unread is frustrating and would surely have helped seal Van Vliet's reputation as a poet. Maybe it was all bluff, but Ace Farren Ford thinks otherwise.

He remembers that in the early Seventies Van Vliet seemed quite serious about publishing a novel, through Singing Ink, *Old Fart At Play* – of which 'Odd Jobs' and 'Hey Garland I Dig Your Tweed Coat' were excerpts – and also a book of poems. As far as Ford was aware it had all been ready to go, but after a while Van Vliet stopped talking about it. Surely someone would have been interested in putting it out. "Is it a concept like you can't publish a book of poems if you're a painter?" Ford muses. "I don't know if that's it but Good Lord, there's got to be volumes of stuff that has certainly got artistic merit and would not detract from his career. I'm sure the reason there are no books of poems and his novel has not been out, is that he decided not to put it out. I'm sure it was, 'Ah, forget that'."

Nowadays, Van Vliet's decision to work at a canvas is a simple affirmation that he is totally in control of what he creates (it also pays better than being a musician or a full-time poet). There are no musicians to be taught material, no need for back-up from the secretaries. He can remain there, like an ass swishing its tail, to his heart's content. Co De Kloet asked him about the difference between music and painting during a radio interview in 1993. Van Vliet answered that painting was "more exciting". He gave his reasons why: "I get to do exactly what I want – not as if I don't anyway – but it's more just on the spot. But it's interesting. I don't have to think about anybody at all." He went on to explain his multiplicity of talents: "The same head does all kinds of things. Tricky brain, I guess you might call it."[5]

That need not in itself mean that there are stylistic similarities between his music and painting, but the parallels are too obvious to ignore. David Breuer feels they are inextricably linked: "If you listen to the music and look at the pictures, you can see how they correspond. The style of his music and a lot of the free jazz music of the late Sixties – people like Albert Ayler, Anthony Braxton and the rowdier ones like Brotherhood Of Breath – it's quite painterly, because they layer a lot of sounds on each other in no particular way. Because it's generally improvised you can actually pick out strands of each particular instrument and make pictures in your mind, as it goes on a linear timescale.

"In between that you've got lots of different things that you can focus on at any given time without distracting from the overall feel of the musical piece. That's a sort of painterly way of approaching it. His music, though composed, is the same thing – it's very confrontational. You can either focus on it as a great big row – in which case it's like being confronted with a massive abstract painting and being blasted away by it – or you can actually follow through the little aspects of it and gradually worm your way in."

Not everyone agrees on this kind of comparison. In an essay in the exhibition catalogue *Stand Up To Be Discontinued*, Luca Ferrari asserts that Van Vliet's music is composed and therefore "conceptual", whereas his painting is "retinic and instinctive".[6] In support of his views, Ferrari puts forward a quote Van Vliet gave to Jim Greer of *Rockstar* in 1991: "I prefer painting to music, because I can spend a whole day on a canvas and then cancel it. Painting over it is a nice feeling."[7]

Van Vliet's music-making was just as instinctive as his art and anything but conceptual. And the rigid musical forms to which Ferrari refers, only became so once they were moulded into their finished structure. One could argue that a painting, or the product of any creative process, also becomes 'rigid' at the point that work on it ceases. Just because Van Vliet can amend his painting doesn't mean that it is a more instinctive way of expression than music – which therefore becomes more 'conceptual' by default. As discussed earlier, self-consciousness and technique seldom got in the way: it's hard to over-intellectualise "going to the bathroom", after all. Van Vliet's main 'concept' was a need to evacuate his mental contents, a manifestation of Bob Dylan's lines on 'From A Buick Six' (from *Highway 61 Revisited*), where he casually announces that he needs a "dump truck" to unload his head.

All of his raw creative material was edited at some point. He is, of course, at liberty to paint over canvas, but similarly he could, and often did, make substantial changes to his music at the last minute. Gary Lucas puts it this way: "He was always editing up to the point of recording – like Penelope at her loom waiting for Ulysses to come home and weaving this beautiful tapestry and ripping it up every day. I really did get that impression, depending on his moods." Van Vliet put his own case unequivocally when he stated: 'I am making music – on canvas.'[8]

Ferrari goes on to write: "Specialist rock critics, who were left the sad task of a retrospective tribute to his career, each time have boldly tried to establish correlations between yesterday's music and today's painting, acting in a way that is markedly 'reparative' and which, implicitly placing diachronic continuity to his basis, has no logical or cultural justification in the Californian artist's experience."[9]

Not only are 'reparative' measures unnecessary, but it is counter-productive to erect an artificial barrier between the two forms of expression. The understanding of the connection between Van Vliet's music and his painting, and to a lesser extent his writing, is crucial in understanding his overall creativity.

Moris Tepper, an artist since his teens and still painting today, offers this appraisal: "There is a sameness, a commonness about the painting in an abstract aesthetic, and the way he composed music that was on that edge. And it's about creating a vagueness, creating a picture that is blurred. It can be blurred by complexity, like mixing colours or by things that don't fit together creating tensions. A blending of those things creates a beauty.

"It strikes this place which is abstract, it isn't intellectual. It's something that's just pleasing in a spiritual, intuitive way. His gift is that it affects the nervous system on a plane that you can't really talk about, and that is what he does in both of those mediums. I see the painting of it [his music], using instruments in a whole new way, creating these textures and palettes that are indescribable but they itch you in a place that you can't scratch."

The most literal relationship between Van Vliet's music and painting is the frequent naming of paintings after songs: 'Japan In The Dishpan' [*sic*] (1984) and 'Golden Birdies' (1988), for example. Titles are also derived from song lyrics, including 'Striped Light' (1985) (words from 'Tropical Hot Dog Night') and 'Parapliers The Willow Dipped' (1987) (words from 'Bellerin' Plain').

Stylistically, Van Vliet skirts around the periphery of Abstract Expressionism and Primitivism. His style of painting is idiosyncratic and individual, if not necessarily unique. After his early, largely abstract work from the Sixties and Seventies, he veered towards figurativism, and his paintings, like his drawings, became populated with animals and anthropomorphic forms. These were often painted onto the raw, unprimed canvas with – in defiance of the first rules of painting taught at school – swathes of white paint added to half-fill the gaps between figures, defining background as an afterthought. This can be clearly seen on the painting

'Royal Hind Deer' (1984). It looks as if he had done the interesting bit and was impatient to get it finished off, although the white "infill" does itself yield some interesting textures. He also broke the art school dictum which proscribes the use of colour straight out of the tube, as the viridian green bodies of the lupine figures in the 'Dilishyeus' series (1984) demonstrate.

The principal reason for Van Vliet becoming more respected as a painter is that his later paintings are much better, in terms of both technique and imagination. From the late Eighties onwards he began with a canvas primed white as a virgin space. And while preserving the energy of his colour fields and gestural marks, the paintings are far more compositionally satisfying. Although vestiges of figurativism still exist, the largely zoomorphic forms are generally reduced to the scale of glyphs and pictographs within the landscape of the canvas – on 'Dry Morning Wind That Jingles Like Fish Bones' and 'Castfat Shadows', for example. Canvases like 'Ten Thousand Pistols No Bumblebees' and 'Dreams In The Daytime Coloured With Sunshine' look ageless, as if they would be as likely to be found painted on the wall of a cave as to be hung in a gallery. Towards the end of the Nineties the paintings were becoming sparser and more purely abstract.

As an adult, he clearly still feels a kinship with the creatures he sculpted in his room as a child, and which he yearned to imbue with life. Now they are the two-dimensional denizens of his paintings. The crow images prominent in works like 'Raven Above, Cross Poked A Shadow of A Crow' and 'Tug' still fascinate Van Vliet. "Right now I'm painting a group of birds called Goatheads," he told Co De Kloet. "They'll actually blow out a tyre. They're that strong. They're pretty good. A good exhibit."[10]

Some stylistic parallels have been drawn between Van Vliet and Dutch/American Abstract Expressionist Willem De Kooning. There are as many differences. Essentially, De Kooning's paintings have a three-dimensional feel, with a sense of movement generated from the paint spilling over from one colour field to another. Van Vliet's, however, are flat, discrete, two-dimensional and contain figurative elements. But typical of his work from the late Fifties and into the Sixties, De Kooning's famous 'Rosy-Fingered Dawn At Louse Point' (1963) has a landscape-like structure which conveys a sense of atmosphere of place, and like Van Vliet's work, the title is used as a signpost into the painting. Generally speaking, Van Vliet is more Expressionist than Colourist – as would befit a self-styled photophobic – but then canvases like 'World Crawled Over The Razor' and 'Wrought Iron

Cactus' are drenched in light and colour. Breuer: "He's one of the few people today working out of landscape and making something fresh for themselves and that's why he's likely to grow in importance."

One genre, almost by definition a non-genre, into which Van Vliet could conceivably fit is that of the Outsider. It is a description coined to encompass stylistically disparate work, the unifying factor being that the artists possess a raw talent and have received little or no formal training. An early conceptualist like Marcel Duchamp, for example, would fit the Outsider criteria – similarly Jean Dubuffet, the originator of Art Brut. Even the early twentieth-century American artist Grandma Moses, who painted naïve landscapes, could be viewed as an Outsider. You don't have to have a degree in literature to write a book, but the art world appears suspicious of the Outsider – unless they can be marketed thus. The art business is as genre-obsessed as the music business, primarily due to the expense and rarity of the commodity. A book or a CD can be bought for a modest amount of money and easily discarded. Not so a piece of art, on which a collector can spend several thousand dollars, only to find out that not only does it fail to match the décor, but it isn't even considered cool.

From one viewpoint, Van Vliet isn't an Outsider any more because he is with a major gallery (and the grouping together of Outsiders does seem rather oxymoronic). But he is an Outsider in terms of his staunch individualism, which he nurtures in seclusion. Putting him in a group of one as a Rural Expressionist wouldn't be far off the mark. John Lane prefers 'Modernist Primitive'. But these are just alternative sets of decals.

Currently, many artists are very immediate, producing quick-fix art with concepts like catch-phrases. The nominees for the annual UK Turner Prize are expected to be, if not outrageous, then at least deliberately provocative – and each year high public interest is counterbalanced by splutterings of horror from traditionalists. All this activity is a world away from Van Vliet, who is distanced from the kind of critical vagaries that find the current styles lauded to the detriment of what has gone before. Breuer gives his view: "He's a one-off, he doesn't mix with anyone, he's not part of any group, he just does what he does and if someone picks up on it, they pick up on it, but if they don't he's certainly not going to change. That's the only way he can do it."

The way Van Vliet paints carries with it an almost old-fashioned purity of expression. That he works in oil is refreshing in itself – like seeing new art in a traditional way. Or vice versa. But there is nothing cosy or sentimental about his art. Indeed, his desire for his music to be an irritant carried through into his painting. He explained to John Yau: "If my paintings don't disturb me I scrap them and I hope that when other people see them the paintings hug them and shake them, because people need to be provoked."[11]

Bryan Biggs was the Director of the Bluecoat Gallery, Liverpool, at the time of Van Vliet's exhibition there in 1972. In a letter to *MOJO* in 1994 he gave these views on Van Vliet's creative endeavours: "Unlike his music, however, Beefheart's art is hardly breaking new ground, and it is perhaps this fact, rather than the difficulties of shaking off his musical mantle, that has denied him any greater critical consideration."[12]

Van Vliet's painting is thoroughly individual, but his music is unique – which is why his reputation largely rests on the latter and why the name 'Captain Beefheart' will continue its regular appearance in the music press. He is an acknowledged influence on musicians in every genre, from avant-rock to pop – Sonic Youth and Pulp to name but two – and beyond to the groups birthed in the techno explosion of the early Nineties like Underworld, whose singer Karl Hyde cites *Trout Mask Replica* as his favourite album.

The popularity of Van Vliet's music is surprisingly widespread. In 1999 a comprehensive survey of the British record-buying public undertaken by HMV record stores, *Trout Mask Replica* was voted number 42 album, one place above David Bowie's *Hunky Dory*. Maybe more people are keen to break up their own catatonic state than had been imagined. That the customers were polled not in specialist music outlets but in the supermarket-sized HMV consumer palaces makes the album's popularity doubly surprising. In their Great Pop Things cartoon on the HMV poll in *New Musical Express*, Colin B. Morton and Chuck Death came up with the wry observation that "If Captain Beefheart is in the chart, then anything not in the chart [i.e. Phil Collins] must be very WEIRD indeed."[13]

Anyone who follows these type of polls will, however, be used to the regular appearance of *Trout Mask*, usually in the top fifty. Both *Trout Mask* and *Clear Spot* appeared in the *MOJO* readers' poll of their hundred best albums of all time in August 1995, at 28 and 64 respectively. As the obsession with ordering musicians and their commodities into lists increased towards the new millennium, the August 1999 issue of *Q* magazine published the results of a readers' poll to find out who, in their opinion, were the Hundred Greatest Stars of the 20th Century. In an utterly ludicrous line-up that included Stravinsky, Debussy and Bongo – sorry, Bono – himself, Captain Beefheart came in at number fifty. In the same issue, *Safe As Milk* was chosen as one of the essential dozen psychedelic albums of all time. In the May 1999 issue of *MOJO*, Captain Beefheart reached number twenty in the readers' all-time top hundred vocalists, and so it goes on. In that feature *MOJO* reader Richard Lodge shared his personal "sublime moment" from *Trout Mask Replica*: 'Moonlight On Vermont'. "When he blasts his command 'Give me some [*sic*] old time religion', he sounds utterly convinced – the listener feels compelled to obey his insistence, if we only knew how."

He has a point. There is a dichotomy between the vast number of musicians he has influenced and the few that sound like Captain Beefheart & The Magic Band except in the most superficial way, and the handful that come near Van Vliet himself on any level. Anyway, this would be extremely difficult and rather pointless. It would be more quintessentially Beefheartian to sound more like themselves. "There's a lot of guys who copied me, and I think they're crazy," Van Vliet told John Rogers in *Associated Press* in 1991. "I think it's a dangerous thing not to be who you are, to try to be somebody else. It doesn't flatter me."[14] Exactly who "copied" him is open to question. He didn't like the idea of people copying him, but then didn't really listen to anyone to see if they were doing so. Devo may have used the same sort of chords, chopped up into similar-sized chunks, but along with The B-52s and Public Image Ltd, two groups who also get dragged into the debate, the overlap is small.

One way in which he was copied was deliberately, through groups doing cover versions of his material, with varying degrees of success. Former Magic Band guitarist Denny Walley appeared with a number of Swedish musicians on a 1995 album *The Music Of Captain Beefheart Live*, which is impressive in terms of musicianship and features a furious version of 'Lick My Decals Off, Baby', but also includes some superfluous jamming – rather Zappa-esque, ironically – and a singer with a hard act to follow who comes off second best. No doubt it was fun seeing the show, and credit to them for keeping the flame alive, but as a CD release it is hardly essential.

With few exceptions, the tribute album *Fast 'N Bulbous*, released on Imaginary Records in 1988, showed how easy it was to slip up when tackling Van Vliet's material. Similarly, Magazine's 1978 version of 'I Love You, You Big Dummy' (B-side of 'You Give Me Everything') finds the song hammered flat in a foursquare rendition amounting to little more than a fame-by-association exercise. The problem that befalls most cover versions is that the musicians just aren't up to grappling with the material, especially the more complex songs.

Some irreverent readings were surprisingly successful. The Edgar Broughton Band – whose leader was audibly indebted to Van Vliet's vocal style – released a single, 'Apache Dropout', in 1971, which sandwiched layers of 'Dropout Boogie' from *Safe As Milk* with The Shadows' 'Apache'. This piece of drollery earned them a number 33 chart placing in the UK. Guitarist Eugene Chadbourne and former Magic Band drummer Jimmy Carl Black have made a habit of treating the songs as raw material to be battered into new shapes, and which still emerge looking good, if decidedly different, particularly on their 1995 paean, *The Jack And Jim Show Present Pachuco Cadaver*. New York big band Doctor Nerve scored another success with their monstrous, horn-powered version of 'When It Blows Its Stacks', from their 1997 album *Every Screaming Ear*.

Musically, Van Vliet has left a living, breathing legacy, not a collection of exhibits to be stored away in a fusty museum or something to listen to because it's good for you. So what audible signs has the 'Beefheartian' influence produced? The epithet has been used in conjunction with all sorts of disparate music-makers, but few have really warranted the tag. Not because they weren't or aren't good at what they do, or because they were barred from earning the accolade, but because Van Vliet's approach to music was so utterly personal that perhaps we should accept that the only true Beefheartian is Beefheart himself.

Tom Waits is often accredited with owing a great deal to Van Vliet. By his 1983 album *Swordfishtrombones*, the cinematic low-life balladry of his early career had mutated into a more adventurous musical mix: theatrical, fairground music cut with antediluvian blues and played on junkyard percussion and marimbas. Waits conceived it as a tribute of sorts of both Beefheart and to American experimental composer and instrument designer Harry Partch, although the words shaped by his impossibly ravaged voice erred more towards a neo-beat folk poetry. Waits's new approach reached an aggressive apogee on his 1992 album *Bone Machine*. His work carries some stylistic overlap with Van Vliet's in that he is also steeped in Americana and enjoys lifting up the stone of the country's contemporary culture to find what might be lurking beneath. But throughout all this, his own idiosyncratic style comes through strongly.

There is a Beefheartian flavour to his work, but there is far more besides.

In the Eighties, The Box, Stump and The Birthday Party – especially when Nick Cave still played sax – were a few of the groups called 'Beefheartian' in that they at least embodied some of his spirit. Arguably, the closest links were in the adrenalised rhythms and splintered guitars of the very earliest incarnation of The Pop Group in 1978, when they were all still teenagers and relatively new to their instruments.

John Peel still regularly identifies Van Vliet's fingerprints on new music. "The extent of the influence of Beefheart's music is that even now I never do a programme when there aren't at least one or two records which have a very plain influence even if the band themselves don't know," he says. "You give a little smile to yourself and think, 'I know where that comes from.'" Although he has been a consistent champion of marginal and exploratory music for over three decades, even his patience is tested by some of the groups keen to be seen as farther out than the rest of the pack by dropping his name "for an excuse for incompetence". On these he says: "I think if Beefheart heard the music he would be very indignant of them making this claim. What's so infuriating is that a lot of people think they do this [sort of music]. I get so many tapes and records from people who say, 'Oh, you'll love our singer – he sounds just like Beefheart,' and you put it on and he growls a bit and you think, 'No, he doesn't – more like the antithesis.'"

Journalists have also fallen prey to overstating the Beefheart case, in their enthusiasm to try and identify the aural evidence of someone who has been so influential, and yet whose overtly audible influence is so rare. In Greil Marcus's book *In The Fascist Bathroom*, he addresses the subject of The Clash's 1978 album *Give 'Em Enough Rope* (recorded at The Automatt, San Francisco, at the same time the Magic Band were recording *Shiny Beast*). This is how he assessed their development: "What you hear now in the storm of their sound is reggae, in the rhythm section, and, in Strummer's furious singing, in Mick Jones's crossing guitar lines, and in the twists and turns of the song structures, Captain Beefheart." Strummer admitted to Marcus: "When I was sixteen *Trout Mask Replica* was the only record I listened to – for a year." But that in itself cannot support this astonishing summary: "The Clash have taken Beefheart's aesthetic of scorched vocals, guitar discords, melody reversals, and rhythmic conflict and made the whole seem anything but avant-garde; in their hands that aesthetic speaks with clarity and immediacy, a demand you have to accept or refuse. It sounds like a promise rock'n'roll has waited years to keep. The sense of confusion and doubt in the sound is still there, along with a sense of triumph."[15] Marcus appears to be willing these connections to exist, to draw a line connecting Van Vliet to a group who were new and important at the time of writing. It is actually hard to imagine any music that sounds less like Van Vliet's, sonically or conceptually, than the blustering big rock sound of The Clash's rather mediocre second album.

Individually and collectively, The Fall have admitted Van Vliet's influence, but contrary to the views of some enthusiasts, from the rhythm section up, there is no shared ground whatsoever. Craig Scanlon, guitarist with the group until the mid-Nineties gave these views to Ben Thompson in 1994: "Beefheart has influenced my guitar playing – just in a liberating way. I wouldn't dare try to copy him. We were asked to play on a tribute album but there's no point."[16]

Underworld reputedly play his music to get fired up before going onstage, but given his avowed hatred of the "mama heartbeat" that pumps through rock'n'roll, Underworld's whomping programmed beats would doubtless have a horrified Van Vliet nervously feeling his heart. In 1999, Pavement's Steve Malkmus made the wry assertion that he had wanted 'Ground Beef Heart', a song pencilled in for inclusion on their album *Terror Twilight*, to sound like a cross between *Lick My Decals Off, Baby* and The Groundhogs' *Split*. Throughout that group's lifespan, comparisons have been made with Van Vliet, but his influence has impinged itself on their elliptical attitude and approach to music rather than their songs and their sound. The crucial effect that his thinking, music, painting and lyrics can have is to make one aware there are no rules other than the ones you choose to accept and that hypothetically, at least, you can do *anything*.

Van Vliet's most radical innovations stand as signposts to an increasingly overgrown path. Few have been able to harness the forces he unleashed and recontextualise them into a new, individual take on his legacy – into a new art-form. Sweden's astonishing Kräldjursanstalten, who released one album, *Voodoo Boogie*, and an EP in 1981, were an exception.

The idea of 'blurred' music is found at all points from Ornette Coleman's *Free Jazz* in the early Sixties to the free flights of ensemble improvising of mid-Seventies progressive experimentalists Henry Cow, and through to the primeval noise overload of nineties Japanese psychedelic group High Rise. But Kräldjursanstalten are one of the rare groups who blur their music in a similar way to that of Captain Beefheart

& The Magic Band – although the little-known south London group The Balloons, also with one eponymously titled album to their credit, have been plotting a similar course for twenty years.

The mama heartbeat, the 'one', was suspended and the blurring came from the mercurial instrumental interactions which, though largely composed, often sounded free. And the group introduced their own European roots into the equation as a substitute for Van Vliet's blues. Michael Maksymenko, who later played with guitarist and Beefheartophile guitarist Henry Kaiser, has proved himself one of the few drummers to take the John French approach to rhythm and make it his own. And importantly it all rocked with a vengeance, as did Van Vliet's music even when the idea of rock was being stretched as far as it could without snapping. The furious cauldron of sound of Kräldjursanstalten's 'Den Stora Coupe Finalen' showed the way rock was ready to go, but was left as another signpost into a rarely visited territory. But then to work on such a level of intra-band empathy takes more time, will and frankly more ability than most groups possess.

Essentially Van Vliet's music is too much of himself to be easily transferable except to the musicians in the various Magic Bands, who put themselves under his tutelage. He came up with no innovations that could be shared by others like the twelve-tone scale, minimalist 'systems', or a concept like Ornette Coleman's harmolodics. He deliberately kept clear of music theory, to the point of coming over as resolutely anti-theory. But he played himself as well as anyone has done. He himself was the sand that irritated the oyster, forcing a number of pearls to pop out. The biggest, *Trout Mask Replica*, will always stand as an index of possibilities in the unfettering of self-expression. He has claimed that the freest harmonica playing he heard was when as a child he held the instrument out of the window of his parents' car and the rushing wind brought it to life. Listening to his best music feels as if you are driving close behind, hyperventilating in his slipstream.

The Brighton leg of the travelling *Stand Up To Be Discontinued* exhibition in 1994 included an installation of music, videos and taped interviews. The Michael Werner Gallery and Van Vliet himself were not initially keen on its inclusion, which is understandable in itself but rather at odds with an exhibition catalogue which contained a number of Captain Beefheart press cuttings. It's inevitable that some of the fans of Captain Beefheart the musician are only interested in Van Vliet the painter because of who he used to be and see his art as a substitute for his dried-up musical output. But overall, interest in the paintings, and Van Vliet as a creative being, should not be underestimated. The Brighton Museum is a small provincial space for exhibiting art, but someone flew in from Switzerland for the preview and then flew back the same night. A few enthusiasts came from Australia, Japan, America and Switzerland. Reading the comments in the visitor's book reveals that opinions were polarised. The artist's wish to provoke had been granted. Here are some examples:

"Utter rubbish."
"Playful, better than the music."
"I like you, but not your paintings."
"Never heard of you before today but your music is very infectious. Will search for your distorted work."
"It's a shame you have to be a pop star to get an exhibition these days."
"Thanks for doing what you needed to, Don."
"I would walk 3,000 miles to see this one."
"The work of a disordered mind. So much trauma."
"Get your band back on the road again, please."
"Beautiful. I drove 110 miles to see the work."
"The figurative work is reminiscent of early Kitaj, however the highly abstract work seems far more interesting."
"Wow, so *angry*."
"Someone stole the drawing he did for me – it could have been the wind, it could have been the sea – it's all still here."
"Enjoyed the music and now the paintings. What next?"

The supposedly "difficult" art on show for the eyes and ears didn't present a problem for some of the audience, as Breuer recollects: "Children really loved it, which was the interesting thing to me. They loved the music, which I found immensely surprising, and they loved the pictures, because there are lots of things in the pictures which require discovery."

The relationship between Van Vliet and The Michael Werner Gallery has been a success and their faith in him has paid off commercially as well as artistically. But his trust in the gallery is paralleled by his lack of interest in the people who buy his paintings – and in some cases the paintings themselves, once they leave his possession.

He told Kristine McKenna: "Most people don't know this, but I was painting throughout the Sixties and Seventies – I never showed my work then because I didn't feel like it. I'm happy to show it now though because the art world is providing a better life for me than music did. It helps not having to deal with the fans and I'm much better off now."[17]

In recent years he has claimed that he no longer thinks about music in a composing sense, preferring to open up his creative channels to visual stimuli. Although he sees his paintings as more important to him now than his music, he is clearly no sentimentalist, telling one associate that he wants them all burnt after his death. His relationship with his recorded legacy is far more difficult to fathom. Although he remains very proud of what he has achieved in music, he is keen that his canon should be left as it is, in the state it was when he gave up recording in 1982. Although the music is his, rather than having it to hand in his studio or dealt with by one gallery like his artwork, it remains in other people's hands. A prime example of this – at the time of writing in 2004 – is that *Lick My Decals Off, Baby* is still unavailable on CD in the UK and the US except on expensive Japanese imports. The convoluted contractual jiggery-pokery that was woven throughout Van Vliet's musical career thwarts the availability of some of his best music to this day. The cumulative effect on Van Vliet is that he now simply says "no" to everything.

The Zappa Estate still own the master tape of *Bat Chain Puller* and had been planning to release it at the end of the Nineties, but out of respect to Van Vliet, asked him if he would sanction its release. One could have been forgiven for thinking that he might jump at the chance of having the record – about which he had been so proud – released so that listeners could at last hear it properly mixed and mastered, and appreciate why it has justly earned the reputation as one of the great lost albums. But the answer that came back was a straight no. Maybe it's because it was too much a relic of the past; maybe because it would have to be mixed by someone else; maybe because he resented the fact that it is still essentially owned by Zappa, but in contrast to his fuck-you attitude to Zappa in 1982 when he used one of its tracks, '81 Poop Hatch', for *Ice Cream For Crow*, he now simply doesn't want to know.

When Revenant Records were compiling their 5-CD box set *Captain Beefheart & His Magic Band Grow Fins: rarities [1965–82]* – a treasure trove of concert tapes, acetates, demos and radio broadcasts with extensive sleeve notes by John French, which was released in 1999 – their attempts to contact Van Vliet were met with silence. He received royalties, as did the featured group members: in many cases, this was the first payment of any kind they had received in connection with the release of Captain Beefheart material. The label's Dean Blackwood says that the set seeks to present the "unguarded moment".

"It happens to be the case that some of the absolutely most compelling moments in Captain Beefheart's recorded legacy were heard by just a handful of people," he explains. Despite Van Vliet's silence, the project was strictly legal, so Revenant decided to proceed. Ideally, they would seek his approval but, in Blackwood's words, "I think our over-riding directive was to be true to the work and the people who made it."

If Van Vliet would not comment on this set, he did, according to a very reliable source, call Rhino Records and complain about *The Dust Blows Forward*, a double CD best-of compilation the label released in 1999 – even though virtually all the tracks were commercially available at the time. In 2000, and after a very lengthy hiatus, Van Vliet resumed contact with John Peel when he heard that the DJ's wife was unwell. Peel mentioned the conversation on his radio show, saying that Van Vliet had told him, "I like rhinos but I don't like Rhino". It's unlikely that *I'm Going To Do What I Wanna Do: Live At My Father's Place 1978*, an internet-only, limited edition, double CD released by Rhino Handmade in 2000, will have endeared him to the company. Taking this as a given, one can only imagine his ire at what has become open season for putting out albums of live material, which are essentially bootlegs, but end up being distributed by major record store chains. *Mersey Trout*, a live album, was recorded at Liverpool during the 1980 UK tour and released on Ozit/Milksafe. Viper Records have released *Magnetic Hands*, another across-the-eras audience tape live collection from the UK, and a sister compilation of similar material from the US called *Railroadism*. But the most notorious is Ozit/Milksafe's *Dust Sucker*, a bootleg version of *Bat Chain Puller* with risible sleeve notes. Although one could argue that it served a purpose in getting the music out into the marketplace, it is essentially a reasonable quality bootleg of the studio sessions, dressed up as if it is an official release. Unfortunately, it has gained such widespread distribution that it is now very unlikely that the Zappa Estate will release *Bat Chain Puller* at all. Although they had respected Van Vliet's initial request not to release the record, information from the Zappa camp hinted that they were also thinking of being true to the work itself – and ultimately recouping a twenty-odd year investment – rather than accede to the wishes of its reclusive and habitually uncooperative creator.

Ozit/Milksafe justified the release of *Dust Sucker* with some implausible tale about Van Vliet giving "his mix" of the sessions to the late DJ and promoter Roger Eagle back in the early Eighties and asking him to release it. Quite why he would have asked someone to independently release an album that had been the single most important cause of the contractual problems that had thwarted his career in the late Seventies – and possibly renewing them – beggars belief. The story is not given any credibility by Magic Band members. In 1980 Virgin released a compilation album of its artists – including Captain Beefheart's 'Dirty Blue Gene' – ironically entitled called *Cash Cows*. Certainly the udders of the Beefheart cash cow are due to become ever more painfully pinched, with more bootleg rag-bags of rarities scheduled for release.

On a more positive note, at the time of writing, Van Vliet's relationship with Rhino has considerably improved. Artist's Ink Editions (a division of Rhino Entertainment) have collaborated with the Michael Werner Gallery in producing *Riding Some Kind Of Unusual Skull Sleigh*, a box set devoted to his work in all media. The limited edition set includes an original signed colour etching, and a fascinating CD of poems and song fragments. There are also two books (one including a collection of photos, lyrics, artworks, cuttings and the text of the pieces on the accompanying CD, the other featuring 60 colour plates of paintings and drawings), and a DVD of Anton Corbijn's short film, *Some Yo-Yo Stuff*. The box retails for $500. Rhino received a number of complaints from purchasers of this pricey set as on some of the etchings, Van Vliet's spidery signature runs off the paper. If Van Vliet really does wish to distance himself from his rock musician past, his choice of material for the CD – surely only of interest to Captain Beefheart devotees – is curious, to say the least.

Only Van Vliet can explain this on/off ambivalence towards his musical career. Initially, he thought that he could effect a major change in the way that people hear music. The changes have been significant, but on a smaller scale than he envisaged. An interview with Jim Greer in *Rockstar* in 1991 showed that he was still disappointed about its marginal status, appearing to hold music critics and gullible public equally responsible: "For my whole life they've repeated to me that I was a genius. They said the same about my childhood sculptures, slapping me on the back... But in the meantime they've also taught the public that my music is too difficult to listen to."[18]

Nowadays Van Vliet is never seen outside his house. The area in which he lives used to be a popular hippie destination in the Sixties and Seventies because of its natural beauty, and he has joked that he doesn't go out in case he meets any Grateful Dead fans. But his desire for seclusion is serious, as he explained to John Rogers: "I've only seen about three other people since I've lived here. And I'm not kidding. But then I don't get out much."[19]

This fuels rumours that he has suffered a serious decline in health. Any such assertions have been brushed aside by himself and The Michael Werner Gallery. His refusal to turn up at the openings of exhibitions in the Nineties has been put down to a fear of flying, a hip injury reported in the Nineties, or an increasing phobia of the urban environment. "I don't like flying either, not since Reagan got rid of all the air traffic controllers," he confided to John Yau. "Besides, I can't paint in airlines, I can't paint in hotels."[20] He later explained to John Rogers why he had not been to any of his exhibitions since 1990: "I don't think being seen in public like that adds anything, I think it's just being commercial."[21]

It is hard to believe that these are the only reasons that Van Vliet is not seen in public. A US TV news clip, broadcast in 1989, shows him at a private view of his exhibition at the Museum of Modern Art, San Francisco, looking very shaky. Although the journalist's first question was edited out, it was not difficult to guess, Van Vliet's curt reply being: "I've done enough music." The sense of frustration was palpable, the same frustration, no doubt, that he had experienced when accosted by Captain Beefheart fans asking for autographs at art shows.

He was then asked what his paintings were about. "Things" was the reply. Its brevity could have been down to the crassness of the line of questioning, but when asked to elaborate, he said, "Good things," in a thin, halting voice. He then walked away with the aid of a stick (with which he had been seen since the exhibition at Waddington's, London, in 1986). There was a further deterioration by the time Ace Farren Ford saw him at an exhibition the following year at the Fred Hoffman Gallery in Santa Monica. It is the last time he has seen or spoken to him. "That was the first time I had actually seen him in a wheelchair, which of course really freaked me out," he remembers. "His condition, I understand now, must have been beginning to manifest during the days of the last tour, because people were helping Don on and off stage, and he was having trouble walking. But we thought nothing of it because of the nature of his persona: Old Captain

Beefheart, the young guy who is actually a thousand years old, that kind of thing. We never even thought that he was actually physically having difficulty. He never talked to anyone about not feeling well, it just seemed like his *routine de jour* at the time."

The perennial party line is that healthwise Van Vliet is OK – he had a new studio built on his property in the early Nineties after all. It is obviously entirely his own business if he does not wish his state of health to be discussed in the media, but some of the reasons given for his reclusiveness seem so half-baked that they create the sort of environment in which rumours flourish.

The semi-corroborated and popularly held belief – if indeed it can be called that – is that Van Vliet is suffering from multiple sclerosis. His reclusiveness is attributed to poor health and mobility as a result of the illness, but in lieu of an official statement, any conclusions will inevitably be speculative. Rick Carr was specific about his condition on National Public Radio in late 1999, stating that he had been diagnosed with multiple sclerosis in the late eighties. In 1994, Van Vliet made a recording of six poems (originally included with the catalogue *Stand Up To Be Discontinued* and later included with Luc Ferrari's sonic book, *Pearls Before Swine, Ice Cream For Crows*). On the seven minutes of material he sounds frail and seems to be having difficulty in enunciating. It certainly came as a shock to Ford. "When I first heard them, I literally cried," he admits. "That was the first real time [I realised] he is sick, he's really not doing well. It was really hard for me to hear those for a while, but I've gotten over that. I still love them still for what they are, but after the years we spent together, that was almost like saying, I guess I'm not going to talk to him anymore. We're not going to have those evenings again."

Elaine Shepherd began making the 1997 BBC TV documentary *The Artist Formerly Known As Captain Beefheart* in 1993. But it soon looked like it might meet a similar fate to a number of other mooted Van Vliet-related projects, where funding was ultimately unforthcoming due to a lack of contribution from the subject. Fortuitously, this problem was surmounted when Van Vliet's friend, the photographer Anton Corbijn, agreed for some of his shots to be used in the documentary. He also shot his own film in 1993 – paid for by the BBC – to accompany the documentary, a 12-minute short entitled *Some Yo Yo Stuff*. Without the involvement of Corbijn – who persuaded Van Vliet that the documentary was OK – there would have been no access to archive film, or clearances for the use of music and paintings in the programme.

Although Jan Van Vliet was co-operative in sending materials, Shepherd never actually spoke to Don – corresponding instead solely with Jan via fax – and when the critically acclaimed documentary was complete, a copy was sent to Van Vliet. But as expected, she received no response. By the early Nineties, Van Vliet was still giving interviews and happy for some sort of exposure, but was also a complete recluse, and acutely sensitive as to how he would come across visually. So although he would not appear in the documentary, the problem was imaginatively solved by *Some Yo Yo Stuff* . This striking and amusing visual essay includes Sue Vliet walking towards the camera holding a cardboard cut-out of her son, which she then introduces to the viewer and plants in the Mojave Desert sand. Film director David Lynch also makes a cameo appearance, asking Van Vliet some questions. When we see Van Vliet, he is seated in a shadowy room wearing shades and smoking a cigar, with his witty and pithy – but shaky – vocal commentary overdubbed. He is presented as positively as possible, but the visual evidence of his physical decline is still clear and came as a shock to many.

In an interview with Corbijn on the London radio station GLR in 1998, the interviewer takes a direct line of questioning: "There's been a lot of worry about his health and everything. He sounds quite slow, as if he's been very ill, in the film [*Some Yo Yo Stuff*]. Is he quite ill at the moment?" Corbijn answers, "Well, he doesn't particularly run the marathon. He is not, I think, in fantastic health, but his mind is very clear. And I think that he just wants to be left alone and paint. And the way I made the film as well I wanted to concentrate on his mind rather than any other things… I haven't seen him since I made the film, actually, but when I talk to him, he's very vibrant."

Corbijn's caginess is echoed in the responses of others who are still close to him. They are either told to be careful of what they say, or decide themselves to act with the utmost discretion. Even those who have lost touch keep promises they made nearly twenty years before not to reveal where he lives, even though, unbeknown to them, that information has been revealed on a number of occasions. Such is the respect he still commands. His reclusiveness is so total that even his closest friends mainly communicate with him by telephone. In the late Nineties Polly Harvey (with whom ex-Magic Band bass and keyboard player Eric Drew Feldman has been a long-time collaborator) told John Peel she had been the recipient of some marathon phone calls from Van Vliet, who is a self-confessed fan of her music. But allegedly, when she was over in the States in 1998, he declined her request to visit him. In 2004 she confirmed that her friendship with Van Vliet was ongoing and that she regularly sent him demos of new material for his critical input.

My ambition to interview Don Van Vliet seemed unrealistic from the outset. Everyone I had contacted who knew him told me he would never speak to me. They were right. Back in 1995, I contacted the Michael Werner Gallery in Manhattan and was informed that Don was not interested in being involved with a book as he only spoke to a few people, it would upset his painting schedule, and he wasn't interested in dredging up the past. But towards the end of the call, I was told that if I managed to avoid the usual recycled stories – which I took to mean anything that was unduly negative – and they were able to see something I had written, then the gallery might be able to put me in touch with useful contacts and, who knows, Don might even participate on the art side of things. I was sent a cuttings file.

A year later, I contacted a close friend of Van Vliet requesting an interview. Provisionally he politely declined, but went on to say that Don would be phoning him next week and he would mention it to him then. I received a fax from the gallery soon after, informing me that it had come to their attention and to that of Don Van Vliet that I had been attempting to solicit material by claiming they were both supporting the project (something I had studiously avoided). I was told to desist from doing so immediately.

In late 1999 I renewed contact, sending a number of chapter drafts and a request for permission to reproduce some artwork – more or less a formality for magazine or newspaper articles. As hope sprang eternal, I also requested an interview. After an ominous delay, I was told that Van Vliet himself had refused permission, apparently because he wanted to distance himself from his musical career. The interview was not mentioned. I then faxed the gallery with a formal interview request and some questions, focusing on his art, for Van Vliet's perusal. It seemed a totally pointless exercise, but I had yet to receive a definite "no". That was not long in coming. The gallery agreed to forward the questions. I received a disappointing but entirely expected answerphone message soon after, informing me that Don wanted nothing whatsoever to do with the project. When revising the book in 2004, I again communicated with the gallery who informed me that it wasn't possible to interview Van Vliet right now, but that he might be open to responding to correspondence by mail if he found the questions interesting. Assessing the chance of getting an interview to be somewhere in the region of infinitesimal, I felt it better to leave him in peace.

In *The Wire* in 1994 John Peel said, "It grieves me more than anything that he's so ill."[22] He speaks for a number of people who have a genuine concern for his well-being because they have been friends with him in the past or because they have been deeply moved by his music – or both. Sadly, this appears to be of little interest to him now. During the research for this book, some people to whom I spoke have Van Vliet's telephone number, but claim the phone is left unanswered and answerphone messages are ignored. These one-time friends, who have a genuine desire to talk to him and give him their best wishes, are unable to do so. As one commented: "I do think it's sad when anyone thinks he can do without old friends. That must be a very sparse existence." Yet Van Vliet told Dave DiMartino in 1993 that he was "as happy as a clam",[23] which is perhaps the best description of his current lifestyle. But put this assertion against accounts from very reputable sources, which tell of callers – whom the Van Vliets knows personally – pulling into his driveway and making their way towards the house only to be greeted by locked doors, suddenly drawn curtains and the ring of the doorbell followed by silence.

In a poignant closing chapter to their troubled friendship, Zappa called him in the early Nineties to tell him that he had terminal cancer. They made up for the last time, Van Vliet telling Zappa of his own health problems. Speaking to John Rogers about his friend's death in 1995, he looked back with sadness: "And then he had to go and die on me. He died too young – way, way too young."[24]

Don Van Vliet is still interested in music and admits he likes to listen to blues and jazz and classical, but not when he's working: "I don't listen to music when I paint. It's silent other than what's going on inside my mind."[25]

Those few people with whom he keeps in contact are still likely to get a call at unpredictable hours that may well include music played over the phone. Moris Tepper recalls a time when he played him Howlin' Wolf's extraordinarily moving late solo recording, 'Ain't Goin' Down That Dirt Road': "I'm talking to Don and I'm like, 'Oh, man' and he's like, 'Oh, my

God.' We were whispering 'cos raw nerve endings had been exposed and he was almost crying. It was not a windy night and all of a sudden my back door slammed open and I jumped and I screamed. I truly thought there was an intruder, a big guy with a gun. And he said, 'What's wrong, man?' and I told him that the door had just slammed open. And he said, 'You know who it is? That's the Wolf. He's done that to me three times.'"

In the *MOJO* feature 'The Best Thing I've Heard All Year', he played his choice for 1994 over the phone to Mark Ellen. "One-string Sam! He's a black hobo! It's either One-string Sam or One-string Jones depending on the neighbourhood! Ha, ha. There's a particularly good one he did called 'He Was A-Fuckin'', recorded quite some time ago. Winged Eel Fingerling [Elliot Ingber] gave it to me to hear, about – oooh – twenty years ago. Yeah! It's pretty good."[26]

Part of the interview also went out in Q. Van Vliet responded to the request to tell a joke with one of his current favourites, although he missed out the part about Chinese men hunting to improve their manhood: "One joke I sure do agree with. It's a joke that the Chinese are killing tigers. They have a pussy problem! I can tell you one more. If you're ever in Japan, don't turn on a big faucet because they eat whales!"[27]

Interviews became rarer, then fizzled out after he spoke to John Rogers in 1995. John Yau, himself a poet, writes, "In this time [where] it falls to artists, writers, and musicians to reveal the myriad ways in which the world exists beyond our understanding, Van Vliet is a truly rare phenomenon."[28] Yau seems to be evoking the spirit of another kind of Outsider, that introduced by Colin Wilson in his 1956 book *The Outsider*. The best-seller can be (very sketchily) summed up as dealing with alienation and creativity in society. Wilson focuses on the notion of the artist as a stranger in a strange land, someone who sits outside a society whose day-to-day runnings he or she is ill-equipped for, but whose vantage point enables him or her to reveal truths which would otherwise go unnoticed.

It came as a considerable surprise, therefore, when the cover of the April 2002 issue of MOJO carried a front cover banner: "Beefheart speaks... to Bono!" The exclamation mark was certainly warranted, not just because he was speaking to the musician about whom he had been so disparaging back in the Eighties, but that he was speaking to anyone at all. Anton Corbijn, a mutual friend, set up the interview as a conference call. The interview followed the format established over the last decade or so in that it was a laconic Q&A, with the interviewer saying largely more than the interviewee. Unless he had undertaken a latterday conversion to U2's music, Van Vliet is extremely gracious throughout. For example, Bono reveals that he would have liked to have followed his father and become a painter, to which Van Vliet answers, "I think you're painting already. You're able to have the song be moving and then you shape it". He even goes so far as to say that U2's 'One' was "fantastic". Maybe the time's long gone when he feels the need to have his guard up all the time, but one would have imagined U2's widescreen rock would have epitomised all that he disliked in contemporary music. Disappointingly Bono's line of questioning rarely goes beyond jocular banter, so we don't really find anything about what Van Vliet is currently doing. But the latter comes out with a few gems. In a bizarre exchange he asks Bono what Hip-hop is, "Hip-hop is how black people use technology to discover Africa," he replies. Van Vliet then veers off onto the subject of animals. "I'm a damn animal freak," he admits. He then asks Bono if he has seen a sunfish. "You must see one," Van Vliet says. "They weigh as much as two cows and look like the head of a fish. Just the head." Bono admits that he has been too shy to approach Van Vliet before now. "Oh no, no way," replies Van Vliet generously, which must come as scant comfort for those who have tried unsuccessfully to contact him.[29]

In September of that year, poet and musician Ivor Kallin got a snippet of information via a brief – and chance – encounter with someone who went way back with Van Vliet, on a railway platform in East Anglia.

"Leaving the train at Stowmarket on the lookout for a bearded ageing uncle whom I'd never previously met, I espied two bearderly men on the platform," recounts Kallin. "One was presumably the sought-after uncle, the other was undoubtedly John Peel. I said to the uncle to put off our meeting for a wee minute whilst I grabbed the opportunity to speak to Peel. 'Mr Peel,' I said, 'I've been an admirer of your show for many decades and have to thank you for being the first person to play Captain Beefheart in this country.' He replied that he was grateful for my kind remarks and said that he had very recently had a phone call from the Captain. He had remembered that it was his birthday and had called to offer best wishes and sing the Robert Johnson song 'Come On In My Kitchen' down the phone. Peel was delighted that the Captain would deign to phone him, had remembered his birthday, and was well enough to remember and make the call."

In 2003 Moris Tepper released a solo album *Head Off*, which contained a big surprise – the lyrics to the song 'Ricochet Man' were written by one Don Van Vliet. His first new musical material in 21 years, 'Ricochet Man' is a pithy portrait of the elusive, fast moving, dice-rolling, gun-toting folkloric character. He is at once romantic and rather sinister, someone who could have walked out of the background action of a song like 'Floppy Boot Stomp' or 'When It Blows Its Stacks'.

Less good news came from an eyewitness report, in late 2003, of a CDF truck and an ambulance arriving at the Van Vliets' house – lights flashing and sirens wailing – and driving Don off to the hospital, followed by Jan in their black Mercedes. But against this background of reclusiveness and ill health, Van Vliet made a surprise return to recording in 2003 – under the name Captain Beefheart. He contributed a 35 second 'Happy Earthday' – a rather cracked a cappella take on 'Happy Birthday' – to the benefit album *Stand For What You Stand On*, compiled by the campaigning environmental organisation, Earthjustice. Other artists featured include Mose Allison, Norah Jones and Van Vliet's early object of musical desire, Ry Cooder.

Equally surprising and at a far higher profile has been the re-emergence of The Magic Band *sans* their Captain. John French had first mooted this idea back in 2001. While working on a book, *Through The Eyes Of Magic*, his personal account of his time in the group, he recalls that the passing of time – and a certain objective distance – found him looking at the music from a different perspective.

"The Internet-sparked resurgence of interest also played a pivotal role in my return to my own musical roots," says French. "My first vision of a reunion was just to get together with my *Trout Mask* comrades [Mark Boston and Bill Harkleroad] and Art Tripp, and perform instrumental versions of *Trout Mask* and *Decals* selections. I mentioned this to BBC producer Elaine Shepherd that year, on one of her visits to California. She spread the word to a few interested parties in the UK and more or less sparked the flame. When actually approached, I was a bit startled that there was a chance my little dream could come to fruition in reality." French brought in Boston and Harkleroad, and Denny Walley, with whom he played in the 1975-76 Magic Band. They began rehearsing for live shows pencilled in for 2002 at California's UCLA, London's Barbican and elsewhere, but the dates collapsed due to contractual difficulties. When Barry Hogan, organiser of the *All Tomorrow's Parties* festivals, made an offer, Harkleroad, a reluctant participant from the outset, dropped out. Finding a replacement who was not only up to playing the parts, but also prepared to put in the time learning them wasn't going to be easy. The problem was solved in August 2002, when Walley witnessed Gary Lucas performing his live score for the 1920s Expressionist silent film *The Golem* in Atlanta, Georgia.

Denny Walley recalled when he and Gary Lucas first worked on their parts in isolation at his home in Atlanta in 2002. "The first thing we played together was 'Steal Softly Through Snow' [from *Trout Mask Replica*] and at the end of it we were just looking at each other with our jaws down as the notes were hanging in the air. We actually started and finished in exactly the same place. From then on we knew we were onto something," he says. "I love it, it's total ecstasy to play," enthuses Lucas, about the piece. "After rehearsing together, Denny and I were very confident. It's the classic rhythm section, and to hear that bottom end and percussion with the guitars, so propulsive and cutting through, was a big thrill to us. We didn't think it would sound this good. It's totally ass kicking and contemporary sounding."

So far, so good, but then a big piece of the puzzle was missing: Van Vliet himself. Considerations were made to draft in guest vocalists, but then who could even learn the more difficult material? Ultimately French, possessed of a bluesy baritone and a fine singer in his own right, volunteered himself for the mentally and physically demanding role. "I had been practising about a dozen songs," he says. "To keep my voice in shape I needed to sing about an hour a day. I rode my bicycle uphill a few times and increased my exercise routine by 50 per cent. Also, I began playing harmonica again, which surprisingly took a great deal of air and so developed my diaphragm. The first couple of weeks I thought I was having heart problems because of excruciating chest pain. Then I realised it was probably my diaphragm crying out from excessive use. One thing I have noticed is increased energy, probably from all that extra oxygen I'm inhaling. The songs became easier to sing. My approach here is not to sing so much in my own style, as to emulate Don. "He is one of the greatest vocalists I've ever heard and his style and delivery is so much a part of the music that it would be ludicrous to attempt to reinvent the vocals. They are the best that could be. His phrasing and tonality is more like acting than singing, in a sense. In the same way that he was influenced strongly by Howlin' Wolf, Muddy Waters, John Lee Hooker and others, I was strongly influenced by Captain Beefheart in the Sixties. I actually was a stand-up singer and harmonica player in a local group and was inspired by Don's charismatic style."

Mark Boston sees it slightly differently. "That music stands on its own, that's why I wanted to do it," he states. "At first we were just going to do it without any vocals as a tribute to Don, but John knows all the songs and he's an excellent singer. But it's still a tribute to Don. John was concerned people would think he was trying to be Don. I said, 'John, there's no way you could be Don, there's no way he could be you. Just sing it to the best of your ability and have fun with it'."[30]

The line-up was augmented initially by Robert Williams on drums when French took over onstage vocal duties, and latterly by Michael Traylor – who briefly joined the Magic Band in the mid-Seventies, but left due to the stasis in which the group found itself. Of course it could never be the real thing, but at least the music was living again and breathing fire rather than gathering dust on collectors' shelves. Interviewing the group individually in early 2003, what came over was their incredible enthusiasm for the music, the respect they still have for Van Vliet, and that they are knitted together by the sort of camaraderie shared by veterans from any difficult campaign. It is also an effective way of dispersing any residual effects of post-Beefheart syndrome. The group recorded an album *Back To The Front*, featuring excellent performances of songs from the Beefheart canon – with more of a 3D sound than the originals. A DVD *Live In Concert* filmed at Shepherd's Bush Empire London, April 2003 has been released together with a documentary about the reunion.

There was no more having to serve time in the barrel, no more fights and psychological warfare, no more ten hour rehearsals where nothing happened. It was more straightforward now, and an enjoyable – and cathartic – experience, which they had all earned. Personally speaking, after seeing songs like 'Click Clack, 'Smithsonian Institute Blues' and 'Moonlight On Vermont' played live, I was quite happy to just put questions of authenticity to one side, throw my head back and howl in affirmation. When the group played an hour-long live set for John Peel's BBC Radio 1 show at the BBC's Maida Vale studios in July 2004, Peel acknowledged there was undoubtedly a "ghost at the feast". He also added, "Here's a thought for you: if a great orchestra plays Beethoven, no one sits there, saying, 'This is only valid if Ludwig's conducting.' And our thanks to the Magic Band for bringing this extraordinary music alive for us tonight". Van Vliet, no doubt, has a different view, but is yet to comment on the group's activities. One also feels that although they are perfectly comfortable in their hard-earned roles in a Captainless Magic Band, it would still mean a lot for them to get a nod of acknowledgement. But that is unlikely.

Van Vliet now relishes the fact that his chosen field of endeavour is one where it's not necessary for him to spend any time with people – in this respect he can do exactly what he wants, which suits him fine. "Give me lack of people," he stated in *Some Yo Yo Stuff*. Buying his plot of land by the sea is the best thing he ever did, he reckons. "I would have lived somewhere like this anyway, but a prod of the feet of humans made me do it sooner," is his summary of the situation.[31]

His situation – geographically at least – sounds idyllic. He described it to Ben Thompson in 1994 as "a painted birdcage above a hacksaw ocean with lovely redwood stalks with zillions of raindrops, falling". The house is small, he admitted, but "a turtle only needs a shell to live in".[32] He also claims that it's helped him cut down on eating salt because he can now simply absorb it by osmosis.

Van Vliet is keen to dismiss the view that he has become cut off from the world. The fact that he now feels that he's got more into it is a clear example of the importance he places on the natural environment above urban landscapes swarming with humans. He told Thompson that he was "cut off just enough to feel well tailored".[31] The following year he explained his reclusiveness to John Rogers: "It's just that I don't like getting out when I could be painting. And when I'm painting, I don't want anybody else around. That's all."[33]

Whatever his state of health, the creative flow carries on unabated in an obsessional relationship with painting. It is as if his philosophy could be crystallised as: "I paint, therefore I am." He claims that he has no choice in the matter. The act of painting, turning himself inside out, is a struggle resulting in hard-won ground, a territory which he is disinclined to share with anyone but his wife, Jan. His maximisation of the time that he spends alone with his brushes, paints and canvases still results in sleepless nights, although he has admitted to making concessions to age by eating and sleeping more: "I usually see the sun and the moon roll around the sky three or four times before going to sleep. I finally hit that point [where sleep is a necessity]. But I fight it."[34]

"I've been painting for four days straight," he told John Yau in 1991. "I finished two paintings in the last couple of days. I won. I actually did something I liked. And that's unusual. I don't need any [sleep]. I've been feeding on the fumes – or dying from them. But it's fun while it lasts."[35]

In 1993, former Magic Band member and long-time friend Bruce Fowler summed up his current lifestyle. To Elaine Shepherd: "I think at this point in Don's life he's most happy just living at his house, having a nice view of nature, being able to just go create, not having to deal with the public so much and having a private life. I do think he's happier being a painter. I meet a lot of people that say, 'Will Don do music again?' I tell them, 'Go look at his art.' He's still there, he's still creating."[36]

His life has gone full circle from the days when he shut himself in his room as a child to create his own space, his clear spot. Of course those accounts may have been fanciful, but now he really does have the "lack of people" he desires and his artistic activity is totally solipsistic. Now he can go as far into himself, into his own creative wellspring as he wants. At least one hopes this is still the case – it does seem rather ominous that no new work has featured in his exhibitions for a number of years now.

Back in the mid-Seventies, Van Vliet described the coastal location of his rented accommodation on Trinidad Bay, enthusing about the whales that swam out in his "fish pond". "They sing and I play the horn to them," he told Vivien Goldman.[37] Nearly two decades later, at the end of the radio interview in 1993, he told Co De Kloet about the whales that he could see out in the bay. He sounded tired, but audibly moved as he described a group of over thirty that had been there one Easter, concluding: "They breed out there, the whales. I can look out my window and see a spout if I'm lucky. They're wonderful."[38] Perhaps in between paintings he might find the time to take his soprano sax out of its case and blast a stream of notes out across the sea to say "Hi", to tell them he's still here.

NOTES

The exact date of some publications is unknown as they have been either reprinted in other publications without comprehensive credits or taken from collections of cuttings that didn't include the date. All quotes not credited come from interviews with the author.

Chapter 1   A Hell Of A Way To Wake Up
Interview with the author: Jim Sherwood

1. Vivien Goldman, *Sounds*, 22 November 1975
2. Caroline Boucher, *Disc and Music Echo*, 1 April 1972
3. Vivien Goldman, *Sounds*, 22 November 1975
4. Paul Rambali, *New Musical Express*, 1 November 1980
5. Elliot Wald, *Oui*, 1 July 1973
6. Lester Bangs, *Voice*, 1–7 October 1980
7. Elliot Wald, *Oui*, 1 July 1973
8. Merete Bates, *Guardian*, 15 Aprll 1972
9. Connor McNight, *Zig Zag*, March 1972
10. Lester Bangs, *Voice*, 1–7 October 1980
11. Caroline Boucher, *Disc and Music Echo*, 1 April 1972
12. Elliot Wald, *Oui*, 1 July 1973
13. Warner Brothers circular, 19 November 1972
14. Caroline Boucher, *Disc Music Echo*, 1 April 1972
15. Patrick Carr, *Crawdaddy*, 19 March 1972
16. Bill Gubbins, *Exit*, 10 May 1974
17. Internet discussion group posting, 1998
18. *Frank Zappa in His Own Words*, Omnibus, 1993
19. Michael Gray, *Mother! The Frank Zappa Story*, Plexus, 1993
20. Jerry Hopkins, *Rolling Stone*, (exact date unknown) 1968
21. *Frank Zappa in His Own Words*
22. Kristine McKenna, *New Musical Express*, 18 September 1982
23. BBC TV interview with Frank Zappa, 1993
24. Sleeve notes, *The Lost Episodes* (Rykodisc) 1996; interview from 1993
25. Ibid.
26. Ibid.
27. Elliot Wald, *Oui*, 1 July 1973

Chapter 2   Ethel Higgenbaum and Her Magic Band
Interviews with the author: Don Aldridge, Jim Sherwood, David Gates, Gary Marker

1. Derek Taylor, *The Great Gnome Biography*, press release by Leonard Grant & Associates, 1966
2. Ibid.
3. Elliot Wald, *Oui*, 1 July 1973
4. BBC TV documentary *The Artist Formerly Known As Captain Beefheart*, first broadcast August 1997; interview from 1993
5. Internet discussion group posting, 1997
6. Drum clinic, Conway Hall, London, 26 May 1996; transcribed by the author
7. *KFWB Hitline*, 28 June 1966
8. *Los Angeles Times*, 1966 (exact date unknown)
9. Internet discussion group posting, 1997

Chapter 3   May The Baby Jesus Shut Your Mouth And Open Your Mind
Interviews with the author: Gary Marker, Don Aldridge

1. BBC TV documentary *The Artist Formerly Known As Captain Beefheart*, first broadcast August 1997; interview from 1995
2. BBC Radio 1, *Guitar Greats*, 1983
3. *Ptolemaic Terrascope*, No. 26, 1998
4. BBC TV documentary *The Artist Formerly Known As Captain Beefheart*, first broadcast August 1997; interview from 1995
5. Ibid.
6. *Zig Zag*, February 1977
7. Drum clinic, Conway Hall, London, 26 May 1996; transcribed by the author
8. *Goldmine*, No. 412, 1996
9. Mike Barnes, *The Wire*, No. 155, January 1997
10. Drum clinic, Conway Hall, London, 26 May 1996; transcribed by the author
11. Elliot Wald, *Oui*, 1 July 1973
12. *Zig Zag*, February 1973
13. Susan Bunn, *Malibu Times* July 6, 2000
14. BBC TV documentary *The Artist Formerly Known As Captain Beefheart*, first broadcast August 1997; interview from 1995
15. Ibid.; interview from 1993
16. Ibid.; interview from 1995
17. *Zig Zag*, February 1977
18. *Zig Zag*, February 1973
19. *Goldmine*, No. 411, 26 April 1996

Chapter 4   Your Psychedelic Seltzer, Sir
Interviews with the author: Gary Marker Don Aldridge, John Peel

1. *Record Mirror*, 1972
2. *Melody Maker*, 1968 (exact date unknown)
3. *Focus*, Autumn 1995
4. *International Times*, early February 1968
5. *Blimp Over Europe*, No. 1, 1995

6. *International Times*, early February 1968
7. *Melody Maker*, 3 February 1968
8. Ibid.
9. *Melody Maker*, 24 February 1968
10. *Record Collector*, May 1990
11. *Drum clinic*, Conway Hall, London, 26 May 1996; transcribed by the author
12. John Ellis, January 1994 phone interview; *Steal Softly Thru Snow*, No. 4, September 1994

Chapter 5   I Want My Own Land
Interviews with the author: Gary Marker, Bill Harkleroad, Jim Sherwood, Lynn Aronspeer, Don Aldridge, Richard Kunc, Mark Boston

1. *DISCoveries*, December 1988
2. Bill Harkleroad, *Lunar Notes*, SAF, 1998
3. John Ellis, January 1994 phone interview; *Steal Softly Thru Snow*, No. 4, September 1994
4. Michael Tearson, January 1972, radio interview; published in *Terminal!*, No. 19, *circa* 1984
5. Bill Harkleroad, *Lunar Notes*
6. David Reitmann, *Rock*, March 15, 1971
7. Roger Ames, source unknown, September 1974
8. Bill Harkleroad, *Lunar Notes*
9. Ibid.
10. Interview on *Supplement*, NOS, Radio 4 (Holland); first broadcast 16 August 1993
11. Alex Duke and Rob DeNunzio, *Hi-Fi Mundo*, Internet magazine, 1998
12. Drum clinic, Conway Hall, London, 26 May 1996; transcribed by the author and published in *Resonance*, Vol. 6, No. 1, 1997
13. Ibid.
14. Ibid.
15. Alex Duke and Rob DeNunzio, *Hi-Fi Mundo*, Internet magazine, 1998
16. Drum clinic, Conway Hall, London, 26 May 1996; transcribed by the author and published in *Resonance*, Vol. 6, No. 1, 1997
17. *Guitar*, September 1995
18. Paul Griffiths, *Modern Music*, Thames & Hudson, 1978
19. *Guitar*, September 1995
20. Ibid.
21. John Ellis, January 1994 phone interview; *Steal Softly Thru Snow*, No. 4, September 1994
22. Interview on *Supplement*, NOS, Radio 4 (Holland); first broadcast 16 August 1993
23. *Mojo* circa 1994, reprinted in *Steal Softly Thru Snow*, No. 4, September 1994
24. Elaine Shepherd, BBC TV documentary *The Artist Formerly Known As Captain Beefheart*, first broadcast August 1997; interview from 1993
25. John Ellis, January 1994 phone interview; *Steal Softly Thru Snow*, No. 4, September 1994
26. Marc Minsker, *Ptolemaic Terrascope*, No. 26, 1998

27. John Ellis, January 1994 phone interview; *Steal Softly Thru Snow*, No. 4, September 1994
28. Drum clinic, Conway Hall, London, 26 May 1996; transcribed by the author and published in *Resonance*, Vol. 6, No. 1, 1997
29. John Ellis, January 1994 phone interview; *Steal Softly Thru Snow*, No. 4, September 1994
30. Writer unknown *Guitar Player* Zappa! special, 1993
31. Alex Duke and Rob DeNunzio, *Hi-Fi Mundo*, Internet magazine, 1998
32. Nigel Leigh, BBC TV interview with Frank Zappa, 1993
33. *Sounds*, 1 April 1972
34. *Zig Zag*, No. 8, 1969
35. *Mojo*, August 1995
36. Nigel Leigh, BBC TV interview with Frank Zappa, 1993

Chapter 6   Out Recording A Bush
Interview with the author: Eric Drew Feldman

1. *Copyright*, No. 5, Spring 1991
2. *New Musical Express*, 1974 (exact date unknown)
3. From sleeve notes to *Howlin' Wolf, The Genuine Article*, Chess/MCA Records, 1997
4. Giles Oakley, *The Devil's Music*, Ariel Books, 1976
5. Edwin Pouncey, *The Wire*, August 1998
6. Greil Marcus, *Invisible Republic*, Picador, 1998
7. Pamela Des Barres, *I'm With The Band – Confessions Of A Groupie*, 1987
8. *Aloha*, No. 1, 6 May 1972; translated from Dutch by Theo Tieman
9. Interview on *Supplement*, NOS, Radio 4 (Holland); first broadcast 16 August 1993
10. John Piccarella, *New York Rocker*, December 1980
11. *Garcia Lorca: Poeta en Nueva York*, Grant and Cutler, 1978
12. Roger Ames, source unknown, September 1974
13. *Rolling Stone*, 27 November 1980
14. John Piccarella, *New York Rocker*, December 1980
15. *Guitar Player*, Zappa! special, 1993
16. Alex Duke and Rob DeNunzio, *Hi-Fi Mundo*, Internet magazine, 1998

Chapter 7   Carp Head Replica
Interviews with the author: Cal Schenkel, John French, Lynn Aronspeer, Richard Kunc, Barry Miles, Michael Smotherman, Gary Marker, John Peel

1. Connor McKnight, *Zig Zag*, February 1973
2. Bill Harkleroad, *MOJO*, August 1995
3. Dick Lawson, *Zig Zag*, July 1969
4. Lester Bangs, *New Musical Express*, 1 April 1978
5. Dave DiMartino, *MOJO*, December 1993
6. Dick Lawson, *Zig Zag*, August 1969
7. Promotional record, Reprise PRO 447
8. Ibid.

9. Barry Miles, *New Musical Express*, 3 January 1976
10. Bill Harkleroad, *Lunar Notes*, SAF, 1998
11. Drum clinic, Conway Hall, London, 26 May 1996; transcribed by the author and published in *Resonance* Vol. 6, No. 1, 1997
12. John Ellis, January 1994 phone interview: *Steal Softly Thru Snow*, No. 4, September 1994
13. *Guitar Player* Zappa! special, 1993
14. Dick Lawson, *Frendz*, 12 December 1969
15. *Blimp Over Europe*, No. 1, 1995
16. Michael Gray, *Mother! The Frank Zappa Story*, Plexus, 1993
17. Interview on *Supplement*, NOS, Radio 4 (Holland); first broadcast 16 August 1993
18. Michael Gray, *Mother! The Frank Zappa Story*
19. Dick Lawson, *Zig Zag*, July 1969
20. *Oui*, 1 July 1973
21. *Disc and Music Echo*, 1 April 1972
22. *New Musical Express*, 1976 (exact date unknown)
23. Promotional record, Reprise PRO 447
24. *Zig Zag* circa December 1969
25. *Goldmine*, No. 411, 26 April 1996
26. Ibid.

Chapter 8   Counting The Passing Cars

Interviews with the author: Barry Miles, Don Aldridge, Bill Harkleroad, Richard Kunc, Moris Tepper, Mark Boston

1. *Sounds*, 1 April 1972
2. *Frendz*, No. 26, 1972
3. *Rock*, 15 March 1971
4. *Rolling Stone*, 14 May 1970
5. Zig Zag, (date unknown)
6. *Frendz*, No. 26, 1972
7. Drum clinic, Conway Hall, London, 26 May 1996; transcribed by the author
8. *Zig Zag*, February 1973
9. Fred Frith, *New Musical Express*, 1974 (exact date unknown)
10. *Melody Maker*, 1971 (exact date unknown)
11. *Rolling Stone*, April 1971
12. Transcription of LA TV show *Eyewitness*, 1980
13. *New Musical Express*, 1 April 1978
14. Justin Sherrill, *Homepagereplica* website, 1998
15. *Zig Zag*, February 1973
16. Lester Bangs, *Voice*, 1–7 October 1980
17. John Orme, *Melody Maker*, 1977 (exact date unknown)
18. *Melody Maker*, 1971 (exact date unknown)
19. Charlie Gillett, *New Musical Express* 1971 (exact date unknown)
20. *Goldmine*, 24 October 1986
21. *Circus*, May 1971
22. Lars Movin, *Copyright*, Spring 1991

23. *Aloha*, No. 1, 6 May 1972
24. *Sounds*, 22 November 1975
25. *Circus*, April 1971
26. Ibid.
27. Warner Brothers circular, 13 March 1971
28. BBC TV documentary *The Artist Formerly Known as Captain Beefheart*, first broadcast August 1997
29. Ibid.
30. Drum clinic, Conway Hall, London, 26 May 1996; transcribed by the author

Chapter 9   Aphorisms, Epigrams and Lugubrious Blues
Interviews with author: Bill Harkleroad, John French, Nick Kent

1. Alex Duke and Rob DeNunzio, *Hi-Fi Mundo*, Internet magazine, 1998
2. *Disc and Music Echo*, 1 April 1972
3. *Crawdaddy*, 19 March 1972
4. *Disc and Music Echo*, 1 April 1972
5. Writer unknown, *Coast FM & Fine Arts magazine*, April 1971
6. January 1994 phone interview; *Steal Softly Thru Snow*, No. 4, September 1994
7. *Coast FM & Fine Arts magazine*, April 1971
8. *Los Angeles Times*, 30 May 1971
9. Nick Kent, *Frendz*, No. 26, 1972
10. *Creem*, 1972 (exact date unknown)
11. *Rolling Stone*, April 1971
12. Paul Rambali, *New Musical Express*, 1 November 1980
13. Steve Peacock, *Sounds*, 1 April 1972
14. *Creem*, 1972 (exact date unknown)
15. *Crawdaddy*, 19 March 1972
16. Ibid.
17. January 1994 phone interview; *Steal Softly Thru Snow*, No. 4, September 1994
18. *New Musical Express Encyclopaedia of Rock*, Salamander Books, 1997
19. *The Devil's Music*, Ariel Books, 1976
20. January 1972 radio interview, *Terminal!*, No. 19, *crica* 1984
21. *Melody Maker*, 1972 (exact date unknown)
22. *New Musical Express*, 1977 (exact date unknown)
23. *New Musical Express*, 21 April 1973
24. *Aloha*, No. 1, 6 May 1972
25. *Zig Zag*, No. 29, February 1973
26. *Crawdaddy*, 19 March 1972
27. *Sounds*, 1 April 1972
28. *Creem*, 1972 (exact date unknown)
29. Alex Duke and Rob DeNunzio, *Hi-Fi Mundo*, Internet magazine, 1998

Chapter 10   Singing For Women
Interviews with the author: Gary Lucas, Gary Marker, Bill Harkleroad, John Peel, Ian Anderson, Michael Smotherman, Nick Kent, Frank Hebblethwaite

1. *Superhebdo*, 11 May 1972
2. Steve Peacock, *Sounds*, 1 April 1972

3. *New York Review of Books*, 11 August 1994
4. *L'Oeuf*, Autumn 1972
5. *Liverpool Daily Post*, 4 April 1972
6. Caroline Boucher, *Disc and Music Echo*, 1 April 1972
7. Bluecoat Gallery press release, 1972
8. Granada TV, 1972 (exact date unknown))
9. *Guardian*, 15 April 1972
10. Ibid.
11. *Creem*, 1972 (exact date unknown)
12. *Sounds*, 1 April 1972
13. *Seconds*
14. *Rolling Stone*, 1 April 1973
15. *Superhebdo*, 11 May 1972
16. *New Musical Express*, 19 July 1975
17. Warner Brothers/Reprise circular, November 1972
18. *MOJO*, August 1995
19. Warner Brother/Reprise circular, November 1972
20. John Ellis, *Goldmine*, 24 October 1986
21. *Unknown Pleasures: Great Lost Albums Rediscovered*, *Melody Maker*, 4 March 1995
22. *New Musical Express*, 1973 (exact date unknown)
23. *Melody Maker*, 1973 (exact date unknown)
24. *New Musical Express*, 1975 (exact date unknown)
25. *Creem*, January 1973
26. *Rolling Stone*, 31 December 1972
27. *Rolling Stone*, 4 January 1973
28. Warner Brothers/Reprise circular, November 1972
29. *Crawdaddy*, 19 March 1972
30. ElliotWald, *Oui*, 1 July 1973
31. Radio interview on KHSU, Arcata, CA, 1972
32. publication unknown, 1973

Chapter 11 You Don't Have To Be Weird To Be Weird
Interviews with the author: Bill Harkleroad. Michael Smotherman, Chris Cutler, Nick Kent, Ace Farren Ford

1. Sleeve notes for CD reissue of *Safe As Milk* (Castle Communications)
2. Ben Watson, *Frank Zappa: The Negative Dialectics of Poodle Play*, Quartet 1994
3. *The Wire*, November 1998
4. Co De Kloet interview on *Supplement*, NOS, Radio 4 (Holland); first broadcast 16 August 1993
5. *Sounds*, 10 December 1977
6. *Exit*, 1 May 1974
7. *Goldmine*, 24 October 1986
8. Ben Edmonds, *Circus*, May 1971
9. Jim Brodey, *Rolling Stone*, 6 June 1974
10. *Melody Maker*, 6 April 1974
11. *New Musical Express*, 1974 (exact date unknown)

12. *New Musical Express*, 1 April 1978
13. *Goldmine*, 24 October 1986
14. John French, letter to *MOJO* dated 17 May 1994
15. *New Musical Express*, 1 June 1974
16. Ibid.
17. Jim Brodey, *Rolling Stone*, 6 June 1974
18. Steve Lake, *Melody Maker*, 1974 (exact date unknown)
19. Steve Lake, *Melody Maker*, 1974 (exact date unknown but later than the above)
20. Martin Hayman *Sounds*, 1974 (exact date unknown)
21. *New Musical Express*, 1 April 1978
22. *New Musical Express*, April 1977
23. *New Musical Express*, 1 June 1974
24. *Melody Maker*, 1974 (exact date unknown)

Chapter 12   The Captain's Holiday
Interviews with the author: Michael Smotherman, Moris Tepper, Barry Miles, Jimmy Carl Black, Nick Kent, Greg Davidson

1. Kris Needs, *Zig Zag*, January 1978
2. *Melody Maker*, 26 October 1974
3. Nigel Leigh, BBC TV interview with Frank Zappa, 1993
4. *New Musical Express*, 3 January 1976 (quotes taken from interviews conducted the previous year)
5. Ibid.
6. *New Musical Express*, 19 July 1975
7. *Rolling Stone*, 19 April 1975
8. Ibid.
9. *New Musical Express*, 26 April 1975
10. Elaine Shepherd, BBC TV documentary *The Artist Formerly Known as Captain Beefheart*, first broadcast August 1997; interview from 1993
11. *Society Pages*, No. 7, September 1991
12. *Sounds*, 12 November 1975
13. Ibid.
14. Nigel Leigh, BBC TV interview with Frank Zappa, 1993
15. Justin Sherrill, *Homepagereplica* website 1998
16. *New Musical Express*, November 1975 (exact date unknown)
17. *Melody Maker*, 18 October 1975
18. *Street Life*, November 1975 (exact date unknown)
19. *New Musical Express*, November 1975 (exact date unknown)

Chapter 13   Pulled By Rubber Dolphins
Interviews with the author: Ian Anderson, Bill Harkleroad, John Thomas, Moris Tepper, John French, Eric Drew Feldman, Denny Walley, Ace Farren Ford

1. *DISCoveries*, December 1988
2. *Zig Zag*, June 1975
3. *Rolling Stone*, 19 April 1975
4. Kate Phillips, *New Musical Express*, 19 July 1975

5. Chris Salewicz, ibid.
6. *Melody Maker*, 18 October 1975
7. Chris Salewicz, *New Musical Express*, 19 July 1975
8. Bill Shumow, publication unknown, May 1976
9. *Wax*, October 1978
10. Ibid.
11. *New Musical Express*, 1976 (exact date unknown)
12. Ibid.
13. Ibid.

Chapter 14   Sequinned Whales and Shiny Beasts
Interviews with the author: Robert Williams, Eric Drew Feldman, Moris Tepper, Denny Walley

1. *Zig Zag*, January 1978
2. Ibid.
3. John Orme, *Melody Maker, circa* 1977/8 (exact date unknown)
4. *New Musical Express*, 8 April 1978
5. Ibid.
6. *Zig Zag*, January 1978
7. *Sounds*, 6 August 1977
8. John Orme, *Melody Maker, circa* 1977/8 (exact date unknown)
9. *Wax*, October 1978
10. *New York Rocker*, December 1980
11. *Creem*, April 1979
12. *New Musical Express*, 1 November 1980
13. *Creem*, April 1979
14. *Downbeat*, 26 January 1979
15. *New Musical Express, circa* 1978/9 (exact date unknown)
16. C. Linstrom, Electricity Web Site, 1999
17. *The Wire*, August 1998

Chapter 15   Rock At The Dada Station
Interviews with the author: Gary Lucas. Bill Harkleroad, Eric Drew Feldman, Moris Tepper, Robert Williams, Rick Snyder

1. *Your Flesh*, Summer 1992
2. *MOJO*, September 1998
3. *Ptolemaic Terrascope*, No. 26, 1998
4. *New Musical Express*, 4 September 1982
5. *New York Rocker*, December 1980
6. *New Musical Express*, 4 September 1982
7. *Voice*, 1–7 October 1980
8. *Sounds*, 1980 (exact date unknown)
9. *Rolling Stone*, 27 November 1980
10. John Pareles, *Musician*, 1980 (exact date unknown)
11. Richard C. Walls, *Creem*, January 1981
12. *Vanity Fair*, April 1983

13. *New Musical Express*, 1 November 1980
14. *New Musical Express*, 8 April 1978
15. *Voice*, 1–7 October 1980
16. *The Wire*, April 1998
17. *New York Rocker*, December 1980
18. *Rolling Stone*, 27 November 1980
19. Ibid.
20. *Musician*, January 1981
21. Internet interview, *Homepagereplica* website, 1995
22. *New Musical Express*, 1 November 1980

Chapter 16   A Kind Whip, A Kind Quip (or Off On An Avantangent)
Interviews with the author: Moris Tepper, Rick Snyder, Gary Lucas, Eric Drew
Feldman, Robert Williams, Cliff Martinez, Denny Walley

1. *Rolling Stone*, 27 November 1980
2. Jim Farber, source unknown
3. *Seconds*, 1995 (exact date unknown)
4. *New Musical Express*, 18 September 1982
5. *New Musical Express*, 9 August 1986
6. *New Musical Express*, 1 September 1982
7. Ibid.
8. *Musician*, October 1982
9. *Sounds*, October 1982 (exact date unknown)

Chapter 17   Exit Pursued By A Giant Mechanical Bear
Interviews with the author: Rick Snyder, Cliff Martinez, Gary Lucas, Moris Tepper,
David Breuer, Ace Farren Ford

1. *Artforum*, February 1983
2. *New York Rocker*, December 1980
3. Reproduced on the sleeve notes of *The Dust Blows Forward And The Dust Blows Back* (Rhino Records, 1999)
4. WBAI radio phone in, broadcast 1984; interview conducted in late 1983
5. *Heavy Metal*, August 1983
6. *Rolling Stone*, 14 May 1970
7. *Rolling Stone*, 27 November 1980
8. *Heavy Metal*, August 1983
9. *Interview*, 1 October 1991
10. *LA Weekly*, 5–11 September 1985
11. Los Angeles Times, 29 July 1990
12. *Observer*, 1986 (exact date unknown)
13. Ibid.
14. *Time Out*, 1986 (exact date unknown)
15. *New Musical Express*, 9 August 1986
16. *New Work*, San Francisco Mueum of Modern Art, 30 November 1988
17. BBC TV documentary *The Artist Formerly Known As Captain Beefheart*, first broadcast August 1997; interview from 1995

18. Kristine McKenna, *MOJO*, December 1983
19. Don Van Vliet, *Stand Up To Be Discontinued*, Cantz 1993
20. Kristine McKenna, *Spin*, January 1988
21. Kristine McKenna, *New Musical Express*, 9 August 1986
22. *Interview*, 1 October 1991
23. *Associated Press*, 22 June 1995
24. *Musician*, January 1981
25. *Copyright*, Spring 1991
26. *Interview*, 1 October 1991

Chapter 18   Beyond The Final Glide Pattern

Interviews with the author: David Breuer, Moris Tepper, Gary Lucas, John Peel, Dean Blackwood, Ace Farren Ford

1. *Copyright*, Spring 1991
2. *Associated Press*, 22 June 1995
3. *Don Van Vliet: Recent Paintings*, 11 November–5 December 1998
4. Lester Bangs, *Psychotic Reactions And Carburetor Dung*, Minerva, 1990
5. Interview on *Supplement*, NOS, Radio 4 (Holland); first broadcast 16 August 1993
6. 'Pearls Before Swine. Ice Cream For Crow. On The Relationship Between Music And Painting In Captain Beefheart's Work', *Stand Up To Be Discontinued*, Cantz 1993
7. *Rockstar*, March 1991
8. Rip Rense, *Chicago Tribune*, 8 January 1989
9. 'Pearls Before Swine. Ice Cream For Crow. On The Relationship Between Music And Painting In Captain Beefheart's Work', *Stand Up To Be Discontinued*, Cantz 1993
10. Interview on *Supplement*, NOS, Radio 4 (Holland); first broadcast 16 August 1993
11. *Interview*, 1 October 1991
12. *MOJO*, March 1994
13. *New Musical Express*, 7 March 1998
14. *Associated Press*, 9 September 1991
15. Greil Marcus, *In The Fascist Bathroom*, Viking 1993
16. *Independent on Sunday*, 21 August 1994
17. *MOJO*, December 1993
18. *Rockstar*, March 1991
19. *Associated Press*, 9 September 1991
20. *Interview*, 1 October 1991
21. *Associated Press*, 22 June 1995
22. *The Wire*, November 1994
23. *MOJO*, December 1993
24. *Associated Press*, 22 June 1995
25. *New Musical Express*, 9 August 1986
26. *MOJO*, January 1995
27. *Q*, January 1995
28. *Cover*, March 1999

29. 'This Is Your Captain Speaking', *MOJO* 101, April 2002
30. Wire issue 230, April 2003, by the author.
31. *Independent on Sunday*, 21 August 1994
32. Ibid.
33. Ibid.
34. *Associated Press*, 22 June 1995
35. *Associated Press*, 9 September 1991
36. *Interview*, 1 October 1991
37. BBC TV documentary *The Artist Formerly Known as Captain Beefheart*, first broadcast August 1997; interview from 1993
38. *Sounds*, 22 November 1975
39. Interview on *Supplement*, NOS, Radio 4 (Holland); first broadcast 16 August 1993

DISCOGRAPHY

None of the Magic Band releases charted in the US.

THE LEGENDARY A&M SESSIONS
Current CD label: Edsel

Producer: David Gates

Engineer: Unknown

Recorded: Sound Recorders, Sunset Boulevard, Hollywood, CA, early 1966

Original release dates as A&M singles: 1) Diddy Wah Diddy b/w 2) Who Do You Think You're Fooling, circa April 1966. 3) Moonchild b/w 4) Frying Pan, circa July 1966. 5) Here I Am, I Always Am, first released in 1984

Don Van Vliet (vocals, harmonica), Doug Moon (guitar), Richard Hepner (guitar), Jerry Handley (bass), Alex St Clair Snouffer (drums on 1–4), PG Blakely (drums on 5)

Comments: All evidence from this era suggests that Here I Am, I Always Am, a rejected b-side, was recorded at a slightly later date, corresponding with the return of PG Blakely.

Released on A&M vinyl EP, October 1984, CD release on Edsel, March 1992

SAFE AS MILK
Original label: Buddah (US), Pye International (UK)

Current label: BMG/Buddha (the label has been reactivated, but with a different spelling)

Producer: Richard Perry & Bob Krasnow

Engineer: Hank Cicalo, Gary Marker

Recorded: Sunset Sound, Hollywood and RCA Studios, CA, April 1967

UK Peak: Did not chart

Release: September 1967 (US). February 1968 (UK)

1) Sure 'Nuff 'N Yes I Do 2) Zig Zag Wanderer 3) Call On Me 4) Dropout Boogie 5) I'm Glad 6) Electricity 7) Yellow Brick Road 8) Abba Zaba 9) Plastic Factory 10) Where There's Woman 11) Grown So Ugly 12) Autumn's Child

Singles: Yellow Brick Road/ Abba Zaba: circa September 1967 (US), January 1968 (UK)

Don Van Vliet (vocals, harmonica, bass marimba), Alex St Clair Snouffer (guitar), Ry Cooder (guitar, bass on 8, 11), Jerry Handley (bass), John French (drums), Russ Titelman (guitar on 12), Milt Holland (log drum on 2, 4). Taj Mahal (percussion on 7), Sam Hoffman (theremin on 6, 7)

Comments: The album has been reissued in numerous formats, but the 1999 Buddha reissue also includes abandoned *Brown Wrapper* material recorded in October/November 1967. The remastering is a vast improvement on any previous version. Extra tracks are Safe As Milk (take 5), On Tomorrow, Big Black Baby Shoes, Flower Pot, Dirty Blue Gene, Trust Us (take 9), Korn Ring Finger

MIRROR MAN

Original label: Buddah

Current CD label: BMG/Buddha as *The Mirror Man Sessions*

Producer: Bob Krasnow

Recorded: TTG Studios, Sunset Boulevard, Hollywood, CA, October/November 1967

UK Peak: 49

Release date: April 1971 (US), May 1971 (UK)

1) Tarotplane 2) 25th Century Quaker 3) Mirror Man 4) Kandy Korn

Don Van Vliet (vocals, harmonica, shenai), Alex St Clair Snouffer (guitar), Jeff Cotton (guitar), Jerry Handley (bass), John French (drums)

Comments: The 1999 Buddha reissue includes more abandoned *Brown Wrapper* material recorded in October/November 1967. Again, the remastering is a vast improvement on any previous version. Extra tracks are Trust Us (take 6), Safe As Milk (take 12), Beatle Bones 'N' Smokin' Stones, Moody Liz (take 8)

STRICTLY PERSONAL

Original label: Blue Thumb (US), Liberty (UK)

Current CD label: Liberty

Producer: Bob Krasnow
Engineer: Gene Shiveley, Bill Lazerus
Recorded: Sunset Sound, Hollywood, CA, 25 April – 2 May 1968
UK peak: Did not chart
Release date: October 1968 (US), December 1968 (UK)
1) Ah Feel Like Ahcid 2) Safe As Milk 3) Trust Us 4) Son Of Mirror Man
– Mere Man 5) On Tomorrow 6) Beatle Bones 'N' Smokin' Stones 7)
Gimme Dat Harp Boy 8) Kandy Korn
Don Van Vliet (vocals, harmonica), Alex St Clair Snouffer (guitar), Jeff
Cotton (guitar), Jerry Handley (bass), John French (drums)

TROUT MASK REPLICA
Original label: Straight (a small number were issued on its sister label,
Bizarre) (US); Straight/Reprise (UK)
Current CD Label: Reprise
Producer: Frank Zappa
Engineer: Dick Kunc
Recorded: Whitney Studios, Glendale, CA and Ensenada Drive, Woodland
Hills, CA, March/April 1969
UK PEAK: 21
Release date July 1969 (US), November 1969 (UK)
1) Frownland 2) The Dust Blows Forward 'N The Dust Blows Back 3)
Dachau Blues 4) Ella Guru 5) Hair Pie: Bake 1 6) Moonlight On
Vermont 7) Pachuco Cadaver 8) Bills Corpse 9) Sweet Sweet Bulbs
10) Neon Meate Dream Of A Octafish 11) China Pig 12) My
Human Gets Me Blues 13) Dali's Car 14) Hair Pie: Bake 2 15) Pena
16) Well 17) When Big Joan Sets Up 18) Fallin' Ditch 19) Sugar 'N
Spikes 20) Ant Man Bee 21) Orange Claw Hammer 22) Wild Life 23)
She's Too Much For My Mirror 24) Hobo Chang Ba 25) The Blimp
(mousetrapreplica) 26) Steal Softly Thru Snow 27) Old Fart At Play
28) Veteran's Day Poppy
Single: Pachuco Cadaver/Wild Life (France Only) 1970
Don Van Vliet (vocals, bass clarinet, tenor sax, soprano sax, simran horn,
musette), Zoot Horn Rollo/Bill Harkleroad (glass finger guitar, guitar,
flute), Antennae Jimmy Semens/Jeff Cotton (steel-appendage guitar),
The Mascara Snake/Victor Hayden (bass clarinet, vocal), Rockette
Morton/Mark Boston (bass & narration), Drumbo/John French
(drums), Doug Moon (guitar on 11)

LICK MY DECALS OFF, BABY
Original label: Straight (US); CBS/Straight (UK)
Current CD label: Bizarre/Straight/Rhino
Producer: Don Van Vliet
Engineer: Phil Schier
Recorded: United Recording Corp., Sunset Boulevard, Hollywood, CA, summer 1970
UK Peak: 20
Release date: December 1970 (US), January 1971 (UK)
1) Lick My Decals Off, Baby 2) Doctor Dark 3) I Love You, You Big Dummy 4) Peon 5) Bellerin' Plain 6) Woe-Is-Uh-Me-Bop 7) Japan In A Dishpan 8) I Wanna Find A Woman That'll Hold My Big Toe Till I Have To Go 9) Petrified Forest 10) One Red Rose That I Mean 11) The Buggy Boogie Woogie 12) The Smithsonian Institute Blues (Or The Big Dig) 13) Space Age Couple 14) The Clouds Are Full Of Wine (Not Whiskey Or Rye) 15) Flash Gordon's Ape
Don Van Vliet (vocals, bass clarinet, tenor sax, soprano sax, chromatic harmonica); Zoot Horn Rollo/Harkleroad (guitar, glass finger guitar); Rockette Morton/Boston (Bassius-o-pheilius) [sic]; Drumbo/French (percussion, broom), Art Tripp (marimba, percussion, broom)
Comments: Long-standing contractual problems have meant that this album has only been available on Japanese import since the mid Nineties

THE SPOTLIGHT KID
Original label: Reprise
Current CD label: Reprise
Producer: Don Van Vliet/Phil Schier
Engineer: Phil Schier
Recorded: The Record Plant, Los Angeles, CA, Autumn 1971
UK Peak: 44
Release date: January 1972 (US), February 1972 (UK)
1) I'm Gonna Booglarize You, Baby 2) White Jam 3) Blabber 'N Smoke 4) When It Blows Its Stacks 5) Alice In Blunderland 6) The Spotlight Kid 7) Click Clack 8) Grow Fins 9) There Ain't No Santa Claus On The Evenin' Stage 10) Glider
Single: Click Clack/I'm Gonna Booglarize You, Baby (US only)
Comments: available on a single CD with Clear Spot
Don Van Vliet (vocals, harmonica, jingle bells), Zoot Horn Rollo/Harkleroad

(glass finger and steel appendage guitar). Ed Marimba/Tripp (marimba, piano, harpsichord), Rockette Morton/Boston (bassius ophelius) [sic], Winged Eel Fingerling/Elliot Ingber (guitar), Drumbo/French (drums), Ted Cactus/Tripp (drums on 1) Rhys Clark (drums on 10)

CLEAR SPOT
Original label: Reprise
Current CD label: Reprise
Producer: Ted Templeman
Engineer: John Landee
Recorded: Amigo Studios, Los Angeles, CA, autumn 1972
UK Peak: Did not chart
Release date: January 1973
1) Low Yo Yo Stuff 2) Nowadays A Woman's Gotta Hit A Man 3) Too Much Time 4) Circumstances 5) My Head Is My Only House Unless It Rains 6) Sun Zoom Spark 7) Clear Spot 8) Crazy Little Thing 9) Long Neck Bottles 10) Her Eyes Are A Blue Million Miles 11) Big Eyed Beans From Venus 12) Golden Birdies
Single: Too Much Time/ My Head Is My Only House Unless It Rains, May 1973
Don Van Vliet (vocals, harmonica, wings on singabus [sic]), Zoot Horn Rollo/Harkleroad (solo guitar, steel appendage guitar, glass finger guitar and mandolin), Rockette Morton/Boston (rhythm guitar, bass on 12), Ed Marimba/Tripp (drums, tattoos and percussion), Oréjon/Roy Estrada (bass), Milt Holland (percussion), Russ Titelman (guitar on 3) The Blackberries (backing vocals on 3, 8), Uncredited Musicians (horns on 2,3,9)
Comments: available on a single CD with The Spotlight Kid

UNCONDITIONALLY GUARANTEED
Original label: Virgin (UK), Mercury (US)
Current CD label: Virgin
Producer: Andy DiMartino
Engineer: John Guess, Jim Callon
Recorded: Hollywood Sound, Los Angeles, early 1974
UK Peak: did not chart
Release date: April 1974
1) Upon The My-O-My 2) Sugar Bowl 3) New Electric Ride 4) Magic Be 5) Happy Love Song 6) Full Moon, Hot Sun 7) I Got Love On My Mind 8) This Is The Day 9) Lazy Music 10) Peaches

Single: Upon The My-O-My/Magic Be (UK), Upon The My-O-My/I Got Love On My Mind (US), April 1974

Don Van Vliet (vocals, harmonica), Zoot Horn Rollo/Harkleroad (guitar, glass finger guitar), Rockette Morton/Boston (bass), Art Tripp (drums, percussion), Alex St Clair Snouffer (guitar), Mark Marcellino (keyboards), Andy DiMartino (acoustic guitar), Del Simmons (tenor sax, flute)

LONDON 1974

Current CD label: Movie Play Gold
Producer: Andy DiMartino
Engineer: Phil Newell, Alan Perkins
Recorded: Drury Lane Theatre, London, 9 June, 1974
UK Peak: did not chart
Release date: 1993

1) Mirror Man 2) Upon The My-O-My 3) Full Moon, Hot Sun 4) Sugar Bowl 5) Crazy Little Thing 6) This Is The Day 7) New Electric Ride 8) Abba Zaba 9) Peaches

Don Van Vliet (vocals, harmonica), Michael Smotherman (keyboards), Dean Smith (guitar), Fuzzy Fuscaldo (guitar), Paul Uhrig (bass), Del Simmons (saxophone, clarinet, flute), Ty Grimes (drums)

BLUEJEANS AND MOONBEAMS

Original label: Virgin (UK), Mercury (US)
Current CD label: Virgin
Producer: Andy DiMartino
Engineer: Greg Ladangi
Recorded: Stronghold Sound Recorders, North Hollywood, CA, Summer 1974
UK Peak: Did Not Chart
Release date: November 1974

1) Party Of Special Things To Do 2) Same Old Blues 3) Observatory Crest 4) Pompadour Swamp 5) Captain's Holiday 6) Rock 'N Roll's Evil Doll 7) Further Than We've Gone 8) Twist Ah Luck 9) Bluejeans And Moonbeams

Don Van Vliet (vocals, harmonica), Dean Smith (guitar and bottleneck guitar), Ira Ingber (bass), Bob West (bass on 3), Michael Smotherman (keyboards and backing vocals), Mark Gibson (keyboards), Gene Pello (drums), Jimmy Caravan (keyboards and star machine), Ty Grimes (drums)

BONGO FURY
(ZAPPA/BEEFHEART/MOTHERS)
Original label: DiscReet
Current CD label: Rykodisc
Producer: Frank Zappa
Engineer: Kerry McNab, Mike Braunstein, Kelly Kotera, Mike Stone, Davey Moire, Frank Hubach
UK Peak: did not chart
US Peak: 66
Release date: November 1975 (US)
Recorded: Live at Armadillo World Headquarters, Austin, Texas, 20–21 May 1975 and Record Plant, Los Angeles, CA 1974–1975
1) Debra Kadabra 2) Carolina Hard-Core Ecstasy 3) Sam With The Showing Scalp Flat Top 4) Poofter's Froth Wyoming 5) 200 Years Old 6) Cucamonga 7) Advance Romance 8) Man With The Woman Head 9) Muffin Man
Frank Zappa (lead guitar, vocals), Don Van Vliet (harp, vocals, shopping bags), George Duke (keyboards, vocals), Napoleon Murphy Brock (sax, vocals), Bruce Fowler (trombone, fantastic dancing), Tom Fowler (bass, also dancing), Denny Walley (slide guitar, vocals), Terry Bozzio (drums, moisture), Chester Thompson (drums on 5 and 6)
Comments: vinyl LP only available on import in UK. First released on CD in 1989

BAT CHAIN PULLER
Original label: unreleased
Producer: Don Van Vliet, Frank Zappa (as executive producer)
Engineer: Kerry McNab
Recorded: Paramount Studios, Los Angeles, CA, spring 1976
1) Bat Chain Puller 2) Seam Crooked Sam 3) Harry Irene 4) "81" Poop Hatch 5) Flavor Bud Living 6) Brickbats 7) The Floppy Boot Stomp 8) A Carrot Is As Close As A Rabbit Gets To A Diamond 9) Carson City 10) Odd Jobs 11) The 1010th Day Of The Human Totem Pole 12) Apes-Ma
Don Van Vliet (vocals, harmonica, sax), Denny Walley (guitar), [Jeff] Moris

Tepper (guitar), John Thomas (electric piano, synthesiser), John French (drums, guitar)

SHINY BEAST (BAT CHAIN PULLER)
Original label: Virgin (UK), Warner Brothers (US)
Current CD label: Virgin
Producer: Don Van Vliet and Pete Johnson
Engineer: Glen Kolotkin, Jeffrey Norman
Recorded: The Automatt, San Francisco, June 6–August 27, 1978
UK Peak: Did not chart
Release date: Autumn 1978 (US), February 1980 (UK)
1) The Floppy Boot Stomp 2) Tropical Hot Dog Night 3) Ice Rose 4) Harry Irene 5) You Know You're A Man 6) Bat Chain Puller 7) When I See Mommy I Feel Like A Mummy 8) Owed T'Alex 9) Candle Mambo 10) Love Lies 11) Suction Prints 12) Apes-Ma

Don Van Vliet (vocals, harmonica, soprano sax, whistling), [Jeff] Moris Tepper (slide guitar, guitar and spell guitar), Bruce Lambourne Fowler (trombone and air-bass), Eric Drew Feldman (synthesiser, [fender] rhodes, grand piano, bass), Richard Redus (slide guitar, bottleneck guitar, guitar, accordion, fretless bass), Robert Arthur Williams (drums, percussion), Art Tripp (marimba, additional percussion)

DOC AT THE RADAR STATION
Original label: Virgin
Current CD label: Virgin
Producer: Don Van Vliet
Engineer: Glen Kolotkin
Recorded: Sound Castle Studios, Los Angeles, CA, June 1980
UK Peak: Did not chart
Release date: August 1980
1) Hot Head 2) Ashtray Heart 3) A Carrot Is As Close As A Rabbit Gets To A Diamond 4) Run Paint Run Run 5) Sue Egypt 6) Brickbats 7) Dirty Blue Gene 8) Best Batch Yet 9) Telephone 10) Flavor Bud Living 11) Sheriff Of Hong Kong 12) Making Love To A Vampire With A Monkey On My Knee

Don Van Vliet (vocals, chinese gongs, harmonica, soprano saxophone, bass clarinet), [Jeff] Moris Tepper (slide guitar, guitar, nerve guitar), Eric

Drew Feldman (synthesiser, bass, mellotron, grand piano, electric piano), Robert Arthur Williams (drums), Bruce Lambourne Fowler (trombone), John French (slide guitar, guitar, marimba, bass and drums on 11, drums on 2), Gary Lucas (guitar on 10, french horn on 8)

ICE CREAM FOR CROW
Original label: Virgin (UK), Epic (US)
Current CD label: Virgin
Producer: Don Van Vliet
Engineer: Phil Brown
Recorded: Warner Brothers Recording Studios, North Hollywood, CA, May/June 1982
UK Peak: 90
Release date: September 1982
1) Ice Cream For Crow 2) The Host The Ghost The Most Holy-O 3) Semi-Multicoloured Caucasian 4) Hey Garland, I Dig Your Tweed Coat 5) Evening Bell 6) Cardboard Cutout Sundown 7) The Past Sure Is Tense 8) Ink Mathematics 9) The Witch Doctor Life 10) "81" Poop Hatch 11) The Thousandth And Tenth Day Of The Human Totem Pole 12) Skeleton Makes Good
Single: Ice Cream For Crow/Light Reflected Off The Oceands Of The Moon (August 82)
Don Van Vliet (vocals, harmonica, soprano saxophone, chinese gongs, prop horn), [Jeff] Moris Tepper (steel-appendage guitar, slide guitar, acoustic guitar, guitar), Gary Lucas (glass-finger guitar, slide guitar, national steel duolian, solo guitar on 5), Richard Midnight Hatsize Snyder (bass guitar, marimba, viola) Cliff R Martinez (drums, shake bouquet, glass washboard, metal drums), Eric Drew Feldman (rhodes piano and synthesised bass on 11)

SELECTED COMPILATION ALBUMS

THE DUST BLOWS FORWARD
(Rhino 1999)
An intelligently compiled 2 CD retrospective, including rarities Light
  Reflected Off The Oceands Of The Moon, and Little Scratch from the
  Clear Spot sessions

GROW FINS: RARITIES 1965–82
(Revenant 1999)
A 5 CD treasure trove of live material and rarities. Included are early, pre-
  Safe As Milk demos, the available material from the famous Frank
  Freeman's' Dancing School, Kidderminster show, the *Trout Mask Replica*
  home recordings at the group's house in Woodland Hills, and a selection
  of live recordings, radio broadcasts. An enhanced CD includes video
  footage from the Amougies Festival, 1969.

FRANK ZAPPA:THE LOST EPISODES
(Rykodisc 1996)
It's unfortunate that the early Zappa/Van Vliet recordings have not all been
  compiled on one disc. This 30-track selection of Zappa obscurata
  features Van Vliet on Lost In A Whirlpool, Tiger Roach, I'm A Band
  Leader, Alley Cat and The Grand Wazoo. A few more early
  collaborations, including Metal Man Has Won His Wings, are found on
  the Frank Zappa Mystery Disc (Rykodisc 1998)

GUEST APPEARANCES

With Frank Zappa: Vocals on Willie The Pimp from *Hot Rats*
  (Straight/Reprise 1970).
Harmonica on San Ber' dino, from *One Size Fits All* (DiscReet 1975)
Harmonica on Find Her Finer from *Zoot Allures* (Warner Brothers,
  November 1976)
With The Tubes: Harmonica on Golden Boy and saxophone on Cathy's
  Clone from *Now* (A&M 1977)
With Ry Cooder and Jack Nitzsche:Vocals on Hard Workin' Man single
  (b/w Coke Machine) (MCA 1978)

RELATED RELEASES

THE MAGIC BAND – BACK TO THE FRONT
Current CD label: ATP
Producer: John French, Bob Weston
Engineer: Bob Weston
Recorded: Paradoxx Sound Studios, Palmdale, CA, Feb 2003
UK Peak: Did not chart
Released: May 2003
1) My Human Gets Me Blues 2) Click Clack 3) Abba Zaba 4) I'm Gonna Booglarize You, Baby, 5) Sun Zoom Spark 6) Alice In Blunderland 7) Steal Softly Thru Snow 8) Dropout Boogie 9) Moonlight On Vermont 10) Circumstances 11) On Tomorrow 12) Floppy Boot Stomp 13) Hair Pie 14) Nowadays A Woman's Got To Hit A Man 15) When It Blows Its Stacks 16) I Wanna Find A Woman Who Will Hold My Big Toe Till I Have To Go 17) Sure 'Nuff 'N Yes I Do

Gary Lucas (guitar), Denny Walley (guitar), Mark Boston (bass guitar), John French (drums, vocals)

DVD

THE MAGIC BAND IN CONCERT/ LIKE BLUEGRASS ONLY WEIRDER (REUNION DOCUMENTARY)
Produced and directed: Elaine Shepherd
Released: September 2004
Live footage of the Magic Band live in the UK 2003, together with an interview-based documentary and archive footage.

DON VAN VLIET – SOME YO YO STUFF (1993)
Directed: Anton Corbijn
Released on DVD September 2003
Twelve minute, black and white short

DON VAN VLIET SOLO AND GROUP EXHIBITIONS

1972
Bluecoat Gallery, Liverpool
Captain Beefheart – Paintings
Solo exhibition

1982
The Museum of Modern Art, New York
Performance Video (*Ice Cream For Crow*)
Group exhibition

1985
New York Studio School, New York
From Organism To Architecture
Group exhibition
Massimo Audiello Gallery
The Chi-Chi Show
Group exhibition
Gallery Schlesinger–Boisante, New York
Fractura
Group exhibition
Galerie Michael Werner, Koln
Don Van Vliet – Sechs Bilder
Solo exhibition
Mary Boone Gallery, New York
Solo exhibition

1986
Waddington Galleries, London
Solo exhibition

1987
Galerie Michael Werner, Koln
Byars, Chamberlain, Salle,
Fischl, Lasker, Van Vliet
Group exhibition

Galerie Michael Werner, Koln
Don Van Vliet – Zehn Bilder
Solo exhibition
Galerie Brinkmann, Amsterdam
Solo exhibition

1988
Galerie Michael Werner, Koln
Accrochage
Group exhibition
Centre d'Art Contemporain,
Abbaye St. Andre, Maymac, Correze
A la surface de la Peinture: Les Annees 80
Group exhibition
Galerie Michael Werner, Koln
Don Van Vliet – Neun Bilder
Solo exhibition
Galerie Lelong, Zurich
Solo exhibition

1989
Galerie Michael Werner, Koln
Accrochage
Group exhibition
Museum Ludwig, Rheinhallen der Kolner Messe, Koln
Bilderstreit, Widerspruch, Einheit und Fragment in der Kunst seit 1960
Group exhibition
Galerie Frank Hanel, Frankfurt/Main
Accrochage
Group exhibition
San Francisco Museum of Modern Art, San Francisco
Don Van Vliet – New Work
Solo exhibition

1990
Kunsthallen Brandts Klaederfabrik, Odense
Bilder des Rock
Group exhibition

Galerie Frank Hanel, Frankfurt/Main
Don Van Vliet 1986/1989
Solo exhibition
Galerie Michael Werner, Koln
Don Van Vliet – Zehn Bilder
Solo exhibition
Fred Hoffman Gallery, Santa Monica
New Paintings and Drawings
Solo exhibition

1991
Michael Werner Gallery, New York
Solo exhibition
Galerie Michael Werner, Koln
Solo exhibition
Kunsthallen Brandts Klaedefabrik, Odense
Solo exhibition

1993
Galerie Michael Werner, Koln
Accrochage
Group exhibition
Galerie Michael Werner, Koln
Solo exhibition

1993/4
Bielefelder Kunstverin, Museum Waldhof, Bielefeld
Don Van Vliet – Stand Up To Be Discontinued
Solo exhibition

1994
Kunsthallen Brandts Klaedefabrik, Odense
Don Van Vliet – Stand Up To Be Discontinued
Solo exhibition
Brighton Museum & Art Gallery, Brighton
Don Van Vliet – Stand Up To Be Discontinued
Solo exhibition
Galerie Michael Werner, Koln

Accrochage
Group exhibition

1995
Stedelijk Museum, Amsterdam
Dancing Girls, in honour of Gustav Mahler, along the edge of Expressionism
Group exhibition
Michael Werner Gallery, New York
Major Works by Georg Baselitz, James Lee Byars, Per Kirkeby, Markus Lupertz, Sigmar Polke, Don Van Vliet
Group exhibition
Michael Werner Gallery, New York
God's Empty Socks and Other Paintings
Solo exhibition
Galleri Aveny, Goteborg
Solo exhibition
Michael Werner Gallery, New York
Solo exhibition

1996
Galerie Michael Werner, Koln
Group exhibition
Galerie Michael Werner, Koln
Solo exhibition

1998
Galerie Michael Werner, Koln
Accrochage
Group exhibition
Michael Werner Gallery, New York
Georg Baselitz, Marcel Broodthaers, Fames Lee Byars, Jorg Immendorff, Eugene Leroy, Markus Lupertz, A.R. Penck, Don Van Vliet: Works on Paper
Group exhibition
Knoedler & Company, New York
Don Van Vliet – New Work
Solo exhibition

1999
Michael Werner Gallery, New York
Works On Paper
Solo exhibition

2000
The Lowe Gallery, Atlanta, Georgia
Solo exhibition

2001
Paintings from the Eighties
Michael Werner Gallery, New York
Solo exhibition

INDEX

Handy, W.C. 88–89
Hansen, Beck 259
'Happy Blue Pumpkin' 166
'Happy Earthday' 340
'Happy Love Song' 187
'Hard Workin' Man' 256
Harkleroad, Bill 60, 64, 68, 69, 70, 74,
    75, 78, 80, 94, 112, 113, 125, 134,
    141, 142, 144, 146, 167, 177,
    178–179, 181, 190–191, 194, 204,
    259, 276; joins CB 64–65; name
    70–71; as musician 76, 77–78, 116;
    relationship with V 71, 82, 83;
    Trout Mask Replica 67, 84, 85, 89,
    91, 101, 105–106, 134, 227;
    musical director 124; *Lick My
    Decals Off, Baby* 125, 126, 127,
    128, 129, 130, 136; *The Spotlight
    Kid* 141, 147, 148, 149, 150, 153,
    155; 1972 tour 157, 159, 162;
    Clear Spot 168, 169–170, 171,
    172–173, 174, 175; *Unconditionally
    Guaranteed* 184, 186, 187, 188;
    leaves CB for Mallard 190; Mallard
    219, 220, 221–222, 223, 231–232;
    reformation of The Magic Band
    340–341
Harkleroad, Margaret 126
Harper, Roy 216
Harris, Derek 98
Harris, Don 'Sugarcane' 111
'Harry Irene' 155, 231, 248
Harvey, Polly 335–336
Hatfield And The North 184
'Have A Whiff On Me' (Mungo Jerry)
    145
Hayden, Victor 67, 114, 116, 201–202,
    236, 237, 284; name 70–71; *Trout
    Mask Replica* 99, 101
Hayman, Martin 194
Hayward, Richie 138
'He Was A-Fuckin'' 338
Head Off (Tepper) 339–340
Heard, Dorothy 21
Hebblethwaite, Frank 'Paco' 180

Hendrix, Jimi 43, 44, 60, 88, 133, 142,
    158, 179
Henry Cow 88, 184, 194, 197, 327
Hepner, Richard 22, 25, 28,
'Her Eyes Are A Blue Million Miles'
    174, 187
'Here I Am, I Always Am' 23, 26, 28,
    36, 69
'Hey, Garland, I Dig Your Tweed
    Coat' (poem) 278, 291, 317, 318;
    as song 291–292
'Hey Joe' (blues) 236
'Hey, Nelda' 12, 14
High Rise 327
Highway 61 Revisited (Dylan) 319
Hill, Ronald 5
Hite, Bob 'The Bear' 60
H.M.S. Bounty 118
'Hobo Chang Ba' 99–100, 115, 157,
    317
'Hoboism' 236, 307
Hoffman, Sam 39
Holland, Milt *Safe As Milk* 36, 41; *Clear
    Spot* 170, 171
The Hollywood Persuaders 12
Hooker, John Lee 27, 88–89, 157, 163,
    164, 342
'The Host The Ghost The Most Holy-
    O' 290
'Hot Head' 261, 262, 274, 279
Hot Rats (Zappa) 111, 120, 122, 123
Hotel (film) 126
Howlin' Wolf 8, 9, 20, 21, 22, 25, 27,
    36, 51, 64, 88, 89, 90, 96, 152,
    158, 161, 162, 163, 342
'How's Your Bird' 12
Huck, Janet *see* Vliet, Jan Van
Huey, Baby And The Babysitters 192
Hunky Dory (Bowie) 323
Hurt, Mississippi John 89, 100, 226
Huxley, Aldous 11
Hyde, Karl 323
Hynde, Chrissie 253

'I'm Glad' 28, 41, 173, 185